Gay and
You

Gay and Lesbian Youth

Gilbert Herdt, PhD
Editor

Gay and Lesbian Youth was simultaneously issued by The Haworth Press, Inc. under the same title as a special issue of the *Journal of Homosexuality*, Volume 17, Numbers 1/2/3/4, 1989, John De Cecco, Editor.

Harrington Park Press
New York • London

ISBN 0-918393-56-6

Published by

Harrington Park Press, Inc., 10 Alice Street, Binghamton, New York 13904-1580
EUROSPAN/Harrington, 3 Henrietta Street, London WC2E 8LU England

Harrington Park Press, Inc. is a subsidiary of The Haworth Press, Inc., 10 Alice Street, Binghamton, New York 13904-1580.

Gay and Lesbian Youth was originally published as *Journal of Homosexuality*, Volume 17, Numbers 1/2/3/4 1989.

Cover design by Marshall Andrews.

Library of Congress Cataloging-in-Publication Data

Gay and lesbian youth.

Simultaneously issued by the Haworth Press, Inc., under the same title, as a special issue of
the Journal of homosexuality, volume 17, numbers 1/2/3/4, 1989.''
1. Gay youth—Cross-cultural studies. 2. Gay teenagers—Cross-cultural studies. I. Herdt,
Gilbert, H., 1949- .
HQ76.25.G38 1989 306.7'66 88-35836
ISBN 0-918393-56-6

This collection was made possible through a grant
from the Kalos Kagathos Foundation,
Laguna Beach, California.

ABOUT THE EDITOR

Gilbert Herdt, PhD, is Associate Professor, Committee on Human Development and The College, The University of Chicago. He was trained in anthropology at the University of Washington and the Australian National University, where he earned his PhD degree in 1978. He did fieldwork in New Guinea between 1974-1985, on which he has written several books, including *Guardians of the Flutes* (New York: McGraw-Hill, 1981), *Rituals of Manhood* (Berkeley: University of California Press, 1982), *Ritualized Homosexuality in Melanesia* (Berkeley: University of California, 1982), and *Sambia: Ritual and Gender in New Guinea* (New York: Holt, Rinehart, & Winston, 1987).

CONTENTS

Adolescent Homosexuality: Preface

Robert W. Deisher, MD

University of Washington School of Medicine

The studies included in this volume are pioneering in their emphasis and scope, offering an urgently needed cross-cultural view of adolescent homosexuality. Those of us who have encountered gay youth in the course of our work have long recognized that received wisdom on adolescent homosexuality largely fails to advance our understanding of this phenomenon beyond the commonly held and crippling myths that so often propel these young people into isolation and diminished self-esteem. Even begging the perennial question of the origins of homosexuality, the limits of our current knowledge concerning its social emergence and early expression are striking. Assumptions about the surface behaviors and social patterns of gay teenagers are loosely supported in the literature by a haphazard accumulation of case studies, incidental findings, and studies of adult populations. Yet until recently, there has been little interest in submitting these impressions to systematic appraisal.

Indeed, proposals to this end have entailed considerable risk, and we are indebted to the authors of this volume not only for their findings, but for their perseverance in the face of a tradition of suspicion and even hostility within their respective professional communities. Too often, the study of adolescent homosexuality has been sidetracked by the inappropriate stigma of putative aberrance among those with legitimate research interests. Too often, the health and social service needs of a young and vulnerable popula-

---

Dr. Deisher is Professor Emeritus of Pediatrics, Division of Adolescent Medicine, University of Washington School of Medicine, Seattle, WA 98195.

xiii

tion have been ignored out of fear that the consequences of collegial disapproval might not be confined to misgivings alone. In reality, advances in our knowledge of adult sexual behaviors make developmental considerations not only appropriate but pressing. Both the methods and conclusions of these studies contribute to an overarching body of knowledge that ultimately encompasses all youth.

Consider how briefly, in intellectual terms, our culture has grappled with homosexuality. In the past 35 years, studies by Alfred Kinsey and Evelyn Hooker have been landmark events in our society's efforts to recognize and assimilate adult homosexuality, but even these significant achievements were limited by the ethnocentricity of their study populations. Sexual expression and its cultural underpinnings are interwoven in a richly detailed tapestry of biological, social, and psychological imperatives. Cross-cultural studies are particularly valuable in dividing such complex behaviors into elements that are universal, variable, endowed by nature, encouraged by nurture, accepted or challenged by ambient culture, and formative or incidental in the life of the individual. The studies that follow are significant not only because their findings are directly applicable in a heterogeneous society, but also because of the broad base they provide for future work.

These issues clamor all the more for our attention when we consider that in the United States alone there are 30 million young people between the ages of 10 and 20, 10% of whom are felt to be predominantly or exclusively homosexual. In spite of their large numbers and the profound difficulties that they confront, few groups of young people have been so ignored, and few evoke so poignantly the aura of quiet desperation to which our statistics on adolescent suicide are such disturbing testimony.

The suggestion that adolescent homosexuality and suicide are causally linked is but one of many controversial assertions that have become part of our poorly buttressed working knowledge of this population. It is important because of its implications for mortality, and because it is so starkly revealing of the issues that are crucial in the lives of these young people: acceptance, denial, self-esteem, isolation despite growing needs for intimacy, the pain of reluctant nonconformity, depression, and inaccessible or absent role models. We cannot yet describe how these difficulties are confronted and overcome, how they are transformed by interactions with parents and significant others, or how they are affected by the hallmark experience of homosexual self-identification, coming out.

These questions define an ambitious agenda for research in adolescent homosexuality, and they suggest as well specific points for engagement in working with gay-identified youth. These young people encounter the developmental difficulties that confront all adolescents, but their conscious conflicts and priorities are shaped by the day-to-day exigencies of interest in same-sex relationships, an interest that vastly complicates the tasks of incorporating intimacy in their lives. For most adolescents, the need for friends and companionship far outweighs the importance of growing sexual needs. However, this distinction is easily lost in the pall of homophobia and isolation that inevitably distorts the connections between sexuality, autonomy, and self-esteem.

It is not surprising that interest in the developmental aspects of homosexuality comes at a time when a worldwide health crisis of staggering dimensions has underscored the complexity and natural variability of human sexual behavior. The perils of AIDS add even greater urgency to our efforts to identify the health and human service needs of gay youth and to respond appropriately. These studies offer knowledge and a perspective from which to build that response.

Gay and Lesbian Youth

Introduction:
Gay and Lesbian Youth,
Emergent Identities,
and Cultural Scenes
at Home and Abroad

Gilbert Herdt, PhD

University of Chicago

SUMMARY. This introduction opens up the field of studies of gay and lesbian adolescents, both with regard to past and present studies in the research literature, and by allusion to the new studies collected in this issue. Historical and crosscultural elements of the context of the "coming out" process are discussed. Four preconceptions of gay youth are critically examined, regarding their heterosexuality, inversion, stigma, and heterogeneity. The anthropological construct of life crisis "rites of passage" is utilized as a heuristic framework for deconstructing attitudes regarding change and constancy in homosexual adolescents. Aspects of age, sex, class, and related variables related to the form and content of the coming out process are then examined in the United States and other societies. Finally, the social problems of gay youth, AIDS and its impact in particular, are briefly considered. The author concludes with a plea for new and urgent research.

Dr. Herdt is Associate Professor, Committee on Human Development at The University of Chicago.

The author wishes to thank his colleagues Barry Adam, Andrew Boxer, Joseph Carrier, John De Cecco, Richard Parker, Michael Ross, and Margaret Schneider for their helpful comments on this paper. He is especially grateful to his "encyclopedic friend" Steve Murray for his comments. Funding for this paper came, in part, from the Spencer Foundation of Chicago, which is gratefully acknowledged.

Correspondence and requests for reprints may be addressed to the author, c/o Committee on Human Development, The University of Chicago, 5730 South Woodlawn Avenue, Chicago, IL 60637.

1

The unprecedented growth of the gay and lesbian community in recent history has transformed our culture and consciousness, creating radically new possibilities for men and women to "come out" and live more openly as homosexuals. This is certainly true of America and Western Europe, where the gay and lesbian population, in hitherto unforeseen ways and in greater numbers, has claimed attention in politics and the media, culture and the arts. Since before the Stonewall riot in New York (1969), the gay perspective had undergone that "significant discontinuity," to use Plummer's (1981) phrase, from being a pathological category to an oppressed minority. Now, gay is identified as more of a social world. Being homosexual — gay or lesbian — now is more understandable, almost recognizable by its positioning within an affluent society, which some call a high culture, one fascinated both with its own hedonism and its "love for human nature" (Sontag, 1982). "Gay" has become a symbolic reality; its emergent identities and new cultural scenes have, in this sense, displaced the old, one-dimensional "sexual culture" of homosexuality in the 1960s and 1970s (Altman, 1973; 1979), not only by shifting the discourse to incorporate new social issues, but also by extending its cultural meanings to reach abroad, to the urban centers of other countries, even those of the Third World.

And yet for all of this, we[1] had not planned upon or fully anticipated an equally unprecedented consequence of the post-Stonewall struggles to construct a gay culture: the emergence of a generation of teenagers who feel themselves to be homosexual and who thus begin the difficult but affirming process of "coming out."[2] Often, lesbian and gay adolescents were felt not to exist or were ignored as a social problem. Today it is estimated, however, that nearly 3 million of our country's 29 million adolescents are gay.[3] When as a social issue teenage homosexuality was studied in the past, it was sometimes psychologized and pathologized, as Martin (1982) suggested, or it was sociologized, as Plummer (1975) showed, with adult subjects' retrospections substituted for teenagers' or young adults' experience. This problem of retrospective bias and distortion, criticized but still not well appreciated in the literature,[4] is inherent in many adolescent studies (reviewed in Boxer and Cohler, herein). Such reductionism and methodological bias presents several formidable roadblocks to understanding gay and lesbian lives: (a) In our post-Stonewall society, gay culture and sexual meanings have changed from a generation ago — this introduces a cohort problem; (b) this generational change is being exacerbated by problems associated with the development of AIDS in a dramatic and deadly way; and (c) the difficulties are even greater when we turn to other cultures, with their own emergent identities as manifested in the lives of homosexual persons. This must include understanding variations in the meaning of "homosexuality" or "gay" and "lesbian" crossculturally, as well as in the contexts of coming out and being socialized into (largely) urban gay scenes around the world (cf. Blackwood, 1986).

The aim of this issue is to address these problems and roadblocks in terms of the words and experiences of adolescents themselves. We use a variety of social science approaches, especially the ethnographic, and the resulting ethnography — as well as the sociology and psychology — are thus meant to redress a gap in the literature. Ours are not only new studies of these young people and their largely untold stories, however; they also represent commentaries on changing relationships across generations in the gay world, itself a part of accelerating social change in the wider society. But the generational problem is most perplexing.

We had not foreseen that the social rights struggles of the 1960s and 1970s — our struggles — might be perceived by youth in a different way, or that, beyond the inheritance of the old stigma surrounding homosexuality, gay youth would also have to contend with the new horrors of AIDS. Nor that, in part because of stigma,[5] and in part due to AIDS, at least as reported in the popular media, teenage gays and lesbians would shun older gays as role models or even as friends.[6] We have the dimming sense that much of post-World War II "gay culture" and folklore are not only gone but may soon be lost, and that the same fate may already have befallen the freewheeling "sexual culture" of the American gay scene (Altman, 1982), post-Stonewall and pre-AIDS (reviewed in Kotarba & Lang, 1986). This is tantamount to suggesting that the knowledge and cultural practices of the gay world, like much of complex and mass culture today, are shifting and ephemeral, having emergent, not fixed, values and meanings. Whether American culture has selected from gay culture its popular tastes and themes (Altman, 1982) is arguable. Nonetheless, only now has gay culture begun to institutionalize "socialization" techniques for the transmission of its cultural knowledge to a younger generation. More will be said of this later.

For the present, however, it suffices to note that neither the formal nor informal substance and contemporary changes in gay life are being readily preserved. Our descriptive studies below document and question these changes. What we want, then, is to preserve the "sensibility" of teenage lives today, which, as Sontag (1982) has said in another context, is the most "perishable" aspect of a culture.[7] To be more precise, however, we can refer to three distinctive historical periods of change in these cultural styles: (a) early 20th century, up to the Gay Liberation movements of the 1960s; (b) the post-Stonewall period after 1969 and up to the early 1980s; and (c) the period following the discovery and objectification of AIDS, circa 1981-1982, as a "gay disease" (Feldman & Johnson, 1986). Each of these is a distinctive cultural marker, particularly in America, for documenting changes in the sensibilities of gay and lesbian youth.

I shall review these issues in this Introduction. My concern is to join the recent efforts of those scholars concerned with the perishable sensibilities of gay consciousness and culture in our time by focusing upon gay youth. This must perforce be limited by space, for this "salvage" anthropology and the study of gay teenagers today involves innumerable psychocultural issues that lead, willy-nilly, onto the study of the wider social field of sexuality.[8] My approach here reflects in part the perspective of an anthropologist and the substantive questions of a gender researcher, which anticipate broader problematics in the field of gender and culture (Herdt, 1984; 1987b; 1987c).

PRECONCEPTIONS AND ASSUMPTIONS

In opening the "problem" of teenage gays (and we must constantly strive to say for whom a "problem" is a problem, society or gays), our concern is to confront, on various levels of action and discourse, four fundamental assumptions, or, to use Gadamer's

(1965) hermeneutic notion, "presuppositions," regarding homo-sexuality and adolescence. These are as follows:

1. Gay/lesbian adolescents are subject to the "assumption of het-erosexuality," of feeling "guilty until proven innocent" in the social arena, to invert our legal principle.
2. Because they are not heterosexual, these teenagers are, there-fore, assumed to be "inverts," according to our cultural pre-sumption of inversion.
3. They are, then, stigmatized as persons, which oppression has real-life consequences for their development and adaptation.
4. Finally, as homosexuals, they are subject to the assumption of homogeneity: the idea that gays and lesbians the *world over* are the same in "coming out" experience, identity, and cul-tural organization.

Let us review each of these problematics in turn.

The Presumption of Heterosexuality

The first preconception with which adolescents must contend in social development concerns being straight: the assumption "that parties to any interaction in straight settings are usually presumed to be heterosexual unless demonstrated to be otherwise" (Ponse, 1978, p. 58). Evelyn Hooker (1965) once referred to this as "het-erosexual ethnocentricity." We should think long on this stereo-type, for if gender theorists are even half-way correct about the power of early experience to shape one's gender identity and even one's world view or sense of existence (Stoller, 1968), the influ-ence of an assumed heterosexuality from before puberty must be profound. Whether sexual orientation is caused by cultural or bio-logical factors, alone or interacting, and the extent to which being "gay" is "constructed" or "essential" in the person's develop-ment are critical related questions (Hoult, 1984), but they do not concern me here. Rather, no matter what the ultimate causes, there will always exist a discordance between the homosexual youths' feeling of being "different" when growing up in a heterosexual environment, and their eventual place in a homosexual world.

The presumption of heterosexuality is identified by many theorists with profound psychosocial problems from the start of adolescent development (Plummer, 1981, and herein). Children who manifest nonconformist gender behavior from an early age are, according to some reports, those most susceptible to parental and peer pressure to change their behavior (Green, 1987; Whitam, 1983), even though they have the greatest likelihood of being gay as adults (Harry, 1982). Such findings highlight the widespread significance of the masculine/feminine dichotomy, which itself underlies the heterosexual/homosexual dichotomy (cf. McIntosh, 1968). Parker's article on Brazil and Carrier's on Mexico herein suggest similar processes at work in Latin American settings.

A variety of ways of feeling different and becoming self-alienated have been correlated with the heterosexual assumption. Among the most powerful of these factors are early homosexual experiences, early puberty or sexual precosity, and disinterests of several sorts, such as disinterest in the opposite sex or in sports. Prior research tends to support these views. Gay men, for instance, do say they feel "very different" from heterosexuals in growing up (based on adult-felt retrospections; see Bell, Weinberg, & Hammersmith, 1981). The age of first sexual contact for gays is younger than heterosexuals (Bell et al., 1981; Roestler & Deisher, 1972), although data show that prehomosexual boys do not develop earlier than heterosexuals (Bell et al., 1981). Harry (1982) has argued that atypical disinterest during adolescence regarding dating and sports reinforce the social alienation of gays. Because heterosexual dating and team sports are two key points of adolescent peer grouping, homosexual youth experience a "major social vacuum" (Harry, 1982) in these key domains. They feel unattached, alienated. They are not integrated and thereby sheltered by peer groups or gangs (Lafont, 1986). Troiden has touched upon this in his excellent review in this issue.

Feeling different and alienated are in turn associated with the earliest aspirations to change identity, which eventually leads to coming out. Both cognition and emotions are involved in such identity change. The very earliest aspect of the process may involve what Weinberg (1983) referred to as the "self-suspicion" of being "different," i.e., of being homosexual. Problems arise here because there is, as Dank (1971) noted in a classic paper, either no "anticipatory socialization" to the gay identity, or else the kind that is inimical as a positive foundation for self-change. Dissonance in cognitions of self and significant others are inevitable, given the presumption of heterosexuality: "Most persons who eventually identify themselves as homosexuals require a change in the meaning of the cognitive category *homosexual* before they can place themselves in the category" (Dank 1971, p. 189). Stigma is obviously sensed and feared in this (Warren, 1980).

One of the initial responses to feeling different in this way is the decline of self-esteem that accompanies harmful alienation, so that teenagers remain isolated and "closeted" (Minton & McDonald, 1983/1984). The well known stage models of development emphasize this trend (reviewed in Cass 1984, see also Coleman, Troiden, herein). Another is to displace self-interest from heterosexual dating and sports into intellectual or artistic performance, which effectively promotes compensatory achievement among gay and lesbian youth (Gagnon, 1979; Harry, 1982). A third possibility is to engage in surreptitious sexual contacts or clandestine same-sex romantic relationships (Jay & Young, 1977, reviewed in Cass 1984; Ponse, 1978; Warren, 1974). Nowadays, the most recent and radical means of dealing with such feelings is for the youth to come out, possibly in the context of a gay or homophile group (Greenberg, 1976). Such a coming out group in Chicago is described from our project (see Gerstel et al.). We shall deal more fully with contemporary cultural scenes and their effects upon identity below.

The Presumption of Inversion

Once feelings of being different are converted into self-suspicion, or into what Troiden (herein) calls a "sensitization stage," another preconception emerges. Before the person's full recognition of internalized stigma and externalized oppression, he or she must work through conflicts of reversal in his or her gender behavior and self strivings. These stem from the stereotype that, not being heterosexual, one must be unnatural: the "invert." Inversion, an old concept, goes back to at least the 19th century, and summons up images of the "disease of effeminancy" in males (Foucault, 1980). Certainly, Freud's work contributed to the popularization of the idea earlier, which even anthropologists un-self-consciously exported to other cultures (see Herdt, 1987b). Lacking what Warren (1974) called "gay knowledge" or what Jay and Young (1977) referred to as the "socializing process" for lesbians, that is, in the absence of explicit knowledge about prevailing positive identities or cultural scenes, the image of inversion, filled with its alienating power of self-preoccupation and psychopathology, comes into play.

First and foremost this is the imagery of the caricature, arising from social stereotypy, secrecy, and guilt, which may produce transitional feelings of existential panic and deterioration of the very foundations of well-being and selfhood. Such images are rooted ultimately in social stigma, to be examined shortly. Their main effect is related to crossgender behavior: feeling that one is not a normative, heterosexual male or female, one must display attributes of the opposite sex in order to attract attention or to "fit in" — hyperfemininity in males and hypermasculinity in females. Is this different than Sontag's (1982, p. 105) "camp," the "love of the unnatural," the avante garde sign that "one should either be a work of art or wear a work of art"? I think so.

Youthful gender transformation today seems to be a playful process, at first staged in a political vacuum, but increasingly indicative of a new awareness that will involve manifesting an open gay lifestyle. Troiden (herein) refers in this context to the "minstrelization" of youthful gays whose gender antics poke fun at society. Gender role stereotypy, class consciousness and psychological ghettoization are also involved, as indicated by the strong correlation between class and often anachronistic gender inversion: working class groups still tend to produce the most exaggerated gender-inverted homosexuals (see Harry, 1982; Murray, 1984; Read, 1980; and Parker, herein). Surely the once popular images of the "Drag Show" and "transvestite queen," produced in part for heterosexual audiences and now associated more with small cities in the Midwest, belong here. They seem a mixture of stereotypic inversion and camp protest against stigma, as Esther Newton once argued in *Mother Camp* (1972). Crossculturally, as Carrier (1980) has shown, the same inversion principle appears elsewhere in what he called sexually restrictive cultures, wherein sexual variations are shunned and those who participate are assigned the inferior status of the dominated. Homophobia, the fear and hatred of homosexuality, is clearly related to this (Weinberg, 1972). Page and Yee (1985) have recently shown that negative images of homosexuality among American heterosexuals remain, that stronger reactions are manifested toward males, and the *strongest* of all are expressed toward masculine gay males (Laner & Laner, 1979). This confirms a prevailing feeling that gay males are more "visible" in popular culture, and, perhaps, the more despised by heterosexual men for their affluence and for forsaking male privilege.

Not until this phase of inversion of the self is reflected upon can a transformation in gay and lesbian awareness emerge, as hinted by Le Bitoux for the youth of Paris (herein). With such a recognition of a homosexual social world beyond the self, either in gay or lesbian peers or social groups, or even among supportive heterosexual friends and networks, the restrictive image of the invert seems to recede.

The invert image presses the imagination up against a perceived "natural law," wherein homosexuality goes against "nature," as reflected most radically in the invert's behavior (Ponse, 1978; Foucault, 1980; cf. Hoffman, 1968; Scruton, 1986). Here, Ponse reminds us, "homosexuality frequently connotes inversion both in common sense thinking and in scientific theories" (Ponse, 1978, p. 31, n. 14). The recent Supreme Court case (*Bowers v. Hardwick*, 1986) upholding the "unnaturalness" of sodomy in state laws reveals at least one side of public opinion: that the invert is an ogre with the power to subvert those around him, especially the young.[9]

Another expression of the inversion stereotype concerns an exclusionary principle: one can be either homosexual or heterosexual, but not both. During this developmental phase, there is a strong tendency in gender-polarized and restrictive cultures, such as America, to rule out bisexual fantasies or activity (Herdt, 1987c). Such a trend runs counter to the surprisingly high rate of bisexuality Kinsey and his colleagues identified in America (cf. Roestler & Deisher, 1972). However, we are dealing here not with empirical patterns, but with folk models, ideal types, that are dualistic. This may be, in part, why the Australian Altman (1982) has referred to recent symbolic changes in our culture as a "homosexualization" of America.

> No other country seems as divided around issues of sexuality:
> the conflict between a repressive puritan heritage and the ethos
> of contemporary hedonism creates a tension that is reflected in
> the passion and all too often the violence that surrounds debate
> over sexuality in America. (p. xii)

According to the prevailing folk ethic, then, someone can be gay or
straight but not both, and the bisexual, so we are told (Paul, 1984),
experiences the greatest pressures of all: to "come clean" and stop
being closeted, by gay friends, or to stop being "adolescent" and
hedonistic, to get married and have children, like "normal"
straight friends. For some persons, the decision to come out is stymied here: some chose to "pass" as straight, for fear of being "inverted," though passing too, has its costs (Lee, 1977). Inversion
creeps beneath these images, never too far from what teenagers and
even adults have to say about "going" gay.

The Recognition of Stigma

The third factor of emergent gay experience, beyond the presumptions of heterosexuality and inversion, is the self's confronta-
tion with the social stigma of homosexuality. No matter in what
direction the analysis of homosexuality proceeds — whether to culture, the self-concept, theoretical debates between constructionists
or essentialists, minority status, sex differences between gays and
lesbians in coming out or in passing as heterosexual — there is a
profound barrier to always be bargained with: recognition of the
stigma and homophobia surrounding homosexuality. Sexism is very
related and should be analyzed in parallel fashion. An immense
literature now surrounds this aspect of the meaning of homosexuality, and it need not be reviewed again here.[10] That stigma exists in
society, in science, and in medical treatment circles regarding homosexuality is a social fact, one that enchants some and disenchants
others across these domains. Stigma is the bastard of oppression
(Warren, 1980). The duality of oppression in social life here concerns domination and heterosexual cooptation (Adam, 1978) in socioeconomic roles and institutional homophobia, on the one hand,
and internalized stigma, stereotypes, and even self-hatred — internal
homophobia (see Savin-Williams, herein) — on the other. De Cecco

(1984) reviewed the many shadow-plays of homophobia to find that these remain a powerful force in contemporary society.

A structural sign of this preconception of stigma is the old stereotype that all homosexual youth are deviant and delinquent. Weeks (1985) reminded us that in the 19th century, the warnings about prostitution and homosexuality effectively placed gays into deviant subgroups. The psychological theory of a previous generation also equated homosexual activity in adolescence to peripherality and antisocial strivings.[11] Even Erik Erikson's (1968) classic work on identity and youth makes the deviant image essential to and almost obligatory for understanding gay youth. "Negative identity prevails in the delinquent (addictive, homosexual) youth of our larger cities," Erikson (1968, p. 88) argued, because of hostility to family and culture. Only through complete identification with such deviant subcultures can relief from psychopathology be found for "cliques and gangs of young homosexuals, addicts, and social cynics" (p. 176). These images derived in part from the Freudian framework, of course, which itself makes a fundamental assumption that anything short of heterosexuality and parenthood are suggestive of pathology (see Isay, 1986). The Freudian model, simplified and mythologized, has become our folk theory, a piece of popular culture.[12] It is not surprising that such folk theory, which conveniently supports the exploitation and pathologizing of homosexuality more broadly, should have resulted in the initial studies of gay youth being done in bars, among male prostitutes or hustlers, prison inmates, and psychiatric patients. Leznoff and Westley (1956) and Reiss (1961) are social science examples; the novels of Rechy (1963) are cultural counterparts.

Plummer (1975) and Weeks (1985), among others, have shown that many generalized Western biases toward homosexuality rest upon stereotypy and stigma of this sort. Many studies have, of course, since questioned these generalizations on empirical grounds. One need only think of Evelyn Hooker's (1957) groundbreaking study of a nonclinical population's positive mental health for counterfindings 30 years ago. Kinsey and his colleagues (1948) paved the way for these revisions in our views by showing the frequency of homosexual contact in the general population of the United States. Yet his biological assumptions and emphasis upon the "sex act," decontextualized from its personal and symbolic meanings, did not fundamentally alter our conceptions of the homosexual (De Cecco, in press). The many "Kinsey-type" studies to follow (e.g., Bell & Weinberg, 1978) further substantiated the "normalcy" of gays, pre- and post-Stonewall. However, these studies have been almost entirely of adults, and, indeed, usually of WASPs. Less effort has been made to show the historical and cultural relationship between the earlier studies and those which followed the momentous events of the 1960s and early 1970s. The many cultural changes that have occurred since then provide a new context for appraisal of stigma, oppression, liberation, and coming out in adolescents and their older gay predecessors.

Such changes have brought positive reinforcements for the coming out process today, with a concomitant decline in psychopathology, at least in certain respects. Secrecy and hiding seem less frequent (Anderson, 1987; Troiden, herein); and casual sex contact does not automatically translate into sexual orientation, be it hetero- or homosexual (Plummer, 1975). Sexualized contact in the cultural scene of the gay bar used to reign supreme in folklore and American literature on homosexuality (Hoffman, 1970), whereas this now seems less so in the fiction of, say, David Leavitt. The overrepresentation of homosexual youth among male hustlers in early studies seems to mirror social stigma here (Roestler & Deisher, 1972), whereas hustling is now a very different theme in the literature (Boyer, herein). Lesbians were much more invisible before, whereas now, some new studies are emerging. Where inversion reigned and transvestism as quintessential homosexual cultural style was common (Read, 1980), today these seem anachronistic. What seems likely, then, is that stigma and oppression combined to make normative homosexual youth, especially lesbians—the most "invisible" (Ponse, 1978) element in the image of the stereotypic "queer"—whom unsympathetic observers interpreted as peripheral "deviants," a token of the homosexuality of the times.[13] The critical papers in this issue by both Boyer and Coleman on teenage male hustlers and their problems speak to this issue.

Social change in the gay world, which challenges stigma and reconstitutes it, making it "minoritized" (now an oppression), has finally placed the issues of gays and lesbians in their rightful judicial arena and political field: society. Involvement by teens and adults in gay groups illustrates this point about social change. Thus, a shift of participation by gays in homophile groups has occurred over time, from the generalized negative avoidance noted by Sagarin (1969) in the late 1960s, to the more positive findings of Plummer (1975) in the mid 1970s, which confirms the greater openness of the post-Stonewall era (Anderson, 1987; Gerstel et al., herein).

Leading up to and growing out of the events of the Stonewall period was a rapid consolidation of the gay community (Murray, 1979). Whereas drinking clubs and bar culture predominated in the lives of gay men following World War II, and may indeed be the main historical foundation for the social formation of the modern gay/lesbian community, other subsequent developments have occurred in urban centers (D'Emilio, 1983; Levine, 1979). These include gay professional and political action groups, reported upon in a plethora of newly founded gay and lesbian newspapers and related periodicals, some produced by local gay organizations. New gay and lesbian religious groups, such as Catholic Dignity, sprang up (see Humphreys & Miller, 1980, for a list of these). Gay merchants and shops emerged and appealed to gay and lesbian clientele, especially in San Francisco and New York. Gay academic unions, social clubs, networks of artists, and special interest groups appeared as never before, providing unprecedented channels of communication and interaction with others, in one's city and elsewhere, too. Many positive signs of cooperation and mutual action existed between homosexual men and women, as anticipated in such manifestos as Altman's classic *Homosexual: Oppression and Liberation* (1973). Class and racial differences seemed less apparent at first than now. The gay world became a satellite culture, Humphries and Miller (1980) suggested, so that by the late 1970s, the largest dozen American cities had recognizable gay neighborhoods, heavily populated by same-sex couples. And beyond the States, mass tourism extended this "homosexual geography" to "all large urban centers" throughout the world (Pollak, 1986, p. 54).

What matters here is that this symbolic world, these special interest communal satellites, became more politically empowered in gay and lesbian struggles against stigma and oppression, and this, in

turn, provided radically new opportunities for teenagers to reconstruct their social realities along different lines. Gay couples and
friends and networks gave added social support to the coming out
processes (McWhirter & Mattison, 1984). These gay communities
became as magnets for hinterland teenagers, whose desire for same-
sex led them to the "promised land." New cultural scenes and
identities were available for their consumption. Gay bath houses,
which at first seemed to be a vanguard of sexual liberation, became
in time the very name of consumerism among gays, and some
would say an oppression of gays through depersonalized sex (Altman, 1981). But these were frequented almost exclusively by
adults, not adolescents. Proximity to urban centers was crucial for
teens, too, especially in accessing homophile support groups while
still living at home and attending high school. Soon, though, some
cracks in this fine mirror began to show, cracks that reflect other
sociopolitical changes in the mainstream society.

D'Emilio (1983) argued that the Gay Liberation movement had
two primary effects in the post-Stonewall period: transformation in
the meaning of the coming out process and its association with the
emergence of a strong lesbian movement.[14] These changes were part
and parcel of the confrontational politics of the 1960s. Their association to "youth protest" (D'Emilio, 1983) seems certain.[15] The relationship between such youth sentiment then, and the low-key gay/
lesbian teenage activism of today, seems less certain, however.
Teenage activists in the 1970s could affirm that:

> The open avowal of one's sexual identity, whether at work, at
> school, at home, or before television cameras,* symbolized
> the shedding of the self-hatred that gay men and women inter-
> nalized, and consequently it promised an immediate improve-
> ment to one's life. (D'Emilio, 1983, p. 235)

But today's youth might well not recognize D'Emilio's next sen-
tence, that "to come out of the 'closet' quintessentially expressed
the fusion of the personal and the political that the radicalism of the

---

* A few teens from the group we have studied in Chicago (see Gerstell et al.,
herein) made a splash on the Oprah Winfrey television show in 1985.

late 1960s exalted'' (p. 235). Gone from the cultural scenes of the gay community are the radical politics of then, but such activism seems to have passed in general from the American scene for the time being. We see glimpses of similar sociopolitical change in Mexico (Carrier) and Paris (LeBitoux) in this collection. While we can therefore agree with Castells (1983), who provides an elegant analysis of the San Francisco history, that ''gay culture is inseparable from gay politics'' (p. 163), such politics today have a different form than a decade ago.

Some observers suggest that where radical politics are gone, gay as chic, and homosexual as decadent and triumphant consumer capitalism, have emerged in their place (Altman, 1982).[16] Perhaps, where the 1950s Mattachine culture of camp sensibility was, as Sontag (1982) suggested, ''disengaged, depoliticized — or at least apolitical'' (p. 107), the recent less activist gay ''community'' has undergone successive changes of increasing bourgeois ''centrism'' and internal factionalism.[17] Gays and lesbians seem more accepted (notwithstanding AIDS) into mainstream Western culture, which is related to their being at the vanguard of middle-class consumerism (Pollak, 1985). Yet as presaged in the mid-1970s by Jay and Young (1977), major divisions had already separated lesbians and gay men.

The nature of the homosexual coming out process today inextricably follows upon these changes: class, racial, and sex differences obviously divide America and therefore the homosexual population, with whites generally doing better than blacks, and men generally better than women, as evidenced in the San Francisco gay community (Castells, 1983).[18] Gentrification of the inner cities provides a case in point, because this made homosexuals economically useful: former run-down neighborhoods were upgraded through work and investment. Here, gentrification caused gays — mostly gay men — to compete with and displace longstanding inner city minorities. Yet, gays did not in turn create ''ghettos'' in the same way as other minorities. They ''choose to live together as a cultural community,'' Castells (1983, p. 139) argued, New York's Greenwich Village and San Francisco's Castro village being obvious examples. Lesbians, however, did not and do not tend to concentrate in given territories in the same way (Castells, 1983; Lockard, 1986), which no doubt reflects the lower social status of women as less privileged persons in a patriarchal culture (reviewed in Blackwood, 1986; Kehoe, 1986; and Warren, 1974). Here, then, we have the conditions for competition between gays and ethnic minorities in gentrification processes, and differential classism and sexism between gays versus lesbians in urban centers, both of which provide conflictual and centripetal structural forces in male and female teenagers' entry into homosexual worlds.

The Assumption of Homogeneity

Overcoming presumptions of heterosexuality and inversion are hard; fighting stigma is harder still. But there is embedded in these preconceptions a deeper, more mature and subtle problem, anticipated in the previous section: the view that gay youth are homogeneous, the same kind of persons.

The sources of this assumption are at once simple and complex. By definition homosexuality is one-dimensional: desire for same sex. The multitude of symbolic realities and states of desire present in our own history and in other cultures today are perceived, in Western discourse, to be but one essence or thing, the homosexual. By the end of the 19th century, as Foucault (1980) and others have shown, this made homosexuality an objectified and monolithic category, akin to a "species of nature." Of course this objectification—or "homosexualization," as Altman (1982) referred to it— issues from the preconceptions of inversion and stigma already outlined above. The nature of this discourse frame, however, creates broader difficulties for internal representations of, and relationships between, adult homosexuals within the gay community, on the one hand; and developmental problems for adolescents who are struggling to come out in society at large. The projected homogeneity derives no doubt from the overemphasis in popular culture on sexual practice as the sole defining characteristic of the moral careers and personhood of homosexuals.

"The most striking thing about sociological studies of homosexuality," Altman (1981) wrote, "is that they are obsessed with sex" (p. 45), a reductionism that poses a problem of great import to the gay world. For, paradoxically, it is this very focus on same-sex erotism that is the rallying point for gay rights activism and resistance to oppression. One cannot easily dismiss the popular stereotypy without undermining the political rhetoric of gays themselves. How are we to turn to the novels of Christopher Isherwood for the larger experience of being homosexual, as Altman might suggest, without finding in them a bedrock of homoeroticism? Moreover, research over the past 20 years or so has tended to emphasize if not homogeneity, then at least vital common concerns (Murray, 1984). Thus, it is hard to shake the centrist view, which in one sense or other is so popular, that homosexual desire, in opposition to normative heterosexual desire, unites gays and lesbians in a common culture. The testimonies of young gays in *One Teenager in Ten* (Heron, 1983) show such a trend in the American context.

And yet there is strong evidence of several kinds to indicate that in spite of same-sex desire, there is not one, but rather many homosexualities. So much is this the case that some find it difficult to see the common denominators in homosexual orientation development (Bell & Weinberg, 1978; Bell et al., 1981; Gagnon, 1979), and the anthropologist Kenneth Read (1980), in search of a language to characterize this diversity, was forced to refer to the multiple cultural behaviors in a gay bar as "styles." The point reveals a widespread difficulty, as noted in the literature (Murray, 1979, 1984): How shall we conceptualize the diversity and uniformity among gays and lesbians? My own deceptive use of such metaphors as "worlds," "communities," "cultures," in regard to gay and lesbian affiliations, is a stop-gap measure that avoids this question.

When it comes to adolescents in our own culture, as the papers below reveal, they are no more clones of each other than the adults. And when teenagers from other cultures are added into the equation, we are indeed confronted with striking diversity. Their social systems and attitudes differ; the symbols they use vary; the contexts and problems to which they must adjust differ even more. Gay youth in other cultures do not necessarily agree on fundamental questions of commitment to and desire for an openly homosexual lifestyle. The sense of gay liberation varies in France and in Mexico, as Le Bitoux and Carrier argue, respectively, because what is being liberated and what remains imprisoned in social conventions varies between these two nation-states. Our Western concepts "gay" and "lesbian" may be alien to them, and other, more fluid categories may substitute for them in culture and experience, as Parker suggests for Brazil. Their responses to parental and peer pressures are quite different from those of Americans, too, and at times we even search in vain for the center of this "Americanness." Teenagers vary as well with regard to how they handle discrimination, homophobia, and stigma, as Michael Ross reveals in his four-country study. These teenagers are only beginning to confront the issue of AIDS, if they are aware of it at all (Remafedi, 1987b). Furthermore, we can expect that AIDS will impact upon the relationship between older and younger gays across generations (Feldman, herein). They are not, to sum up, made from the same mold, or molded into the same roles, self-conceptions, and contexts.

Sexual identities and meanings are, like other areas of human life, profoundly shaped by culture and social structure. They are also constructed out of our life histories. Personal and social identities, be they gay or straight or something else, are no different in this regard, as Stoller (1985) suggested in his essay on meanings of the term homosexuality. We are forever in danger of forgetting this, because we assume from cultural ideals or political rhetoric that what *seems to be* is. When a homogeneous category such as "gay" or "lesbian" is available for self-identification and social attribution, the temptation to leave the "splitters" of cultural relativism and join the "lumpers" of universalist social classification becomes very great.

A simple illustration shows, however, the fallacy in this tendency to the lumping of universalism. "Female" is a sexual type in morphology, whereas "feminine" is a gender category whose meanings vary enormously (Rosaldo & Lamphere, 1973). To say "she is a black female" compresses cultural factors of both the gender- and color-codes of a culture. To add "she is a black feminist" further splits the categorization. And to conclude that "she is a black lesbian," but not a "black feminist lesbian," reveals an enormously complex system of differing identities and cultural scenes to which the person is oriented. Many other examples could be adduced to make the same point in our own culture: gays and lesbians do share things in common, by virtue of their general cultural tradition and their particular sexual orientations, but there are many other ways in which they are also distinct. Deborah Wolf examined such nuances in her important study *The Lesbian Community* (1979), which newer studies have expanded upon (Kehoe, 1986).

Now when we turn to the question of cross-cultural variations, the problems multiply because the "surface structures" of shared cultural meanings are no longer constant. This leaves only sexual orientation as a common denominator of homogeneity cross-culturally. Yet, having recognized that sexual identities and meanings are, in certain respects, also culturally constructed, we are left with what would seem to be very little homogeneity—essence—at all (see Blackwood's 1986 critical collection in this regard).

To return to the above example, to say of our "black lesbian" that she is a Brazilian greatly compounds the illustration, and to locate further her relevant identity and contexts of real-life action, we need to know something about her class and education and generation. What is the link between her politics and sexual orientation?[19] This strains the example to the point that we must wonder: In what way is her black lesbian identity like that of an American at all? And is the term "lesbian" her own or was it imposed upon her by outsiders?

These issues in the interpretation of meanings beset the understanding of homosexuality in many times and places. For some, such as the historian John Boswell (1980), "gay" is such a universal category (or perhaps an essence) that he sees as present across the centuries in reference to identities of persons, even in Archaic societies. Many have disagreed with this usage (reviewed in Greenberg & Bystryn, 1982; Herdt, 1987b; Murray, 1984); others are more sympathetic. My point, however, is that the homogenizing of same-sex desire goes too far when it is argued that variations in culture and history are mere accretion or residue in the understanding of such different lives.

The similarities between gays and lesbians who themselves adopt these words as their identities in urban centers around the world, whether Western or Third World, provide new support for the idea of cross-cultural continuities, however. The mere presence of the lexemes "gay/lesbian" is not sufficient to interpret the related identities and meanings as homologous, as Murray (1984) has suggested before and as Carrier notes herein. To what extent are Western tourists a primary cause of this increasingly visible gay category abroad, especially in large cities such as Paris, Rome, Hong Kong, and Buenos Aires? We cannot yet be sure, for there are other structural and world system forces at work that clearly are homogenizing the shape of sexual categories around the world (Adam, 1987; Aries, 1986; Foucault, 1980; Harris, 1982; Murray, 1984; Weeks, 1985; see below Parker, Ross, herein). Nonetheless, the local knowledge and symbolic values of homosexually identified persons determine in many ways not only the structural form of their sexual identities and same-sex relationships, but also the cultural content of their sensibilities, or, to return to Sontag's concept, the richness or impoverishment of their consciousness and communicative styles as these are woven into their particular homosexualities.

We must avoid the dangers, both conceptual/intellectual and political, of assuming too much or too little homogeneity. We cannot settle the matter of whether those homosexuals who themselves self-identify as gay/lesbian are more alike or more different in their essence, their "is-ness" (Plummer, 1981), or in their behavior; such closure would, at present, be premature. Indeed, the studies reported herein throw into new relief basic questions surrounding assumptions about the "essentialism" and "constructionism" of this subspecies of homosexuality: the emergent adolescent identity "gay/lesbian," here and abroad. But to sharpen our analysis, and more fully consider the preconceptions reviewed, let us now highlight the coming out process among this younger generation.

VARIATIONS IN THE COMING OUT PROCESS

Perhaps no aspect of adolescent homosexuality is as weighty or rich in its cultural sensibilities as that of the coming out process, the declaration of one's sexual orientation, across cultures. And, just as well, no other element of the present body of gay and lesbian research is as badly and urgently in need of new models and fresh ideas.[20] We do not know very well whether coming out has changed much over the past few years. For example, shall we consider coming out to mean "out to the self," or only "out to others"? Disclosure may occur to friends but not to family. And the teenager faces the question of whether to come out in high school, to heterosexual peers, and in contexts of work and religion. Here all of the previously mentioned preconceptions historically at play can be understood as they are experienced and practiced in the lives of adolescents and their social worlds.

We can place this coming out discourse in a new light if we think of coming out as a rite of passage in the anthropological sense of the term. Rites of passage, as Van Gennep (1960) argued long ago, typically structure life crisis events among traditional peoples. Their recurrent processes seem to involve (a) separation from the society as a whole; (b) isolation into a special or liminal (from the French word *limin*, for threshold or door) period, with taboos and restrictions of a sacred character; (c) followed by reaggregation or assimilation back into secular society. Life crisis events necessitate ritualization by their effect upon social status changes: from childhood to adulthood, by the onset of puberty, with birth and death and marriage. Each transformation in social state utilizes ritual process to adjust people's behavior to new and appropriate rights and duties, knowledge and identities, as these refashion social relationships with others. Transition rights also change the persons' interior and exterior, thus linking their psychological states and cultural knowledge to their new moral and sociopolitical responsibilities. Van Gennep himself used a house with many rooms as the key image of society, each room representing a social state or developmental stage, each life transition requiring passage through a threshold, the timeless and formless liminal ritual period, that led onto, and in its turn affected, all the other rooms or social roles. In spite of all the differences ostensibly separating the situation of gay teenagers from those of tribal initiates, such as the Sambia with whom I have worked in New Guinea (Herdt, 1981), there are useful parallels to be drawn from the image.

Teenagers today are "betwixt and between" (Turner, 1967) different social worlds as never before. For lesbian and gay youth, this inbetweeness is represented by the ordinary heterosexual lifestyles of their parents, on the one hand, and the adult gay and lesbian community, on the other. To feel different and then direct oneself into new contexts opens up basic challenges of the life crisis sort, as suggested by Van Gennep. The closer young people are to puberty, or to separating from their parents' households, the more acutely will they experience their situation as crisis (see Boxer & Cohler, herein). The life crisis, it is true, may begin only in their heads, by the kind of self-suspicion or the cognitive dissonance mentioned earlier. But then, there is real-life action: the exciting and difficult opportunities, or lack of such, to explore, probe, and experiment with new feelings and ideas (Plummer, herein). Thus, more than metaphor are references in the literature, such as Jay and Young's (1977), to the coming out process as a "rite of passage."

Teenagers may at first feel isolated or depressed or worse. They may feel desperate to change their situation (Robertson, 1981). Or they may not, in which case they may postpone their developmental change until after high school, or college, until a heterosexual marriage, or to some later point in adulthood (Lee, 1977). Whatever the case, youth must deal with the increasing disparity between their own inner desires and desired external objects—romantic partners, new cultural roles—and a working through of the preconceptions that increasingly frustrate and even strangle them: heterosexual ethnocentrism, inversion, stigma, homogeneous cloning. Secrecy is a significant but poorly understood part of this liminal transition (see Martin, 1982; Warren, 1980). Their eventual changes, as outcome variables, depend upon several factors, including their mental well-being, age, sex, socioeconomic status, ethnicity, urban or rural ambiance, and the degree of support from their familial and cultural systems. We shall touch upon these factors presently.

But to continue on rites of passage, the anthropological analogy would seem to falter in two ways for gay youth. First, they experience the life crisis in isolation, apart from significant others, seemingly not initiated by formal procedures nor as part of an age set or cohort, and even unsupported by the society at large. Second, our society has traditionally suppressed and ignored the social state of being homosexual, especially among adolescents, so that apart from the stigma and being pariah, they have no clear "room" into which they can move and be recognized as esteemed social actors.

To the first objection, it can be argued that social and technological changes have made media and periodical images of the gay world available to many adolescents, even those in rural areas. Gay groups, especially supportive homophile self-help groups (Anderson, 1987), today serve essentially as liminal cohorts and contexts for coming out. Other contexts of coming out, such as the armed services, are also available but more problematical, as noted variously by the large social surveys of homosexuality (Bell & Weinberg, 1978; Jay & Young, 1977).

To the second objection, that our society is a house without room for the homosexual status traditionally, we can offer the signs of some social change. The gay and lesbian world, however oppressed and dehumanized, now presents an alternative social reality for the teenager, in contrast to other normative lifestyles. Society has added a small and perhaps rather poorly furnished back room (some might say a jail cell), but this nevertheless exists, and its existence is surely vital in easing the identity transition process, as Lillian Faderman (1981) argued in writing that those women who come out now are spared some of the painful experiences of those who did so prior to the late 1960s and early 1970s. Political gains of the last two decades have enabled this, and ultimately, political sovereignty rests upon cultural sovereignty. Plummer (1981) also suggested that the existence of this other cultural world, even in the face of stigma, permits young homosexuals now to "rewrite" their personal histories, by "adapting to and creating homosexual meanings . . . [and then] incorporating these into one's life pattern" (p. 93). The revised cultural context gives expanded personal meaning to the coming out process for young gays.

There is another dimension of contemporary coming out that should be mentioned here: its younger, adolescent age, which links the problems of gay youth to those of adolescence in our mainstream culture. Since the time of Dank's (1971) classic study on coming out, studies have shown that the mean age of coming out has dropped, at least in urban areas. Dank (1971, N = 179, nonrandom sample) reported a mean age of 19.3 years. Troiden and Goode (1980) more recently reported a mean of 16.3 years for age of first self-definition as homosexual, and Coleman (1982) reported age 15 for males, and age 20 for females coming out. Remafedi (1987a) recently reported a mean age of 14, among gay youth who self-identify as such. Michael Ross (herein) reports on the mean age of realization of coming out in four countries: Sweden (14.1 years), Australia (12.5 years), Finland (13.9 years), and Ireland (15.6

years). The more sexually restrictive the culture, the later age at which one will discover one's own homosexuality. The mean age of becoming homosexually active, however, is much later, between 5 and 7 years later for these countries, respectively. These studies are suggestive but problematic, in that the coming out process is not always defined identically.

Male and female age differences are and always have been significant in coming out, as Troiden reports herein, for lesbians have tended to come out later than their male counterparts, although this pattern is changing (see Schneider, herein). This adolescent age range raises adjustment problems that are similar to those of heterosexual teenagers, including the emergence of the sexual (Gagnon, 1979) in girls and boys, with its attendant social conflicts. Other issues are separation from home, entry into college or work, and the quest for adult goals. Yet gay youth experience the stigma and burden of coming out on top of all this. The wonder is the relatively good mental health of gays and lesbians (Cohen & Stein, 1986; Gonsiorek, 1982).

Ironically, most accounts of normative adolescent development have been conceptualized within the conflict and crisis model (Blos, 1962; A. Freud, 1958). Empirical studies, such as those by Offer and Offer (1975) and Vaillant (1971), however, increasingly suggest that the conflictual emphasis is inaccurate. Other studies have reported positive relationships with peers and parents among heterosexual teens, though sexuality was not a central issue (Douvan & Adelson, 1966; Kandel & Lesser, 1972). Nevertheless, a recent commentary suggested that the experience of adolescence is more difficult than ever (Hamburg, Nightingale, & Takanishi, 1987). The conflictual nature of the homosexual adolescent's experience is also prominently noted in the literature (Anderson, 1987; Troiden, 1979; and see Boxer & Cohler, herein). Surely, cultural and generational changes have influenced this. But precisely how are things more or less conflictual now? What research increasingly suggests is that, as the age of coming out, of the life crisis transition, lowers for gay youth, additional developmental age-related pressures may overburden the gay or lesbian teenager. This has greater psychosocial costs, and it raises risk factors, such as suicide, that should be studied more intensively, a later point of discussion.

Very often the question of coming out has been posed as one in which we can infer from the empirical data normative stages of youth identity development among gays and lesbians. The concern here is with charting a territory of homosexual development, in part as counterpoint to that of heterosexuality (Plummer, 1981); that is, identity formation as a process. Troiden's paper reviews and reconsiders important findings from this research genre. He argues, in relation to the decreasing age of coming out, that if it is to emerge, the sense of being gay is "probable" by late adolescence (see Remafedi, 1987a). Moreover, once this awareness emerges, he suggests that invariant psychosocial phases, which he labels as sensitivity, individuation, consolidation, and acceptance, occur and must be passed through, on the way to the expression of a mature gay/lesbian identity consonant with the prevailing cultural lifestyle of the local population (cf. also Coleman, herein; Cass, 1984; Plummer, 1981). It is assumed by some (e.g., Silverstein, 1981) that these phases will spontaneously emerge at no matter what actual age the person comes out.

To what extent are such identity development stages the same for males and females? Are they universal and applicable to other societies? Tremble and his colleagues point up differences in the process based on sex, ethnicity, and religious conventions. The majority of our data are on males, however; an unfortunate slant that is to be found throughout the literature. We need more research on younger lesbians. The validity of these stage models in the final analysis is critical, but remains to be fully tested cross-culturally to understand how identity is not only a process, but also a product of particular cultural contexts.

Other contemporary factors of coming out among teenagers are also illuminating: significant life events, contexts, and relationships can be seen as macrolevel factors that influence microfactors, such as sex and class. Of course these cannot be decontextualized from the total sociocultural systems in which they are embedded, but for the sake of heuristic clarity, I shall treat them here as somewhat separate elements of gay youth development.

The sex of the person, as hinted above, has been shown to structure the coming out process in various ways (reviewed in Jay & Young, 1977; Ponse, 1980). A global dimension of this aspect

cross-culturally concerns the subordinate status of females in patriarchal cultures (Faderman, 1981; Rubin, 1975). A significant empirical difference between males and females has been shown to be
how sex versus love enters into their differential coming out processes. Males tend more often to define themselves as gay in contexts of same-sex erotic contact, whereas females experience their
lesbian feelings in situations of romantic love and emotional attachment (reviewed in Troiden, herein; Ponse, 1978). Such a sex difference reminds us of the contrast in moral voices through which
females versus males speak (Gilligan, 1982). Where females emphasize attachment and personal orientations, males stress independence and positional relationships in public. We can recognize easily how this sex-related difference is structurally based, in the sex
roles of our society, in that the normative contexts for exploration
of same-sex experience are culturally structured, too. Many of the
contexts of sexual exploration listed by Dank (1971), such as the
army, public toilets, dormitories, and boy scouts, are available only
to males. Females were, as we know, made more invisible in the
domestic domain until very recently (Abbott & Love, 1972; Kehoe,
1986), and Schneider has documented the consequences of this for
young lesbians in narrative accounts. Moreover, the gender roles
and life expectations of the sexes are very different, with their reproductive and parenting roles creating contrary developmental and
social problems. The pressures on young girls to conform to heterosexual roles are very great (Kehoe, 1986), particularly in more traditional societies, such as those of Latin America and Europe,
where social roles create quite distinct adaptations in the sexes (Carrier, 1980).

Socioeconomic status is another critical, but still largely unknown contributor to the coming out process as a rite of passage.
Class is significant in structuring gender codes and roles. The more
male/female roles are dichotomized, the greater the tendency of the
inversion preconception to manifest itself in cross-gender behavior
(Harry, 1982; Whitam, 1983), a point that Carrier has critically
examined here as elsewhere (Carrier, 1980). More traditional non-
Western polarized societies seem closer to the working class norms
of Western culture in this rule-bound restrictiveness (Harry, 1985).
Both education and class-related attitudes affect the timing of first

sexual contact, via attitudes toward sexual activity before adulthood (reviewed in Pollak, 1985). Plummer indicates this to some extent in his article on the relationship between gays and youth culture, showing differential class responses to "punk" styles. The androgyny of punk provides a fluidity which in some ways mediates sex role dichotomies and class barriers.[21] The relationship between urbanized gay gentry and middle- and upper-middle-class consumer norms is well known (Altman, 1979; Cassells, 1983; Pollak, 1985). The large disposable incomes of gay men, which presumably have led to the term "guppy" (gay urban mobile young professional), have been commented upon, as have their professionality and higher education norms (Bell & Weinberg, 1978). One wonders about the representativeness of these samples, however (Carrier, 1979).

The impact of the coming out process on education in gay youth is an area that has been neglected. The literature is contradictory on this point: Harry (1982) argued that gay males "compensate for their negative feelings about their homosexuality through the acquisition of higher education" (p. 173). Class is clearly a factor, for in Harry's sample, blue-collar persons tend to feel more guilt than white-collar persons regarding their homosexuality, and guilt makes the engine run, in Harry's view (see also Levitt & Klassen, 1974). A West German study (Reichert & Dannecker, 1977) seems to support Harry's finding. However, Saghir and Robbins (1973) found, on the other hand, that homosexual men are more likely than heterosexuals to drop out of college before graduation. We may have a cohort effect here: How far these findings apply to gay (and lesbian) teenagers and young adults in the mid-1980s is unclear. Here is an area of research desperately in need of careful study.

The disadvantages of ethnic minorities in coming out today are only very dimly known (Adam, 1978). Tremble shows the effects of coming out in a multicultural context in Canada. One suspects that a greater degree of acceptance of variation in cultural standards and life styles may underlie the response of heterosexual Canadians to gay and lesbian youth there (cf. Soares, 1979; Vasquez, 1979). By contrast, Gerstell and her colleagues hint that race is a powerful force for segregation and boundary maintenance in interactions between gay and straight youth in the Chicago area, with blacks being suspected of gay inclinations merely by associating with white teen-agers (cf. Vernon, 1971). Echos of this ethnic/class barrier can also be found in Carrier's study. Here is a factor of gay identity con-struction and maintenance that begs to be studied in multiethnic social fields (see Bass-Hass, 1968; Hidalgo & Christensen, 1976; and Rich, 1979).

The difference between coming out in rural versus urban areas is another, largely unknown, dimension of the total developmental situation, though it has long been believed to influence significantly the age and characteristics of the gay experience in American soci-ety. Howard Brown (1976), for instance, provided poignant por-traits of "homosexuals in small towns," attempting to counteract the attitude of some gays, to wit: "Let them move to the cities" (p. 89). Silverstein (1981) suggested that males in rural communi-ties can grow up naive of their own eroticism, and thus "be pre-vented from even knowing that they are gay" (p. 107). They have no label and role for their experience (Troiden & Goode, 1980). The large social surveys done on urbanized adult gay men reveal their attitude about residing in gay urban communities for harmony and protection (Bell & Weinberg, 1978). Now, Lynch (1987) has told us, "non-ghetto" gays have moved back to the suburbs.[22]

The coming out literature generally suggests that youth in close proximity to urban centers have more opportunities for making sup-portive homosexual contacts, particularly those that derive from the recent appearance of homophile coming out groups (Anderson, 1987). Our Chicago study provides a new account of such a group (Gerstell et al.). So much is the situation for gay youth better in the cities that Rose Robertson (1981), in a recent essay on young gays, suggested that those in urban areas are "lucky," and "workers in this field will be aware of the absolute despair of young people in isolated small towns who feel themselves to be homosexual" (p. 172). Such a dismal picture does seem warranted based upon what is known from America, though Silverstein (1981) provided a more positive report.

The chapters that follow, on England and France, Mexico, and Brazil, the comparative project undertaken by Ross, and the Cana-dian studies of Schneider and her colleagues, suggest that the urban scene in other countries tends to be freer and more supportive of the emergence of alternative sexual orientations elsewhere, too. We must take care in interpreting these trends, and in understanding their causes, as indicated above. Not all of these youth self-identify as gay or homosexual, or the appropriate kindred cultural identity. The presence of Western and local tourists has surely contributed to this trend (Pollak, 1986). Yet the studies by Carrier, and Parker, respectively, clearly reveal how local "gay" movements provide their own infrastructural support for the coming out process in teens. How widespread are such local gay support systems? (For reviews see Adam, 1987; Lauritsen & Thorstad, 1974; and Murray, 1984.)

In a short piece on the Sulu Islands near Borneo, Nimmo (1978) reported on a traditional form of male transvestism that was usually indicative of adult homosexuality. Nimmo found that in the process of urbanization, other Sulu males not only did not manifest this form of homosexuality, they even became reluctant to engage in any same-sex contact because of having internalized negative Western stereotypes of "the homosexual" in the cities. Nimmo's paper reminds us that a gloomy and perhaps decadent image of the city, involving crime, pollution, degeneracy, is prevalent in Western mythology, and that the history of Western homosexuality in Western cities is embedded in it (Aries, 1986). One point to draw from such examples is that the phenomenon of gay youth is rapidly changing in our "global village" and that it results from many complex forces that create unusual events and contexts for the affirmation of homosexual desires.

What role does the family system contribute in the process of coming out today? Familial factors of all kinds are always shaped by the broader cultural environment. Attitudes toward homosexuality, and the presence of homophobia within family members, often reflect general social norms and values (see Ross, herein). Most of our studies herein touch upon this in myriad ways. Yet the importance of parental attitudes, as a directive force in the everyday lives of teenagers, cannot be exaggerated. And here, the preconceptions outlined earlier, particularly the assumption of heterosexuality, still reign. "The grasping at straws by so many parents is significant. It demonstrates the still widely held belief that all young people are heterosexual and can only be corrupted into homosexuality by contact with homosexuals" (Robertson, 1981, p. 174).

Martin (1982) commented in this context on the generalized

"pernicious equation of homosexuality and danger to children" (p. 54), a reflection of the stereotypes mentioned above (see Warren, 1980). Such attitudes result in prohibitions on contact with gays and lesbians, teenagers or adults. The stigma, however, particularly transfers by association with gay adults, which accounts, in the adolescent experience, for the early and still prevailing distance between gay groups and the individual, as role models (Martin, 1982). But there are new signs of hope, as revealed through stories of parents of gays and lesbians, stories which tell of frustration, courage, and the capacity of parents to transcend stereotypes through love of their children (Muller, 1987; Rafkin, 1987).

Contact with peers is as significant for gay youth as for straight peers, and these peers are less suspect than older gays. Open rebellion against parents is also an option, but one that sometimes creates grave social and financial hardships for youth, who may be forced out of their homes. Extreme emotional responses may accompany this rejection, including suicide. Part of the attraction to present-day peer groups is their fluid, unisex character, which may bewilder parents. The nature of punk culture dovetails with the coming out process, as Plummer shows below, emphasizing mutual acceptance by peers: "Where being yourself was acceptable, whether that was gay, straight, bisexual, or cucumber freak," Aaron Fricke wrote (1981, p. 49). Today, youth gangs are remarkable in how age outweighs gender as the key mode of membership and identification (Lafont, 1986). Fluctuations in societal gender roles and norms underlie this androgyny, signaling an overall change in adolescent sensibilities with regard to being lesbian or gay. Indeed, Aries (1986) suggested that this is a transcultural trend:

> The unisex fashion is a clear indication of a general change in society. Tolerance of homosexuality is the result of changes in the way the sexes present themselves to the world, in their actions, in their professional lives, in their families, but especially in their function as symbolic figures. (p. 64)

Foucault (1980) would probably have agreed with this summary, though he might have added that it is the product of many structural and infrastructural forces, which include various localized homosexual or gay liberation movements around the world. Or, to cite

Parker's perspective from Brazil on the matter, these alternative youth scenes and groups provide "multiple discourses and realities" on society and sexuality for the construction of gay adolescent lives.

A final issue concerns the understanding of social problems among gay youth. Such was the bias of an earlier day that the social problems of gay and lesbian youth were inflated by the stereotyped preconceptions already noted, or else completely ignored and denied. We must make no mistake about it: This is purely a result of homophobia and ghettoization. To take but one example, Berger found, in his study *Gay and Gray* (1982), that "when gerontologists talk about the elderly, they mean heterosexual elderly" (p. 13). The gay and lesbian elderly have been terribly ignored, it is true, because they are structurally invisible (Kehoe, 1986); but more significantly because their *existence has been psychologically denied* — in the minds of health care providers, researchers, government agencies, and the public at large. Yet, in his study, Berger (1982) found "striking similarities" between elderly gays and other older Americans, which argues for increased care-giving to the elderly homosexual. The general point could be extended to encompass gay teenage problems of adjustment, grief, depression, drug abuse, school achievement, and so forth. Paradoxically, gays present a "social problem" to society, but when particular social problems are studied, gays are often ignored.

The "problems" of the gay teenager must be understood in this sense. In an unpublished report, Gibson (n.d.) highlighted the issues in understanding gay teenage suicide, which is alarmingly high and must be a cause for great concern. Between 20 and 35% of gay youth have made suicide attempts, the best available statistics show (Gibson, p. 2). Youthful gays often internalize negative stereotypes and images of themselves. And when you have been told that you are "sick, bad and wrong for being who you are," you begin to believe it, Gibson wrote (p. 5). Peers, older gays, and especially supportive family members can help relieve this terrible pattern.

More than anything else, the impact of AIDS is changing social attitudes regarding homosexuality and gay youth. Much new research is presently underway to understand and fight the disease (Feldman & Johnson, 1986). Meanwhile, fear of contagion, hysteria, and hatred have spread. AIDS is creating new and unique problems in society and in the gay world (Herdt, 1987a), problems the likes of which we can still only imagine. It will undoubtedly produce far-reaching changes in the nature and meaning of same-sex behavior and relationships. Much has already been demonstrated about the effects of the disease upon the gay population, including the media presentations of it (Baker, 1986). AIDS is now a global problem, requiring global solutions and unprecedented international cooperation.

Yet I fear that not enough emphasis has been placed upon our understanding of AIDS risks and prevention in teenagers, a point made clearly in a recent Surgeon General's report. As with fashions and school performance, teenage suicide, and drug use, peer culture can influence sex behavior and awareness of AIDS (Fullilove, 1987). We urgently need research on adolescent populations and their perceptions and handling of AIDS. Feldman (herein) shows that American adolescents are still woefully ignorant of what constitutes "safe sex" behavior. Millan and Ross (1987) concluded similarly of Australian youth.

Equally important, AIDS is no doubt affecting the coming out process in ways that are yet unknown. Fear of AIDS has made parental acceptance more complicated than ever (Robinson & Walters, 1987). It has changed self-acceptance, too. As one teenager recently told me in our Chicago study: "I never wanted to be gay. Now, with AIDS, I have even less reason to feel positive about that part of myself." We urgently need new studies of this problem.

AIDS has exacerbated an already existing generational difference between older and younger gays. This, too, must be seen in perspective, as but one piece of a larger mosaic of oppression of gays across societies. Berger (1982) noted, for instance, that the invisibility and peripheralization of elderly gays have isolated them from their peers — not just their heterosexual, but also their homosexual counterparts. These older gays are isolated from youth as well. Furthermore, the fear of AIDS contact has seemingly alienated teenagers from younger and middle-aged adults (Feldman, herein), not merely as role models, but just as companions and friends. This is regrettable for many reasons, not the least of which is that older gays and lesbians could help in the reduction of AIDS risks to teens. Let us strive and work for a change in this unfortunate trend. For, as

Damien Martin (1982) concluded, "Stigmatization of the gay adolescent has evolved from centuries of misinformation and fear. Education through direct teaching and the example of role models will be the best way to attack discrimination at its root" (pp. 63-64).

CONCLUSION

We have just begun to open a new discourse on understanding homosexuality and adolescence. The papers that follow represent some of the best and newest knowledge we have on the lives and problems of gay youth. And yet, there is so much that remains unknown; we have barely scratched the surface of the sensibilities and culture of these young people. There are many controversies involved in these studies, for this road to understanding is filled with potholes and intellectual bumps and political landmines. More could have been said about some topics and less about others. We have, in such discourse, the feeling that we have failed to capture much of what we were looking for, or that what we found is not exactly what we might have expected, or even wanted to find. Yet our papers show growth, crisis, and change—always the wellsprings of human life—and they have helped to move us beyond what Plummer (1981) referred to as that notorious preoccupation with the childhoods of homosexuals, whose lives seemed to end in their potentiality at age 5. We look forward to many new contributions to follow from this one, which will surely not be the end but rather the beginning of an era of research on gay youth.

NOTES

1. This "we" must stand for the gay and lesbian community, the social science establishment, and—notwithstanding the "bicultural" identity of the gay/social scientist (Murray, 1984)—the public gay laity studied mainly by the gay researchers now being studied themselves by (mostly gay and lesbian) historians.
2. Altman, 1982:

> But at the same time there is a sense in which style and fashion mold behavior, and to this extent the impact of gays is changing American society . . . [though] much of what I have to say applies to other Western

countries. . . . the new homosexual affirmation can be found in Sydney, Strasbourg, and even São Paulo, as well as in San Francisco. (p. xii)

3. Dr. Kenneth Sladkin, Chairman, Section on Adolescent Health, American Academy of Pediatrics. Cited in *Pediatric News*, December 1983, p. 34.

4. Reviewed in Ross (1980), and recently raised by Risman (1984) in objection to the entire foundation of Joseph Harry's *Gay children grown up* (1982).

5. "The denial of role models is an essential part of the total stigmatization process" (Martin, 1982, p. 55). See also Silverstein (1981).

6. See, for instance, Hippler (1986).

7. Sontag, 1982:

The sensibility of an era is not only its most decisive but also its most perishable aspect. One may capture the ideas (intellectual history) and the behavior (social history) of an epoch without ever touching upon the taste which informed those ideas, that behavior. (p. 106)

8. See, for example, Adam, 1987; Martin, 1982; Plummer, 1975, 1981; and for the longer historical view, see Foucault, 1980.

9. Shepard, 1987:

This is why societies like Britain and the U.S.A. have had such an exaggerated horror of homosexuality — the sexual invert is assumed to have subversive political attitudes as well, should be banned from high office, and until recently was considered not merely as a potential, but as an actual criminal. (p. 264)

10. See De Cecco's (1984) edited volume on this. What remains obscure, however, are present forms of homophobia among youth.

11. Thus, Ollendorff (1966), in a period work that is typical, stated, "We feel, therefore, that *the occurrence of adolescent homosexuality is a product of a wrong social setting* [italics in original] . . . and is a presenting factor of major importance in most psychiatric illnesses" (p. 51).

12. Ann Muller (1987) referred to these Freudian stereotypes as the "trolls of psychiatry" in her narrative account of the parents of gays and lesbians.

13. By contrast, though homosexuality was illegal in Germany after 1871, lesbianism was ignored there and elsewhere, and the Nazis' "counter-revolution" in criminalizing all forms of homosexuality primarily affected males (Heger, 1980). Elsewhere, Lauritsen and Thorstad (1974) argued that the homosexual rights movement had the same dual effects upon Germany after the turn of the century, both of which the Nazis were to undo by the late 1930s.

14. D'Emilio (1983):

Gay liberation used the demonstrations of the New Left as recruiting grounds and appropriated the tactics of confrontational politics for its own ends. The ideas that suffused youth protest found their way into gay liberation, where they were modified and adapted to describe the oppression of homosexuals and lesbians. The apocalyptic rhetoric and the sense of impending revolution then made a public avowal of their sexuality seem insignificant. (p. 233)

15. Gays, some commentators (Altman, 1982; Aries, 1986) have said, put sex back into polite mixed company, whereas for straights, the themes of the consumer and procreative age still reign. When Michel Foucault visited the West Coast before his death, he is reported to have complained of dining with heterosexual yuppies, who, over dinner, seemed only to discuss their personal computers and their children.

16. No doubt the terrible rise of AIDS during the past several years has had an impact upon these trends, perhaps reversing them. Because the social effects of this are so rapidly unfolding, we cannot be sure of even their near-term outcomes.

17. Steve Murray (personal communication, March 1, 1987) reminded me that the residential North Beach area in San Francisco may have created the early critical mass of gays necessary to mobilize and reject the then prevailing stereotypes of homosexuality.

18. The lesbian and women's culture literature does not emphasize the erotic in the same way as does the gay male scene (cf. Krieger, 1982). The lesbian experience seems to emphasize love and attachment to women (Jay & Young, 1977) as much as the erotic. And Marg Schneider (personal communication, March 11, 1987) reminded me that feminist issues may ultimately divide gay men from women in ways that transcend the affinities of sexual orientation.

19. Weeks (1987) pointed out that the link between lesbianism as political or sexual identity seems tenuous and more of a choice in longstanding evocative trends in the literature.

20. The existing literature on coming out, so extensive and fruitful, has not been fully tapped for new concepts and syntheses. Troiden's invaluable review, herein, is a marvelous tool in rethinking it. But my suggestion for new research arises mainly from the sense that the problem has been, at once, too broadly and too narrowly defined; broad in the sense that we need more microscopic studies of the full range of homosexualities beyond that of American WASPS (Carrier, 1979), and narrow in the sense that the ideas are constrained too much by the folk concepts of Western psychology and sociology, as represented by the primary body of work done in these disciplines in the U.S. When an anthropology of the coming out process emerges, we shall have passed a critical conceptual roadmark in the understanding of homosexuality for humans, one which could transcend the increasingly threadbare dichotomizing of essentialist/constructionist models.

21. See Fricke's (1981) vignette on the "Rocky Horror Show" film and its cult followers: Here is a common urban gay youth context.

22. Interestingly enough, Lynch's (1987) study of suburban gays (mean age of coming out around 30) suggested that distance from urban areas does indeed postpone the coming out process.

REFERENCES

Abbott, S., & Love, B. (1972). *Sappho was a right-on woman*. New York: Stein & Day.

Adam, B. (1978). *The survival of domination*. New York: Elsevier.

Adam, B. (1987). *The rise of a gay and lesbian movement*. Boston: Twayne.

Altman, D. (1973). *Homosexual: Oppression and liberation*. New York: Avon Books.

Altman, D. (1979). *Coming out in the seventies*. Sydney: Wild & Woolley.

Altman, D. (1981). *Coming out in the seventies*. Boston: Alyson. (Shortened version of 1979 edition).

Altman, D. (1982). *The Americanization of the homosexual, the homosexualization of America*. New York: St. Martin's Press.

Anderson, D. (1987). Family and peer relations of gay adolescents. *Adolescent Psychiatry, 14*, 165-178.

Aries, P. (1986). Thoughts on the history of homosexuality. In P. Aries & A. Bejin (Eds.), *Western sexuality* (pp. 62-75). London: Basil Blackwell.

Baker, A. J. (1986). The portrayal of AIDS in the media: An analysis of articles in the New York Times. In D. Feldman & T. Johnson (Eds.), *The social dimension of AIDS* (pp. 179-196). New York: Praeger.

Bass-Hass, R. (1968). The Lesbian Dyad. *Journal of Sex Research, 4*, 108-126.

Bell, A., & Weinberg, M. S. (1978). *Homosexualities: A study of diversity among men and women*. New York: Simon & Schuster.

Bell, A. P., Weinberg, M. S., & Hammersmith, S. (1981). *Sexual preference*. Bloomington, IN: Indiana University Press.

Berger, R. (1982). *Gay and gray*. Urbana, IL: University of Illinois Press.

Blackwood, E. (1986). Breaking the mirror: The construction of lesbianism and the anthropological discourse on homosexuality. In E. Blackwood (Ed.), *Anthropology and homosexual behavior* (pp. 1-17). New York: The Haworth Press.

Blos, P. (1962). *On adolescence: A psychoanalytic interpretation*. New York: The Free Press-Macmillan.

Boswell, J. (1980). *Christianity, social tolerance and homosexuality*. Chicago: University of Chicago Press.

Brown, H. (1976). *Familiar faces: Hidden lives*. New York: Harcourt, Brace, Jovanovich.

Carrier, J. (1979). [Review of *Homosexualities: A study of diversity among men and women*, by A. Bell & M.S. Weinberg, 1978]. *Journal of Homosexuality, 4*, 296-298.

Carrier, J. (1980). Homosexual behavior in crosscultural perspective. In J. Marmor (Ed.), *Homosexual behavior: A modern reappraisal* (pp. 100-122). New York: Basic Books.

Cass, V. (1984). Homosexual identity: A concept in need of a definition. *Journal of Homosexuality, 9*(4), 105-126. New York: The Haworth Press.

Castells, M. (1983). Cultural identity, sexual liberation and urban structure: The gay community in San Francisco: In *The city and the grass roots: A cross-cultural theory of urban social movements* (pp. 138-172). London: Edward Arnold.

Cohen, C. J., & Stein, T. S. (1986). Reconceptualizing individual psychotherapy with gay men and lesbians. In C. J. Cohen & T. S. Stein (Eds.), *Contemporary perspectives on psychotherapy with lesbians and gay men* (pp. 27-54). New York: Plenum.

Coleman, E. (1982). Developmental stages in the coming out process. *Journal of Homosexuality, 7*(2/3), 31-43.

Dank, B. (1971). Coming out in the gay world. *Psychiatry, 34*, 180-197.

Darrow, W. W., Gorman, E. M., & Glick, B. P. (1986). The social origins of AIDS: Social change, sexual behavior and disease trends. In D. Feldman & T. Johnson (Eds.), *The social dimensions of AIDS* (pp. 95-110). New York: Praeger.

De Cecco, J. P. (1984). *Bisexual and homosexual identities: Critical theoretical issues*. New York: The Haworth Press.

De Cecco, J. P. (in press). Sex and more sex. In D. McWhirter (Ed.), *Homosexuality and heterosexuality*. New York: Oxford University Press.

D'Emilio, J. (1983). *Sexual politics, sexual communities*. Chicago: University of Chicago Press.

Douvan, E., & Adelson, J. (1966). *The adolescent experience*. New York: John C. Wiley & Sons.

Erikson, E. (1968). *Identity, youth and crisis*. New York: W. W. Norton.

Faderman, L. (1981). *Surpassing the love of men*. New York: William Morrow.

Feldman, D. A., & Johnson, T. M. (1986). Introduction, *The Social dimensions of AIDS: Methods and theory* (pp. 1-12). New York: Praeger.

Foucault, M. (1980). *The history of sexuality*. New York: Pantheon.

Freud, A. (1958). Adolescence. *Psychoanalytic study of the child, 13*, 255-278.

Fricke, A. (1981). *Reflections of a rock lobster*. Boston: Alyson.

Fullilove, M. (1987, Spring). Teens rap about drugs, STDs, and AIDS. *Multicultural Inquiry and Research on AIDS*, p. 1.

Gadamer, H. G. (1965). *Truth and method*. New York: Crossroad.

Gagnon, J. (1979). The interaction of gender roles and sexual conduct. In H. A. Katchadourian (Ed.), *Human sexuality* (pp. 225-245). Berkeley: University of California Press.

Gibson, P. (n.d.). Gay male and lesbian youth suicide. Unpublished manuscript.

Gilligan, C. (1982). *In a different voice*. Cambridge: Harvard University Press.

Gonsiorek, J. (Ed.). (1982). *Homosexuality: Social, psychological and biological issues*. Beverly Hills, CA: Sage Publications.

Green, R. (1987). *The "sissy boy syndrome" and the development of homosexuality*. New Haven, CT: Yale University Press.

Greenberg, D., & Bystryn, M. (1982). Christian intolerance of homosexuality. *American Journal of Sociology, 88*, 515-548.

Greenberg, J. (1976). A study of the self-esteem and alienation of male homosexuals. *The Journal of Psychology, 83*, 137-143.

Hamburg, D. A., Nightingale, E. O. & Takanishi, R. (1987). Facilitating the transitions of adolescence. *JAMA, 257*, 3405-3406.

Harris, M. (1982). *America now*. New York: Simon & Schuster.

Harry, J. (1982). *Gay children grown up*. New York: Praeger.

Harry, J. (1985). Defeminization and social class. *Archives of Sexual Behavior, 14*(1), 1-12.

Herdt, G. (1981). *Guardians of the flutes: Idioms of masculinity*. New York: McGraw-Hill.

Herdt, G. (1984). Ritualized homosexuality in the male cults of Melanesia, 1862-1982: An introduction. In G. Herdt (Ed.), *Ritualized Homosexuality in Melanesia* (pp. 1-81). Berkeley, CA: University of California Press.

Herdt, G. (1987a, March). AIDS and anthropology. *Anthropology Today*.

Herdt, G. (1987b). Homosexuality. *Encyclopedia of religion*, Vol. 3. Macmillan Religion Encyclopedia (17 vols.). New York: Macmillan.

Herdt, G. (1987c). *Sambia: Ritual and gender in New Guinea*. New York: Holt, Rinehart, & Winston.

Herger, H. (1980). *The men with the pink triangle* (D. Fernbach, Trans.). London: Gay Men's Press.

Heron, A. (1983). *One teenager in ten: Testimony by gay and lesbian youth*. New York: Warner Books.

Hidalgo, H. A., & Christensen, E. H. (1976). The Puerto Rican lesbian and the Puerto Rican community. *Journal of Homosexuality, 2*, 109-121.

Hippler, M. (1986, September 16). The problem and promise of gay youth. *The Advocate*, Issue 455.

Hoffman, M. (1968). *The gay world*. New York: Basic Books.

Hoffman, S. (1970). The cities of night: John Rechy's city of night and the American literature of homosexuality. In H. M. Ruitenbeek (Ed.), *Sexuality and identity* (pp. 390-402). New York: Delta.

Hooker, E. (1957). Adjustment of male homosexuals. *Journal Proj. Tech*, 21: 18-31.

Hooker, E. (1965). An empirical study of some relations between sexual patterns and gender identity in male homosexuals. In J. Money (Ed.), *Sex research: New developments* (pp. 24-52). New York: Holt, Rinehart, & Winston.

Hoult, T. F. (1984). Human sexuality in biological perspective: Theoretical and Methodological Considerations. *Journal of Homosexuality, 9*(2/3), 137-155.

Humphreys, L., & Miller, B. (1980). Identities in the emerging gay culture. In J. Marmor (Ed.), *Homosexual behavior* (pp. 142-156). New York: Basic Books.

Isay, R. A. (1986). The development of sexual identity in homosexual men. *The Psychoan. St. Child, 41*, 467-489.

Jay, K., & Young, A. (1977). *The gay report*. New York: Summit.

Kandel, D., & Lesser, G. (1972). *Youth in two worlds*. San Francisco: Jossey Bass.

Kehoe, M. (1986). Lesbians over 65: A triple invisible minority. *Journal of Homosexuality, 12*(3/4), 139-152.

Kinsey, A., Pomeroy, W. B., & Martin, C. E. (1948). *Sexual behavior in the human male*. Philadelphia: W. B. Saunders.

Kortaba, J. A., & Lang, N. G. (1986). Gay lifestyle change and AIDS: Preventive health care. In D. A. Feldman & T. A. Johnson (Eds.), *The social dimensions of AIDS* (pp. 127-144). New York: Praeger.

Krieger, S. (1982). Lesbian identity and community: Recent social science literature. *Signs, 8*, 91-108.

Lafont, H. (1986). Changing sexual behavior in French youth gangs. In P. Aries & A. Bejin (Eds.), *Western sexuality: Practice and precept in past and present times*. Oxford: Blackwell.

Laner, M. R., & Laner, R. H. (1979). Personal style or sexual preference? Why gay men are disliked. *Intl. Rev. Mod. Soc., 9*, 215-228.

Lauritsen, J., & Thorstad, D. (1974). *The early homosexual rights movement*. New York: Times Change Press.

Lee, J. A. (1977). Going public: A study in the sociology of homosexual liberation. *Journal of Homosexuality, 3*, 49-78.

Levine, M. (1979). *Gay men*. New York: Harper & Row.

Levitt, E., & Klassen, A. (1974). Public attitudes toward homosexuality. *Journal of Homosexuality, 1*, 29-43.

Leznoff, M., & Westley, W. (1956). The homosexual community. *Social Problems, 2*, 257-263.

Lockard, D. (1986). The lesbian community: An anthropological approach. In E. Blackwood (Ed.), *Anthropology and homosexual behavior* (pp. 83-95). New York: The Haworth Press.

Lynch, F. R. (1987). Non-ghetto gays: A sociological study of suburban homosexuals. *Journal of Homosexuality, 13*(4), 13-42.

McIntosh, M. (1968). The homosexual role. *Social Problems, 16*, 182-192.

McWhirter, D. P., & Mattison, A. (1984). *The male couple*. Englewood Cliffs, NJ: Prentice-Hall.

Martin, A. Damien. (1982). Learning to hide: Socialization of the gay adolescent. *Adolescent Psychiatry, 10*, 52-65.

Millan, G., & Ross, M. W. (1987). AIDS and gay youth: Attitudes and lifestyle modifications in young male homosexuals. *Community Health Studies, 11*, 52-53.

Minton, H., & McDonald, G. J. (1983/1984). Homosexual identity formation as a developmental process. *Journal of Homosexuality, 9*(2/3), 91-104.

Muller, A. (1987). *Parents matter*. New York: The Naiad Press.

Murray, S. O. (1979). The institutional elaboration of a quasi-ethnic community. *Intl. Rev. Mod. Sociol. 9*, 165-177.

Murray, S. O. (1984). *Social theory, homosexual realities*. New York: Gai Sabre Books.

Newton, E. (1972). *Mother camp*. Toronto: Prentice-Hall.

Nimmo, H. (1978). Relativity of sexual deviance: A Sulu example. *University of Oklahoma Papers in Anthropology, 19*, 91-97.

Offer, D., & Offer, J. B. (1975). *From teen-age to young manhood: A psychological study*. New York: Basic Books.

Ollendorff, R. (1966). *The juvenile homosexual experience and its effects on adult homosexuality*. New York: Julian Press.

Page, S., & Yee, M. (1985). Conception of male and female homosexual stereotypes among university undergraduates. *Journal of Homosexuality, 12*(1), 109-118.

Paul, J. (1983/84). The bisexual identity: An idea without social recognition. *Journal of Homosexuality, 9*(2/3), 45-63.

Plummer, K. (1975). *Sexual stigma*. Boston: Routledge & Kegan Paul.

Plummer, K. (1981). Homosexual categories: Some research problems in the labelling perspective of homosexuality. In K. Plummer (Ed.), *The makings of the modern homosexual* (pp. 53-75). London: Hutchinson.

Pollak, M. (1986). Male homosexuality—Or happiness in the ghetto. In P. Aries & A. Bejin (Eds.), *Western sexuality: practice and precept in past and present times*. London: Basil Blackwell.

Ponse, B. (1978). *Identities in the lesbian world: The social construction of the self*. Westport, CT: Greenwood.

Ponse, B. (1980). Lesbians and their worlds. In J. Marmor (Ed.), *Homosexual behavior:A modern reappraisal* (pp. 157-175). New York: Basic Books.

Rafkin, L. (1987). *Different daughters: A book by mothers of lesbians*. Pittsburgh: Cleis.

Read, K. (1980). *Other voices*. Toronto: Chandler & Sharpe.

Rechy, J. (1963). *City of night*. New York: Grove.

Reichert, T., & Dannecker, M. (1977). Male homosexuality in West Germany. *Journal of Sex Research, 13*, 35-53.

Reiss, A. (1961). The social integration of queers and peers. *Social Problems, 9*, 102-120.

Remafedi, G. (1987a). Male homosexuality: The adolescent's perspective. *Pediatrics, 79*, 326-330.

Remafedi, G. (1987b). Adolescent homosexuality: Psychosocial and medical implications. *Pediatrics, 79*, 331-337.

Rich, A. (1979). Disloyal to civilization: Feminism, racism, and gynephobia. *Chrysalis, 7*, 9-27.

Risman, B. J. (1984). [Review of *Gay Children Grown Up*, by J. Harry]. *Contemporary Sociology, 13*, 469-470.

Robertson, R. (1981). Young gays. In J. Hart & D. Richardson (Eds.), *The theory and practice of homosexuality* (pp. 170-176). London: Routledge & Kegan Paul.

Robinson, B., & Walters, L. (1987, April). The AIDS epidemic hits home. *Psychology Today*, pp. 48-52.

Roestler, T., & Deisher, R. W. (1972). Youthful male homosexuality. *Journal of American Medical Association, 219*, 1018-1023.

Rosaldo, M. A., & Lamphere, L. (Eds.). (1973). *Woman, culture and society*. Stanford, CA: Stanford University Press.

Ross, M. (1980). Retrospective distortion in homosexual research. *Archives of Sexual Behavior, 9*, 523-531.

Rubin, G. (1975). The traffic in women: Notes on the "Political Economy" of Sex. In R. R. Reiter (Ed.), *Toward an anthropology of women* (pp. 157-210). New York: Monthly Review Press.

Sagarin, E. (1969). *Odd man in*. Chicago: Quadrangle.

Saghir, M., & Robbins, E. (1973). *Male and female homosexuality*. Baltimore: Williams & Williams.

Scruton, R. (1986). *Sexual desire*. New York: The Free Press.

Shepherd, G. (1987). Rank, gender, and homosexuality: Mombasa as a key to understanding sexual options. In P. Caplan (Ed.), *The cultural construction of sexuality* (pp. 240-270). London: Tavistock.

Silverstein, C. (1981). *Man to man: Gay couples in America*. New York: William Morrow.

Sladkin, K. E. (1983). Commentary. *Pediatric News, 14*, 3-6.

Soares, J. V. (1979). Black and gay. In M. Levine (Ed.), *Gay men: The sociology of male homosexuality*. New York: Harper & Row.

Sontag, S. (1982). Notes on camp. In *A Susan Sontag reader*. London: Penguin.

Stoller, R. J. (1968). *Sex and gender*. New York: Science House.

Stoller, R. J. (1985). *Presentations of gender*. New Haven, CT: Yale University Press.

Troiden, R. R. (1979). Becoming homosexual: A model for gay identity acquisition. *Psychiatry, 42*, 362-373.

Troiden, R. R., & Goode, E. (1980). Variables related to acquisition of gay identity. *Journal of Homosexuality, 5*, 383-392.

Turner, V. (1967). Les Rites des Passage. In *Forest of symbols*. Ithaca, NY: Cornell University Press.

Vaillant, G. (1971). Theoretical hierarchy of adaptive ego mechanisms. *Archives of General Psychiatry, 24*, 107-115.

Van Gennep, A. (1960). *Rites of passage*. Chicago: University of Chicago Press.

Vasquez, E. (1979). Homosexuality in the Context of the Mexican-American Culture. In D. Kuhnel (Ed.), *Sexual issues in social work: Emerging concerns in education and practice* (pp. 131-147). Honolulu: University of Hawaii School of Social Work.

Vernon, R. (1971). Growing up black and gay. *Gay Sunshine, 6*, 14-17.

Warren, C. (1974). *Identity and community in the gay world*. New York: John C. Wiley.

Warren, C. (1980). Homosexuality and stigma. In J. Marmon (Ed.), *Homosexual behavior: A modern reappraisal* (pp. 123-144). New York: Basic Books.

Weeks, J. (1985). *Sexuality and its discontents*. London: Routledge & Kegan Paul.

Weeks, J. (1987). Questions of Identity. In P. Caplan (Ed.), *The Cultural Construction of Sexuality* (pp. 31-51). New York: Tavistock.

Weinberg, G. (1972). *Society and the healthy homosexual.* New York: St. Martin's.

Weinberg, T. S. (1983). *Gay men, gay selves.* New York: Irvington.

Whitam, F. L. (1983). Culturally invariable properties of male homosexual. *Archives of Sexual Behavior, 12,* 207-222.

Wolf, D. G. (1979). *The lesbian community.* Berkeley, CA: University of California Press.

The Formation of Homosexual Identities

Richard R. Troiden, PhD

Miami University

SUMMARY. This paper uses sociological theory to develop an ideal-typical model of homosexual identity formation. The four-stage model outlined here represents a synthesis and an elaboration on previous research and theorizing on homosexual identity development. The model describes how committed homosexuals, lesbians and gay males who see themselves as homosexual and adopt corresponding lifestyles, recall having acquired their homosexual identities. Often repeated themes in the life histories of gay males and lesbians, clustered according to life stages, provide the content and characteristics of each stage.

This paper describes how committed homosexuals, men and women who have defined themselves as homosexual and adopted homosexuality as a way of life, recall having arrived at perceptions of self as homosexual in relation to romantic and sexual settings. More specifically, I introduce a sociological perspective toward sexuality; differentiate the key concepts of self-concept, identity, and homosexual identity; define and describe ideal types; summarize the homosexual identity formation literature; present a four-

Dr. Troiden, an AASECT certified Sex Educator and Sex Counselor, is Professor with the Department of Sociology-Anthropology, Miami University.

The author wishes to thank Dr. Karen Feinberg for her editorial assistance. A short version of this paper was presented at a Symposium on Gay and Lesbian Adolescents sponsored by the Department of Pediatrics, University of Minnesota Medical School, Minneapolis, MN, May 30-31, 1986.

Correspondence and requests for reprints may be addressed to the author, c/o Department of Sociology-Anthropology, Miami University, 344 Hoyt Hall, Oxford, OH 45056.

stage ideal-typical model of homosexual identity formation; and describe qualifications to the model.

THEORETICAL PERSPECTIVE

Sexual conduct is primarily social in origin (Gagnon, 1977; Gagnon & Simon, 1973; Plummer, 1975; Ponse, 1978; Simon & Gagnon, 1984). Existing sociocultural arrangements define what sexuality is, the purposes it serves, its manner of expression, and what it means to be sexual.

People learn to be sexual pretty much as they learn everything else. Women and men are born with an open-ended, diffuse, and relatively fluid capacity for bodily pleasure that is shaped and expressed through sexual scripts. These scripts are learned and organized during adolescence along lines previously laid down during gender-role socialization. Males, for example, are taught to see sex in active, genitally focused, and goal-oriented terms; females are encouraged to view sexuality in reactive, emotionally focused, and process-oriented ways (Laws & Schwartz, 1977; Levine, 1987).

Sexual scripts are articulated by the wider culture and are similar to blueprints: they shape, direct, and focus sexual conduct by providing sexuality with its affective and cognitive boundaries (Gagnon & Simon, 1973). Sexual scripts provide sexuality with its affective or emotional boundaries by specifying what kinds of feelings are sexual. "The mind has to define something as 'sexual' before it is sexual in its consequences" (Plummer, 1975, p. 30). In addition, sexual scripts designate the cognitive limits of sexuality by indicating appropriate and inappropriate sexual partners (*the whos*), proper and improper sexual behavior (*the whats*), permissible and nonpermissible settings for sex (*the wheres*), positively and negatively sanctioned motives for sex (*the whys*), and appropriate and inappropriate sexual techniques (*the hows*) (Gagnon, 1977; Gagnon & Simon, 1973; Simon & Gagnon, 1984). This is not to deny a biological substratum to sexuality, but to emphasize the powerful role of social forces in shaping sexual conduct. Because sexual learning occurs within specific historical eras and sociocultural settings, sexual conduct and its meanings vary across history and among cultures.

Today, in the research tradition established by Alfred Kinsey and his associates (Kinsey, Pomeroy & Martin, 1948; Kinsey, Pomeroy, Martin & Gebhard, 1953), sexuality experts generally view heterosexuality and homosexuality as matters of degree rather than kind. People are described as occupying various points along a continuum in their sexual behaviors and responsiveness from exclusive heterosexuality (Kinsey 0s) through bisexuality (Kinsey 3s) to exclusive homosexuality (Kinsey 6s). Whether sexual orientations are established before birth (Bell, Weinberg & Hammersmith, 1981a, 1981b; Whitam & Mathy, 1986), grow out of gender-role preferences established between the ages of three and nine (Harry, 1982), or organized out of experiences gained with gender roles and their related sexual scripts (Gagnon & Simon, 1973), the meanings of sexual feelings are neither self-evident nor translated directly into the consciousness. People construct their sexual feelings to the extent that they actively interpret, define, and make sense of their erotic yearnings using systems of sexual meanings articulated by the wider culture.

Sexual identities, perceptions of self as homosexual, heterosexual, or bisexual in relation to sexual and romantic contexts, are constructed similarly. People learn to identify and label their sexual feelings through experiences gained with gender roles and their related sexual scripts. Women and men decide what types of feelings they have, their significance and predominance, and whether they are personally relevant and salient enough to warrant self-definition as heterosexual, homosexual, or bisexual. I shall describe how committed lesbians and gay males recall having constructed their homosexual identities after I have differentiated key theoretical concepts, discussed ideal types, and briefly summarized the homosexual identity formation literature.

KEY CONCEPTS

The differences between self-concept and identity are revealed in the ways the two concepts are defined. Self-concept refers to people's mental images of themselves: what they think they are like as people. Defined in this way, self-concept is similar to the concept of identity as used traditionally by psychologists. Identity, on the other hand, refers to perceptions of self that are thought to represent the self definitively in specific social settings (such as, the "doctor" identity at work, the "spouse" identity at home). Self-concept is broader in scope than identity and encompasses a wider range of social categories; identity encompasses only situationally relevant dimensions of self-concept. Stated somewhat differently, self-concept and identity differ in the sense that identity requires reference to a specific social setting (imagined or real), and self-concept does not (Troiden, 1984/1985).

Social situations are structured normatively: people's expectations of how they and others should act often depend upon the contexts in which they find themselves. Situationally based expectations place limits on the range of identities and roles that may legitimately be expressed: identities are mobilized in situations where they are relevant. Once removed from a situation, the relevant identity becomes dormant or latent: part of the bundle of potentially relevant identities that make up a person's self-concept.

Identities perceived and experienced as relevant in many social situations are transsituational identities. The stigma surrounding homosexuality and the perceived need to keep homosexuality a secret may infuse homosexual identities with transsituational significance.

The homosexual identity is one of several identities incorporated into a person's self-concept. A homosexual identity is a perception of self as homosexual in relation to romantic or sexual situations. A perception of self as homosexual is an attitude, a potential line of action toward self and others, that is mobilized in settings (imagined or real) defined as sexual or romantic. Depending upon the context, the homosexual identity may function as a self-identity, a perceived identity, a presented identity, or all three (Cass, 1983/1984).

The homosexual identity is a *self-identity* when people see themselves as homosexual in relation to romantic and sexual settings. It is a *perceived identity* in situations where people think or know that others view them as homosexual. It is a *presented identity* when people present or announce themselves as homosexual in concrete social settings. Homosexual identities are most fully realized, that is, brought into concrete existence, in situations where self-identity, perceived identity, and presented identity coincide—where an agreement exists between who people think they are, who they claim they are, and how others view them.

IDEAL TYPES

Ideal types are not real; nothing and nobody fits them exactly. They represent abstractions based on concrete observations of the phenomena under investigation. Ideal types are heuristic devices, ways of organizing materials for analytical and comparative purposes, and are used as benchmarks against which to describe, compare, and test hypotheses relating to empirical reality (Theodorson & Theodorson, 1969). Described somewhat differently, they are frameworks for ordering observations logically. Ideal types are similar to stereotypes, except that they are examined and refined continuously to correspond more closely to the empirical reality they try to represent. At best, ideal models capture general patterns: variations are expected and explained, and often lead to revisions of ideal types.

The four-stage model of homosexual identity formation outlined here describes only general patterns encountered by committed homosexuals, women and men who see themselves as homosexual and adopt corresponding lifestyles. Often repeated themes in the life histories of lesbians and gay males, clustered according to life stages, provide the content and characteristics of each stage. Progress through the various stages increases the probability of homosexual identity formation, but does not determine it fully. A shifting effect is involved: some men and women "drift away" at various points before stage four. Only a small portion of all people who have homosexual experiences ever adopt lesbian or gay identities and corresponding lifestyles (Kinsey et al., 1948, 1953).

Homosexual identity formation is not conceptualized here as a linear, step-by-step process in which one stage precedes another and one necessarily builds on another, with fluctuations written off as developmental regressions. Instead, the process of homosexual identity formation is likened to a horizontal spiral, like a spring lying on its side (McWhirter & Mattison, 1984). Progress through the stages occurs in back-and-forth, up-and-down ways; the characteristics of stages overlap and recur in somewhat different ways for different people. In many cases, stages are encountered in consecutive order, but in some instances they are merged, glossed over, bypassed, or realized simultaneously.

LITERATURE SUMMARY

During the past decade, several investigators have proposed theoretical models that attempt to explain the formation of homosexual identities (Cass, 1979, 1984; Coleman, 1982; Lee, 1977; Ponse, 1978; Schäfer, 1976; Troiden, 1977, 1979; Weinberg, 1977, 1978). Although the various models propose different numbers of stages to explain homosexual identity formation, they describe strikingly similar patterns of growth and change as major hallmarks of homosexual identity development.

First, nearly all models view homosexual identity formation as taking place against a backdrop of stigma. The stigma surrounding homosexuality affects both the formation and expression of homosexual identities. Second, homosexual identities are described as developing over a protracted period and involving a number of "growth points or changes" that may be ordered into a series of stages (Cass, 1984). Third, homosexual identity formation involves increasing acceptance of the label "homosexual" as applied to the self. Fourth, although "coming out" begins when individuals define themselves to themselves as homosexual, lesbians and gay males typically report an increased desire over time to disclose their homosexual identity to at least some members of an expanding series of audiences. Thus, coming out, or identity disclosure, takes place at a number of levels: to self, to other homosexuals, to heterosexual friends, to family, to coworkers, and to the public at large (Coleman, 1982; Lee, 1977). Fifth, lesbians and gays develop "increasingly personalized and frequent" social contacts with other homosexuals over time (Cass, 1984).

The four-stage model developed here is a revision of my earlier work, which synthesized and elaborated Plummer's (1975) model of "becoming homosexual." The revised model incorporates insights provided by Barbara Ponse's (1978) and Vivienne Cass's (1979, 1984) theorizing and research on homosexual identity formation. The first stage, sensitization, is borrowed from Plummer.

Stage two, identity confusion, combines insights borrowed from Plummer, Cass, and my earlier model. The third stage, identity assumption, incorporates Cass's hypothesized stages of identity tolerance and acceptance. The fourth stage, commitment, posits identity disclosure (Cass, 1979, 1984) as an identity option (rather than as a separate stage) and as an external indicator of commitment to homosexuality as a way of life. Theoretical insights borrowed from Ponse (1978) are incorporated throughout the model. (See Troiden, 1988, for an extended description and criticism of the various models of homosexual identity formation.)

THE MODEL

Sociological analysis of homosexual identity formation begins with an examination of social contexts and patterns of interaction that make homosexuality personally relevant. "Becoming homosexual" involves the accumulation of a series of sexual meanings that predispose people to identify themselves subsequently as homosexual (Plummer, 1975). The meanings of feelings or activities, sexual or otherwise, are not self-evident. Before people can identify themselves in terms of a social condition or category, they must: (a) learn that a social category representing the activity or feelings exists (e.g., homosexual preferences or behavior); (b) learn that other people occupy the social category (e.g., that homosexuals exist as a group); (c) learn that their own socially constructed needs and interests are more similar to those who occupy the social category than they are different; (d) begin to identify with those included in the social category; (e) decide that they qualify for membership in the social category on the basis of activity and feelings in various settings; (f) elect to label themselves in terms of the social category, that is, define themselves as "being" the social category in contexts where category membership is relevant (e.g., self-definition as homosexual); and (g) incorporate and absorb these situationally linked identities into their self-concepts over time (Lofland, 1969; McCall & Simmons, 1966; Simmons, 1965).

STAGE ONE:
SENSITIZATION

The *sensitization* stage occurs before puberty. At this time, most lesbians and gay males do *not* see homosexuality as personally relevant, that is, they assume they are heterosexual, if they think about their sexual status at all. Lesbians and gay males, however, typically acquire social experiences during their childhood that serve later as bases for seeing homosexuality as personally relevant, that lend support to emerging perceptions of themselves as possibly homosexual. In short, childhood experiences sensitize lesbians and gay males to subsequent self-definition as homosexual.

Sensitization is characterized by generalized feelings of marginality, and perceptions of being different from same-sex peers. The following comments illustrate the forms that these childhood feelings of difference assumed for lesbians: "I wasn't interested in boys"; "I was more interested in the arts and in intellectual things"; "I was very shy and unaggressive"; "I felt different: unfeminine, ungraceful, not very pretty, kind of a mess"; "I was becoming aware of my homosexuality. It's a staggering thing for a kid that age to live with"; "I was more masculine, more independent, more aggressive, more outdoorish"; and "I didn't express myself the way other girls would. For example, I never showed my feelings. I wasn't emotional" (Bell et al., 1981a, pp. 148, 156).

Similar themes of childhood marginality are echoed in the comments of gay males: "I had a keener interest in the arts"; "I couldn't stand sports, so naturally that made me different. A ball thrown at me was like a bomb"; "I never learned to fight"; "I wasn't interested in laying girls in the cornfields. It turned me off completely"; "I just didn't feel I was like other boys. I was very fond of pretty things like ribbons and flowers and music"; "I began to get feelings I was gay. I'd notice other boys' bodies in the gym and masturbate excessively"; "I was indifferent to boys' games, like cops and robbers. I was more interested in watching insects and reflecting on certain things"; and "I was called the sissy of the family. I had been very pointedly told that I was effeminate" (Bell et al., 1981a, pp. 74, 86).

Research by Bell et al. (1981a) found that homosexual males

(N = 573) were almost two times more likely (72% vs. 39%) than heterosexual controls (N = 284) to report feeling "very much or somewhat" different from other boys during grade school (grades 1-8). Lesbians (N = 229) were also more likely than heterosexual controls (N = 101) to have felt "somewhat or very much" different from other girls during grade school (72% vs. 54%).

Childhood social experiences play a larger role in generating perceptions of difference during sensitization than events encountered in the spheres of emotionality or genitality. Both lesbians and gay males in the Bell et al. (1981a) sample saw gender-neutral or gender-inappropriate interests, or behaviors, or both as generating their feelings of marginality (the social realm). Only a minority of the lesbians and gay males felt different because of same-sex attractions (the emotional realm) or sexual activities (the genital realm).

More specifically, lesbians in the Bell et al. (1981a) study were more likely than heterosexual controls to say they felt different because they were more "masculine" than other girls (34% vs. 9%), because they were more interested in sports (20% vs. 2%), or because they had homosexual interests, or lacked heterosexual interests, or both (15% vs. 2%). Moreover, fewer lesbians than heterosexual controls (13% vs. 55%) reported having enjoyed typical girls' activities (e.g., hopscotch, jacks, playing house), but lesbians were much more likely (71% vs. 28%) to say they enjoyed typical boys' activities (e.g., baseball, football).

In a similar vein, homosexual males were more likely than heterosexual controls to report that they felt odd because they: did not like sports (48% vs. 21%), or were "feminine" (23% vs. 1%), or were not sexually interested in girls, or because they were sexually interested in other boys (18% vs. 1%). Gay males were also significantly more likely than heterosexual controls (68% vs. 34%) to report having enjoyed solitary activities associated only indirectly with gender (e.g., reading, drawing, music). Moreover, homosexual males were much less likely than heterosexual controls (11% vs. 70%) to report having enjoyed boys' activities (e.g., football, baseball) "very much" during childhood.

Although a sense of being different and set apart from same-sex age mates is a persistent theme in the childhood experiences of lesbians and gay males, research indicates that only a minority of gay males (20%) and lesbians (20%) begin to see themselves as sexually different before age 12, and fewer still, only 4% of the females and 4% of the males, label this difference as "homosexual" while they are children (Bell et al., 1981b, pp. 82-83). It is not surprising that "prehomosexuals" used gender metaphors, rather than sexual metaphors, to interpret and explain their childhood feelings of difference: the mastery of gender roles, rather than sexual scripts, is emphasized during childhood (Doyle, 1983; Tavris & Wade, 1984). Although they may have engaged in heterosexual or homosexual sex play, children do not appear to define their sexual experimentation in heterosexual or homosexual terms. The socially created categories of homosexual, heterosexual, and bisexual hold little or no significance for them. Physical acts become meaningful only when they are embedded in sexual scripts, which are acquired during adolescence (Gagnon & Simon, 1973). For these reasons, prehomosexuals rarely wonder, "Am I a homosexual?" or believe that homosexuality has anything to do with them personally while they are children.

The significance of sensitization resides in the meanings attached subsequently to childhood experiences, rather than the experiences themselves. Since sociocultural arrangements in Anglo-American society articulate linkages between gender-inappropriate behavior and homosexuality, gender-neutral or gender-atypical activities and interests during childhood provide many women and men with a potential basis for subsequent interpretations of self as possibly homosexual. Childhood experiences gained in social, emotional, and genital realms come to be invested with homosexual significance during adolescence. The reinterpretation of past events as indicating a homosexual potential appears to be a necessary (but not sufficient) condition for the eventual adoption of homosexual identities.

STAGE TWO:
IDENTITY CONFUSION

Lesbians and gay males typically begin to personalize homosexuality during adolescence, when they begin to reflect upon the idea that their feelings, behaviors, or both could be regarded as homosexual. The thought that they are potentially homosexual is dissonant with previously held self-images. The hallmark of this stage is *identity confusion*, inner turmoil and uncertainty surrounding their ambiguous sexual status. The sexual identities of lesbians and gay males are in limbo: they can no longer take their heterosexual identities as given, but they have yet to develop perceptions of themselves as homosexual.

Cass (1984) describes the early phase of identity confusion in the following way:

> You are not sure who you are. You are confused about what sort of person you are and where your life is going. You ask yourself the questions "Who am I?," "Am I a homosexual?," "Am I really a heterosexual?" (p. 156)

By middle to late adolescence, a perception of self as "probably" homosexual begins to emerge. Gay males begin to suspect that they "might" be homosexual at an average age of 17 (Troiden, 1977, 1979; Troiden & Goode, 1980); lesbians at an average age of 18 (Schäfer, 1976). Cass (1984) describes the later phase of identity confusion in the following manner:

> You feel that you *probably* are a homosexual, although you're not definitely sure. You feel distant or cut off from [other people]. You are beginning to think that it might help to meet other homosexuals but you're not sure whether you really want to or not. You prefer to put on a front of being completely heterosexual. (p. 156)

Several factors are responsible for the identity confusion experienced during this phase: (a) altered perceptions of self; (b) the experience of heterosexual and homosexual arousal and behavior; (c) the stigma surrounding homosexuality; and (d) inaccurate knowledge about homosexuals and homosexuality.

Altered perceptions of self are partly responsible for the identity confusion experienced during this phase. Childhood perceptions of self as different crystallize into perceptions of self as sexually different after the onset of adolescence. Whereas only 20% of the lesbians and the gay males in the Bell et al. (1981a) study saw themselves as sexually different before age 12, 74% of the lesbians and

84% of the gay males felt sexually different by age 19, as compared to only 10% of the heterosexual female controls and 11% of the heterosexual male controls. For both homosexual women and men, the most frequently cited reasons for feeling sexually different were either homosexual interests, or the lack of heterosexual interests, or both. Gender atypicality was mentioned, but not as frequently. Thus, genital and emotional experiences, more than social experiences, seem to precipitate perceptions of self as sexually different during the stage of identity confusion.

Another source of identity confusion is found in the realm of sexual experience itself. Recent investigations of homosexuality have revealed consistently that homosexuals exhibit greater variability in their childhood and adolescent sexual feelings and behaviors than heterosexuals (Bell & Weinberg, 1978; Bell et al., 1981a; Saghir & Robins, 1973; Schäfer, 1976; Weinberg & Williams, 1974). By early to middle adolescence, most lesbians and gay males have experienced both heterosexual and homosexual arousal and behavior. Only a minority of the Bell et al. (1981b) sample, for example, 28% of the gay males and 21% of the lesbians, were *never* sexually aroused by the opposite sex, and only 21% of the males and 12% of the females reported never having an opposite-sex encounter they or others considered sexual. Thus, significant majorities of lesbians and gay males experience heterosexual and homosexual arousal and behavior before age 19. Because Anglo-American society portrays people as either homosexual or heterosexual, it is not surprising that adolescent lesbians and gay males are uncertain and confused regarding their sexual orientations.

As a general rule, gay males are aware of their same-sex attractions at earlier ages than lesbians. Males report awareness of their same-sex feelings at an average age of 13 (Bell et al., 1981a; Dank, 1971; Kooden, Morin, Riddle, Rogers, Strang & Strassburger, 1979; McDonald, 1982). The corresponding average age for lesbians is between 14 and 16 (Bell et al., 1981a; Riddle & Morin, 1977). Gay males first act on their sexual feelings at an average age of 15 (Bell et al., 1981a; Kooden et al., 1979; McDonald, 1982; Troiden, 1977, 1979; Troiden & Goode, 1980), whereas lesbians first act on their sexual feelings at an average age of 20, 4 to 6 years after first awareness of their same-sex attractions (Bell et al., 1981a; Riddle & Morin, 1977; Schäfer, 1976).

The stigma surrounding homosexuality also contributes to identity confusion because it discourages adolescent (and some adult) lesbians and gay males from discussing their emerging sexual desires, or activities, or both with either age mates or families. As Plummer (1975) has noted, the societal condemnation of homosexuality creates problems of guilt, secrecy, and difficulty in gaining access to other homosexuals. Moreover, the emphasis placed on gender roles and the general privatization of sexuality compounds the experience of identity confusion and aloneness.

Ignorance and inaccurate knowledge about homosexuality also contributes to identity confusion. People are unlikely to identify themselves in terms of a social category as long as they are unaware that the category exists, lack accurate information about the kinds of people who occupy the category, or believe they have nothing in common with category members (Lofland, 1969). In other words, before they can see themselves as homosexual, people must realize that homosexuality and homosexuals exist, learn what homosexuals are actually like as people, and be able to perceive similarities between their own desires and behaviors and those of people labeled socially as homosexual. Today, accurate information about homosexuality has been circulated and distributed throughout society, making it easier to identify homosexual elements in feelings and activities (Dank, 1971; Troiden, 1979; Troiden & Goode, 1980). Lesbians and gay males first understand what the term "homosexual" means at approximately the same time, at the average ages of 16 or 17 respectively (Riddle & Morin, 1977). Knowledge of what the term "homosexual" means may be acquired more rapidly in urban areas, where homosexuality is more likely to be discussed, than in rural areas, where conversation is less apt to focus on the topic.

Lesbians and gay males typically respond to identity confusion by adopting one or more of the following strategies: (a) denial (Goode, 1984; Troiden, 1977); (b) repair (Humphreys, 1972); (c) avoidance (Cass, 1979); (d) redefinition (Cass, 1979; Troiden, 1977); and (e) acceptance (Cass, 1979; Troiden, 1977).

Lesbians and gay males who use *denial*, deny the homosexual component to their feelings, fantasies, or activities.

Repair involves wholesale attempts to eradicate homosexual feelings and behaviors. Professional help is sought to eliminate the homosexual feelings, fantasies, or activities.

Avoidance is a third overall strategy for dealing with identity confusion (Cass, 1979). Although avoidant women and men recognize that their behavior, thoughts, or fantasies are homosexual, they see them as unacceptable, as things to be avoided. Avoidance may assume at least one of six forms.

Some adolescent (and adult) men and women inhibit behaviors or interests they have learned to associate with homosexuality: "I thought my sexual interest in other girls would go away if I paid more attention to boys and concentrated more on being feminine"; "I figured I'd go straight and develop more of an interest in girls if I got even more involved in sports and didn't spend as much time on my art" (author's files).

A second avoidance strategy involves limiting one's exposure to the opposite sex to prevent peers or family from learning about one's relative lack of heterosexual responsiveness: "I hated dating. I was always afraid I wouldn't get erect when we petted and kissed and that the girls would find out I was probably gay"; "I felt really weird compared to the other girls. I couldn't understand why they thought guys were so great. I dated to keep my parents off my back" (author's files).

A third avoidance strategy involves avoiding exposure to information about homosexuality. People may avoid accurate information because they fear that the information may confirm their suspected homosexuality: "Your first lecture on homosexuality awakened my fears of being homosexual. I cut class during the homosexuality section and skipped the assigned readings. I just couldn't accept the idea of being a lesbian" (author's files); "One ingenious defense was to remain as ignorant as possible on the subject of homosexuality. No one would ever catch me at the 'Ho' drawer of the New York Public Library Card Catalog" (Reid, 1973, p. 40).

A fourth avoidance strategy involves assuming antihomosexual postures. Some adolescent (and adult) women and men distance themselves from their own homoerotic feelings by attacking and ridiculing known homosexuals: "At one time I hated myself because of my sexual feelings for men. I'm ashamed to admit that I made a nellie guy's life miserable because of it"; "I really put down masculine acting women until I came out and realized that not all lesbians act that way and that many straight women do" (author's files).

Heterosexual immersion is a fifth avoidance strategy. Some teen-aged lesbians and gay males establish heterosexual involvements at varying levels of intimacy in order to eliminate their "inappropriate" sexual interests: "I thought my homosexual feelings would go away if I dated a lot and had sex with as many women as possible"; "I thought my attraction to women was a passing phase and would go away once I started having intercourse with my boy friend" (author's files). In some cases, an adolescent girl may purposely become pregnant as a means of "proving" that she couldn't possibly be homosexual.

A sixth avoidance strategy involves escapism. Some adolescent lesbians and gay males avoid confronting their homoerotic feelings through the use and abuse of chemical substances. Getting "high" on drugs provides temporary relief from feelings of identity confusion, and may be used to justify sexual feelings and behaviors ordinarily viewed as unacceptable.

A fourth general means of reducing identity confusion involves *redefining* behavior, feelings, or context along more conventional lines. Redefinition is reflected through the use of special case, ambisexual, temporary identity (Cass, 1979), or situational strategies.

In the special case strategy, homosexual behavior and feelings are seen as an isolated case, a one-time occurrence, part of a special, never-to-be-repeated relationship: "I never thought of my feelings and our lovemaking as lesbian. The whole experience was too beautiful for it to be something so ugly. I didn't think I could ever have those feelings for another woman" (author's files).

Defining the self as ambisexual is another redefinitional strategy: "I guess I'm attracted to both women and men" (author's files).

This strategy may or may not reflect an individual's actual sexual interests.

A third redefinitional response is the temporary identity strategy. Here, people see their homosexual feelings and behaviors as stages or phases of development that will pass in time: "I'm just passing through a phase, I'm really not homosexual" (author's files).

People who adopt the situational redefinitional strategy define the situation, rather than themselves, as responsible for the homosexual activity or feelings: "It only happened because I was drunk"; "It would never have happened if I hadn't been sent to prison."

A fifth overall strategy is *acceptance*. With acceptance, men and women acknowledge that their behavior, feelings, or fantasies may be homosexual and seek out additional sources of information to learn more about their sexual feelings. For men and women who always felt different because they felt that their thoughts, feelings, and behaviors were at odds with others of their sex, the gradual realization that homosexuals exist as a social category and that they are "probably" homosexual diminishes their sense of isolation. The homosexual category provides them with a label for their difference. "From the time I was quite young I felt different from other girls and I felt more masculine than feminine. When I learned that lesbians existed I had a word that explained why I was different from other girls" (author's files). "The first name I had for what I was, was 'cocksucker.' 'Cocksucker' was an awful word the way they used it, but it meant that my condition was namable. I finally had a name for all those feelings. I wasn't nothing" (Reinhart, 1982, p. 26).

Perceptions of self anchored in the strategies of denial, repair, avoidance, or redefinition may be sustained for months, years, or permanently. Bisexual (ambisexual) perceptions of self, for example, a redefinitional strategy, may be maintained or undermined by a person's social roles, position in the social structure, intimate relationships, and by the perceived strength, persistence, and salience of the homosexual feelings. Although individuals may use several different stigma-management strategies, they characteristically use some more than others.

STAGE THREE:
IDENTITY ASSUMPTION

Despite differences in stigma-management strategies, a significant number of women and men progress to *identity assumption*, the third stage of homosexual identity formation, during or after late adolescence. In this stage, the homosexual identity becomes both a self-identity and a presented identity, at least to other homosexuals. Defining the self as homosexual and presenting the self as homosexual to other homosexuals are the first stages in a larger process of identity disclosure called "coming out" (Coleman, 1982; Lee, 1977). The earmarks of this stage are self-definition as homosexual, identity tolerance and acceptance, regular association with other homosexuals, sexual experimentation, and exploration of the homosexual subculture.

Lesbians and gay males typically define themselves as homosexual at different ages and in different contexts. Retrospective studies of adult homosexuals suggest that gay males arrive at homosexual self-definitions between the ages of 19 and 21, on the average (Dank, 1971; Harry & DeVall, 1978; Kooden et al., 1979; McDonald, 1982; Troiden, 1979). Retrospective studies involving small samples of adolescent gay males indicate a younger age at the time of self-identification as homosexual: age 14, on the average (Remafedi, 1987). Adult lesbians recall reaching homosexual self-definitions slightly later, between the average ages of 21 and 23 (Califia, 1979; Riddle & Morin, 1977; Schäfer, 1976; Smith, 1980).

The contexts in which homosexual self-definition occurs also vary between the sexes. Lesbians typically arrive at homosexual self-definitions in contexts of intense affectionate involvements with other women (Cronin, 1974; Schäfer, 1976). Seventy-six percent of the lesbians interviewed by Cronin, for example, defined themselves as lesbian in contexts of meaningful emotional involvements with other women. Gay males, on the other hand, are more likely to arrive at homosexual self-definitions in sociosexual contexts where homosexual men are reputed to gather for sexual purposes: gay bars, parties, parks, YMCAs, and men's rooms (Dank,

1971; Troiden, 1979; Warren, 1974). Only a minority of gay males, roughly 20%, appear to define themselves in contexts of same-sex love relationships (Dank, 1971; McDonald, 1982; Troiden, 1979). Today, I suspect that young men are more likely to arrive at homosexual self-definitions in romantic contexts than in sexual settings. For many men, the possibility of AIDS infection has reduced the perceived desirability of sexual experimentation.

Patterns laid down during sex-role socialization explain why lesbians define themselves in emotional contexts; gay males in sociosexual contexts: "Male sexuality is seen as active, initiatory, demanding of immediate gratification, and divorced from emotional attachment; female sexuality emphasizes feelings and minimizes the importance of immediate sexual activity" (de Monteflores & Schultz, 1978). For males, admitting a desire for homosexual activity implies the label of homosexual; for females, intense emotional involvement with the same sex has similar implications.

Although homosexual identities are assumed during this stage, they are tolerated initially rather than accepted. Cass (1984) describes people who tolerate their homosexual identities as follows:

> You feel sure you're a homosexual and you put up with, or tolerate this. You see yourself as a homosexual for now but are not sure about how you will be in the future. You usually take care to put across a heterosexual image. You sometimes mix socially with homosexuals, or would like to do this. You feel a need to meet others like yourself. (p. 156)

Self-definition as homosexual may occur just before, at the same time as, or shortly after first social contact with other homosexuals (Cronin, 1974; Dank, 1971; Ponse, 1978; Troiden, 1977, 1979; Weinberg, 1977, 1978). Initial contacts may have been engineered consciously (e.g., deciding to go to a homosexual bar) or accidentally (e.g., learning that a respected friend is homosexual). Only a minority of lesbians and gay males appear to define themselves as homosexual without having direct contact with one or more homosexuals. Self-designation as homosexual in the absence of affiliation with other homosexuals (e.g., as a consequence of reading about homosexuality) has been referred to as *disembodied affiliation* (Ponse, 1978).

The quality of a person's initial contacts with homosexuals is extremely important (Cass, 1979). If initial contacts are negative, further contact with homosexuals may be avoided and nonhomosexual perceptions of self will persist, maintained through the strategies of denial, repair, ambisexuality, or temporary identity described earlier. Perceptions of the increased risks of living as a homosexual (e.g., fear of blackmail or AIDS) in a homophobic society may also encourage individuals to cling to nonhomosexual perceptions of self.

Positive contacts with homosexuals, on the other hand, facilitate homosexual identity formation. Favorable contacts provide lesbians and gay males with the opportunity to obtain information about homosexuality at first hand. Direct positive exposure provides a basis for re-examining and re-evaluating their own ideas about homosexuality, and for seeing similarities between themselves and those labeled "homosexual." The meanings attributed to the homosexual label begin to change in a more favorable direction.

Personally meaningful contacts with experienced homosexuals also enable neophytes to see that homosexuality is socially organized, and that a group exists to which they may belong, which diminishes feelings of solitude and alienation. Experienced homosexuals provide neophytes with role models from whom they learn: (a) strategies for stigma management; (b) rationalizations that legitimize homosexuality and neutralize guilt feelings; (c) the range of identities and roles available to homosexuals; and (d) the norms governing homosexual conduct.

Once they adopt homosexual identities, lesbians and gay males are confronted with the issue of stigma and its management. They may adopt one of several stigma-evasion strategies during identity assumption: capitulation, minstrelization, passing, and group alignment (Humphreys, 1972).

Women and men who *capitulate* avoid homosexual activity because they have internalized a stigmatizing view of homosexuality. The persistence of homosexual feelings in the absence of homosexual activity, however, may lead them to experience self-hatred and despair.

Individuals who use *minstrelization* express their homosexuality along lines etched out by the popular culture. They behave as the wider culture expects them to behave, in highly stereotyped, gender-inappropriate fashions.

Passing as heterosexual is probably the most common stigma-evasion strategy (Humphreys, 1972). Women and men who pass as heterosexual define themselves as homosexual, but conceal their sexual preferences and behavior from heterosexual family, friends, and colleagues, "by careful, even torturous, control of information" (Humphreys, 1972, p. 138). Passers lead "double lives," that is, they segregate their social worlds into heterosexual and homosexual spheres and hope the two never collide.

Group alignment is also adopted commonly by neophyte homosexuals to evade stigma. Men and women who evade stigma through affiliation become actively involved in the homosexual community. The perception of "belonging" to a world of others situated similarly eases the pain of stigma. Other homosexuals are looked upon as sources of social and emotional support, as well as sexual gratification. Yet an awareness of "belonging" to the homosexual subculture also fosters an awareness of "not belonging," perceptions of being excluded from the worlds of opposite-sex dating, marriage, and parenthood. As Ponse (1978) has noted, people may deal with this alienation by immersing themselves completely in the homosexual subculture, by avoiding heterosexual settings that remind them of their stigma, by normalizing their behaviors (i.e., minimizing the differences between heterosexuals and homosexuals), or by aristocratizing their behaviors (i.e., attaching a special significance to homosexual experience). Other lesbians and gay males may nihilize heterosexual experience, that is, define heterosexual patterns as deviant (Warren, 1974).

To recapitulate, positive homosexual experiences facilitate homosexual self-definition; unrewarding experiences reinforce negative attitudes toward homosexuality. Undesirable homosexual experiences may prompt people to reject the identity ("I am not homosexual"), abandon the behavior ("I'm not really homosexual if I avoid the behavior"), or reject both identity and behavior ("I'm not homosexual. I can learn to behave heterosexually").

By the end of the identity assumption stage, people begin to accept themselves as homosexual. Cass (1984) describes acceptance of the homosexual identity as follows:

> You are quite sure you are a homosexual and you accept this fairly happily. You are prepared to tell a few people about being a homosexual but you carefully select whom you will tell. You adopt an attitude of fitting in where you live and work. You can't see any point in confronting people with your homosexuality if it's going to embarrass all concerned. (p. 156)

STAGE FOUR:
COMMITMENT

A commitment is a feeling of obligation to follow a particular course of action (Theodorson & Theodorson, 1969). In the homosexual context, *commitment* involves adopting homosexuality as a way of life. For the committed homosexual, "it becomes easier, more attractive, less costly to remain a homosexual" than to try and function as a heterosexual (Plummer, 1975, p. 150). Entering a same-sex love relationship marks the onset of commitment (Coleman, 1982; Troiden, 1979).

The main characteristics of the commitment stage are self-acceptance and comfort with the homosexual identity and role. Commitment has both internal and external dimensions. It is indicated *internally* by: (a) the fusion of sexuality and emotionality into a significant whole; (b) a shift in the meanings attached to homosexual identities; (c) a perception of the homosexual identity as a valid self-identity; (d) expressed satisfaction with the homosexual identity; and (e) increased happiness after self-defining as homosexual. It is indicated *externally* by: (a) same-sex love relationships; (b) disclosure of the homosexual identity to nonhomosexual audiences; and (c) a shift in the type of stigma-management strategies.

The fusion of same-sex sexuality and emotionality into a meaningful whole is one internal measure of a person's commitment to homosexuality as a way of life (Coleman, 1982; Warren, 1974; Troiden, 1979). The same sex is redefined as a legitimate source of love and romance as well as sexual gratification. Homosexuals themselves see same-sex romantic preferences as differentiating "true" homosexuals from those who are merely experimenting (Warren, 1974).

Another internal measure of commitment to homosexuality as a way of life is reflected by the meanings attached by homosexuals to the homosexual identity. The homosexual subculture encourages both lesbians and gay males to perceive the homosexual identity as an "essential" identity, a "state of being" and "way of life" rather than merely a form of behavior or sexual orientation (Ponse, 1978; Warren, 1974; Warren & Ponse, 1977). Lesbian feminists are especially likely to view lesbianism as all-encompassing: "A lesbian's entire sense of self centers on women. While sexual energies are not discounted, alone they do not create the lesbian feminist" (Faderman, 1984/1985, p. 87).

The perception of the homosexual identity as a valid self-identity is also a sign of internal commitment. Homosexual identities and roles are seen as growing out of genuine, deep-seated needs and desires. Homosexual expression is reconceptualized as "natural" and "normal" for the self. Committed homosexuals find the homosexual identity "a more valid expression of the human condition than that afforded by a heterosexual one" (Humphreys, 1979, p. 242).

The degree of satisfaction people express about their present identities is another measure of internal commitment (Hammersmith & Weinberg, 1973). When Bell and Weinberg (1978) asked their sample of homosexuals whether they would remain homosexual even if a magic pill would enable them to become heterosexual, 95% of the lesbians and 86% of the gay males claimed they would *not* take the magic pill. In addition, 73% of the gay males and 84% of the lesbians indicated they had "very little or no" regret about their homosexuality. Only 6% of the male and 2% of the female homosexuals felt "a great deal" of regret. Societal rejection, punitiveness, and the inability to have children were the most frequently mentioned sources of regret.

Increased happiness is another indication of an internal commitment to homosexuality. When asked, "At this time would you say you are more, less, or about as happy as you were prior to arriving at a homosexual self-definition?" 91% of the gay males I interviewed indicated they were more happy, 8% stated they were about as happy, and only one person said he was less happy (Troiden, 1979).

A same-sex love relationship is one external sign of a commitment to homosexuality as a way of life, a concrete manifestation of a synthesis of same-sex emotionality and sexuality into a meaningful whole (Coleman, 1982; Troiden, 1977, 1979). Lesbians appear to enter their first same-sex love relationships between the average ages of 22 and 23 (Bell & Weinberg, 1978; Riddle & Morin, 1977), a year or less after they define themselves as lesbians. Gay males typically have their first love affairs between the average ages of 21 and 24 (Bell & Weinberg, 1978: McDonald, 1982; Troiden, 1979), roughly two to five years after they define themselves as homosexual.

In keeping with their gender-role training, males are much more likely than lesbians to gain sexual experiences with a variety of partners before focusing their attentions on one special person (Troiden, 1979). Lesbians, on the other hand, are more likely to explore the homosexual community and gain sexual experiences in the context of emotional relationships with one woman or a series of "special" women (Cronin, 1974; Smith, 1980).

Disclosure of the homosexual identity to heterosexual audiences is another external measure of commitment to homosexuality as a way of life. As mentioned earlier, coming out involves disclosure of the homosexual identity to some of an expanding series of audiences ranging from self, to other homosexuals, to heterosexual friends, family, or both, to coworkers, to employers, to public identification as homosexual by the media (Lee, 1977).

Homosexual identity formation is characterized over time by an increasing desire to disclose the homosexual identity to nonhomosexual audiences (Cass, 1984). Few people, however, disclose their homosexual identities to everybody in their social environments. Instead, they fluctuate "back and forth in degrees of openness, depending on personal, social, and professional factors" (de Monteflores & Schultz, 1978).

Lesbians and gay males appear more likely to come out to siblings or close heterosexual friends, than to parents, coworkers, or employers. Fifty percent of the gay males and 62% of the lesbians interviewed by Bell and Weinberg (1978) said they had told "some or all" of their siblings about their homosexuality. Regarding disclosure to heterosexual friends, 54% of the lesbians and 53% of the gay males claimed that "some or most" of their heterosexual friends knew about their homosexuality. Fewer had told their parents about their homosexuality. Forty-two percent of the gay males and 49% of the lesbians said they had come out to their mothers, and 37% of the lesbians and 31% of the gay males said they had told their fathers.

Bell and Weinberg's (1978) respondents exercised even greater discretion in disclosing their homosexual identities to coworkers and employers. Sixty-two percent of the gay males and 76% of the lesbians stated that "few or none" of their coworkers knew they were homosexual, and 85% of the lesbians and 71% of the gay males claimed that their employers were unaware of their homosexuality. Lesbians and gay males appear reluctant to come out in the workplace for two reasons: fear of endangering job credibility or effectiveness, and fear of job or income loss (Kooden et al., 1979; Riddle & Morin, 1977).

Those lesbians who disclose their homosexual identities to nongay friends begin to do so at an average age of 28 (Riddle & Morin, 1977); gay males between the average ages of 23 and 28 (McDonald, 1982; Riddle & Morin, 1977). Gay males who disclose their homosexual identities to their parents do so at age 28, on the average; lesbians at an average age of 30 (Riddle & Morin, 1977). Those who come out in professional settings do so at even later average ages, 32 for lesbians, 31 for gay males (Riddle & Morin, 1977). The AIDS epidemic, however, has amplified the stigma surrounding homosexuality. As a result, younger gay males and lesbians may be less willing today than in the past to disclose their homosexual identities to nonhomosexual audiences.

A third external indicator of commitment is a shift in stigma-management strategies. Covering (Humphreys, 1972) and blending appear to replace passing and group alignment as the most common strategies, with a minority opting for conversion (Humphreys, 1972).

Women and men who *cover* are ready to admit that they are homosexual (in many cases because it is obvious or known), but nonetheless take great pains to keep their homosexuality from looming large. They manage their homosexuality in ways meant to demonstrate that although they may be homosexual, they are nonetheless respectable. "Imitation of heterosexual marriage, along with other roles and lifestyles designed to elicit praise from straight segments of society," typifies this form of stigma evasion (Humphreys, 1972, p. 139). Like people who blend, people who cover turn to other homosexuals for social and emotional support as well as sexual gratification, and disclose their homosexual identities selectively to significant heterosexuals.

People who *blend* act in gender-appropriate ways and neither announce nor deny their homosexual identities to nonhomosexual others. They perceive their sexual orientations as irrelevant to the kinds of activities they undertake with heterosexuals, and cloak their private lives and sexuality with the shroud of silence. When quizzed or challenged about their sexual orientations or behavior, they are likely to respond: "What's it to you?" or "It's none of your business." Women and men who blend affiliate with the homosexual subculture and present themselves as homosexual to other gay males and lesbians, and to carefully selected nonhomosexuals.

Lesbians and gay males who *convert* acquire an ideology or world view that not only destigmatizes homosexuality, but transforms it from a vice to a virtue, from a mark of shame to a mark of pride. People who convert confront rather than evade the homosexual stigma. Formally or informally, they attempt to inform the general public about the realities of homosexuality and the special contributions made to society by homosexuals. Their goal is to eliminate oppression through education and political change (e.g., equal rights in jobs and housing). A few lesbians and gay males adopt conversionist strategies during the identity assumption stage when they define themselves as homosexual.

Stigma-evasion strategies are situational rather than constant, that is, personal, social, or professional factors may prompt individuals to blend or cover in some situations, disclose their homosexual identity openly in others, and switch to conversionist modes in yet other contexts. Selective and relatively nonselective self-disclosure have important consequences for the self. Identity disclosure enables the homosexual identity to be more fully realized, that is, brought into concrete existence, in a wider range of contexts. A more complete integration between homosexuals' identities and their social worlds is made possible when they can see and present themselves as homosexual and be viewed as such by others. Cass (1984) describes *identity synthesis* in the following way:

> You are prepared to tell [almost] *anyone* that you are a homosexual. You are happy about the way you are but feel that being a homosexual is not the most important part of you. You mix socially with homosexuals and heterosexuals [with whom] you are open about your homosexuality. (p. 156)

In the final analysis, homosexual identity is emergent: never fully determined in a fixed or absolute sense, but always subject to modification and further change. Homosexual identity formation is continuous, a process of "becoming" that spans a lifetime, a process of "striving but never arriving" (Plummer, 1975). For this reason, commitment to the homosexual identity and role is a matter of degree. Homosexuals span a continuum from low to high levels of commitment on both internal and external dimensions, which may vary across time and place. Thus commitment is always somewhat inconsistent, strengthened, or weakened at various points and contexts by personal, social, or professional factors.

QUALIFICATIONS

More research is needed to determine more clearly the variables that help and hinder homosexual identity formation. A number of factors implicated in homosexual identity formation appear to influence the ages at which samples of homosexuals recall having experienced events related to homosexuality (e.g., first same-sex arousal, first same-sex sexual activity, homosexual self-definition, first same-sex love relationship). Below, I have indicated a number of issues in need of further attention and investigation.

First, the average ages outlined for each stage should be viewed as approximations or rough guidelines. Since these ages are based on averages, variations are expected and should not be treated as developmental regressions.

Second, sample characteristics may also influence reported rates of homosexual identity formation: the mean ages of respondents in the studies cited here vary, for example. In retrospective samples consisting of relatively older lesbians and gay males, the respondents recall having encountered various events (e.g., self-definition as homosexual) at relatively higher ages than younger informants, thus raising the average ages at which the various events seem to occur. Older informants grew up during a time when homosexuality was rarely discussed, and then only in highly stereotypical terms.

Research obtained in the 1970s (Dank, 1971; Troiden, 1977, 1979; Troiden & Goode, 1980) and 1980s (Remafedi, 1987) indicates that adolescent lesbians and gay males today acquire their homosexual identities at lower average ages than did their older counterparts. More specifically, homosexuals under 25 recall having encountered the various events (e.g., first same-sex love relationship) associated with homosexual identity formation at significantly lower average ages than the ones reported here. Increased openness, tolerance, and accurate information about homosexuality may have made it easier to perceive similarities between self and "homosexuals."

On the other hand, the onset of the AIDS epidemic may have the opposite effect: it may delay homosexual identity formation (at least among males) because it has amplified the stigma surrounding homosexuality. The possibility of contracting AIDS may defensively motivate people to deny their erotic feelings, to delay acting upon them, or to express them only in the context of committed love relationships. In addition, identity integration and a positive sense of homosexual identity may be undermined. To avoid being seen as potential disease carriers, lesbians and gay males may choose not to disclose their homosexual identities to nonhomosexual audiences. Identity fear may replace identity pride. Fears of infection may promote erotophobia, a fear of sexual relations, and cause people to avoid homosexual behavior completely or to reduce their sexual experimentation.

Gender-inappropriate behavior (Harry, 1982), adolescent homosexual arousal and activity, and an absence of heterosexual experiences (Troiden & Goode, 1980) facilitate progress through the various stages. Gender-atypical, homosexually active, heterosexually inexperienced adolescent lesbians and gay males encounter less identity confusion than other "prehomosexuals" because Anglo-

American gender conventions articulate linkages between all three characteristics and adult homosexuality. Conversely, adolescent gay males and lesbians who are gender-typical, heterosexually active, and homosexually inexperienced encounter more confusion regarding their sexual identities because their characteristics are at variance with prevailing stereotypes.

Supportive family and friends may also facilitate homosexual identity formation. Individuals may feel more comfortable acting upon their sexual feelings when they believe that those close to them will accept them for themselves. Conversely, lesbians and gay males with nonsupportive families and friends may find it more difficult to acknowledge and act upon their sexual feelings. Fears of rejection appear to inhibit homosexual identity formation to various degrees.

Educational level and prevailing atmosphere of the workplace also facilitate or hinder homosexual identity formation. Highly educated lesbians and gay males in homophobic professions may fear that they have more to lose by acknowledging and acting upon their sexual feelings than their less educated counterparts. Fears of job or income loss, or concerns about endangering professional credibility, inhibit homosexual identity formation (Kooden et al., 1979; Troiden, 1977). Conversely, lesbians and gay males with less education, and those who work in more supportive occupational structures, may find it easier to act upon and integrate their sexual feelings into their overall lives because they feel they have less to lose.

CONCLUSIONS

This paper has developed an ideal-typical model of homosexual identity formation using a sociological perspective. The stigma surrounding homosexuality was shown to affect powerfully the formation and management of homosexual identities. Homosexual identity formation was described as occurring over a protracted period and involving a number of growth points or changes, which were ordered into a series of four ideal-typical stages. Among committed homosexuals, that is, lesbians and gay males who define themselves as homosexual and adopt corresponding lifestyles, childhood perceptions of self as different crystallize into views of self as sexually different during middle to late adolescence. Positive contacts with other homosexuals facilitate self-definition and acceptance of self as homosexual. Continued involvement with the homosexual identity and role fosters commitment to homosexuality as a way of life and an increased desire to disclose the homosexual identity to nonhomosexual audiences. Selective and nonselective identity disclosure permit the homosexual identity to be realized more fully across a wider range of situations and contexts, which enables gay males and lesbians to integrate their homosexual self-identities more completely with their social worlds. Differences in gender-role socialization explain differences between gay males and lesbians in the homosexual identity formation process. I concluded by listing factors that may promote or hinder rates of homosexual identity formation and that are in need of further research.

REFERENCES

Bell, A.P., Weinberg, M.S. (1978). *Homosexualities: A study of diversity among men and women.* New York: Simon & Schuster.

Bell, A.P., Weinberg, M.S., & Hammersmith, S.K. (1981a). *Sexual preference: Its development in men and women.* Bloomington, IN: Indiana University Press.

Bell, A.P., Weinberg, M.S., & Hammersmith, S.K. (1981b). *Sexual preference: Its development in men and women: Statistical appendix.* Bloomington, IN: Indiana University Press.

Califia, P. (1979). Lesbian sexuality. *Journal of Homosexuality, 4,* 255-266.

Cass, V.C. (1979). Homosexual identity formation: A theoretical model. *Journal of Homosexuality, 4,* 219-235.

Cass, V.C. (1983/1984). Homosexual identity: A concept in need of definition. *Journal of Homosexuality, 9,* 105-126.

Cass, V.C. (1984). Homosexual identity formation: Testing a theoretical model. *The Journal of Sex Research, 20,* 143-167.

Coleman, E. (1982). Developmental stages of the coming-out process. In W. Paul, J.D. Weinrich, J.C. Gonsiorek, & M.E. Hotvedt (Eds.), *Homosexuality: Social, psychological and biological issues* (pp. 149-158). Beverly Hills, CA: Sage Publications.

Cronin, D.M. (1974). Coming out among lesbians. In E. Goode, & R.R. Troiden (Eds.), *Sexual deviance and sexual deviants* (pp. 268-277). New York: William Morrow & Sons.

Dank, B.M. (1971). Coming out in the gay world. *Psychiatry, 34,* 180-197.

de Monteflores, C., & Schultz, S.J. (1978). Coming out: Similarities and differences for lesbians and gay men. *Journal of Social Issues, 34,* 59-72.

Doyle, J.A. (1983). *The male experience.* Dubuque, IA: Wm. C. Brown.

Faderman, L. (1984/1985). The "new gay" lesbian. *Journal of Homosexuality, 10,* 85-95.

Gagnon, J.H. (1977). *Human sexualities.* Glenview, IL: Scott, Foresman.

Gagnon, J.H., & Simon, W. (1973). *Sexual conduct: The social sources of human sexuality.* Chicago: Aldine.

Goode, E. (1984). *Deviant behavior* (2nd. ed.). Englewood Cliffs, NJ: Prentice-Hall.

Hammersmith, S.K., & Weinberg, M.S. (1973). Homosexual identity: Commitment, adjustments, and significant others. *Sociometry, 36,* 56-78.

Harry, J. (1982). *Gay children grown up: Gender culture and gender deviance.* New York: Praeger.

Harry, J., & DeVall, W. (1978). *The social organization of gay males.* New York: Praeger.

Humphreys, L. (1972). *Out of the closets: The sociology of homosexual liberation.* Englewood Cliffs, NJ: Prentice-Hall.

Humphreys, L. (1979). Being odd against all odds. In R.C. Federico (Ed.), *Sociology* (2nd. ed.) (pp. 238-242). Reading, MA: Addison-Wesley.

Kinsey, A.C., Pomeroy, W.B., & Martin, C.E. (1948). *Sexual behavior in the human male.* Philadelphia: W.B. Saunders.

Kinsey, A.C., Pomeroy, W.B., Martin, C.E., & Gebhard, P.H. (1953). *Sexual behavior in the human female.* Philadelphia: W.B. Saunders.

Kooden, H.D., Morin, S.F., Riddle, D.L., Rogers, M., Strang, B.E., & Strassburger, F. (1979). *Removing the stigma: Final report of the board of social and ethical responsibility for psychology's task force on the status of lesbian and gay male psychologists.* Washington, DC: American Psychological Association.

Laws, J.L., & Schwartz, P. (1977). *Sexual scripts: The social construction of female sexuality.* Hinsdale, IL: The Dryden Press.

Lee, J.A. (1977). Going public: A study in the sociology of homosexual liberation. *Journal of Homosexuality, 3,* 49-78.

Levine, M.P. (1987). *Gay macho: Ethnography of the homosexual clone.* Unpublished doctoral dissertation, New York University.

Lofland, J. (1969). *Deviance and identity.* Englewood Cliffs, NJ: Prentice-Hall.

McCall, G.J., & Simmons, J.L. (1966). *Identities and interactions: An examination of human associations in everyday life.* New York: The Free Press.

McDonald, G.J. (1982). Individual differences in the coming out process for gay men: Implications for theoretical models. *Journal of Homosexuality, 8,* 47-60.

McWhirter, D.P., & Mattison, A.M. (1984). *The male couple: How relationships develop.* Englewood Cliffs, NJ: Prentice-Hall.

Minton, H.L., & McDonald, G.J. (1983/1984). Homosexual identity formation as a developmental process. *Journal of Homosexuality, 9,* 91-104.

Plummer, K. (1975). *Sexual stigma: An interactionist account.* London: Routledge & Kegan Paul.

Ponse, B. (1978). *Identities in the lesbian world: The social construction of self.* Westport, CT: Greenwood Press.

Reid, J. (1973). *The best little boy in the world.* New York: G.P. Putnam's Sons.

Reinhart, R.C. (1982). *A history of shadows*. New York: Avon Books.

Remafedi, G. (1987). Male homosexuality: The adolescent's perspective. *Pediatrics, 79*, 326-330.

Riddle, D.I., & Morin, S.F. (1977, November). Removing the stigma: Data from individuals. *APA Monitor, 16*, 28.

Saghir, M.T., & Robins, E. (1973). *Male and female homosexuality: A comprehensive investigation*. Baltimore, MD: The Williams & Wilkins Company.

Schäfer, S. (1976). Sexual and social problems among lesbians. *The Journal of Sex Research, 12*, 50-69.

Simmons, J.L. (1965). Public stereotypes of deviants. *Social Problems, 13*, 223-232.

Simon, W., & Gagnon, J.H. (1984). Sexual scripts. *Society, 22*, 53-60.

Smith, K.S. (1980). *Socialization, identity, and commitment: The case of female homosexuals*. Unpublished master's thesis, Miami University.

Tavris, C., & Wade, C. (1984). *The longest war: Sex differences in perspective*. New York: Harcourt Brace Jovanovich.

Theodorson, G.A., & Theodorson, A.G. (1969). *A modern dictionary of sociology*. New York: Thomas Y. Crowell.

Troiden, R.R. (1977). *Becoming homosexual: Research on acquiring a gay identity*. Unpublished doctoral dissertation, State University of New York at Stony Brook.

Troiden, R.R. (1979). Becoming homosexual: A model of gay identity acquisition. *Psychiatry, 42*, 362-373.

Troiden, R.R. (1984/1985). Self, self-concept, identity, and homosexual identity: Constructs in need of definition and differentiation. *Journal of Homosexuality, 10*, 97-109.

Troiden, R.R. (1988). *Gay and lesbian identity: A sociological analysis*. New York: General Hall.

Troiden, R.R., & Goode, E. (1980). Variables related to the acquisition of a gay identity. *Journal of Homosexuality, 5*, 383-392.

Warren, C.A.B. (1974). *Identity and community in the gay world*. New York: John Wiley & Sons.

Warren, C.A.B., & Ponse, B. (1977). The existential self in the gay world. In J.D. Douglas, & J.M. Johnson (Eds.), *Existential sociology* (pp. 273-289). New York: Cambridge University Press.

Weinberg, M.S., & Williams, C.J. (1974). *Male homosexuals: Their problems and adaptations*. New York: Oxford University Press.

Weinberg, T.S. (1977). *Becoming homosexual: Self-disclosure, self-identity, and self-maintenance*. Unpublished doctoral dissertation, University of Connecticut.

Weinberg, T.S. (1978). On "doing" and "being" gay: Sexual behavior and homosexual male self-identity. *Journal of Homosexuality, 4*, 143-156.

Whitam, F.L., & Mathy, R.M. (1986). *Male homosexuality in four societies: Brazil, Guatemala, the Philippines, and the United States*. New York: Praeger.

Widening Circles:
An Ethnographic Profile of a Youth Group

Camille J. Gerstel, MA

University of Chicago

Andrew J. Feraios, MEd

University of California, Berkeley

Gilbert Herdt, PhD

University of Chicago

SUMMARY. This article introduces work-in-progress on the ethnography of a gay and lesbian youth group in Chicago. The surrounding neighborhood is sketched and aspects of the supporting agency, within which the group functions, are described. Both are seen as contributing contexts for the "coming out" process here. The youth group is described in part, including the age, ethnicity,

Ms. Gerstel is in the Department of Anthropology, Mr. Feraios is in the Department of Psychology, and Dr. Herdt is on the Committee on Human Development.

Data drawn upon in this paper derive from an ongoing project entitled "Sexual orientation and cultural competence in Chicago," conducted by Gilbert Herdt, Andrew Boxer, and Floyd Irvin, and funded by the Spencer Foundation, whose support is gratefully acknowledged. Support for the writing of this article came, in part, from the Clinical Research Training Program in Adolescence, Michael Reese Hospital, under NIMH 2T32 MHJ14668-12, and this assistance is also gratefully acknowledged. For their comments and criticisms of this article, the authors wish to thank Andrew Boxer and Adam Katz. We are especially grateful to Chicago Horizons Community Services, Inc., its Board, and Director, Bruce Koff, for their help and support of our project.

Correspondence and reprint requests may be addressed to Dr. Herdt at the University of Chicago, Committee on Human Development, 5730 South Woodlawn Avenue, Chicago, IL 60637.

75

and related factors of its composition. Youth are found to be involved in a process of dual socialization entailing roles and knowledge in the gay and straight normative communities.

This article presents work-in-progress that is part of an ongoing interdisciplinary study of a group of gay and lesbian teenagers in Chicago. Gay youth can be said to derive from every ethnic, religious, and class background. What they share is the experience of growing up alienated from, yet shaped by, the social institutions, roles, and norms of their wider societies. In constructing identities and networks, and in learning to manage a variety of social tasks in different contexts, gay and lesbian adolescents are unique in that their parents almost never have the same sexual orientation as themselves. Even parents who are aware and supportive of teenagers' developing gay identities lack personal experience of, and strategies for responding to, related problems (Martin, 1982; Muller, 1987). Gay adolescents must look outside of the family for help in negotiating their sexual identities.

Until very recently, media representations of gay characters were minimal or negative; mainstream institutions of American society, such as religious and health care organizations, traditionally pathologized gay persons and homoerotic emotions, or ignored them as peripheral (see Herdt, herein). This is still largely the case in Chicago, and it contributes to a vast sense of isolation, of the feeling that "I am the only one in the world like this." Because of the fear and loneliness created by mainstream attitudes toward gays, many young (and not so young) gay people feel forced to hide their sexual identities, to live in the "closet." "Coming out" or "coming out of the closet" is thus a dual process of accepting oneself and of sharing knowledge of one's sexual identity with widening circles of others: family, friends, peers, co-workers, strangers. The subjects in our study participate in a social and support group for gay youth who have embarked on this life-long process. They are, therefore, a highly select sample of adolescent homosexuals, in that many are coming out in the context of this gay-identified group. Many American cities are witnessing the formation of such groups (see Anderson, 1987). However, for the vast majority of both closeted and more openly gay teenagers nationally, such supportive groups are absent, too difficult, or too risky for them to attend.

Identity formation involves a complex process of assimilation to social roles and the self-interpretation of social norms via individual experience (see Troiden, herein). Organizing a gay identity is a dual process: It involves socialization into mainstream society, which assumes heterosexuality to be at the foundation of adult roles, and socialization into gay cultural settings, which establishes differential norms that reflect upon and against the mainstream culture. No gay population in Western culture is a simple "reverse image" of mainstream straight society, but neither can any construct itself in isolation from the wider society (Adam, 1978; D'Emilio, 1983). Gay adolescents must therefore negotiate an understanding of self and society from two conflictual but synergistic perspectives.

We shall introduce the context of, and the resources available to, a small group of Chicago's gay adolescents who are at present coming out. The Youth Group, its sponsoring agency, and the largely gay neighborhood surrounding it are briefly described. The neighborhood offers positive role models of personal and professional aspects of adult gay life; it provides various opportunities for social interaction with other gay teenagers. The agency provides social services oriented toward the gay population. Because it draws its resources from that population, it fosters attitudes of self-sufficiency and a sense of community. Within the group itself, teenagers encounter other gay youth from diverse backgrounds; for many, this is their first socialization into a gay cultural setting. Our article highlights impressions of this process as revealed through initial interviews and participant observations.

NOTES ON CONTEXT AND METHODS

Our Chicago Gay and Lesbian Youth Project provides a naturalistic study of gay adolescents through participant observation and interviews built around open-ended questions. Psychological and sociological studies in the past have generally drawn their samples from clinical patients or prostitutes. They have often relied upon adult participants for retrospective histories, the memories of which, as we know, are filtered through later social experiences that differ qualitatively from and, in turn, influence the retrospectives (Ross, 1980). Further, many studies by white male researchers of adult white male populations have overgeneralized their findings to represent all gay and lesbian persons (Carrier, 1979). By contrast, our Chicago population is extremely heterogeneous, as described below and our own research staff is male, female, and multiracial. Because the teenagers themselves use the term "gay" to refer to both males and females, we follow their convention. When males or females in particular are indexed, the sex will be specified.

The Youth Group from which participants are drawn is organized by Chicago Horizons Community Services, a nonprofit social services agency that provides the context for our Project. The Youth Group itself thus serves as a social center for the teenagers, many of whom cannot be open about their sexual orientation anywhere else. In addition to the supportive and confidential environment Horizons provides for their coming out, youth can also turn to the agency at any time for other social or psychological services.

The interview component of our Youth Project utilizes in-depth, semistructured interviews, that examine familial, peer, and romantic relations and coming-out experiences. Unlike prior studies of homosexuality, ours invites teenagers to construct their experiences as open-ended narratives. We also examine demographic factors (ethnic and religious background, residence community, household membership), same-sex emotions, sexual orientation through a modified Kinsey scale, same and opposite-sex sexual experience, personal definitions of "coming out" and related experiences with family and friends' attitudes toward gays prior to "gay" self-identification, awareness of and role models concerning cultural representations of gays; awareness of AIDS and AIDS prevention, selected assessments of mental well-being using a variety of psychosocial measures for this, and the effects of the Youth Group on the coming-out process, identity formation, and future life goals.

This interview information is supplemented by participant observation of the Youth Group meetings and the neighborhood environs of Horizons. Here we have begun to describe informal networks of friends and related local cultural settings of gay youth. Work is in progress on the history of the Group, as revealed through interviews with past and present facilitators (Group leaders), Horizons administrators, and with adolescents themselves. Historical and cultural materials will be utilized later to examine links between our teenage cultural contexts and the broader Chicago gay and lesbian population.

THE NEWTOWN NEIGHBORHOOD

The Horizons agency is located in the Newtown neighborhood of Chicago, populated by artists, young singles, significant black and Hispanic concentrations, and the city's largest gay core. Directly west of Lake Michigan on Chicago's northside, the neighborhood includes both quiet residential streets and popular shops, restaurants, and many of the city's well-known regional theaters. Housing is primarily in rental buildings of 6 to 30 units. Gay adults are sporadically openly affectionate in public, sometimes kissing or holding hands. Various gay-identified businesses and organizations, peppered among the neighborhood shops, provide examples of career role models of successful gay adult lifestyles for younger people.

Gay teenagers have found several places to socialize, meet with friends, or just "hang out" in the area. There are several fast-food restaurants near Horizons, and an urban mall offers food, boutiques, and busy lobbies protected from the weather. The lakeshore a few blocks away, which is faced with stepped rock slabs, is popular in summer for sunning and swimming. Here again the example of openly gay adults on the beach reinforces positive adolescent images of gay life. Night life is more complicated. There is a mixed gay and straight "juice bar"/dance club, and a few of the area nightclubs do host occasional "all-ages" nights, when liquor is not served. But the difficulty for Chicago gay youth in locating evening spots to congregate is further complicated because many do not feel accepted by, or desire to be openly gay around, their straight peers—whom they may unexpectedly meet, causing embarrassment or even harassment.

Newtown thus provides a circle of acculturation to gay adult norms by revealing models of visible gay lifestyles integrated within a more broadly mixed neighborhood. While there are the usual gay bars and clubs, there are also bookstores, clothing and card shops, restaurants (ranging from diners to the elegantly international), laundries, florists, and travel agencies owned by openly gay proprietors. Gay lawyers, accountants, and doctors (among whom is a recent candidate for city alderman) certainly challenge culturally received stereotypes of homosexuals as prostitutes, child molesters, or "dirty old men." Adolescents cannot help but be exposed to positive alternative role models, including persons of diverse ethnic and political backgrounds, within the gay population. This complex urban world provides a radically new context for the gay teenager: one that can change his or her feeling of being alone and help realize a whole range of feelings, ideas, and relationships, including some shared by fellow youth and esteemed adults.

Gay publications in Chicago provide organizational signs of an adult gay community. The weekly magazine *Gay Chicago* includes legal, medical, and advice columns, reviews of the arts, calendars of events, and lists of gay-identified bars, services, and businesses. The weekly newspaper *Windy City Times* provides local gay-related news, as well as national and international articles, personals, opinion and society columns, and a "letter to the editor" section as a forum for readers. *Outlines* is a newer publication that provides items of interest, expanded news and local interview columns, and more information of interest to lesbians. It also includes a directory of gay businesses and contact information for various services and hotlines. By supplying this free information to youths who may be afraid of or unprepared to discuss their awakening gay identities with straight family, friends, or professionals, such weeklies provide a valuable communicative and socializing service to gay youth. Indeed, these media may be a teenager's first exposure to the concept of a "gay community," which transcends the old "sexual culture" of same-sex attractions and behaviors. The sense of there being an "us" helps adolescents to counteract the isolating and peripheralizing images engendered by mainstream society and the mass media.

Newtown, then, exposes youth to a number of alternative gay lifestyles and, consequently, to more verbal and physical harassment. Experiencing such attacks, either as witnesses or as victims, reawakens fears, even as positive models soothe them. Recent news has unfortunately warned of attacks on gays as a "backlash" for AIDS.

One such incident occurred at our fieldsite, reminding us of the history of violence surrounding gay lifestyles in our own society.

A significant message of the neighborhood is that "being gay" is not a monolithic state; teenagers observe that gay and lesbian adults are individuals with their own tastes, talents, and goals that they have developed and now apply to the task of living their lives. Newtown becomes a place for gay teenagers to socialize informally and to formulate their own mode of socialization.

HORIZONS – THE UMBRELLA AGENCY

Chicago Horizons Community Services, Inc. lies within the neighborhood and is easily accessible via public transportation from other parts of the city. Founded in 1973 to provide a wide range of services to the gay community, Horizons is staffed by a paid executive director and over 230 volunteers, including psychologists, social workers, lawyers, and administrators. The agency works to identify the social service needs of metropolitan Chicago's gay and lesbian population, and to establish programs and referrals providing for those needs. Horizons emphasizes the resources already available among the gay population, and draws upon these resources whenever possible. It sees itself as "engendering opportunities for self-help, growth, and maturity" (as described in its publications), so that Horizons not only serves, but in some ways represents the gay community.

Horizons offers training and educational services to professional organizations, City of Chicago agencies, schools, and other community groups. It also sponsors special events, such as public conferences and workshops on topics of special interest to lesbians and gay men. AIDS information is made available through a number of services and educational materials, provided at Horizon's offices and distributed to health care agencies through its outreach program in the City. Education about AIDS as a disease and about prevention and "safe-sex" practices are included in all Horizons programs, with outreach to those perceived to be at highest risk. The Telephone Help Line operates nightly, providing information and access to Horizon's programs. As a further information service, volunteer attorneys offer free initial consultation, secondary referrals, and public education.

Horizons also addresses gay mental health needs with counseling services. Professionally trained and supervised peer counseling is provided both in person and over the telephone, to couples as well as individuals. For those needing in-depth counseling, Horizons offers the services of professional psychotherapists. P.A.S.S.-A.G.E.S. conducts support and educational groups for gay men at risk of AIDS, including those contemplating being tested for the AIDS antibody, or those who have taken the test and who now seek support regarding their concerns about the results. Horizons extends other services for personal growth and support as well. Discussion groups for men and women, led by facilitators, cover broad-ranging topics such as couplehood, coming out, friendships, and relationships. A group for parents and friends of gays, the local arm of the national organization P.F.L.A.G., provides discussions, social events, and special activities for parents and children. Horizons Youth Group, the focus of our study, offers a safe, supportive, and comfortable environment in which youth aged 14 to 21 can deal with the emergence of their sexual orientation, familial problems, and other issues. Through this range of services, then, Horizons sees itself as fulfilling its commitment to affirming the lives of lesbians and gay men.

The attitudes of youth stimulated by the Horizons context are perhaps as important, symbolically, as the provision of these services. Horizons stresses self-help, both by the individual and within the gay community; feelings of isolation, loneliness, and dependence engendered elsewhere are thus reversed. A key idiom we often hear, in the socializing process, is that one has a "family of choice," connoting the security and confidence that arise from the sense of belonging to a vital and affirming community, caring for itself and reinforcing positive values and norms.

THE INNER CIRCLE: THE YOUTH GROUP

The Horizons Youth Group was founded in 1978-1979 to provide a supportive environment for young people in the greater Chicago area. Horizon's founders recognized that conventional supports for adolescents through school, church, and the community did not serve the special needs of youth struggling to identify themselves as lesbian or gay. The Youth Group operates on the premise that sharing experience with peers who are undergoing similar processes enhances self-esteem and promotes emotional growth. The Group does not force a gay identity on those who are uncertain of their sexualities. Rather, it provides a noncritical environment in which participants may explore their own feelings and gay peers' reactions regarding sexual orientation and sexual identity, as well as family and peer relationships.

For a decade the Youth Group has provided a predictable, supportive, group structure that teenagers can rely on. The Group meets every Saturday at noon, after which members go off with their friends to local fast-food restaurants for lunch and informal get-togethers. Many come from long distances—some from as far as Indiana or Wisconsin—and thus may be unable to attend every week or to call ahead of time to verify meetings. The stability of the group meeting time offsets the fluidity of its membership, which seems psychologically and symbolically important for those unable to attend all the time. The Group thus functions as a contact center, where friends of different neighborhoods, ethnic backgrounds, and towns can meet, talk, and forge bonds.

The Saturday meetings are semistructured. Newcomers are welcomed; anyone attending for the first time is introduced and applauded, which constitutes their intentional recognition by the group. Meetings open with general announcements about events, and new activities are planned and discussed. Youth make announcements regarding events of local interest, such as bake sales and parties. Sometimes, to get acquainted and reacquainted, everyone gives their first names, as group composition shifts from week to week. But people are free to introduce themselves however they wish, and some use nicknames and pseudonyms. New members, those who have attended less than five meetings, break off into a separate "newcomers" group, that focuses explicitly on coming-out issues. The larger group offers a choice of topics for discussion that may be taken up in one larger or several small rap groups. For the latter, teenagers select the topic that interests them and form small groups of about 10, each of which is led by at least one facilitator. Occasionally, a women's group meets to discuss issues of particular relevance to them. A break is scheduled about half-way, so friends in different groups that week can consolidate their social plans for afterwards. In addition to the Saturday meeting, the group now holds a Wednesday evening "drop-in" unstructured time for teenagers to meet and socialize in an open, supportive environment.

One theme of the Group is "self-help" and encouraging teenagers to take responsibility for themselves. Program selection is a dynamic aspect of this, in which the adolescents actively participate. While facilitators may suggest topics or offer guidance, it is the teenagers themselves who make the choices. In the announcements period of a recent meeting, for instance, topics that had arisen in the women's meeting and which seemed to have broader implications were designated as general discussion topics for a later meeting. The newly formed Youth Council, an informal elected group of representatives who provide leadership for the Group, is another aspect of self-help. The Council meets separately and plans and coordinates activities for the Group as a whole. The names of the new officers were recently published in *Windy City Times*, enhancing the Youth Group's visibility in the adult gay community. The Youth Group thus shows itself to be not a counseling agency, but an avenue for teenage self-affirmation and development, generating leadership skills and peer networks within a future adult cohort, a symbolic theme to which we shall return.

Although many Chicago neighborhoods are racially segregated, in the Youth Group we have observed blacks, whites, Hispanics, and Asians mixing comfortably. Racial tension, if present, seems very muted. Interracial friendship in the Group is a feature of its social life. This is so different from the city itself, where interracial friendship in certain neighborhoods is so rare that one young black informant's family recently confronted him regarding his sexuality because of it: they suspected he was gay when he began bringing home white friends.

Membership is not only racially, but sexually varied because unlike many parallel adult groups, the Youth Group strives to have the same number of males and females. This was not always so. In its earlier years, only a few members of the group were female. Today the number of women members is much higher. Some past members and facilitators attribute the change to the addition of new adult women facilitators; others see the new facilitators as a response to the perceived needs of more female members. The women's movement has certainly contributed here, influencing the goals and expectations of young women *and* men. Strong cross-gender friendships are common in the Youth Group; during the meetings young men and women hug, tease one another, and share chairs. Most of our respondents name at least one member of the opposite sex as one of his or her three closest friends, indicating that this trend extends beyond the Horizons environment. It will be particularly interesting to see if such friendships continue into adulthood, with its separate gay male and lesbian domains in our society (see Herdt's introduction, herein).

To sum up, the youth come from all socioeconomic classes and from a number of geographic settings: urban, small-town, inner-city, suburban. The diversity of members itself reflects the diversity of American society on the one hand, and the heterogeneity of gay adults and communities on the other. And just as the gay and lesbian population encompasses many styles and subcultures, so does the Youth Group. Members may be rich or poor, go to private high schools or work full-time at 16; come from many racial and ethnic backgrounds, live with their parents or in college dormitories far from their home towns. They are linked together by a deep sense of feeling different from straight peers, and a desire to understand how their sexual orientation determines their place in the mainstream of society.

There are almost as many paths into the Group as there are members. Some have seen or heard Youth Group members interviewed in the local media, such as television's "Oprah Winfrey Show" and Phyllis Levy's radio program "Sex Talk." Others have friends who introduced them to the Group. Still others hear of the Horizons agency or see notices of it in gay publications, and then call its Help Line. Some find the Horizons number in the telephone book, while searching madly for the words "gay," "lesbian," and "homosexual."

After they have found the Group, their next step is to attend a meeting. Some are prepared to meet other gay teenagers and thus go the next Saturday. Others, however, describe months of walking about with the address in their pockets before committing themselves, because, as one teenager explained, his presence at the meeting constituted an open declaration to himself of his sexual orientation.

The Youth Group, by custom, leads the Chicago Gay Pride Parade, which is held every June to commemorate the 1969 Stonewall riots. For many gay adults, these adolescents represent not only the future continuity of their community, but also a level of self-awareness and gay openness inconceivable in their own adolescence.

The teenagers themselves express a different symbolic focus, as shown in the following comments.

> We're like pioneers. We know there weren't groups like this 20 years ago, but some of that is [because] . . . there weren't people ready to go to them. We're a lot older than our parents were when they were teenagers; there's more to deal with. It's a different world. We're making a difference.

The Group has become for many a focus for activism. Gay teenagers who appear on local media and at Chicago rallies supporting gay rights measures express the *adolescent* gay's aspirations for the community in a very different example: Some youth initially expressed concern about our study, not to protect themselves, but to see that it was helpful to others. They were eager to participate, but only if our data were used to help educate the public at large, rather than merely becoming objects in a study produced for "musty old professors." Recently, a teenager said of the study after being interviewed, "I liked it. . . . It can be used to help straight people understand gay people. . . . That we're not so different. Maybe there would be less rejection of us."

Youth Group members identify the Group as the catalyst for new perceptions, not only regarding themselves, but also their position in relation to society. It provides ways both to affirm the self and to transform their shared identification as members of an oppressed minority. Perhaps for other minority groups, such social consciousness derives at first from their parents. But as Barry Dank (1971) initially argued in this context, gays are unique in belonging to a stigmatized category to which their parents almost never belong.

On the contrary, for many adolescents, the most difficult people to come out to are family members.

WIDENING CIRCLES OF COMING OUT

Coming out symbolizes a key dimension of gay life. The idiom "coming out" implies a single event. In many ways, though, temporally, spatially, and socially, coming out is a process of identifying one's sexual orientation to widening circles of persons, beginning with the self. This process may entail several discrete steps leading to an uncertain outcome. Some teenagers describe coming out as self-identification alone. Others say they have come out only if they have discussed their orientation with intimates, or, again, only if they are emerging into a gay lifestyle. For the most open of them, the circle describing "out" becomes increasingly public and includes a gay identity openly expressed to everyone: family, friends, colleagues, and strangers. Each person, in his or her own terms, negotiates a balance between levels of concealment (suggesting denial) and levels of openness (creating vulnerability to harassment and discrimination), in degrees that are adaptive to the self at present. This adolescent balance may of course shift over the life course, with coming out symbolizing a process of continuous revelation and becoming.

Fear of being shunned or rejected is, according to our informants, at its greatest at the beginning of the coming-out process. Even negative reactions, once endured, may be interrupted to reaffirm the knowledge that one can cope with and live beyond the early frost. However, adolescents are still dependent for emotional and financial support upon their parents. Fears of coming out to family reveal internal fears of emotional rejection, as well as external threats of being thrown out of the home, being forced into psychotherapy, or even being physically abused. Aside from these fears, though, many teenagers, who feel that their parents would never harm them, struggle with guilt because they fear disappointing their parents' hopes and projected plans for them. Some adolescents thus avoid coming out to the very people society regards as their main source of advice and comfort.

Adolescents locate and interact with gay peers through the major venues mentioned above, the urban mall and lakeshore areas. A day at the beach is easy to account for in summer, and a day of shopping at the mall during colder weather provides an equally plausible story to tell parents. After Group meetings comes fast food and gossip, and opportunities for teenagers to make new friends. Other contexts, neither as structured as the Horizons Group nor as dependent on local "in-crowd" knowledge of "good places to hang out," provide possibilities. For example, several of our female informants mentioned first discovering Newtown, and even Horizons, through women's organizations, feminist support or political groups that include in their membership lesbians with whom the younger women made contact. Some of the state and private colleges in the Chicago area also have gay students' groups, and their parties and social events frequently include outsiders of college age who are not enrolled. Some college-bound high school students find their needs better met in such groups than at Horizons. Some Youth Group members attend local colleges and also belong to such campus groups.

Two of these local colleges base their curricula in the arts and are known to have large gay student populations. Libraries, cafeterias, and campus-sponsored events provide them with many places to socialize. Arts groups in general have been mentioned by several respondents; some made most of their gay contacts through volunteer or paid work with theaters and writers workshops. One teenager, who had been frequently harassed at school, told us, "I'm switching to a gay high school." The school he referred to focuses on the arts and, according to the respondent, is "75 to 80% gay, and the rest don't care." In fact, the actual number of gay students need not be higher than that of other high schools. The important thing is the gay students' openness about being gay, and the positive attitudes of straight peers. Artistic communities seem to embrace alternative lifestyles, making it less acceptable to harass students for their gay sexual orientations. Some of our teenagers are thus also in the arts, and they expect to, and do find other youth with similar interests, in these settings.

The "magnet school" system in Chicago has several side effects that color the formation of gay cohorts within the schools. Several high schools are set aside for talented or academically gifted students; entrance is by competitive examinations. Students there go to school not with the teenagers from their own neighborhoods, but with a citywide cross section. As a result, the student bodies are more racially integrated, and more importantly, religious or ethnic norms that might be upheld within a neighborhood are de-emphasized. Behaviors, therefore, are less easily stereotyped. One woman mentioned her interracial high school clique, which included several openly gay students. Because of the magnet school atmosphere, this diverse group was easy to maintain; in her neighborhood they would have been harassed.

Over the last few years, changes in media presentations of gay themes and cultural roles point to shifts in norms both within and regarding gay populations. Other changes, located in mainstream society, affect Group members. For instance, some of our youth refer to gay characters on television and in movies; both male and female respondents mentioned and identified heavily with television's *Consenting Adult*, in which a college freshman comes out to himself, his parents, and friends. Gay characters and stories raise the awareness of, and create dialogue with, mainstream society. For those who have not yet come out, the message that other people with same-sex attractions exist and can be accepted is invaluable. Two rock groups have also been important: The Communards and Bronski Beat are both gay-identified, and popular not just in the closed circuits of gay clubs, but as part of the New Wave music scene in general. Gay teenagers and their straight peers see videos and hear songs by these groups every day. Gay adolescents have songs and singers to identify with directly in mainstream environments, and straight teenagers, in turn, have positive images through which to empathize when gay friends come out to them.

Not all contemporary media images enhance hopes of a positive future as a gay adult. Portrayals of AIDS color both the perceptions of older gay cohorts and teenagers' own expectations. Some of these changes are reflected in the language of participants. For example, for most people in their 20's and beyond, "old gay" refers to people who came out before the Stonewall riots in 1969, which ushered in the gay liberation movement. For Youth Group members, "old gay" means people who came out and were sexually active before AIDS became an issue in Chicago, roughly about

1982-1983. Many teenagers interpret these adults as riskier sexual partners than teenage peers. Due to the media emphasis on males as more at risk than females, some lesbian group members view any sexual act with another lesbian as safe. One woman defined "safe sex" as not sleeping with bisexual women. Group members coming out in the context of AIDS structure their realities in terms of the disease itself and misinformation surrounding it. Not only current behavior, but also future expectations depend upon folk conceptions of AIDS. When asked to project his life as an older gay man, one respondent said:

> If a cure for AIDS has been found, then I think it'll be . . . for me a lot more secure. I'll feel that heterosexuals will accept us the same way they should have by now. If it weren't for AIDS I think we'd be so far along. . . . If a cure for AIDS is not found, I'll be more secluded, maybe go back in the closet and turn out the light, but I'll never get heterosexually married.

Another social change reflected in Group membership is the degree of cross-gender behavior, described by a long-time facilitator as less common in the Group now, compared to 5 years ago. Cross-gender behaviors may indicate underlying factors in Chicago as elsewhere: rebellion by gays or straights against too-rigid gender roles, testing of peer reactions to a possibly gay identity, or announcement of a gay sexual orientation. Before Stonewall, individuals were seen as having a "condition" or "sickness," that of homosexuality. Homosexuality was, in turn, closely identified in cultural stereotypes with cross-gender behavior, so that many individuals with same-sex orientations who felt no urge to express cross-gender mannerisms or tastes never self-identified as homosexuals. At the same time, adopting such behaviors was a means of expressing one's sexual orientation, both to potential partners and to society as a whole. One member mentioned a similar point when she appeared on the "Oprah Winfrey Show" with other Group members. Discussing male friends who did not adopt cross-gender dress or mannerism, she said:

Some of my friends are not feminine, just normal, everyday Joe, and they find it hard to find boyfriends. Some of them don't like being so average. They like it because people don't look at them, but they don't like it because they don't get dates. They're not really ready to say, "Hey, will you go out with me?"

Particularly in segments of society upholding rigid gender roles, where harassment of gays is reinforced for straight aggressors, cross-gender behaviors evoke a negative response. It may expose gays to abuse, but at the same time reassure potential partners of one's orientation and affirm self-identification. The two positive aspects of cross-gender behavior may be particularly important for adolescents lacking regular access to openly gay environments. At this stage of our research, we cannot know how much these factors hold for Group members, or to what degree other influences, such as socioeconomic class differences observed among older cohorts of gays, may impinge upon Youth Group members in particular, and upon contemporary gay adolescents in general.

Life goals and transitions are undoubtedly influenced by the adolescent nature of the Youth Group. Where teenagers are expected to go to college, for instance, there may be less pressure from families to "settle down" with a heterosexual partner. And simultaneously, an adolescent questioning his or her readiness to come out may see college far from home as an ideal venue for creating a new identity, and thereby defer part or all of the coming-out process until later. Alternatively, teenagers from working-class or small-town environments may feel that parents expect them to marry quickly and live nearby. Such pressure may force teenagers either to the cities or to early confrontations with parents, or drive them to go to extraordinary lengths to conceal their emerging gay identities.

Integration into those mainstream and gay contexts that constitute a gay adolescent's world requires personal reflection and a highly personalized sorting of values, preferences, and the symbolic messages of public actions. The complex process of coming out demands all the tasks of adolescence: the shedding of childhood norms and acquisition of adult values, coping with puberty and awakening sexuality, and choices about future educational and career goals. In addition, for the self-identifying gay teenager, coming out adds learning that other gay people exist, finding them, working out mainstream stereotypes about gay life, and transcending heterosexual roles in the development of gay roles that fulfill needs unaddressed by socialization at school, church, and by parents. Until very recently, no structured supports have been available to gay adolescents involved in this process. The appearance of the Horizons Youth Group, and similar organizations for other age groups in the gay population, are positive signs of a growing awareness in mainstream society of the presence and contributions of gay communities, and of those communities' commitment to assisting their youngest members.

BIBLIOGRAPHY

Adam, B. (1978). *The survival of domination*. New York: Elsevier.

Anderson, D. (1987). Family and peer relations of gay adolescents. *Adolescent Psychiatry, 14*, 162-178.

Carrier, J. (1979). Review of *Homosexualities: A study of diversity among men and women*, by A. Bell and M. S. Weinberg (1978). *Journal of Homosexuality, 4*, 296-298.

Dank, B. (1971). Coming out in the gay world. *Psychiatry, 34*, 180-197.

D'Emilio, J. (1983). *Sexual politics, sexual communities*. Chicago: University of Chicago Press.

Martin, A. Danien (1982). Learning to hide: Socialization of the gay adolescent. *Adolescent Psychiatry, 10*, 52-65.

Muller, Ann. (1987). Retrospective distortion in homosexual research. *Archives of Sexual Behavior, 9*, 523-531.

Ross, M. (1980). Retrospective distortion in homosexual research. *Archives of Sexual Behavior, 9*, 523-531.

Parental Influences on the Self-Esteem of Gay and Lesbian Youths: A Reflected Appraisals Model

Ritch C. Savin-Williams, PhD

Cornell University

SUMMARY. Based on a population of 317 gay and lesbian youths, the current investigation explores the appropriateness of a reflected appraisals perspective in predicting the degree to which parental attitudes, as perceived by youth, affects their self-esteem and comfortableness being gay. A lesbian was most comfortable with her sexual orientation if she also reported that her parents accepted her homosexuality; these variables did not, however, predict her level of self-esteem. Among the gay males, parental acceptance predicted comfortable being gay if the parents were also perceived as important components of a youth's self-worth; a male most comfortable with his sexual orientation had the highest level of self-esteem. Results are discussed in terms of: (a) sex of parent, (b) sex-role development, (c) comparisons of gays and lesbians, and (d) research on gay and lesbian youth.

In American society it is taken as an axiom that we are social animals, responding almost without recourse to the attitudes and

Dr. Savin-Williams is Associate Professor of Social/Personality Development in the Department of Human Development at Cornell University.

For this research, the author received the Mark Freedman Memorial Award in August 1986, in recognition of his outstanding research on gay and lesbian issues. Dr. Savin-Williams wishes to express his appreciation to undergraduate students Beth Burlingame, Andrea Butt, Jay Coburn, Richard Goldberg, and Rala Massey[1] for their invaluable assistance in the data collection process.

Correspondence and requests for reprints may be addressed to the author, c/o Department of Human Development, MVR Hall, Cornell University, Ithaca, NY 14853.

actions of others in the environment. This particular theoretical stance is assumed in part by a position referred to as "reflected appraisals" (Rosenberg, 1979):

> Reduced to essentials, the principle holds that people, as social animals, are deeply influenced by the attitudes of others toward the self and that, in the course of time, they come to view themselves as they are viewed by others. (p. 63)

The present study focuses on one aspect of that social environment, the parent-child dyad. In particular, based on a sample of gay and lesbian youths, the research explores the degree to which parental attitudes toward their son's or daughter's sexual orientation, as perceived by the youth, affects the youth's comfortableness with that sexual orientation and in turn his or her self-esteem. The specific theoretical perspective tested in predicting the nature of these relationships is a reflected appraisals formulation as articulated by Rosenberg (1979), with an emphasis on Cooley's (1912) looking-glass self theory.[2] Cooley's contribution was to stress the "imagination" rather than the reality of how one appeared to another person and the "imagination" of that person's judgment to conceptions and evaluations of the self.

A number of investigators have documented the seemingly critical importance of parental variables for predicting, if not determining, an adolescent's self-esteem (Gecas, 1971; O'Donnell, 1976; Openshaw, Thomas & Rollins, 1984; Watkins & Astilla, 1980). Consistent with Cooley's (1912) principle of the looking-glass self, more critical than the actual attitudes of the parents for the development and maintenance of an adolescent's self-evaluation is the youth's perception of those attitudes. Thus, the emphasis is not on the actual attitudes of the parents, but on how the adolescent perceives those attitudes toward himself or herself. These perceptions are believed to be particularly significant in family relationships. For example, Gecas and Schwalbe (1986) reported that adolescent global self-esteem was more related to the adolescent's perceptions of parental attitudes and behaviors toward the adolescent than to the parents' report of their attitudes and behavior toward their child.

In addition, the importance of individuals to the subject mediates the relationship between the self and self-evaluation (Rosenberg, 1979). ". . . not all significant others are equally significant, and those who are more significant have greater influence on our self-concepts (p. 83)." Although research studies may assume significance, especially of parents, significance is in the eye of the beholder (Rosenberg, 1979). Thus, in the current study it is not assumed that parents are necessarily important for the self-esteem of a youth: rather, this assumption is tested by integrating it into the causal model. The study participants were asked if their parents were significant contributors to their sense of self-worth: the valuation rather than the credibility aspect of significance.[3]

The period of middle to late adolescence was selected for investigation because, according to Rosenberg (1979), it is the time immediately succeeding the increase of self-concept disturbance and self-consciousness of early adolescence, the assumed pubertal blues. By this account, during early adolescence self-esteem is extremely unstable and susceptible to the stresses of pubescence and various transitions in social contexts that occur, such as the change from elementary to junior high school for girls (Simmons, Blyth, Van-Cleave & Bush, 1979). Although this view is debatable, the research goal was to avoid these confounding influences and to focus on the years when self-esteem is assumed by most researchers to be relatively stable but not static, so as to better project a causal model (O'Malley & Bachman, 1983; Savin-Williams & Demo, 1984).

The decision to test a reflected appraisals theory with a sample of gay and lesbian youths was based on several considerations. First, to my knowledge there are relatively few, if any, research studies that empirically investigate self-evaluation among young gays and lesbians. Those in this age group with a gay or lesbian orientation would appear to be nearly invisible to psychologists and sociologists, except in retrospect (e.g., Bell, Weinberg & Hammersmith, 1981). Second, there is a public belief that gay and lesbian youth, because of their social if not psychological deviancy, are particularly susceptible to experiencing self-hatred and to internalizing external attitudes toward themselves. (This literature is reviewed in Savin-Williams, in preparation.) Third, previously published investigations of reflected appraisals theory involving the parent-adolescent dyad *assumed* heterosexual samples. Finally, regardless of the causal explanation of homosexuality, whether psychoanalytic, social conditioning, or biological, most theories of homosexuality include in their formulations the importance of the parents in the development of sexual orientation. Thus, for gay and lesbian youth the parental relationships would appear to be particularly salient in developing evaluations of the self.

This point of view has been theoretically articulated by several writers who attempted to explain why gay persons have low self-esteem. For example, in Hoffman's (1968) revelations of the gay world, low self-esteem among homosexuals is said to result from their internalization of the homophobic values and reflected appraisals of others as they grew up, especially those of parents, siblings, and teachers. Weinberg (1983) noted, "The way people feel about themselves intimately relates to the kinds of feedback that they perceive they are getting from others" (p. 244). Heterosexuality is assumed and encouraged; homosexuality is either invisible or condemned. This is the message given to the child, and later accepted by the child as an adolescent and as an adult. As a result, the gay person's self-esteem suffers. One need not experience the negative reaction directly; sometimes the imagined sense of a negative sanction is more powerful than an actual assault on one's self-image (Weinberg & Williams, 1974).

Based on a reflected appraisals perspective the following model is proposed: For those lesbian and gay adolescents who view their parents as an important source for their sense of self-worth, the degree to which the youths report that their parents have accepted (or would accept if they knew) their homosexuality will determine the level at which the youths will feel comfortable being gay or lesbian. The greater the perceived acceptance rather than rejection, the less likely that adolescents will want to give up their homosexuality. Because relationships with parents are not always equal, this hypothesis will be examined separately for mother and father. Finally, the more youths feel comfortable with their sexual orientation, the higher self-esteem will be. Although there is little reason to expect the sexes to differ in fulfilling the reflected appraisals model, analyses will be conducted separately for the lesbian and gay youths to test this assumption.

METHODS

Participants

Of the 317 respondents completing the questionnaire, 214 (68%) are gay men and 103 (32%) are lesbians. They range in age from 14 to 23 years, with 78% between the ages of 19 to 22 years. Many (78%) were in college during the study period. Table 1 below describes the status of the sample when data were collected.

The population is primarily Caucasian (91%), but it is diverse in religious affiliation: Catholic (34%), Protestant (32%), none (17%), Jewish (15%), and Eastern (2%). The nonwhites are Hispanic (3%), Black (2%), Asian-American (2%), Native American (1%), and International (1%).

When questioned concerning their home town community, the population reflected a rural, small town (44%) flavor. The others are from medium-sized towns (27%), small cities (12%), and large metropolitan areas (17%). Most of the families are professional (34%) or lesser professional/managerial (35%) in occupational sta-

Table 1
Age and Education Levels of the Sample

Category	Age	Education Completed	N
In School			
High School	14-17	8-11	10
College Freshmen	17-22	12	26
College Sophomores/ Juniors	17-23	13-14	111
College Seniors	20-23	15	86
Graduate Students	21-23	16	25
Out of School			
No College	16-23	9-12	25
Some College	19-23	13-15	17
College Graduates	21-23	16	17

tus; 18% are blue collar in status and 7% are clerical/sales (5% represented missing data).

The vast majority of the youths are either predominantly (31%) or exclusively (46%) homosexual in sexual orientation (5s or 6s on the Kinsey scale). The other participants reported a significant degree of heterosexual interest. Fourteen (4%) of the youths said that they were not "out" to any heterosexuals; 59 (19%) were out to any heterosexuals who care to know. In between these two extremes, 49% of the youths said there were a few, while 27% said there were a large number of heterosexuals "I do not want to know I am gay." Slightly less than half (48%) were currently in a self-defined love affair.

Measures

Gay and Lesbian Questionnaire (GAL Q). The Blumstein-Schwartz (1983) and Weinberg-Williams (1974) questionnaires incorporated most of the items of interest in this research project and thus formed the core of the questionnaire used in the current study. Several questions were added concerning parenting, love affairs, physical development, and athletics. Completing the 10-page GAL Q took 15 to 30 minutes.

Rosenberg Self-Esteem Scale (RSE). The RSE is a 10-item Likert-type scale that addresses issues of global self-esteem (i.e., "On the whole, I am satisfied with myself"), explicitly distinct from specific contexts. The scoring method, developed by Schilling and Savin-Williams (in preparation), is a 4-step scoring system with a person separation index of .89. Interitem reliability and the RSE's correlation with other self-report self-esteem scales are consistently high (Demo, 1985: Savin Williams & Demo, 1984).

Procedures

The GAL Qs were distributed by the author and five undergraduate research assistants to gay and lesbian youths through a variety of methods (see Table 2 below).

At the lesbian and gay picnic sponsored by the local gay bar, The Common Ground, the GAL Qs were placed in a box with pencils by the food table for one hour. Another box beside the other was

Table 2
Sources of Sample Recuitment

		Males		Females		Total	
		N	%	N	%	N	%
1)	A community picnic sponsored by the local Common Ground Bar	13	6	10	10	23	7
2)	Gay organization meetings on university campuses	44	21	5	5	49	15
3)	Female undergraduates who gave to their friends and their networks	19	9	37	36	56	18
4)	Male undergraduates who gave to their friends and their networks	69	32	9	9	78	25
5)	Contact persons in other states	27	13	16	16	43	14
6)	Attendees of a North-East Conference of Gay and Lesbian Student Activists	42	20	20	19	62	20
7)	A university sexuality class	0	0	6	6	6	2
		214		103		317	

marked "Completed Questionnaires." Although there were over 200 in attendance, most were involved in eating, drinking, playing softball or volleyball, and watching the wet T-shirts or wet shorts contests; they did not notice the research agenda. Less than one third of the completed GAL Qs returned could be used, primarily because respondents were older than 23 years of age.

The three gay campus meetings sampled were open to both men and women, though they were strikingly male dominated. The GAL Qs were distributed after a business meeting (Iowa State), a wine and cheese reception (SUNY Binghamton, New York), and a discussion meeting (University of Minnesota). All in attendance at these times completed the questionnaires.

Almost one half of the total responses came from friendship networks. We gave the GAL Qs to friends and asked those friends to distribute the questionnaires to their friends. The GAL Qs were either returned immediately to the researcher or, as was the case in nearly three quarters of these occasions, returned in a preaddressed, sealed envelope. This technique was the most anonymous and the most preferred (it was our impression), by those most uncomfortable with public knowledge of their sexual orientation. Because our friendship networks were quite unique, this procedure enhanced the diversity of the sample.

To increase geographic diversity, that is, a nonupstate New York population, the six of us sent 10 questionnaires to a friend in another state. The friends were requested to give the questionnaires to gays and lesbians they knew who were 23 years of age or younger. Positive responses were received from several states in the Midwest, South, and East. Nearly one fifth of the sample came from these mail-away sources.

Of the 180 students registered for the activist conference, 67 attended the workshop that I conducted, and where the GAL Qs were distributed. Of those, 62 returned a completed questionnaire. The participants were students from 27 colleges in eight states in the East and Mid-Atlantic who are active members of the political lesbian and gay communities.

Finally, a few questionnaires were returned from a human sexuality class. GAL Qs were distributed to the class of 200, but only 6 female students claimed to be other than heterosexual. Those females rated themselves between 2 and 6 on the sexual orientation scale and were included in the sample.

Variables

From the GAL Q and the RSE the following variables were delineated.

Parental Importance. On a scale of 1 to 9 the study participants rated how important their parents were to their sense of self-worth. The continuum ranged from extremely not important (1) to extremely important (9).

Parental Acceptance. Each adolescent was asked on the GAL Q, "How has your mother/father reacted (or how do you think she or

he would react) to the fact that you are gay?'' The 4-point continuum included the options: rejecting, intolerant (but not rejecting),
tolerant (but not accepting), and accepting (or it would not matter).

Comfortableness. Two scales were totaled for the comfortable
being gay dimension: (a) ''I would not give up my homosexuality
even if I could'' and (b) ''I feel my life would be much easier if I
were heterosexual.'' The scales ranged from 1 (strongly disagree)
to 9 (strongly agree). Respondents' answers were combined after
reversing scores on the second scale.

Self-Esteem. Evaluation of the self was assessed by the Rosenberg Self-Esteem Scale (RSE). On a 4-point scale, from strongly
agree to strongly disagree, respondents indicated the degree to
which the five positively stated and five negatively stated sentences
characterized them.

Data Analysis

Regression analyses were computed for each sex separately and
for mother and father variables; missing data cases for each analysis
were omitted. In the first series of regressions, ''comfortableness''
was the dependent variable, and mother or father ''acceptance''
was the independent variable. Next, ''importance'' and its interaction with ''acceptance'' were placed in the model to test for the
significance of the parental relationship.

In the self-esteem regression analyses both ''comfortableness''
and mother or father ''acceptance'' were inserted as independent
variables, separate for each sex and for each parent. Finally, ''importance'' and its interactions with both ''comfortableness'' and
''acceptance'' were added to the model.

RESULTS

Predicting Comfortableness

Based on a reflected appraisals perspective, it was expected that
the greater the degree of mother and father acceptance of the adolescent's homosexuality the more likely the adolescent will feel comfortable being gay. This expectation was confirmed for females but
not for males, as shown in Table 3.

Table 3
Predicting Comfortableness Being Gay for Male and Female Youths Based on Their Perceptions of Mother and Father Acceptance

		N	Mean square	Degrees of freedom	Explained variance	F values	p values
Males							
	Mother	199	2.60	2	1%	.59	.445
	Father	193	.51	2	1%	.12	.733
Females							
	Mother	97	18.65	2	5%	5.35	.023
	Father	93	24.47	2	6%	7.22	.009

Furthermore, this relationship should be stronger when the importance of the parent is considered: The more significant the parent is perceived to be for one's sense of self-worth, the greater should be his or her impact on comfortableness (and self-esteem). Adding "importance" and its interaction effects with "acceptance" had little impact on predicting female adolescent comfortableness with mother acceptance (increasing the attributed variance to 7%), but had the expected effect (increasing explained variance to 11%) with father acceptance. The correlation between father acceptance and comfortableness was .33 ($p = .003$) for lesbians who reported that parents are important, but .03 ($p = .895$) for those who said parents are relatively not important. Adding the variable "importance" to the male adolescent models strengthened both the mother acceptance ($F = 3.19, 3df, p = .024$) and the father acceptance ($F = 2.90, 3df, p = .034$) relationship to the level of significantly predicting male comfortableness being gay (contrasted with nonsignificant F values in Table 3). The correlations between mother acceptance and comfortableness ($r = .14, p = .087$) and father acceptance and comfortableness ($r = .11, p = .181$) are considerably higher for the "important" than the "not important" groups ($r = .04, p = .77$ and $r = -.14, p = .352$, respectively).

Predicting Self-Esteem

It was hypothesized that self-esteem would be highest among those who felt most comfortable being gay because their parents accepted their sexual orientation. For the lesbian youths this was clearly not the case (Table 4), for either the mother acceptance or father acceptance models. Adding importance and its interactions dimensions did not increase the adjusted R-square in the former, but did in the latter (to 6%; $F = 2.24, 5df, p = .057$). This addition was in terms of the father acceptance-importance interaction ($t = 1.83, p = .071$): adding importance increased the positive relationship between father acceptance and self-esteem.

For gay males, however, the model was strongly confirmed (Table 4), primarily because of the direct effect of "feeling comfortable" on positive self-esteem. Adding importance and its interactions had relatively little effect, except to mediate the effect of

Table 4
Predicting Self-Esteem Among Gay and Lesbian Youths from the Dimensions Comfortableness and Parental Acceptance

	N	Mean square	Explained variance	F	p	t	p
			Full Model			Parameters	
Males							
Mother							
Acceptance	197	268.19	10%	10.64	.0001	2.00	.047
Comfortable						4.03	.0001
Father							
Acceptance	192	243.83	9%	9.45	.0001	1.62	.106
Comfortable						3.99	.0001
Females							
Mother							
Acceptance	95	12.31	1%	.58	.561	.53	.600
Comfortable						.81	.419
Father							
Acceptance	91	28.77	3%	1.40	.253	1.14	.259
Comfortable						.90	.368

mother and father acceptance because of their high intercorrelation. Thus, the direct effect of acceptance on self-esteem is reduced to nonsignificance when importance is added to the models (mother acceptance: $t = 1.47, p = .144$; father acceptance: $t = 1.33, p = .185$).

DISCUSSION

The reflected appraisals perspective received mixed support, with several significant limitations and refinements. First, in terms of support, congruent with the reflected appraisals prediction, a lesbian youth felt most comfortable with her sexual orientation if she also reported that her mother and father accepted (or would accept if they knew) her sexual orientation. Adding importance to the model increased this relationship with father acceptance but not with mother acceptance. Apparently, acceptance by the mother was important for a lesbian to feel comfortable with her sexual orientation, regardless of how important the parents were for the youth's sense of self-worth.

The reflected appraisals perspective was more fully supported among the gay males than the lesbians: Mother and father acceptance predicted comfortableness of a gay male *only* if the parents were perceived as important components of the youth's sense of self-worth. This supported Rosenberg's (1979) claim that not all significant others are significant for one's self-evaluation. The reflected appraisals prediction of self-esteem was further supported by the finding that gay males who were most comfortable with their sexual orientation had the highest levels of self-esteem.

In terms of limitations, the reflected appraisals model was not supported in the prediction of self-esteem among lesbians for either the mother or the father acceptance model. Adding "importance" changed little in the mother acceptance-comfortableness-self-esteem model, but it altered the father acceptance model such that it approached statistical significance.

Finally, several refinements of the reflected appraisals model were supported by the current study. Adding "importance" of the parental relationship to one's sense of self-worth was of far greater significance in predicting a youth's comfortableness with being gay than in predicting his or her self-esteem. Comfortableness may be far more transitory than is self-esteem, and thus more easily influenced by situational events. Comfortableness is a feeling, a state of being; self-esteem would appear to be more of a stable component of the person through the adolescent and adult years (Dusek & Flaherty, 1981; O'Malley & Bachman, 1983; Savin-Williams & Demo, 1984). Thus, the significance of the ''other'' in affecting a dependent variable may depend on the characteristics of that variable, such as its permanence for an individual's personality.

As a second refinement, it proved particularly important to consider the sexes separately. A reflected appraisals approach worked far better for the gay males than it did for the lesbians. This is somewhat surprising because the reflected appraisals of significant others assess more adequately ''inner'' than ''outer'' self-esteem (Franks & Marolla, 1976), supposedly an issue of far greater concern for adolescent females than males. Consequently, one would expect the discriminating power of a reflected appraisals approach to be more sensitive to the self-esteem of females. Although this relationship may be characteristic of heterosexual adolescents, perhaps among gay youth a different pattern is normative. In a separate analysis of these data (Savin-Williams, in preparation), the two sexes were *equal* in self-assessed psychological masculinity and femininity. Furthermore, femininity among the gay males did not lead to low self-esteem as is universally reported in studies of heterosexual adolescents (e.g., Lamke, 1982; Whitley, 1983), but to high self-esteem. Lesbians who were ''average'' in masculinity had the highest self-esteem level among the females. Perhaps in regard to self-evaluation the gay and lesbian adolescents in this sample did not follow the traditional sex-role stereotypes, but created a unique pattern that requires additional empirical documentation and a more expansive theoretical explanation than is possible with reflected appraisals.

The third refinement is that it mattered whether the reference was to the perceived attitudes of the mother or of the father. For example, the perception of acceptance by the mother was crucial for a lesbian to feel comfortable with her sexual orientation regardless of whether the parents were important or unimportant components of the youth's sense of self-worth. The more important the parents were, the greater the lesbian youth felt comfortable with her homosexuality; father acceptance predicted her self-esteem. This was not a characteristic relationship for the gay male. Thus, separating the parents provided additional information that distinguished the attitudes of the male and female youths. Especially significant, it illustrated the importance of the mother-daughter bond for a lesbian's self-esteem.

This study did not assess the actual or would-be attitudes of the parents toward their offspring's homosexuality, primarily because of Cooley's (1912) contention that the adolescent's perceptions of others' attitudes toward himself or herself are more important in affecting self-evaluation than are the actual attitudes. This research did not empirically test this assumption, but it did affirm the connecting link among multiple positive perceptions. If reflected appraisals is essentially a perplexing manner of stating that good things go together, this study affirmed this for the self-esteem of gay males and for feeling comfortable with one's sexuality for both gay and lesbian youths.

Perhaps the most important contribution of this study and this volume in general will prove to be not the substantive findings reported here and elsewhere but their contribution in reducing the invisibility of gay and lesbian youth for social scientists and eventually for the lesbian and gay communities (Gonsiorek, 1986). At a recent conference on gay and lesbian youth (Remafedi, 1986), many speakers noted that the paucity of research on gay and lesbian adolescents is both prevalent and appalling. Among the contributing factors is the hesitancy of social scientists to confront the stigmatic, legal, and moral issues involved in studying gay and lesbian minors. To many, gay and lesbian youth do not exist; they are instead only homosexually behaving adolescents who are temporarily detained from their heterosexual destination. In addition, gay and lesbian youth are frequently invisible to themselves, another factor that compounds the difficulty of finding them as research participants. Given these problems, social scientists either ignore gay and lesbian youth or rely on retrospective data gathering techniques (e.g., Bell, Weinberg & Hammersmith, 1981) that make particular and often debatable assumptions concerning the accuracy of recall data (Ross, 1980).

In very important ways, gay and lesbian youth are similar to other adolescents. Gays and lesbians, too, internalize and incorporate into their self-image their perceptions of external others, such as family members. If indeed it proves to be the case that sexual orientation produces minimal differences in developmental processes, then we need far fewer gay-versus-straight comparisons and more intragay population studies that focus on unique patterns within a homosexual sexual orientation. For example, some gay males and lesbians do not always follow traditional sex-role patterns, as suggested in the current study. With this effort, social scientists increase the likelihood of learning about normal development in all of its manifestations.

NOTES

1. The five undergraduate research assistants varied by sex, college, age, degree of openness, sexual orientation, life goals, and family and socioeconomic background.

2. This restriction omits two other dimensions of the reflected appraisals perspective: direct reflections and the generalized other (Rosenberg, 1979, p. 63). Direct reflections refer "to how particular others view us" and its omission is discussed in the text; the second, the generalized other, which refers "to the attitudes of the community as a whole," is not examined because of the developmental rather than sociological orientation of this paper.

3. According to Rosenberg (1979) valuation includes the opinions of those we care about, who make a difference to us, and to whom we desire to be favorable. On the other hand, credibility is the confidence that we have in the judgment of the other.

REFERENCES

Bell, A. P., Weinberg, M. S., & Hammersmith, S. K. (1981). *Sexual preference*. Bloomington, IN: Indiana University Press.

Blumstein, P., & Schwartz, P. (1983). *American couples: Money, work, sex*. New York: William Morrow.

Cooley, C. H. (1912). *Human nature and the social order*. New York: Scribners.

Demo, D. H. (1985). The measurement of self-esteem: Refining our methods. *Journal of Personality and Social Psychology, 48*, 1490-1502.

Dusek, J. B., & Flaherty, J. F. (1981). The development of the self-concept during the adolescent years. *Monographs of the Society for Research in Child Development, 46*(4, Serial No. 191).

Franks, D. D., & Marolla, J. (1976). Efficacious action and social approval as interacting dimensions of self-esteem: A tentative formulation through construct validation. *Sociometry, 39,* 324-341.

Gecas, V. (1971). Parental behavior and dimensions of adolescent self-evaluation. *Sociometry, 34,* 466-482.

Gecas, V., & Schwalbe, M. L. (1986). Parental behavior and adolescent self-esteem. *Journal of Marriage and the Family, 48,* 37-46.

Gonsiorek, J. C. (1986, May), *Mental health problems of gay and lesbian youth.* Paper presented at the Symposium on Gay and Lesbian Adolescents, Minneapolis, MN.

Hoffman, M. (1968). *The gay world.* New York: Basic Books.

Lamke, L. K. (1982). The impact of sex-role orientation on self-esteem in early adolescence. *Child Development, 53,* 1530-1535.

O'Donnell, W. J. (1976). Adolescent self-esteem related to feelings toward parents and friends. *Journal of Youth and Adolescence, 5,* 179-185.

O'Malley, P. M., & Bachman, J. G. (1983). Self-esteem: Change and stability between ages 13 and 23. *Developmental Psychology, 19,* 257-268.

Openshaw, D. K., Thomas, D. L., & Rollins, B. C. (1984). Parental influences on adolescent self-esteem. *Journal of Early Adolescence, 4,* 259-274.

Remafedi, G. (Organizer). (1986, May). Symposium on Gay and Lesbian Adolescents, Minneapolis, MN.

Rosenberg, M. (1979). *Conceiving the self.* New York: Basic Books.

Ross, M. W. (1980). Retrospective distortion in homosexual research. *Archives of Sexual Behavior, 9,* 523-531.

Savin-Williams, R. C. (In preparation). *Forgotten and invisible: Gay and lesbian youth.*

Savin-Williams, R. C., & Demo, D. H. (1984). Developmental change and stability in adolescent self-concept. Developmental Psychology, 20, 1100-1110.

Schilling, S. G., & Savin-Williams, R. C. (In preparation). *The assessment of adolescent self-esteem stability: A new application of the beeper technology and the Rasch measurement model.*

Simmons, R. G., Blyth, D. A., VanCleave, E. F., & Bush, D. M. (1979). Entry into early adolescence: The impact of school structure, puberty, and early dating on self-esteem. *American Sociological Review, 44,* 948-967.

Watkins, D., & Astilla, E. (1980). Self-esteem and family relationships: A Filipino study. *International Journal of Sociology of the Family, 10,* 141-144.

Weinberg, M. S., & Williams, C. J. (1974). *Male homosexuals: Their problems and adaptations.* New York: Penguin.

Weinberg, T. S. (1983). *Gay men, gay selves.* New York: Irvington.

Whitley, B. E., Jr. (1983). Sex role orientation and self-esteem: A critical meta-analytic review. *Journal of Personality and Social Psychology, 44,* 765-778.

Sappho Was a Right-On Adolescent: Growing Up Lesbian

Margaret Schneider, PhD, C Psych

Ontario Institute for Studies in Education, Toronto, Canada

SUMMARY. Beginning with the interaction between the coming-out process and adolescent development, this paper explores the young lesbian experience. The words and perceptions of over 20 young lesbians are used to depict the experience from their own points of view.

As Adrienne Rich (1980) once wrote, "The lesbian experience [is] a profoundly *female* experience" (p. 650). Indeed, research indicates that lesbians have more in common with their heterosexual counterparts than with gay men in matters that include, expectations of relationships, equality, and the development of sexual awareness (Dailey, 1979; Peplau, Cochran, Rook, & Padesky, 1978; Simon & Gagnon, 1967). Yet, in the study of homosexuality, as is often the case in social sciences research, the male experience is frequently taken as the norm. In recognition of the underrepresentation of the lesbian experience in current research, this paper focusses on the lives of young lesbians, as females and as adolescents.

Research on lesbian and gay identity formation describes the

Dr. Schneider is Assistant Professor of Applied Psychology at the Ontario Institute for Studies in Education.

The author would like to thank David Kelley and Bob Tremble for their contributions in collecting the data for this paper, and Lesbian and Gay Youth Toronto for helping to contact research participants.

Correspondence and reprint requests may be addressed to Dr. Schneider, c/o Ontario Institute for Studies in Education, 252 Bloor Street W., Toronto, Ontario Canada M5S 1V6.

111

coming-out process beginning with first awareness and delineating the stages that culminate in identity consolidation. The psychological and situational factors that facilitate movement through these stages are identified (Cass, 1979; Coleman, 1982; Cronin, 1974; Ponse, 1978; Schäfer, 1976). The present research differs in that it examines coming out in the context of the developmental process and describes experiences once lesbian identity has been established, during the stages that Cass labeled Identity Acceptance, Identity Pride, and Identity Synthesis.

TORONTO AND THE GAY AND LESBIAN COMMUNITY

Toronto, a city of over 2,000,000, resembles many large, North American cities. The downtown core offers a rich mixture of business, stores, and entertainment, including performing and visual arts, museums, galleries, sporting events, and a variety of restaurants. The main streets are dotted with buskers and vendors selling crafts, food, and souvenirs. Although the surrounding suburban areas have developed self-sufficiency in many respects, downtown Toronto remains where the action is, particularly for youth.

Toronto is unique due to its ethnic diversity. A variety of ethnic groups are represented, each having its own self-contained local neighborhood, which includes commerce, entertainment, and shopping. The city is also unique because of the mixed-use characteristic of most neighborhoods. Most areas combine commercial and residential use, with businesses along the main streets and residential buildings along the side streets. Types of residences include highrise and low-rise apartment buildings, Victorian mansions converted into flats and apartments as well as single family dwellings. Even the downtown core constitutes a neighborhood, resulting in lots of people on the streets at all times. Thus, the city is relatively safe because it is populated at most times of day and night. Toronto is also remarkably clean.

The putative gay area is located in the northeast corner of the downtown area with focal points on two parallel streets, Church and Parliament. The latter marks the boundary of Cabbagetown, a neighborhood once inhabited by poor Irish and Scottish immigrants. It has undergone extensive gentrification during the past ten years. It is now one of the preferred residential areas for well-to-do gay men, and is very expensive. The area looks much like the trendy, upscale part of any city; however, many subtle signals identify it as the center of gay community life.

The gay and lesbian community consists of over 100 organizations that include recreational, political, and social service organizations. Among these are: peer support groups; counselling services; organized sports leagues; political action groups; theatre companies; a number of gay, lesbian, and feminist publications; and a youth group, Lesbian and Gay Youth Toronto (LGYT). Many of these organizations meet at a local community center on Church Street.

LGYT is the only niche for youth in the homosexual community. It is a peer support group which meets once a week at the community center. It is organized by a steering committee and has a changing membership of over 200 young men and women at any given time. Apart from this group, the only alternatives for socializing are the bars.

Like many identifiable gay and lesbian communities, Toronto's visible community represents only the tip of the iceberg of the city's gay and lesbian population. This visible element is white, middle-class, youthful, and generally male dominated. The composition of the remainder of the population and the networks through which individuals socialize is anyone's guess. Its existence is only surmised by extrapolating from the statistics that estimate the percentage of gays and lesbians in the general population. This scenario is much the same throughout urban North America.

METHOD

Participants

The research participants were 25 self-identified lesbians, ages 15 to 20. They were contacted through friendship networks, word-of-mouth, a coming-out group, and through LGYT. Only two of the women were black, from the West Indies. The rest were Caucasian. The majority came from the middle socioeconomic bracket, and were raised in suburban Toronto, although three had moved to Toronto from rural communities. Some of these women had rarely or never gone downtown until their first LGYT meeting.

About one-third lived with their parents. The remainder lived on their own, downtown, sharing accommodation with friends. Of the latter, some have moved to be closer to the community, others were kicked out when their parents found out they were lesbians, and a few left in order to avoid lying to their parents. A portion of these young women moved frequently, crashed with friends, or had friends crashing with them. One of the support functions of LGYT is to make sure, in an informal way, that everyone has a place to sleep.

Some of the youngsters work full-time at unskilled jobs. Those who go to high school or community college work part-time. They are a mixed group, preppy, punk, ordinary, unusual. They are generally articulate. They have found lesbian peers and a niche in the lesbian community. They are at least fairly comfortable with their sexual orientation. They are not necessarily representative; they speak for themselves, but through their words we may come to a better understanding of the young lesbian.

Procedures

The data reported here were gathered over a period of two years, beginning in the summer of 1984, as part of a larger study of coming out among male and female adolescents. Particular attention was paid to stresses and coping mechanisms.

Participants were asked to take part in a study of coming out. They were paid $10.00; although most, if not all, would have participated without renumeration.

A relatively unstructured interview was used, lasting from 1 to 3 hours, averaging about 1 1/2 hours. Participants were asked to describe (a) how they realized they were lesbians, (b) what they did about it, and (c) how they felt about it at different points in the process. Interviews were conducted by the author or a male research assistant, usually in the author's office at a children's mental health center, or at the local community center. The choice of interviewer was determined by whomever made the initial contact with a particular youngster.

Rapport was established by attending LGYT and other meetings to talk about the research. This enabled potential participants to get to know us before they consented to the interview. Participants consented enthusiastically once they knew a friend had participated. They seemed to enjoy talking about their coming-out experiences, and some utilized the opportunity to talk to an adult about things that were troubling them. In anticipation of this, we were prepared to refer young people to appropriate professional services, if necessary.

The data presented here represent a preliminary and qualitative examination of the interviews with young lesbians. Themes that became conspicuous through repetition in a number of interviews are reported here, and the quotations are those which, in the opinion of the author, illustrate the themes articulately and often poignantly. Emerging from the data is an indication that adolescent development is atypical for young lesbians (as well as for gay males). By focussing on the subjective experiences of these young women we can identify major issues in coming out and growing up.

ADOLESCENT DEVELOPMENT AND THE COMING-OUT PROCESS

Being both lesbian and adolescent means that two interrelated processes are taking place simultaneously, coming out and growing up. These processes provide a framework for conceptualizing the experiences of young lesbians as well as gay males.

Coming out is defined as "the developmental process through which gay people recognize their sexual preferences and choose to integrate this knowledge into their personal and social lives" (De Monteflores & Schultz, 1978, p. 59). It involves at least five interrelated areas of development: (a) the growing awareness of homosexual feelings and identity, (b) developing a positive evaluation of homosexuality, (c) developing intimate same-sex romantic/erotic relationships, (d) establishing social ties with gay and lesbian peers or community, and (e) self-disclosure. Disclosure is reached once labelling takes place, a gay-positive feeling develops, sexual orientation is appropriately placed in perspective relative to the individual's entire identity, and friendships and intimate relationships are established with gay and lesbian peers. These tasks take place in the larger context of general life issues. For example, developing social ties with gay or lesbian peers is part of establishing a community of friends (gay or straight), at work, at leisure, and in the neighborhood. Self-disclosure is one aspect of delineating boundaries between the private and public aspects of life.

To some extent, the tasks of coming out parallel major developmental tasks of adolescence that include: (a) establishing a sense of identity, (b) developing self-esteem, and (c) socialization, including learning how to form and maintain friendships and, in the context of a growing sexual awareness, finding meaning and a place in life for intimacy. Coming out adds a new dimension to these tasks. How do the two processes interact?

Adolescence is a time for identity consolidation (Erikson, 1963), for asking the question, "Who am I?" The lesbian adolescent must also ask, "What does it mean to be a lesbian?" She may also wonder about her place among both heterosexual women and gay men. These are complex issues. Beyond same-sex attraction, being lesbian holds diverse meaning for different individuals (Eisner, 1982; Golden, 1985), and the experiences shared with gay men are accompanied by profound differences. Furthermore, lesbians have much in common with heterosexual women (Cronin, 1974; Rich, 1980). There are pitfalls in arriving at answers. The young person may feel compelled to act out the ubiquitous myths and stereotypes. The characteristic "lesbian" may be allowed to obscure all the other important attributes that comprise the individual. The task for the young lesbian is to put sexual orientation into an appropriate perspective, which is exemplified by Cass' (1979) description of Indentity Synthesis, "With the developmental process completed, homosexual identity is integrated with all other aspects of self. Instead of being seen as *the* identity, it is now given the status of being merely one aspect of self" (p. 235).

In a world which tells lesbian youngsters that they are criminals, sinners, or mentally ill, self-esteem becomes a major issue. Until gay-positive feelings emerge, lesbian youngsters have difficulty feeling good about anything they do in school, at home, or in social situations. With gay-positive feelings come self-esteem in other areas of life. Conversely, successes in other parts of life form a foundation on which to build gay-positive feelings.

Socialization for young lesbians is atypical in many respects. They may "date" heterosexually in response to peer pressure and in an attempt to fit in. Confused, conflicted youngsters may engage in promiscuous heterosexual behavior to try to make themselves straight, or to make absolutely sure that they really are lesbians (Schneider & Tremble, 1985). Pregnancy among teenage lesbians is becoming a conspicuous phenomenon (J. Hunter, personal communication November 18, 1986).[1] Those who are involved in an intimate same-sex relationship must keep it a secret. Thus, lesbian adolescents have little opportunity to date, develop intimate same-sex relationships, or experiment sexually in the safe, socially sanctioned context in which heterosexual youngsters develop their social awareness. "At a time when heterosexual adolescents are learning how to socialize, young gay people are learning how to hide" (Hetrick & Martin, 1984, p. 6).

The following discussion will examine the interaction between these two simultaneous processes from the perspective of these young lesbians. How do their experiences compare to those of older lesbians or their young gay male counterparts? What are the pitfalls and what are the strengths to be drawn upon? What are the responsibilities of adults in the lesbian community and in the larger community to respond to the needs of these growing young people?

Identity

In spite of the increased visibility of gays and lesbians, the myths and stereotypes of homosexuals are extant. These images are a source of confusion for gay and lesbian youngsters who erroneously believe that they must adhere to the stereotypes (Schneider & Tremble, 1985). Eventually, as part of the coming-out process, they realize that life-style and personal style involve options and choices.

Is the lesbian stereotype relevant to the lives of these young women? A few felt pressured to conform to standards that reject

---

1. Joyce Hunter is Director of Social Services at the Hetrick-Martin Institute in New York.

traditional femininity. A particularly attractive 19-year-old remembered:

> I was criticized for looking politically incorrect. I dressed the way I wanted to and the way I felt most comfortable, and in the way that would attract other women, and it certainly did! I didn't want to have to live by anybody else's standards. I heard so many times, "You look straight." I thought that was stupid. Looking straight! What's looking straight, what's looking gay? Give me a break. I told them that they were trying to get rid of stereotypes and then creating their own.

A few went through a phase of acting out a stereotype:

> I don't dress butch anymore because I decided that's not what I wanted. But I used to walk down the street with "Women are Powerful" on my leather jacket. That jacket for the past couple months has just been hanging in my closet. It's not that I'm going through a femme phase now. It's that I'm wearing things that are more comfortable. I realized that I don't have to make a statement about what I am. Straight people don't have to go up to people and say, "Hey, I'm straight." (Beth, 16 years old)

Generally, the stereotypical masculine image of the lesbian is perceived as a thing of the past.

> I guess the older people are so used to the stereotype because that's all they had to go on, whereas now we have ourselves to go on. There are some people who look butch all the time. But that's them. They don't do it to look butch. (Emma, 18 years old)

These young women were more interested in being comfortable and having fun with the way they looked. For lack of a better term, they referred to this style as femme. A 19-year-old art student explained:

Being butch you've got one leather jacket, one pair of jeans, one pair of cowboy boots. That would bore me out of my mind. But being femme you've got a great closet and you can go through all your stuff. Look at it that way and it just seems more interesting.

Ann, age 17 explained, "I don't think I have to change in order to look like a lesbian. If there is a lesbian look, it's comfortable casual clothes and short hair. It's preppy. And lesbians don't wear heels!"

Some noted that the young gay males are the ones more likely to act out a stereotype by being effeminate. Some young women hypothesized that this was a way for males to advertise their sexual availability when they first come out. Others believed it to be a backlash to the heterosexual demands to fit a masculine, macho image. It may also indicate a greater confusion among males between sexual orientation and gender role. In addition, playing the stereotype might serve as a distancing technique for males who, in spite of their sexual orientation, are like heterosexual males in that they are not used to expressing affection for other males. For whatever reason, the salience of the stereotype is one major difference that exists between the contemporary experience for gay males and lesbians.

Adolescents are coming out now at a time when some pop culture figures are openly identifying themselves as gay or lesbian, and when rock songs occasionally refer to same-sex eroticism. Sometimes this is the youth's first indication that she is not alone:

When you first become aware of your feelings, you think you're the only person in the world. And when Carol Pope sang in "High School Confidential" that she was in love with a woman, at least I knew there was someone on the same planet that felt like me. (Maria, age 18)

Furthermore, unlike the gay males, young women are coming out in a subculture of lesbian and feminist music, art, humor, and political thought. For example, women's music has emerged as a major component of the subculture over the past decade. Exemplified by the work of performers such as Cris Williamson, Holly Near, and Meg Christian, the music began as a reflection of the lesbian and feminist experience and as a celebration of womanhood. Although much of woman's music has transcended these boundaries by appealing to a wider audience, it still remains woman-identified.

To what extent is women's culture relevant to these young people? It depends on personal interests. As one art student pointed out, "People pursue lesbian culture in their own way. I identify with the art, and it helped me to come out, seeing my feelings on canvas. The art I do is lesbian. It focusses on women." Women's music is not especially youth-oriented. It is not their sound. Concerts and records tend to be expensive and not particularly accessible. Nonetheless, the fact of its existence is important. A punk rocker (age 15) comments, "The music is too mellow. I'm not into mellow. I'm into anger. But I think it's great that women have their own music and can do it on their own."

To some, the feminist movement itself is passé. From the perspective of young women who have not experienced the full impact of being a woman in society today, the movement seems to have fulfilled its purpose and it seems to them time to move on the other issues. For others, the feminist movement is still alive; although it poses some conflict for the more politically involved young women. Carrie, a radical lesbian feminist at age 16 explained:

> The feminist movement has helped lesbians a lot, but leading feminists never mention the work of lesbians. We don't belong in the gay movement because we're women, and we don't belong in the feminist movement because we're gay. These feminists, who are supposed to have the best interests of women in mind, don't like lesbians because they don't want anyone to think they're lesbians.

In spite of some ambivalence and occasional indifference to women's culture, it is a source of pride. It may be something that these adolescents grow into. At the very least it provides older lesbian role models for young lesbians, something that is missing from their day-to-day lives. They need to see adults who are happy and productive. Without role models, lives and relationships are difficult to imagine:

I can't imagine being 65 and still with the same person, but I could imagine being with a man for that long. Long term relationships is a concept that straights have. I just can't get hold of it. I can't imagine being older and being with a woman. (Maria, age 18)

I worry about being alone ten years down the road. I see a lot of young lesbians out there. What happens when you get old? What happens to old lesbians? I don't know. I mean, do they live together and move out to the suburbs or something? (Naomi, age 18)

In summary, identity issues for these young lesbians are somewhat different than issues for their female predecessors or their gay male peers. They seem less influenced by the prevailing stereotypes. They have the advantage of a women-identified subculture, which may become increasingly relevant as they get older and the subculture evolves. However they are lacking appropriate adult lesbian role models, an important component of identity development for young lesbians.

Self-Esteem

The young lesbians in this study had all developed a positive lesbian identity. This was accomplished through a combination of personal resources and external supports.

Some brought to the coming-out process a trust in their own feelings, which shielded them from society's proscriptions:

I never really thought there was anything wrong with appreciating a poster of a woman instead of a man. I just accepted that that was what I thought. I never put a label to it. I never said, "Hey, I'm a lesbian." It was just what I was doing. (Maria, age 18)

I knew enough of the negative beliefs to know not to talk about it. But this feeling was so natural, I guess I trusted my own feelings enough not to believe anybody else's negative ones. Because I felt that if what I'm doing is what they're saying is

sick and bad, well, they must be sick and bad. Because I felt
so good about it. (Naomi, age 18)

Most youngsters, lesbian or straight, grow up with a sense of
being different. That sense is accentuated for the young lesbian.
How she feels about being different will influence her self-esteem.
Some can make peace with feeling different:

> There are people at school who don't like me and my girlfriend
> because we're gay. But they wouldn't like us anyway. They
> can just put a name to it now. I don't care, but I just don't like
> people who are scum feeling like they have something on us.
> Like guys come up to me and say, "I'd ask you out, but I
> know you're not into guys," as if I'd go out with them if I
> was. (Punk rocker)

> I was always different. I read a lot more than most kids. I
> played sports more than my girlfriends. All the things that
> made me feel different were also the things that made me feel
> good. When I started thinking I was gay it was just one more
> difference. (Brenda, age 17)

More youngsters than we realize had serious difficulty:

> There was a total rejection of the idea of being a lesbian. Just a
> total and utter rejection of it. There was absolutely no way that
> I wanted to feel different and I felt very different from every-
> one and I didn't want that. So I didn't feel normal unless I had
> alcohol or drugs in me. (Sarah, age 20)

External support had to complement internal resources. When it
was forthcoming the path was easier. When it was absent, life was
painful:

> It's painful, but if you have a positive image about yourself,
> you pick the right friends and your family's really supportive,
> and even if your family's not, you'll generally find friends
> who will be, if they're good friends. Just keep your chin up.
> (Adrienne, age 16)

Connecting with people my own age who were lesbians would have made my life a lot easier, or being told that it was okay. I didn't know where to go to find them. I didn't know if I wanted to find them on my own, alone. I needed someone to say, "It's okay. It's okay to feel confused or to be a lesbian." And all around me were girls my own age who were dating guys, who seemed to be enjoying that, and my parents who are heterosexual. I was surrounded by all that. So I felt like there was a part of me that wasn't being acknowledged. That it didn't exist, and it made me feel alone and depressed. (Theresa, age 19)

Thus, contact with other lesbians was frequently a milestone:

I hadn't met any lesbians up until then. I knew they were somewhere, but I felt isolated. Then I got involved with this lesbian group at the community center and I realized that these women were feeling the same things that I felt and what I'd been reading about lesbians was, in fact, what I am. That's when I started feeling really good. (Brenda, age 17)

When you find friends who are supportive, not only supportive, but in the same boat as you, and you can see for yourself that their life isn't hell and that a lot of things you hear about gay lifestyle and gay people isn't true, and you find there's nothing really different about them. Then you think, "Gee, it's okay." (Sarah, age 20)

Like any life crisis, coming out provides the context for developing and honing coping skills and personal strengths that in turn contributed to self-esteem. A 20-year-old business student explained:

I feel that I am the terrific person I am today because I'm a lesbian. I decided that I was gay when I was very young. After making that decision, which was the hardest thing I could ever face, I feel like I can do anything.

For lesbians, coping competency becomes a feminist as well as a personal issue, as young women prepare for life outside of a traditional heterosexual relationship without a male provider to depend upon. Patty, who spent some time as a street kid, observes:

You have to protect yourself. Straight women think, "I have a man to protect me," but for me, it's just me. You've got to stick up for yourself and survive every day—just having the strength and using it. (Patty, age 17)

You can't turn to men for typical things. You have to depend on yourself, and on other women. Men tell you that you can't do things on your own, that you need a man. I don't need a man to help me with anything because I can do it myself. I may depend on other women, but it's not being dependent. (Jackie, age 18)

Assaults on self-esteem can be managed with a combination of personal resources and external support. The struggle often results in increased coping competency. In this the young lesbian differs little from her male counterpart. However, her struggle takes place within the larger context of feminist issues. Her strength and independence as a lesbian is merely part of being a strong and independent female at a time when all women are divesting themselves of their traditional dependent posture.

Socialization: Friendship, Intimacy, and Community

Making friends, working in groups, or earning a living are among those aspects of socialization that can be fulfilled for the young lesbian in a heterosexual context: in the home, at school, and in the community. However, coping in a largely rejecting society requires lesbian peers and role models who provide a forum for problem-solving and comparing experiences. The young lesbian also requires a safe context for exploring intimacy and relationships. The visible lesbian community provides that milieu; although, in many respects, it is an atypical environment for young people.

The young women in this study, including the 15-year-old, consider themselves lucky that they can pass for 19, the legal drinking age in Ontario. A fake I.D. and some makeup gains them access to "the hot meeting places," but not necessarily to the adult world. Older lesbians seem reluctant to have much to do with under-aged lesbians, primarily out of fear of being accused of recruitment or seduction of minors, a charge that all gays and lesbians are particularly vulnerable to. What seems self-preservation to some adults is often interpreted by youth as rejection, ageism, and envy:

> When my teacher discovered I was gay, I was thrown out of the closet. I was 15. I had had a lover for six months and I had no interest in the lesbian community. But when I was forced out and what happened became public, then I had to start finding the community and the support. I'm lucky, because I look 19 and I can talk my way out of anything. So getting to know people wasn't easy, but it was easier than it could have been. But I swear to God, people will support you if they think you're 19. They'll sleep with you. They'll do anything with you. They hear you're 16, and nothing. (Kathy, age 16)

> The older people are so tight together because they had to work so hard together. Young people are coming out now in a society that is more accepting of being gay and they're a bit jealous and angry, in a way, that they never had that. (Jan, age 17)

The impropriety of the bar scene for adolescents is evident to the youths themselves:

> We need some sort of hang-out-in-the-mall atmosphere, like, you go from hanging out in the mall with your boyfriend to going out to a bar with your girlfriend. Like overnight. It's such a change. What you need . . . is somewhere that the casual comfortableness is still there. (Brenda, age 17)

> The bar scene was good because it was my first chance to really meet other lesbians; although most people were just interested in one night stands. But once you meet people at the beginning and make the connections, you don't need the bars as much. But you do at first. (Angie, age 19)

Carrie, age 16, explained, "Let's face it. It's loud, it's smoky, and you drink a lot. It's not healthy. And it's expensive. I'm a student and so are my friends. We don't have that kind of money." And Beth, who is 16, told us, "In the straight world you don't have

to go to a bar to meet people. In the gay world you sort of have to.
. . . It's the only way you know that people are gay.''
    Still others said:

> They [the adult gay and lesbian community] don't realize how
> many 15- and 16-year-olds they have in the bars. If they really
> cared, if they truly cared, they would find other ways for kids
> to socialize away from the bars. (Susan, age 18)

> I'd spend Friday after school at my lover's house. We'd make
> love and then go out to the bar. I'd ride my bike home to
> Rosedale and have breakfast on Saturday morning with my
> family, who had no idea where I'd been. I'd look around the
> table and feel like screaming. (Mary-Anne, age 17)

> I spent most weekends with these women, most of whom were
> a lot older than me. I'd play hockey and go to the bars even
> though I was only 16. Then I'd go back to school on Monday.
> What could I say when people talked about their weekends? I
> felt like I was two different people during the week and then
> on the weekends. (Wendy, age 18)

These words reflect an ambivalence to the bar scene. It is where
the action is. It is a place to meet people, but going special places
just to meet lesbians seems artificial. The alcohol-focussed, sexually loaded environment is, admittedly, not appropriate for young
people, and they themselves know it. The experience is akin to
culture shock, suddenly moving from a straight, adolescent world
to the fast lane in the adult lesbian scene. Little wonder that many
describe a schizophrenic sense of living in two separate worlds. It
creates problems at home, as well. As Damien Martin, Executive
Director of the Hetrick-Martin Institute (formerly the Institute for
the Protection of Lesbian and Gay Youth), points out, even parents
who accept their gay or lesbian youngster will become understand-
ably concerned when their teenager starts going to bars and coming
home late at night.
    Yet, these youngsters continue to frequent the bars, which are,
after all, places to dance, meet friends, and are springboards to the
rest of the lesbian community. They are drawn downtown from the

suburbs and bedroom communities by the noise and excitement of the downtown core and the need for a lesbian community. To youth, the bars exemplify that community.

Alternatives to the bar scene include organized sports, political groups, and outdoors groups. To varying degrees, these activities are open to young lesbians, but they are largely populated by adults. Twenty-five-year-old lesbians and 16-year-old lesbians have about as much in common as their heterosexual counterparts. While socializing among teenagers and adults can be rewarding for both groups, it leaves much to be desired if it is the sole option for adolescents. At the end of the day, when the team goes out for a beer, is the 16-year-old permitted to join in? The young lesbian is in a double bind. She is out of place with her heterosexual friends at times, and there are few comfortable places for her in the lesbian community.

What alternatives do these young women envision? They "want somewhere to go to be normal and gay. I would like to do regular, normal things with other lesbians." They want to go on short trips, go dancing, camping, or simply hang out in casual surroundings with their lesbian friends. Their recreational needs are much the same as those of heterosexual youngsters, with the additional need to spend a portion of time in a completely lesbian environment. Unlike their heterosexual counterparts, their friendship networks are not large enough to support some of these activities, and their geographical dispersion over a large area mitigates against spontaneous get-togethers. Yet, outside of the weekly LGYT meeting there are no places for young lesbians to go to gather and socialize openly among themselves.

As adolescents in an adult environment, these young lesbians are out of place. Their abrupt introduction to an alcohol-focussed and sexually loaded environment bypasses the gradual and safe ways in which most heterosexual youngsters learn to deal with alcohol and sexual intimacy. Yet, they need lesbian adults in their lives, not as peers, but as role models. They are not surrounded, as are heterosexual youngsters, by an adult presence which reassures them that life ahead can be happy and productive. Role models of stable lesbian relationships are conspicuously absent in their lives.

Older lesbians, for their part, remain largely unaware, not uncaring, of the dilemma for youth. The social service providers and community developers in the lesbian community are often stymied in outreach to youth by legalities, limited funds, and manpower. Young lesbians, like most youth in an adult-oriented society, feel that adults are largely unresponsive to their needs. "They don't listen to us," is a common theme for all adolescents, but in the microcosm of the lesbian community it is magnified to far greater proportions.

CONCLUSION

These youth share some common experiences of growing up and coming out. Yet, the meaning of the experiences is different for each of them. What does it mean to them to be a lesbian?

> You have to drop a lot of options. Like economic security. Women don't usually have a lot of money. (Wendy, age 18)

> It's a real love and trust of women, and respect. It's something inside me that I can't explain. (Brenda, age 17)

> I have the same goals and dreams. Those don't change because of your sexuality. You don't have different goals just because you're gay. (Shannon, age 17)

> It's just realizing something about yourself that's different. You're not going to get married and live the way your parents want you to. (Beth, age 16)

> It's not that important. Like, it's the most important unimportant issue. It's not a way of life. It's just a part of my life. You have to sneak around. It's difficult that way. (Ann, age 17)

> I don't want it to be a central part of my life. But it keeps coming up. Like when someone asks how come you don't have a boyfriend yet. It means a lot of lying. (Patty, age 19)

> My soul feels more comfortable. It feels right. (Shannon, age 17)

> It means a certain amount of independence and dependence on women. . . . a sense of democracy, and strength and power in women. (Carrie, age 16)

Being a lesbian means being strong, secretive, nonconforming. It is full of contradictions. It means being different and simultaneously being the same. "The most important unimportant issue," captures the ultimate contradiction in coming out: that the characteristic "lesbian" is a private, personal issue, far from being the mainstay of identity; yet it becomes a central focus for organizing identity and life-style as the result of the need to hide, lie, and to be accepted. In the end, these young women almost unanimously wanted me to express their need and desire for acceptance. I will let them express it for themselves:

> For the straights who are reading it, just to accept us. I don't consider myself different from the average 16-year-old. Except instead of talking about guys I talk about women, or I don't talk about it at all. (Beth, age 16)

> We aren't asking for the world. We're asking to be accepted for what we are as human beings. You don't have to care about our privacy, our sexual pleasures. We're human. (Sandy, age 18)

> We've been through a lot to accept what we are. I'd like them to respect the choice and to appreciate people for what they are, not to judge them by what they do sexually. (Deb, age 17)

> Let them realize how hard it is and just to give us a chance to be who we are. Just to give a human being a chance. I mean, that's who we are. And to other gay kids: don't give up! (Emma, age 18)

REFERENCES

Cass, V.C. (1979). Homosexual identity formation: A theoretical model. *Journal of Homosexuality, 4*(3), 219-235.

Coleman, E. (1982). Developmental stages in the coming-out process. *Journal of Homosexuality, 7*, 31-43.

Cronin, C.S. (1974). Coming out among lesbians. In E. Goode & R.R. Troiden (Eds.), *Sexual deviance and sexual deviants*. New York: Morrow.

Dailey, D.M. (1979). Adjustment of heterosexual and homosexual couples in pairing relationships: An exploratory study. *Journal of Sex Research, 15,* 143-157.

De Monteflores, C., & Schultz, S.J. (1978). Coming out: Similarities and differences for lesbians and gay men. *Journal of Social Issues, 34,* 59-72.

Eisner, M. (1982). *An investigation of the coming-out process, lifestyle, and sex-role orientation of lesbians.* Unpublished doctoral dissertation. York University, Downsview, Ontario.

Erikson, E. (1963). *Childhood and society.* New York: Norton.

Golden, C. (1985, April). Diversity and variability in lesbian identities. In J. Russotto (Chair), *Developmental milestones in the lives of gay men and lesbians.* Symposium conducted at the Annual Meeting of the American Orthopsychiatric Association, New York.

Hetrick, E., & Martin, D. (1984). Ego dystonic homosexuality: A developmental view. In E. Hetrick & T. Stein (Eds.), *Innovations in psychotherapy with homosexuals.* Washington: American Psychiatric Press.

Peplau, L.A., Cochran, S., Rook, K., & Padesky, C. (1978). Loving women: Attachment and autonomy in lesbian relationships. *Journal of Social Issues, 34,* 7-27.

Ponse, B. (1978). *Identities in the lesbian world: The social construction of the self.* Westport, CT: Greenwood Press.

Rich, A. (1980). Compulsory heterosexuality and lesbian existence. *Signs: Journal of Women in Culture and Society, 5,* 631-660.

Schäfer, S. (1976). Sexual and social problems of lesbians. *Journal of Sex Research, 12,* 50-69.

Schneider, M., & Tremble, B. (1985). Gay or straight? Working with the confused adolescent. *Journal of Social Work & Human Sexuality, 4,* 631-660.

Simon, W., & Gagnon, J. (1967). The lesbians: A preliminary overview. In W. Simon & J. Gagnon (Eds.), *Sexual deviance.* New York: Harper & Row.

The Development
of Male Prostitution Activity
Among Gay and Bisexual Adolescents

Eli Coleman, PhD

University of Minnesota

SUMMARY. The current research literature regarding male-juvenile prostitution activity is reviewed. An attempt is made to develop some theoretical understanding of the development of this activity among gay and bisexual adolescents. A predisposition, resulting from faulty psychosexual and psychosocial development, appears to make these boys vulnerable to the situational variables that they encounter. More severe disruptions in psychosexual and psychosocial development seem to result in more destructive and non-ego-enhancing prostitution activities. A clinical case study is presented which illustrates the development of this activity. Recommendations are made to help reduce the amount of self-destructive prostitution activity among male adolescents.

Dr. Coleman is Associate Professor at the Program in Human Sexuality, Department of Family Practice and Community Health, Medical School, University of Minnesota. He is Editor of the *Journal of Psychology & Human Sexuality* and two recent books published by The Haworth Press entitled *Psychotherapy with Homosexual Men and Women: Integrated Identity Approaches for Clinical Practice* and *Chemical Dependency and Intimacy Dysfunction*.

Earlier versions of this paper were presented at the National Conference for Family Violence Researchers sponsored by the University of New Hampshire in Durham on July 21-24, 1981 and the 15th Annual Meeting of the American Association of Sex Educators, Counselors and Therapists (AASECT), New York City, March 13, 1982. The author would like to acknowledge the research assistance on this paper by Daniel Andersen and the editorial assistance received from Orlo Otteson.

Correspondence and requests for reprints may be addressed to the author, c/o Program in Human Sexuality, 2630 University Avenue, S.E., Minneapolis, MN 55414.

ON THE GAME

Watch for punkers
Learn the score
Money first
Then his pleasure
Make the punter
Want you more
Be the weakness
For his strength
Be the child
He's yet to have
Be the strength
For his weakness
Apologize
For saying "Dad"

Anonymous[1]

Obviously, not all gay and bisexual adolescents engage in prostitution. For those who do, this activity creates certain social problems. Many questions remain in the minds of professionals: What do we know about these boys; the motivations behind their activity? What are the effects of this activity on later psychosocial, psychosexual and identity development and psychological functioning?

The answers to these questions are not exactly clear based upon the extant literature. We know that male prostitution is as old as female prostitution. Benjamin and Masters (1964) have provided us with an excellent history and a cross-cultural look at male prostitution. And, there are many types of male prostitution, including homosexual and heterosexual prostitution. Homosexual prostitution mostly involves adolescent males; heterosexual prostitution is more prevalent among adult males. This paper addresses juvenile male prostitution and focuses on homosexual forms of prostitution.

Kinsey, Pomeroy, and Martin (1948) in their study of male sexual behavior found that:

there is . . . a homosexual prostitution among males who provide sexual relations for other males, and such homosexual
prostitutes are, in many larger cities, not far inferior in numbers from females who are engaged in heterosexual prostitution. (p. 596)

There are several problems in interpreting the literature, and fortu-
nately, more recent research has taken these problems into account.
First, there is the problem of defining prostitution. Prostitution can
be viewed in a narrow or broad sense. The author's preference is to
use the broad-based definition formulated by Maloney (1980):

Any juvenile male who engages repeatedly in sexual activity
with another male person or persons with whom he would not
otherwise stand in any special relationship and for which he
receives currency and/or the provision of one or more of the
necessities of life.

These necessities could include food, shelter, clothing, and protection. Maloney (1980) also includes cigarettes and drugs, which
are not actual necessities in life; they are, however, often perceived
by the juvenile to be necessities, and, therefore, are major curren-
cies for prostitution.

Another problem in interpreting the literature is whether these
boys can be defined as gay, bisexual, or heterosexual. The task of
identifying sexual orientation is extremely difficult for a couple of
reasons. First, the development or clarification of an adult homosexual identity has been shown to take place at an age later than
chronological adolescence (Coleman, 1981/1982). Second, sexual
orientation is not necessarily a stable element throughout one's life,
and it certainly cannot be ascertained by behavior alone (Coleman,
1987).

There are many types of prostitutes, and many different typolo-
gies have been presented in the literature. Maloney (1980) identified seven types: the punk, the drag prostitute, the brothel prostitute, the kept boy, the call boy, the bar hustler, and the street
hustler. "Punk" is a prison term for males used sexually by other
inmates who reward their punks with protection, cigarettes, and

drugs. The drag prostitute is a transvestite or a presurgery male-to-female transsexual who poses as a female prostitute and who usually engages in oral sex in order to conceal their true biological gender.

There are two types of brothel prostitutes. One type is "employed" by a house of heterosexual prostitution for clients who sometimes prefer homosexual activities. The second is employed by an all-male house of prostitution run by a male "madam." These houses cater mainly to male clients. There are, apparently, few of these houses in existence, and very little is known about them.

The kept boy, described by Caukins and Coombs (1976), has the highest status; achievement of this status is often a stated goal of young juvenile prostitutes. The kept boy is one who has developed a relationship with a client that is long lasting and that provides an affluent lifestyle, including living expenses, clothing, transportation, travel, entertainment, and a life of leisure. Clients may or may not have expectations of sexual favors and the duration of the relationship may vary from weeks to years. In these relationships the "sugar daddy" often provides a "parenting" role to the young male prostitute (Shick, 1981).

Call boys have been described by Caukins and Coombs (1976) as physically attractive, well-built, easygoing, sexually versatile, dependable, successful, and "well-hung." These individuals work through an agency that acts as a go-between for the customer and the prostitute. The call boy usually goes to the location that the client has arranged. Other call boys are self-employed and advertise in newspapers and magazines with gay circulations.

Bar hustlers work in heterosexual or homosexual bars and hustle bar patrons. Certain bars in almost every city attract male prostitutes, and these bars are known as "hustler bars."

Finally, there is the street hustler, who, according to Ross (1959), has the lowest status of all male prostitutes. (Bar hustlers have a higher status than street hustlers; call boys have the highest status.) The street hustler is the most common, most observable and most likely to draw the attention of the law officials and the general public, and is more likely to be a juvenile than are any of the other types.

Fisher, Weisberg, and Marotta (1982) of the Urban and Rural Systems Associates (URSA) described another typology that is based upon the juvenile's relative dependence on hustling to survive (see also Weisberg, 1985). This activity can be situational (motivation is created by economic need), habitual ("addiction" to excitement, fast living, and street comradery), vocational (professional, in control, and usually not of juvenile age), and avocational (part-time professionals). These URSA researchers found 42% of their sample to be situational, 37% habitual, 13% vocational, and 8% avocational. They identified three types of male prostitutes: those who work in the sex trade zone, those who work in the gay ghetto zones and those who travel in the high class zone. Self-esteem is reported to be greater among the juvenile prostitutes who are avocational and vocational types and work in the gay ghetto.

Each of these zones attracts a certain type of hustler. Those who feel conflicted about themselves and neglected by mainstream society, come from the lowest classes, and tend to work in the sex trade zone — struggling to make enough money to survive. Those with developing gay identities from middle-class homes are more likely to be found in the gay ghetto zones. Young men who are particularly attractive and who are looking for good money, and entry into the institutions of the upper class, frequent the high-class bars or neighborhoods (Fisher, Weisberg, & Marotta, 1982).

AGE

The ages of the juvenile prostitutes who have been studied vary, but the mean and modal age is 17 or 18 years old. The average age of the first hustling experience is around 14 years old; more active hustling begins at ages 15 and 16 (Allen, 1980; Fisher, Weisberg, & Marotta, 1982). Most adolescent males who begin regular hustling activity do so within a year of their first hustling experience.

SOCIOECONOMIC BACKGROUND

Several studies showed that whereas male juvenile prostitutes come from every socioeconomic strata, the majority come from working class and lower socioeconomic backgrounds (Harris, 1973;

Reiss, 1961; Gandy & Deisher, 1970; Ginsburg, 1967; Allen, 1980; Fisher, Weisberg, & Marotta, 1982). They tend to have little education: the average educational level of those studied by Fisher, Weisberg, and Marotta (1982) was 10th grade. Consequently, much of the literature points out the need for vocational rehabilitation and education. Many of these boys have little or no knowledge of municipal, state, or private services that could assist them (Fisher, Weisberg, & Marotta, 1982).

FAMILY CHARACTERISTICS

The male prostitute's family life is chaotic and disorganized. For example, Butts (1947) found that although broken homes and homes containing both parents were equally represented in his study, most of the boys interviewed reported feeling unwanted or misunderstood at home. MacNamara (1965) found that out of 103 prostitutes interviewed most had highly traumatic family backgrounds that included broken homes, illegitimacy, rejection, alcoholism, brutality, inadequate schooling, and insufficient income. Craft (1966), Ginsburg (1967), Deisher, Einser, and Salzbacher (1969), Gandy and Deisher (1970), Coombs (1974), and Allen (1980) all reported similar backgrounds among their subjects. Allen (1980) observed that family problems are much more characteristic among the habitual street hustlers than among the part-time hustlers. In the URSA study, three-fourths of the subjects were runaways who left home at an average age of 15. Most reported that they left because of family conflicts and a desire for freedom and adventure.

The URSA researchers (as well as Gandy & Deisher, 1970) found that the homosexuality of many of the young male prostitutes precipitated many of the family problems and the decisions to run away or to be thrown out. Unlike their female counterparts, who often flee their homes, the males were often thrown out because of their family's inability to accept their son's homosexuality. The URSA report suggests that much of the family violence and physical abuse of the child is precipitated by the family's response to learning of their son's homosexuality.

SEXUAL ORIENTATION

Earlier researchers (Jersild, 1956; Ginsburg, 1967; Craft, 1966; Coombs, 1974) indicated that few, if any, of the subjects were homosexual; however, Shick (1981) and Furnald (1978) reported about two-thirds of their sample had a homosexual orientation. Furnald was able to provide data comparing sexual orientation, as determined by behavior and self-concept, before and after the hustling experience. He found greater homosexual orientation after the hustling activity began. Approximately one-third of the male prostitutes he studied, however, maintained a heterosexual or bisexual identity.

Similarly, in the URSA study, the majority were either gay identified, struggling to find a place in the gay male subculture, or both. Only 15% of the youth regarded themselves as "straight." Although many of the habitual and situational prostitutes in the URSA study identified themselves as gay, few were able to report any kind of permanence in their homosexual relationships. The researchers found that for many of these boys, intimacy was thwarted by their fears of closeness and affection, their "promiscuous past," and their dislike for control or restriction in relationships. They found that the avocational and professional prostitutes were more integrated in their gay identity and had more capacity for intimate relationships with other males.

Allen (1980) also reported that the type of prostitute was correlated to sexual orientation identity. The call or kept boys were the most homosexual in their stated homosexual interest (as measured by Kinsey-scale ratings); the group of delinquent boys who often exploit male homosexuals were least stated. Overall, 50% of Allen's subjects considered themselves to be predominately homosexual (Kinsey, 4, 5, 6), 28% bisexual (Kinsey 3), and 19% predominately heterosexual (Kinsey 1 or 2). These results indicate that at least an incidental homosexual arousal or a psychic response or both is present in male juvenile prostitution, and most have more than an incidental homosexual response (Kinsey 2-6).

Although an incidental physical or psychic response is present in most of these boys, this does not assume that they are all homosexual nor that they will all become so (Hoffman, 1972). Though many, who initially deny their homosexual interests and justify their behavior as simply a pursuit of money, later come to define themselves as gay (Hoffman, 1972).

GENDER IDENTITY

Furnald (1978) seems to be the only researcher who asked questions about gender identity. Overall, subjects in his study had a strong male gender identity, but a number of the prostitutes had thought about becoming women. We can probably assume that a significant amount of gender and sex-role dysphoria would exist among drag prostitutes and less so among other types.

EFFECTS OF SITUATIONAL VARIABLES

Learning to survive in a big city is a challenge for anyone, especially the economically and socially disadvantaged. For the gay adolescent coming from a low socioeconomic background and a disrupted home, alienated from their families and other institutions, and without economic power, prostitution provides some power and control over their lives. The URSA study also shows that the gay hustling environment provides comradery for the boys, which must serve a welcome relief for those who have been alienated from their family members or thrown out of their homes. The URSA report states that they learn quickly from others on the street that turning tricks is one way to survive. They also report a sense of kinship, which is derived from their similar pasts and current circumstances. In contrast to female prostitutes, young male prostitutes are often seen on the street in groups: creating their own kinship system and in some ways replacing the family system from which they have been ostracized (Fisher, Weisberg, & Marotta, 1982).

MOTIVATIONS FOR HUSTLING

The male prostitute reports that money is his prime motivation. In the URSA study, 69% reported money, 29% reported sex, 19% reported fun and adventure, and 1% reported socializing as the prime motivating factor. This study also revealed that the motivation is different for different types of prostitutes. For example, the situational hustler perceives the activity as temporary. Given the socioeconomic class from which he often emerges, this is understandable because many juvenile prostitutes are runaways and in need of money to survive. In fact, many observers believe that the experiences of running away and juvenile prostitution are closely related.

For some prostitutes, the activity is simply an integral part of their lives, as are drugs and alcohol, petty thefts, minor assaults, and other acts of criminality. However, researchers suggest that there are underlying motivations, including the need for finding someone to take care of them, the need to flee from a bad family situation, the need for affection from male figures, the lure of excitement and adventure, and the need for a way of dealing with a homosexual identity (Maloney, 1980).

The development of prostitution activity has been hypothesized to involve a number of situational variables combined with a number of feedback loops that determine the development of or disengagement from prostitution behavior or other delinquent or criminal behavior (Pieper, 1979). Pieper hypothesized a model for the development of these behaviors. Pieper (1979) noted that many prostitutes define their activity as noncriminal behavior, and they see this activity as a preferable alternative to other criminal acts. Although the threat of police intervention is real, the level of intervention and punishment is relatively less for prostitution activities than it is for other kinds of criminal behavior. Sociocultural factors alone do not explain why individuals choose to enter the world of prostitution (Pieper, 1979).

DRUG USE AND ABUSE

A study of 200 juvenile and adult prostitutes showed that alcohol and other drugs were strongly present in the subjects' family of origin and in the early and later stages of prostitution (Silbert, Pines, & Lynch, 1982). These researchers note a pattern of victimization that appears to be perpetuated from their severely disturbed

THEORETICAL MODEL

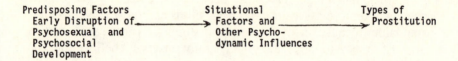

Predisposing Factors	Situational	Types of
Early Disruption of	Factors and	Prostitution
Psychosexual and	Other Psycho-	
Psychosocial	dynamic Influences	
Development		

backgrounds to their own self-destructive behavior, sense of help-lessness, negative self-concept, and psychological paralysis.

In one of the studies on male juvenile prostitution, Shick (1981) found that 20% of his 144 subjects eventually overdosed on heroin. Furnald (1978), in his study of male juvenile prostitution, also found a significant history of drug abuse among the subjects, especially after entry to hustling. Similarly, Allen (1980) found that 29% of his sample were regular users of hard drugs and 42% were heavy drinkers or alcoholics. Drug dealing is common. Allen (1980) and Fisher et al. (1982) found that the degree of drug use is related to the type of prostitution—with habitual prostitutes being the heaviest users. Many of these boys use drugs while they are hustling (76% in the URSA study).

INCIDENCE OF CHILD ABUSE

The experience of child abuse among juvenile prostitutes has been correlated with the development of prostitution activity. For example, in a study by James (1978) of 136 female juvenile prostitutes and 100 female delinquents, 63% of the prostitutes had experienced physical abuse in their childhood. Thirty-seven percent of the prostitutes and 33% of the nonprostitutes were molested prior to their first intercourse by a person at least 10 years older. In 17% of the prostitutes and 14% of the nonprostitutes, the molester was a relative. Forty-seven percent of the prostitutes and 32% of the nonprostitutes had been raped. Nearly half of the prostitutes had been raped more than once.

Furnald (1978) found that most of the male prostitutes in his study had had their first sexual experience with a much older man. All of the subjects had had sexual experiences with slightly older persons as part of their early sexual experimentation. Moreover, two-thirds of the sample had been raped. In the URSA study, 25% of the male prostitutes reported that they had been sexually abused, and 10% of them reported sexual abuse by a family member.

In Allen's (1980) study of 128 male juvenile prostitutes, the range in age of first sexual experiences was 5 to 16 years, with a median age of 13.5. In the one-third of the boys who had had their first experiences with a girl, 66% described this experience as a "seduction" by an older female. Those for whom the first sexual experience was with a male (two-thirds of the sample), 56% said that they had been "seduced" by an older man. Another study of 21 adolescent male prostitutes (street hustlers) showed that 29% had a history of physical abuse, and 43% had a history of sexual abuse, both before and after their prostitution behavior (Paperny & Deisher, 1983).

A large scale study of child sexual abuse in Canada showed that many preteen and young adolescents who were sexually abused needed to run away in order to escape emotional, physical, and sexual abuse. Prostitution, for these children, became a way of survival. Unfortunately, these prostitution experiences invariably lead to further physical and sexual abuse (victimization) (Bagley, 1985).

Janus, Scanlan, and Pierce (1984) studied 28 males (ages 12 to 25) who were involved in prostitution. Nineteen (68%) reported that their earliest sexual experiences had been "coercive." In most cases, these first coercive experiences occurred repeatedly. Eight of the youths reported that they were seven or less when these coercive experiences took place.

When Janus et al. (1984) compared a group of male prostitutes to a group of boys who were involved in other forms of street life (delinquency), they found that the main difference in their histories was an absence of coercive sexual experiences among the delinquent group (nonprostitutes). These authors concluded that childhood sexual assault serves as a premature introduction into adult sexuality and teaches the child to use sex to meet adolescent-nonsexual needs.

Incidence rates of childhood physical and sexual abuse are high among male prostitutes. It should be noted that studies of incidence rates have relied on self-reports from boys who are currently involved in prostitution. It is my clinical experience that many of these boys do not remember their early childhood abuse experiences, and that some do not become consciously aware of this trauma until they reach adulthood. There is a cultural taboo against admitting this kind of abuse. However, because it seems to be a significant factor in the etiology of female prostitution, it would not be surprising to find it a significant factor in the development of male prostitution. However, this phenomenon needs to be studied more closely.[2]

Male juvenile prostitution is considered by many to be a form of child sexual abuse (even though there is usually verbal, consensual agreement between the young prostitute and his customer). The power differential between the socioeconomically deprived and psychosexually and psychosocially underdeveloped adolescent and the "john" is great and it is difficult to see the experience as a "consenting relationship." The incidence of venereal disease among these juveniles (up to 50% in most studies) can also be considered a form of child abuse and the vulnerability of these young men to AIDS looms large, since their partners rarely give them the opportunity to engage in safer-sex practices. Consequently, the street hustlers are more at risk to AIDS and other sexually transmitted disease than are other types of prostitutes.

THEORETICAL UNDERSTANDING

To understand the development of male juvenile prostitution behavior, one must take into account sociocultural factors, situational variables, types of prostitution activities, and early developmental factors that disrupt psychosexual and psychosocial development.

Using Erikson's (1968) eight stages of human development is helpful in understanding the impact of various psychodynamic as well as sociocultural factors found to be correlated with prostitution. It is also helpful in understanding some of the etiology of prostitution behavior, especially the effects of early disruption of psychosocial and psychosexual development. For those who have negatively resolved the psychosocial stages of development identified by Erikson, they are particularly vulnerable to finding prostitution activity as a logical expression of their unsuccessful psychosex-

PIEPER'S MODEL

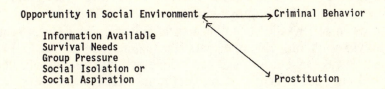

ual and psychosocial development. With this predisposing factor and the vulnerability of these young boys, exposure to situational variables that show them the way into prostitution and resulting experiences determine the development, continuation or elimination of the behavior. The author also hypothesizes that the degree of disruption of early psychosexual and psychosocial development and quality of the situational factors influence the type of prostitution activity. Essentially disruption in healthy resolution of Erikson's earlier developmental stages will lead to types of prostitution that are more self-destructive and non-ego-enhancing.

CASE STUDY

This clinical case study illustrates the point. Jeff, a 21-year-old man, came to our clinic immediately following chemical dependency treatment. During his treatment, he began to recall incidences from his childhood. First of all, he remembered that both his parents drank excessively; these drinking episodes often led to violence in the home. His father physically abused his mother and his father and mother both physically abused the children. Verbal fighting and abuse were common. Jeff also said that he could not remember any physical affection or expression of love from either of his parents except when he was ill. There were very few experiences to foster the development of trust, initiative, or autonomy.

Although there was no reported overt incest with his mother, a covert incestuous relationship developed. His mother would use Jeff as a close confidant. During drinking episodes, she would tell him her problems. She would relay, in great detail, her past physical abuse by her own father and her continued problem with her husband. As much as she relied on Jeff for emotional support, she continued to accuse him of not loving her. Jeff felt very frustrated because he could not prove his love to her, but kept trying.

When Jeff was 10, his oldest sister began trying to have sexual activity with him. He remembers resisting her efforts. She told him that it was OK because she had "done it" with his older brother. She continued to persist at different times over the next three years until Jeff finally gave in at age 13. He remembers he decided to have sex with her because he had been concerned about his homosexual feelings and felt a need to prove otherwise. Shortly after this first sexual experience, his sister began to develop seizures and Jeff was convinced that he had caused them. He also realized that his sister's illness diverted his mother's attention away from him, and he felt incredibly jealous. Shortly after his sexual experience with his sister, he began to use drugs. His use included marijuana, LSD, amphetamines, cocaine, heroin, and alcohol. All of his adolescent sexual experiences were associated with drug use.

From the ages of 6 through 13, Jeff cross-dressed extensively. He was extremely embarrassed and ashamed about these experiences. He had wondered as a child if he was really a girl. For some reason, which we could not determine, this activity stopped. Although he stopped thinking he might be a woman, he continued to have fears about his masculinity and homosexuality.

His first same-sex experience occurred when he was 15. He met a man on the street and went to this man's apartment to engage in sexual activity. They began to see each other regularly. A short time after the relationship began, the man started to physically abuse Jeff. The man also drank heavily and was most abusive when he was drunk. Jeff left the relationship after the man tried to strangle him.

Jeff found his way into prostitution. He first learned to "turn a trick" when he was hitchhiking and received offers for money or drugs in exchange for sexual activity. This continued on a regular basis for several years. His activity was localized to the "sex trade zone." During this period, Jeff did not identify himself as gay. His prostitution activity ended when he went into treatment for chemical dependency. By this time, Jeff had been quite dysfunctional, both socially and psychologically. He was addicted to alcohol and marijuana.

Treatment was extensive. The course of therapy lasted for 2 years. Treatment focused on the healthy resolution of his early developmental stages. Although the therapy did not systematically progress from a recapitulation of one Erikson stage to the next, in many ways, the flow of therapy did progress along those lines.

Consistent care and unconditional positive regard was critical in the early stages of therapy. Focus was also placed on understanding family dynamics and the source of his mistrust of other people. It took at least 6 to 8 months for him to trust me. For many months he had fantasies that I was going to hit him.

His shame and doubt about himself was the source of many self-destructive and suicidal thoughts. Besides his suicidal ideation, Jeff had many fantasies of hitting himself and on several occasions he came into therapy sessions with self-inflicted bruises on his face.

From the very beginning, Jeff was involved in vocational rehabilitation, but he experienced great difficulty in his training. This was clearly a result of his lack of positive resolution of earlier developmental stages. His mistrust of people, his shame, and his guilt served as a barrier to his functioning in the workplace. As he developed greater trust and less shame about himself, he was able to function better at school even though it continued to be an incredible struggle for him. His vocational rehabilitation was, though, a critical feature in his development. I encouraged him as much as I could. In addition, I supported his setting of goals, reinforced his efforts, and acknowledged his progress.

In working with his identity, we focused on his homosexuality. Positive conceptions were built. His gender and sex-role identities were also clarified.

When Jeff began to feel better about himself, I encouraged him to bring family members into therapy. However, his parents refused to come. Two of his seven brothers and sisters came in for one session each. Even though we were not successful in getting his family into therapy, the process of trying was very therapeutic. Jeff realized how little support he had from his family. He also realized how little they were accepting of his homosexuality or alcoholism. When he attended family gatherings, they would offer him drinks.

As a result, Jeff decided to terminate relations with his parents first — and then with the rest of his family. This was a very difficult process, even though he felt no support or love from them.

The development of intimacy skills started with the therapeutic relationship. An important adjunct to therapy was his involvement with Alcoholics Anonymous, which helped him maintain sobriety and develop intimacy skills with others in the group setting. As we worked on these developmental issues, Jeff began to develop an intimate relationship with another man. At first, he was very frightened of the relationship and reluctant to even talk about it. The relationship grew. There was good communication, openness, honesty, and a marked lack of abuse. After approximately 6 months, they decided to commit themselves to a long-term relationship.

This is obviously a sketch of the therapeutic course over 2 years. It, however, gives an idea of how the therapeutic issues were addressed using an Eriksonian framework. The development of his prostitution activity could be understood from the disruption in his psychosocial and psychosexual development. Although he stopped his prostitution activity, many developmental issues needed to be addressed in therapy and in his life. Through using an Eriksonian approach to therapy, many of his early developmental stages were successfully resolved. He was then able to work on later stages of industry, intimacy and the further adult stages of development.

CONCLUSION AND RECOMMENDATIONS

1. This case study and the extant research supports the hypothesis that disruption in healthy resolution of Erikson's earlier developmental stages can lead to types of prostitution that are more destructive and non-ego-enhancing; however, this hypothesis needs to be investigated further.
2. The issue of food, clothing, medical care, educational opportunities, job training and placement, supervised living and prolonged and consistent contact with nurturing adults are a prerequisite to the counseling process.
3. From a clinical perspective, in working with males who have been involved in juvenile prostitution, efforts at restoration of positive ego functioning is essential.
4. We also must find from research some ideas of how to treat

or prevent individuals who are engaging in prostitution in a self-destructive manner.

5. We need more preventative activities so children have more successfully resolved earlier stages of ego development before they reach adolescence.

6. Boys who have been abused as children and who are exposed to situational variables that make prostitution activity a logical survival mechanism are individuals at high risk for developing self-destructive prostitution activities. Prevention activities must be directed toward these boys.

7. We need more and effective outreach programs to street hustlers to build trust, and encourage vocational rehabilitation.

8. We need to help adolescents involved in prostitution activity, clarify their sexual orientation, and offer opportunities for socialization and development of intimacy skills. They must not be assumed to be homosexual because they engage in homosexual activity. They need to clarify this identity on their own over time. Given that they must have at least some psychic or physical pleasure from homosexual activity, this needs to be understood and not become a source of homophobic anxiety.

9. For those with a predominant or exclusive homosexual identity, we need to provide mechanisms for these adolescents to socialize in a manner and setting that can be ego-enhancing and can teach them trust and intimacy skills. They need to learn how to develop positive conceptions of themselves and their sexual orientation.

10. We need to help families and society remove the stigma from homosexuality to reduce conflicts within families over this issue. This will result in greater opportunities for positive psychosexual and psychosocial development of boys with bisexual or homosexual sexual orientation identities.

NOTES

1. This poem came to my attention in materials prepared by Richie J. McMullen of "Streetwise," P.O. Box 185, London, SW5 9JR, England.

2. There is some controversy in the literature about the effects of early sexual experiences with adults on later adult development and functioning. Some research indicates that subjects do not report any lasting effect as a result of these

early sexual experiences; in fact, some report these to have been positive (see Jay & Young, 1979; Constantine, 1980). However, the bulk of the research provides evidence of negative reactions and serious disruptions in emotional and behavioral development (see Constantine, 1980).

REFERENCES

Allen, D. M. (1980). Young male prostitutes: A psychosocial study. *Archives of Sexual Behavior, 9*, 399-426.

Bagley, C. (1985). Child abuse and juvenile prostitution: A commentary on the Bagley report on sexual offences against children and youth in Canada. *Journal of Public Health, 76*, 65-66.

Benjamin, M., & Masters, R. E. L. (1964). *Prostitution and morality*. New York: Julian Press.

Butts, W. M. (1947). Boy prostitutes of the metropolis. *Journal of Clinical Psychopathology, 8*, 673-681.

Caukins, S. E., & Coombs, N. R. (1976). The psychodynamics of male prostitution. *American Journal of Psychotherapy, 30*, 441-451.

Coleman, E. (1981/1982). The developmental process of coming out. *Journal of Homosexuality, 7*(2/3), 31-43.

Coleman, E. (1987). Assessment of sexual orientation. *Journal of Homosexuality, 12*(1/2), 9-24.

Constantine, L. L. (1980). The impact of early sexual experience: A review and synthesis of outcome research. In J. M. Samson (Ed.), *Childhood and sexuality*. Montreal, Quebec: Editions Etuides Vivantes.

Coombs, N. R. (1974). Male prostitution: A psychosocial view of behavior. *American Journal of Orthopsychiatry, 44*, 782-789.

Craft, M. (1966). Boy prostitutes and their fate. *British Journal of Psychiatry, 112*, 1111-1114.

Deisher, R., Einser, V., & Salzbacher, S. I. (1969). The young male prostitute. *Pediatrics, 43*, 936-942.

Erikson, E. H. (1968). *Identity: Youth and crisis*. New York: Norton.

Fisher, B., Weisberg, D. K., & Marotta, T. (1982). *Report on adolescent male prostitution*. San Francisco, CA: Urban and Rural Systems Associates.

Furnald, R. (1978). Male juvenile prostitution. Unpublished master's thesis. University of Southern California, Los Angeles, CA.

Gandy, P., & Deisher, R. (1970). Young male prostitutes: The physicians role in social rehabilitation. *Journal of the American Medical Association, 212*, 1661-1666.

Ginsburg, K. N. (1967). "The meat rack": A study of the male homosexual prostitute. *American Journal of Psychotherapy, 21*, 170-185.

Harris, M. (1973). *The dilly boys*. London: Croom Helm Ltd.

Hoffman, M. (1972). The male prostitute. *Sexual Behavior, 2*, 16-21.

James, J., & Meyerding, J. (1978). Early sexual experience as a factor in prostitution. *Archives of Sexual Behavior, 7*, 31-42.

Janus, M. D., Scanlon, B., & Prince, V. (1984). Youth prostitution. In A. W.

Burgess (Ed.), *Sex rings and child pornography*. Lexington, MA: D. C. Heath.

Jay, K., & Young, A. (Eds.), (1979). *The gay report: Lesbians and gay men speak out about sexual experiences and lifestyles*. New York: Simon & Schuster.

Jersild, J. (1956). *Boy prostitution*. Copenhagen: G.E.C. Gad.

Kinsey, A. C., Pomeroy, W. B., & Martin, C. E. (1948). *Sexual behavior in the human male*. Philadelphia: W. B. Saunders.

MacNamara, D. E. J. (1965). Male prostitution in an American city: A pathological or socio-economic phenomenon? *American Journal of Orthopsychiatry, 35*: 204.

Maloney, P. (1980). Street hustling: Growing up gay. Unpublished manuscript.

Paperny, D. M., & Deisher, R. W. (1983). Maltreatment of adolescents: The relationship to a predisposition toward violent behavior and delinquency. *Adolescence, 18*, 499-506.

Pieper, R. (1979). Identity management in adolescent male prostitution in West Germany. *International Review of Modern Sociology, 9*, 239-259.

Reiss, A. J. (1961). The social integration of queers and peers. *Social Problems, 9*, 102-120.

Ross, H. L. (1959). The "hustler" in Chicago. *Journal of Student Research, 1*, 13-19.

Schick, F. (1978). Service needs of hustlers. Unpublished manuscript. Available from the author, 111 N. Wabash #1320, Chicago, IL 60602.

Silbert, M. H., Pines, A. M., & Lynch, T. (1982). Substance abuse and prostitution. *Journal of Psychoactive Drugs, 14*, 193-197.

Weisberg, D. K. (1985). *Children of the night: A study of adolescent prostitution*. Lexington, MA: D.C. Heath.

Male Prostitution
and Homosexual Identity

Debra Boyer, PhD

Women Studies Program, University of Washington, Seattle, Washington

SUMMARY. The documentary film on transvestites, *The Queen*, has a scene where a young man tells a friend about a recent job interview (Litvinoff, 1968). His friend asks, "Did you tell them you were a homosexual?" The young man, who did not get the job, answers, "No, they told me." What this interaction reflected was not just the fact of the young man's homosexuality, but the social fact: What it means to be homosexual in his culture and society. In this paper, I discuss the conduct of prostitution as one enactment of those meanings: Prostitution, as a social fact in the life of adolescent gay males, is understood by them to be linked with their homosexual identity.

In recent decades, a dramatic rise in the number of adolescents involved in street corner societies has brought male prostitution to public attention.[1] An accessible and visible street-corner market of male prostitutes is relatively new, but male homosexual prostitution is not. There are references to a transvestite and male prostitution

---

Dr. Boyer is Research Associate in the Women Studies Program at the University of Washington in Seattle, WA and a cultural and applied anthropologist in private practice in Seattle, WA. She is presently doing research on the relationship of physical and sexual victimization of adolescent parents to child maltreatment in Washington state. She is providing consultation to several institutions and social services to integrate developmental approaches in program design for street youth, prostitutes, and incarcerated youth. Her research populations have included female offenders, adolescent street youth, prostitutes, pregnant and parenting adolescents, and substance abusers.

Correspondence and requests for reprints may be addressed to the author at 2235 Fairview Avenue East, #11, Seattle, WA 98102.

subculture in France as early as the 1700s. The meeting places where homosexual encounters were available have been described by Jeffery Weeks (1981):

> In this world of sexual barter, particularly given the furtiveness, the need for caution and the great disparities of wealth and social position among participants, the cash nexus inevitably dominated. (p.119)

Contemporary descriptions of public territories of gay male subcultures generally include terms such as "trade" and "market," which refer to characteristic impersonal sexual interactions (Read, 1980; Rechy, 1977; Marotta, 1981). Researchers in the early part of the 20th century (e.g., Freud, 1905; Ellis, 1912, 1936; Bloch, 1909; and Hirschfeld, 1936) refer to their observations of the prevalence of prostitution among homosexuals. This pattern has been observed and described by several researchers in recent decades. Evelyn Hooker (1967) has used the concepts of "sexual market" and "market mentality" to describe gay bars in Los Angeles:

> I conceive of homosexual bars as free markets which could only arise under a market economy in which buyers and sellers are governed by rules whereby the right to enter in is determined by whether the buyer has the wherewithal. The term market as applied to bars has two meanings: 1) as a business enterprise in which leisure is accomplished via the market: gain from the sale of liquor and entertainment is legitimate; and 2) as a metaphor to conceive of transactions between homosexuals, a set of terms relating to the negotiation of an exchange of sexual services. (p.174)
>
> I turn now to the second meaning of the term market as applied to "gay" bars, that is, as a sexual market: a place where agreements are made for the potential exchange of sexual services, for sex without obligation or commitment, the "one night stand." (p. 174)

Hustling, promiscuity, and cruising are major themes found in any comprehensive discussion of homosexuality one may choose to read (Kinsey, Pomeroy, & Martin, 1948; Hooker, 1967; Gagnon & Simon, 1973; Plummer, 1975; Tripp, 1975; Bell & Weinberg, 1978; Masters & Johnson, 1979; Marmor, 1980). Several researchers (Bell & Weinberg, 1978; Humphreys, 1970; Rechy, 1977; Leznoff & Westley, 1956; Kinsey et al., 1948) have described "cruising" as the principal method for finding sexual partners in public territories of the male homosexual subculture. Although these relationships do not always imply an exchange of money for anonymous sex, prostitution is not an uncommon basis for an encounter. Habitual promiscuity makes payment for sex less noteworthy. Cory (1951), for example, asserts the willingness to "buy love" in the first descriptions of the hustling scene in the contemporary American gay male subculture (p.129). Read (1980) has described the public territories of male homosexuality as "steeped in the lore of hustling" (p.75).

The idea that homosexual expression is confined to impersonal and economic exchange is a widely held notion. The interdependence of homosexual expression and prostitution has led some researchers to argue that homosexuality and prostitution are perceived as inseparable, if not synonymous phenomena (Weeks, 1981). Contemporary research and literature on gay lifestyles have by now demonstrated otherwise. Gay relationships are, of course, as varied as heterosexual ones and include long-term and monogamous associations. Admittedly, gay males involved in prostitution for support or as a lifestyle comprise only a small subset of the gay male population. The issue I am addressing is how one adapts to life as a homosexual within a particular cultural context that has stigmatized homoerotic behavior. One's first association with the homosexual subculture will serve as a role model and reference group, which is important to identity formation and management. In this paper, I demonstrate how gay adolescents who are exposed to the public territories of male homosexuality (Read, 1980) may develop a self-understanding that links their homosexual identity with prostitution.

REVIEW OF PAST STUDIES

Historical studies of homosexuality have indicated that "writings on male prostitution emerged simultaneously with the notion of homosexuals as an identifiable breed of persons with special needs, passions, and lusts" (Weeks, 1981, p.113). Yet contemporary studies are most remarkable for their ambivalence toward the sexual orientation of male prostitutes. Sexual orientation of male prostitutes is the subject of contradictory findings. The question: "Are they or aren't they homosexual?" is of paramount concern to researchers, but homosexuality is generally excluded as a motivation for prostitution by males.

Reiss (1961), for example, described homosexual prostitution among his sample as a reflection of the greater sexual experience of lower class males, who did not define themselves as homosexual. Coombs (1974) described 72% (n = 41) of his sample as heterosexual. As for the others, Coombs states: "Actually he probably is not homosexual. Many subjects were supermasculine in appearance. Only 6% defined themselves as homosexual" (p.783). Coombs supported his statements by suggesting that those who reported to be homosexual were overcompensating for their social failings. In a later article, Caukins and Coombs (1976) conclude that most hustlers insist they are not homosexual (p.444).

Craft (1966), in another well-known study, interviewed 33 males under the age of 16 who "persistently" prostituted, and 17 young males who participated in homosexual activity within an institution. It is unclear if the latter prostituted within the institution or were identified for the study because of their known homosexual activity. The ambiguity is interesting because Craft seems to assume that prostitution and homosexuality are synonymous. Craft does not pursue the possibility that a homosexual orientation may be a plausible factor in the homosexual behavior of his sample. He suggested that poor parenting and bad home environments result in personality disorganization. Prostitution is an incidental feature of social and personal maladjustment.

MacNamara's (1965) study of 37 male prostitutes suggested that they were homosexual, but that sexual preference is attributed to socioeconomic factors. Ginsburg (1967) likewise did not view individual prostitutes as homosexual. He concluded that male hustlers are motivated by psychological needs that can only be achieved through physical relationships. According to Ginsburg (1967), the motivation of the hustler in the sexual act is different from the homosexual, although hustlers may "convert" in time to homosexuality.

Given the negative cultural valuation of homosexuality, I suggest that in the years before the gay liberation movement, researchers may have been unwilling to accept the existence of stable and permanent homosexual identities. Subjects were quick to affirm "it" (homosexuality) was not true for them. I suspect findings that refute a homosexual orientation (as opposed to the perhaps unavailable construct of "identity") among male prostitutes affirm a social desire and not a social reality: subject and researcher agreed upon a mutual denial of homosexuality.

More recent studies have reported a larger percentage of gay identified youth among male prostitutes (Allen, 1980; Fisher, Weisberg & Marotta, 1982). In Fisher et al.'s (1982) study of 79 male prostitutes, only 16.5% identified themselves as heterosexual. Fisher concluded that male prostitution was becoming "gayer." Fisher did not dispute the conclusions of earlier studies, but suggested that male prostitution is a post-World War II phenomenon that has emerged only with the contemporary gay subculture. This conclusion runs counter to historical evidence given by Weeks (1977) and others who have demonstrated that the Western tradition of homosexual subcultures were organized around prostitution.

The more recent research asks us to assume the plausibility of a causal relationship between the post-World War II growth of a gay subculture and homosexual involvement in male prostitution, without a discussion of the social, cultural, and historical processes involved. We are left with questionable descriptions of: who male prostitutes are, their sexual identity, and the individual and cultural processes involved in male prostitution. Most of all, we are left with an incomplete understanding of the relationship of male prostitution to homosexuality in this culture.

DESCRIPTION OF RESEARCH

In 1980, I began work on a 2-year study of adolescent male prostitution in Seattle, Washington (James, 1982; Boyer, 1986a). The information I present here is based on interviews and observations of 47 of these prostitutes. The young men I interviewed were identified primarily by the parameters of the perceived "social problem" as defined by the media, social services, and the criminal justice system. They were male prostitutes who could be seen hustling on the corners of downtown. They were contacted in several ways: (a) referrals from outreach workers, (b) personal contact during field work, (c) probation officer or caseworker identification and referral, (d) self-disclosure during interviews, and (e) charge-at-arrest as noted on daily census sheets at the youth detention center.

A control group of 50 adolescent males, who were delinquent but not prostitutes, were interviewed in the detention center. The control group of delinquents was interviewed for comparison with the prostitutes to determine what factors might motivate a delinquent pattern that included prostitution.[2]

Demographic Characteristics

Previous studies have described male prostitutes as: 15 to 23 years of age, unemployed, drifters, unskilled, and high school dropouts. They are from all socioeconomic backgrounds, but often reported lower economic status (MacNamara, 1965; Fisher et al., 1982). Male prostitutes tend to come from deprived, neglectful, or broken homes (Cory & LeRoy, 1963; Deisher, Esner, & Sulzbacker, 1969; Ginsburg, 1967; Fisher et al., 1982). Incidences of physical and sexual abuse, greater than expected, have also been reported for male prostitutes (Fisher et al., 1982; Coombs, 1974; Caukins & Coombs, 1976; Harlan, Rodgers, & Slattery, 1981).

The young men I interviewed were not unlike those who participated in past studies. The average age of the male prostitutes was 16.2 years; the average age at first prostitution was younger, 14. (See Table 1.1 for mean ages of the young men at critical junctures in the process of involvement in prostitution.)

The ethnic representation of the sample resembles the general population; a majority were Caucasian (70.2%). Blacks, in comparison to the area's population of 4.2%, were overrepresented (14.9%). Contrary to observations by the police at the time of this study, 8.5% of my sample were Native American.[3] There were two Samoans (2.1%) and one Hispanic (1.5%). There were no Asians.

Prostitutes described family-of-origin incomes of "above average," whereas most controls reported "average" family incomes. The occupations of the head-of-household were generally not in the

Table 1.1
Average Age at Time of Event

EVENT	HetP	HomP	Het Control	Hom Control
Interview	16	16.5	16.1	15
Sexual Involvement	10.1	10.1	11.7	12
First Sexual Partner	14.1	16.1	12.7	13
First Sex with Male	13.4	11	-	12
First Male Partner	32.6	20.2	-	13
Rape	14	12.2	14 (n=2)	-
Regular Sexual Activity	12.7	13.3	13.6	15
First Arrest	12	13.5	13.2	9
Second Arrest	12.9	14	14.1	14
Third Arrest	13.7	14.4	14.8	14
Prostitution Arrest	14.4	14.6	-	-
First Alcohol Use	10	11.4	11.9	11.5
First Marijuana Use	9.4	12.1	11.9	13.5
Awareness of Prostitution	11.5	13.1	11.9	12.5
Prostitution Involvement	14.3	14.4	-	-
Grade Left School	9.4	9.8	-	-
Grade Began Dating	7	7.5	-	-

professional category. Education levels of parents were seldom beyond high school. Divorced or separated parents were reported for 83% of the prostitutes and 74% of the control group. Of the prostitutes, 87.2% were not in school, in contrast to 54% of the controls. In both groups the young men left school in the ninth and tenth grades.

Family relationships in both the prostitute and delinquent groups were riddled with conflict and instability; although family problems were more severe among the prostitutes. Prostitutes reported significantly more physical abuse, $p < .05$; sexual abuse, $p < .00001$; and psychological abuse, $p < .008$, than the controls.

Sexual Orientation

In contrast to many studies, I found the most significant factor discriminating male prostitutes from other delinquents, and from many other adolescents, was their sexual identity: most are homosexual. Of the prostitutes, 70% (33) identified themselves as either homosexual or bisexual in comparison to only 4% (2) of the control group. Thirty percent (14) of the prostitutes identified themselves as heterosexual, in comparison to 96% (48) of the control group.

Sexual preference was determined by responding to two questions. They were first asked to place themselves on Kinsey's (1948) 7 point scale to determine the balance of their heterosexual to homosexual involvement. Next, they were asked to state their primary sexual orientation: heterosexual, homosexual, bisexual, asexual, or uncertain. Tables 1.2 and 1.3 list the responses.

Kinsey (1948) found that homosexual experience spread across his 7 point scale. He concluded the following:

> From all of this, it should be evident that one is not warranted in recognizing merely two types of individuals, heterosexual and homosexual, and that the characterization of the homosexual as a third sex fails to describe any actuality. (p.647)

Although I accept Kinsey's argument that categories for sexual orientation are arbitrary and heuristic, I have used them for these reasons: (a) the small sample size, (b) the lack of diversity within the heterosexual group, and (c) the research focus on individual perceptions. These categories function as organizing principles for individuals and society in Western culture. They are, in fact, part of the institutionalized reality that confronts individuals and are used in determining one's self- and social definition.[4]

To summarize, the factors that most strongly discriminated between prostitutes and controls were: (a) homosexual or bisexual identity, (b) sexual victimization, and (c) a dysfunctional and rejecting family. In the remainder of this paper, I discuss these factors

Table 1.2
Primary Sexual Orientation

	P n=47	HomP n=33	HetP n=14	C n=50
Heterosexual	29.8 (14)	0	100	96
Homosexual	51.1 (24)	72.7	0	4
Bisexual	19.1 (9)	27.3	0	0

Table 1.3
Kinsey Scale

	P (n=47)	HomP (n=33)	HetP (n=14)	C (n=50)
Exclusively heterosexual	10.6% (5)	0	35.7	86
Mainly heterosexual	6.4% (3)	0	21.4	10
Mainly heterosexual/ substantial degree of homosexual	14.9% (7)	6.1	35.7	0
As much heterosexual as homosexual	12.8% (6)	18.	0	0
Mainly homosexual/ substantial degree of heterosexual	10.6% (5)	15.2	0	0
Mainly homosexual	17% (8)	24.2	0	2
Exclusively homosexual	25.5% (12)	36.4	0	2
No answer	2.1% (1)	0	7.1	0

as social constraints upon male prostitutes within the context of the sex and gender constructs of Western society.

THE CULTURAL CONSTRUCTION
OF HOMOSEXUALITY

Homosexuality constitutes a separate sexual category of moral and symbolic significance. As a matter of moral concern, homosexuality has been subject to intervention and regulation. The symbolic power of homosexuality is referential in so far as "homosexuality" is subject to social definitions from which individuals are assigned a status. The symbolic power of the concept of homosexuality also has a productive dimension. As individuals avail themselves of the meanings of homosexuality, the category is constantly recreated and reconstituted. A young man, who is or becomes homosexual, has been born into a social world with a configuration of sexual meanings that he will experience as the "objective reality" of homosexuality (Plummer, 1975).

Elements of the objective world that shape the context of homosexuality include: religion, law, medicine, psychiatry, and normative sexuality, which include family and gender role expectations (Foucault, 1980; Berger & Luckman, 1967). These are sources of stigmatization that form the individual and collective responses to homosexuality. These elements can be found in the lives of the young men described below.

Religion

The antisexual philosophy of Judeo-Christian tradition is complex, but the ultimate message is not. Although these attitudes predate this religious tradition, the assertion of spiritual values in opposition to "sins of the flesh" singles out Christianity for its long history of hostility and taboos against all forms of homosexuality, and much of heterosexuality (Foucault, 1985; Plummer, 1975; Tripp, 1975; Weeks, 1979). Certain sexual activities, such as masturbation ("spilling of the seed") and especially sodomy, have been construed as "crimes against nature." Thus, homosexuality has been referred to as "the crime not to be named among Christians" and as "a disgrace to human nature" (Weeks, 1979, p.99). Religion has ordered sexual behavior according to what is "natural" and what is "unnatural." The first information received on homosexuality by many of the young men in this study came from religious sources or can be seen as based upon religious principles.

Case Studies

Matthew is 16, Caucasian, and says that he is gay. He lived most of his life in a small city in the eastern part of Washington. His parents were divorced before he entered school. Matthew felt an attraction for males at an early age. His first memory of sexual play was at age 7 with a male cousin. At age13, Matthew was raped by an older man, a stranger. Following the rape, Matthew's problems at home worsened. He endured a childhood of physical abuse associated with his mother's alcoholism. He was placed in a boys' home for two years. This was not a happy time for him:

> I was hassled for being gay. It was terrible. The owner of the boys home was "anti-gay." The staff were mostly old Christian people. I'm not knocking it (religion) down but it looks down on homosexuality. They said it was a sin.

Mark is 17, black, and says he has not made a final decision, but he "might still be homosexual." He described his father as an alcoholic who often beat his mother. Sometimes Mark slept with his mother because of nightmares, and sometimes because his mother wanted protection from his father. When Mark was 13, his father died in a truck accident: soon after he dropped out of school.

Mark remembers having strong sexual feelings for males all of his life. He enjoyed wearing makeup and his mother's nightgowns as a child. Mark wonders if he is a transvestite and if he should have a sex change operation. There have been many times when he wanted to die, he talks about suicide often. Thinking about a sex change operation occupies his thoughts, but he has not made any decisions yet:

I might still be homosexual or something but I want to think about my future and my religion. We're really against that stuff. I feel like I have two marks against me because I am black and I am gay. I started to feel bad about myself because of society and stuff; it was basically because of my religion, you know, that's what it was.

In the following quotes we see more examples of how exposure to religious attitudes shaped young men's feelings about themselves and their homosexuality:

My parents are Mormon. We just never talked about it (homosexuality). It's like you must not talk about it, but I get the impression they don't want me to be gay even though we never talked about it.

When I was young we used to have home bible study night and we read from the book of Mormon. A couple of times homosexuality was the subject and my father would read where God said that it was unnatural and condemned.

Homosexuality is a problem for me psychologically, mostly from religion. It was read in pamphlets and books and in the bible. I thought that if I really did want to get into religion, I'd have to stop (homosexual activity).

The encounters these young men had with religious doctrine began to shape their understanding of cultural attitudes toward persons with homoerotic feelings or experiences. The message was clear: homosexuality is bad. Homosexuals, as a category of persons, stood in an anomalous position to the natural order of things and were in violation of fundamental religious traditions (Plummer, 1975; Tripp, 1975).

Law

What had been understood in a religious context as sinful sexual behavior was to further unfold as criminal behavior. Religious traditions that acted to protect reproductive sexuality and to regulate nonprocreative sexual activity provided the basis for legal regulation of homosexual behavior (see Weeks, 1977, 1979; Crompton,

1976; Knutson, 1980; and Katz, 1976 for reviews of the legal history of homosexuality). By the beginning of the 19th century, all male homosexual activity, public or private, was illegal.

It has been said of the United States that the number and breadth of statutes, policies, regulations, and judicial decisions provide the most fervently antihomosexual laws in the western world (Knutson, 1980). Recent efforts by gay rights activists have resulted in localized law reform, but the majority of laws in the United States that address homosexuality clearly maintain the original intent of prohibiting and punishing "unnatural acts and sexual practises." A 1986 decision by the United States Supreme Court gave new life to these sentiments. The Court rejected arguments that Georgia State's statutes against sexual activity defined as sodomy were in violation of constitutional rights of privacy. Laws criminalizing oral and anal sexual activity between heterosexual couples were upheld in this decision.

These young men, though, did not refer to the legal texts of homosexuality as directly as they did to the religious texts. That is not to say the repressive legal atmosphere toward homosexuals did not affect them. The time and location of my study coincided with litigation in a neighboring county that challenged discrimination against homosexuals in the military and in public schools. In *Gaylord v. Tacoma School District* (559 P.2d 1340 [Wash. 1977]), dismissal of a male homosexual teacher was upheld because "his status as a homosexual" was an unquestionable violation of the law (Knutson, 1980, p.7). In another case a male homosexual was unsuccessful in stopping his military discharge. The media attention given to these cases clearly reflected the reality prescribed for homosexuals by law. Gagnon and Simon (1973) have also made this point: "The law is at the center of a good many of the male homosexual's dilemmas because it converts an unchosen condition into a legal disability" (p.161).

The path joining homosexual behavior with criminal behavior is ordained by law. Homosexuality is illegal both as an activity, and consequently, as an identity. The legal restrictions on homosexual activity channeled the young men in this study toward a world in which sexual activity is commensurate with cruising, hustling, and soliciting. These are all illegal acts that forced the expression of their homosexuality into an illegal lifestyle and personhood. A criminal subcultural world has been called into existence to provide access to socially outlawed sex and a safety zone for persons identified as homosexual.

Medicine and Psychiatry

Homosexuality has been perceived as both sinful and criminal. It has also acquired an analytic permanence with pathological implications. The recasting of homosexual behavior in medical terms was informed, as were legal sanctions, by the religious model. Nonprocreative sexual behavior was viewed as sinful and its transformation to a medical pathology was first rationalized by beliefs regarding the loss of semen (Foucault, 1985; Bullough, 1976). Eventually it came to be understood that only a sick person would engage in nonprocreative sexual behavior.

The psychogenic perspective on homosexuality led to its objectification as a clinical entity and subsequent subjection to psychotherapeutic treatment. Theoretical developments in this area have been directed toward etiology, which in turn suggests appropriate therapy. Medical and psychiatric definitions of homosexual activity have many implications for scientific inquiry and for individual homosexuals, not the least being the variety of change therapies homosexual individuals have been subjected to. They have ranged from hormone and aversion therapy to various forms of psychotherapy. As has been found repeatedly, there is no "cure" for homosexuality (Ross, Rogers, & McCullough, 1978; Tripp, 1975; Freund, 1977). Scientific research has not produced reliable theories on either the cause or the cure of homosexual behavior. The cultural ideology of homosexuality as an illness, however, still prevails.

Case Studies

David is 16, Caucasian, and describes himself as gay. He has prostituted for six years and feels he will never be able to do anything as well as he prostitutes. David describes his parents as wealthy and strict Catholics. At age 11, he moved to Seattle from out of state to live with his sister. By moving, David was attempting to hide his homosexuality from his parents. He said he was afraid to tell his mother that he was gay because he thought she would want to send him to a psychiatrist. David says "no parents expect their children to turn out gay and if they (the children) do, it is a total shock."

David's sister soon felt she could not be responsible for David and had him placed in foster homes. In one home, David was raped by his foster father. After the incident, David returned to his sister's home and told her of the assault. David said: "The worst thing that ever happened to me was being raped and not being believed."

David's sister decided he needed psychiatric help because his homosexuality could no longer be overlooked. David made one visit to a psychiatrist: "She (sister) did take me to psychiatrist and the psychiatrist said it (homosexuality) was abnormal behavior."

In the example cited above, the young man seemed successful in resisting arguments relating homosexual desires with mental illness. In this case, the young man had been in contact with other gay people who provided an alternative point of view. Although this young man was given competing and more favorable messages by gay friends, I think it would be a mistake to dismiss the power of psychiatric pronouncements in an overall understanding of the self. As we see in continuing case studies, a self-doubt lingered.

Gender Socialization and Social Sex Role

A convention of the gender system of Western society is the triple attribution relating gender, sex role, and erotic preference (Harry, 1982). The perception of effeminate males as homosexuals, and of homosexual males as effeminate, is a corollary to the conventional understanding of sex and gender scripts. The products of research on sex and gender often reflect the assumption that homosexuality is related to deficiencies of masculinity or femininity. Prominent researchers in the field maintain that homosexuality is "rooted in gender incongruity" and that transsexualism, transvestism, and homosexuality are functions of opposite sex identification (Money & Erhardt, 1968, 1972; Green, 1975, 1976, 1980). Several studies by these researchers have found associations between cross-gender role preference in childhood and adult sexual orientation

(Bell, Weinberg, & Hammersmith, 1981; Green & Money, 1966; Green, 1975, 1976, 1980; Lebovits, 1972; Stoller, 1967, 1968).

In the studies cited above, a biological origin for cultural effects is often assumed. Causal links are made between what our culture deems effeminate behavior in males and a potential for homoerotic preference. Of course, a predisposition toward a specific gender role is not necessary or sufficient to predispose one toward a sexual preference. The equation of effeminate behavior in men with homosexuality is, nevertheless, a major principle of the gender system of western society.

Part of the objective reality confronting a young man who is or is to become homosexual, is that effeminate behavior signifies a homosexual preference. Identification with the feminine has a "spillover" effect, meaning that it is a potential source for homosexual identification (Plummer, 1975). Meanings associated with nonconforming sex role behavior are linked with meanings associated with sexual object preference. As the case studies below show, gender confusion may be precipitated by conflicts associated with body image for boys who are smaller than average, or for those who are disinterested in activities dictated to be masculine such as hunting or sports (Saghir & Robins, 1973; Green, 1976; Harry, 1982).

Case Studies

Mark rated himself as not very masculine because: "I'm not very coordinated and not very good in sports." Mark also believed he was less masculine than other males because he did not fight, he liked to play with girls, and he liked to read.

> I guess I was feminine. I was. I had a lot of feminine qualities about me. I'm not saying they were from my mother. It is just that I always had them.

John described himself as not very masculine and felt his parents would have rated him the same. As an after thought he said, "I am just not very good at sports." At one point, John's mother told him: "they were going to knock the woman out of me." John reasoned:

> I guess I was femininish when I was younger. I tended to get along better with girls than with boys. I liked the way women looked and acted. I don't like to be around people who can't be sociable without fighting.

When John was seven he was called a queer at school. He asked his older brother what it meant. He was told it was "someone who acts like a girl or woman." It was then that John said he began to think he was different.

The young men in this study found themselves in conflict with the cultural demands of male sex role behavior. Their innermost feelings ran counter to those prescribed by religious, legal, and medical authority. They began to discover they were different. These differences were translated as sexual differences and from them emerged the self-understanding that they belonged to a stigmatized category: homosexuals (Plummer, 1975).

INTERSUBJECTIVE WORLD OF HOMOSEXUALITY

What is internalized for a young man who has identified himself as a homosexual? Once there is a mutual acknowledgement between a young man and the members of his social world that he is homosexual, he faces implicit condemnation and increasing stigmatization. A hostile and rejecting world unfolds for homosexuals in which the objective understanding they have of homosexuality as unnatural, abnormal, and despised becomes a statement of self-definition. These interactions are particularly influential because they take place within the major socializing contexts for humans, that is family and peers.

Case Studies

Matthew, who was placed in a religiously oriented boy's home following a rape, described the reactions he encountered to his homosexuality:

> I was hassled for being gay. It was terrible. "B" (a friend) and
> I got caught experimenting sexually with each other and it got
> around the boy's home. I was called boof, buttfucker, faggot,
> and queer. I went through 2 years of torment. I was teased and
> punched on. I felt that if I was gay then I would end up being
> beaten up all my life. I was hit on, spit on, had eggs thrown at
> me and shaving cream, all kinds of things happened to me.

After 2 years in the boy's home, Matthew moved back home with
his mother. Her alcoholism and physical abuse continued. At the
same time, he was experiencing more negative reactions to his homosexuality at school.

> My friends were mostly females. Most of the guys called me
> boof. I went out with a lot of girls. As long as I kissed them
> they thought I was straight.

Luke's father told him that queers were the most hated people in
the world. He left school because he was reputed to be a "fag" and
was miserable.

> It's terrible, I was really self-conscious about even walking
> down the street. I didn't like walking down the street because I
> was afraid someone was going to holler "queer," because it
> happened quite a bit. I thought I was gay but I wasn't sure and
> I still had girlfriends and stuff. I was, I guess, feminine, be-
> cause I was around my mother for so long. Just like my hands
> and the way I hold my cigarette and the way I talk.

The young men in this study who identified as gay reported "facing fag patrols" and "faggot beaters" in school. Indeed, a heterosexual control identified himself as part of a "faggot beater" gang.
The young men recalled being afraid to walk down the halls at
school for fear someone would yell "queer." They were afraid to
be on the street because people might recognize them as homosexuals "just by looking at them." One young man stated "I don't
want to look like a screaming queen." Others reported walking by
groups of peers and having them break into chants such as: "He's
gay, stay away, he's gay, stay away."

The responses of families to the homosexuality of their sons ranged from strong condemnation to total rejection, for example "it's disgusting"; "we refuse to accept it"; "we don't want to talk about it"; "that's it, you are leaving." These young men suffered outright rejection from their families and were often literally thrown away as sullied human beings.

The meaning of homosexuality for male prostitutes in this study should be clear by now. They held beliefs about themselves that were similar to those presented to them by their society and culture. The quotes below reflect the ambivalence they had of their homosexual identification and of a developing sense of shame and self-hate.

> I would like to be bisexual, but I find myself being homosexual. I've only had sex with one woman and it did not work out very well. I guess I'm homosexual until I find the right woman.

> I'd rather be heterosexual. I'm bisexual, but I think homosexuality is unnatural. I played a rejection trip on myself after I was raped. I though I might be bisexual. (The young man quoted here described himself as being antigay.)

> I was more worried about being found a homosexual than a prostitute.

> I feel guilty about having sex with men. I don't know why but I just feel guilty.

The case studies illustrate the young men's experiences of stigma and their attempts to manage their "spoiled identity" (Goffman, 1963). Matthew attempted to "cover" his homosexuality by continuing to go out with girls. Luke's reputation was based on selected elements of his behavior that were considered to be signs of his femininity. His feminine behavior became a visible symbol that conveyed social information signifying his sexual preference. All of the young men experienced the phenomenon of others fearing the spread of their stigma through association. Peer relationships were terminated and parents worried about the exposure of younger children to gay siblings.

Goffman (1963) has argued that "the central feature of the stigmatized individual's situation is the pursuit of acceptance." The often desperate and extreme measures that characterize the drive for acceptance gives the stigmatized person a "proneness to victimization." Below I discuss experiences of sexual victimization among male prostitutes.

Sexual History

Studies of female prostitutes have shown strong associations between early sexual victimization and prostitution involvement (James & Meyerding, 1979; James, 1980; Boyer & James, 1983; Silbert, 1980). I expected to find a high incidence of sexual abuse among the prostitutes, but the differences between the groups is stunning (see Tables 1.4 and 1.5). Of the prostitutes, 83% had at least one negative sexual experience in contrast to 12% of the control group. The frequency of abusive incidents in the childhood of prostitutes is remarkably greater than the 2.5% to 8% found in the general population (Finkelhor, 1984).

Table 1.4
Incidence of Sexual Abuse

	One Abuse includes attempts	One Abuse excludes attempts	Two or more abuses excludes attempts
Prostitutes (n=46)	83.0% (n=38)	63.0% (n=29)	52.0% (n=24)
HomP (n=32)	87.0% (n=28)	72.0% (n=23)	60.0% (n=19)
HetP (n=14)	71.)% (n=10)	43.0% (n=6)	36.0% (n=5)
Controls (n=50)	12.0% (n=6)	6.0% (n=3)	2.0% (n=1)

I dropped one HomP case in this table because there were problems with the recording and coding of the responses (n=46 for P and n=32 for HomP).

Table 1.5
With Whom Did You Have Your First Sexual Experience?

	P n=47	C n=50	HomP n=33	HetP n=14
No answer	2.1	0	3	
No sexual experience	0	4	0	
Father/stepfather	2.1		3	
Sister	6.4		3	14.3
Male relative	12.8		18.2	
Female relative	4.3		6.1	
Male acquaintance	21.3	4	30.3	
Female acquaintance	34	86	18.2	71.4
Male stranger	2.1		3	
Female stranger	0	2	0	
Parent's male lover	2.1		3	
Male authority figure	4.3		6.1	
Female authority figure	2.1	4	0	7.1
Customer	6.4		6.1	7.1

The frequency of rape was very high in the prostitute population: 42.6% had been raped once or more; 23.4% had experienced attempted rape. Just over 42% of the homosexual prostitutes had been raped and 21.4% of the heterosexual prostitutes. No rapes occurred among nonprostitutes; 6% reported attempted rapes, however. Both prostitute groups reported being raped by strangers most often, 27.7%; and 12.8% reported being raped by customers. Of those rapes occurring among the prostitutes, only 14.9% were street related. Thus experiences of sexual victimization generally preceded street involvement.

The youths were also asked if they had been molested by someone at least ten years older than they were before their first sexual activity. Of the prostitutes, 29.7% had been molested; 36.3% of the homosexual prostitutes were molested; and 14.2% of the heterosexual prostitutes were molested.

Cultural myths regarding the etiology of homosexuality influence how one interprets the experience of sexual victimization. A cultural myth that is available to all boys, regardless of how fixed their sexual orientation may be, is that a homosexual experience may result in "becoming" a homosexual.[5] This myth is available as a potential source for interpreting experiences and shaping both self-understanding and social identity. Due to the stigma associated with homosexuality, males who have been sexually abused seldom report the abuse. Consequently, they seldom receive the help they need to resolve the incident. But most importantly, the sexually abused possess knowledge and experience other delinquents may not have. They know there is a market for certain kinds of sexual activity.

Case Studies

Mark was molested by an adult male when he was 7. At age 10, he was raped in a group home by a 13-year-old boy, and later by a customer when he was prostituting.

Luke's first sexual experience was at age 8 with a 15-year-old male cousin. At about the same time, he became the focus of attention of two married men who were brothers. They molested Luke, who described it as "playing around." At age 16, Luke was raped by a stranger who grabbed him and threw him to the ground. Luke did not report the assault because he felt: "it wouldn't do any good because I am gay." Luke was also raped by a customer.

John was sexually assaulted at age 15 by an uncle who was a few years older than he. At about the same time, he was forced to have sex with two men at a party. John stated, "I was just too afraid to do anything." He had also been molested by a minister:

> One time I was stuck in town and I went over to his house and I stayed there until morning. At the time I didn't know it (his interest in John) was sexual. He said I could sleep on his bed. He really didn't try anything, he just put my hand on his crotch. I woke up and he had his hand on my crotch I didn't

believe it. I felt picked out as someone who would be willing to do something like that.

David's first sexual experience was as a prostitute with a customer. He was held and drugged by him for three weeks.

Another young man I will call Eddie, was molested at age 9 by a man 23. He reported the incident to his mother, but was disappointed by her response:

> She didn't do nothing. So I went to the police and told them. They came up and questioned him (the offender). He (the offender) said he didn't do nothing, but they took him to jail. My mom bailed him out though. I felt like killing my mom.

In another example, a young man was molested from age 7 to 10 by a stepuncle who was 19. After this relationship, he was abused by his stepfather and described the experience in this way:

> It's just that he was my stepfather and he had oral sex with me, you know, and then he tried to make me do it to him and I just, I don't know what it was. I had never even masturbated before, you know. I already had an aversion toward him because he would always beat me up. He said you can't ever tell anybody and if you were to tell your mother she'd have me arrested. I just kept it inside and I kind of avoided him for awhile and never looked at him for quite awhile. I just kept my eyes downcast all the time. I was always sad anyway when I was younger.

Long-term effects of sexual abuse are linked to prostitution through sexual learning, negative attributions, and psychic trauma. Sexual abuse defeats the developmental process of individuation. Prostitution is an expression of that defeat; it is both a loss of self and an attempt to reassert self-definition (Boyer & James, 1983). It is through sexual violations and stigma that prostitutes were first diminished. And, it is through sexuality that prostitutes attempt to reclaim themselves.

The sexual activity of prostitution can be understood in several ways. One is that prostitutes have failed to achieve the sex role ideal dictated by culture. Male prostitutes have failed as "men." They are homosexual, an ipso facto deviation. If they were heterosexual and abused, they failed to protect themselves and felt the stigma of homosexuality as well. Prostitution may be a compulsive reenactment of the earlier tragedy in which they are trying to regain control of their bodies (Miller, 1984). They are also attempting to create a positive male role. Prostitutes couple their experience with cultural stereotypes of men as virile. As one young man put it: "I can still be a stud on the street corner." The effects of sexual abuse can also be seen in the continued victimization of young men once they are involved in prostitution.

Subculture

The increased number of adolescent males prostituting may be related to the greater influence of the gay community. In contemporary times it has become possible to organize one's entire life around the facts of homoerotic sexual orientation. Homosexuality, or "being gay," is more often referred to as a lifestyle than an individual condition (Humphreys & Miller, 1980). Partially due to the successes of the homophile movement, the homosexual subculture provides not just sexual partners, but a total identity. Foucault (1980) has referred to the phenomenon of gay people developing their own sense of identity and consciousness as "reverse discourse":

> Homosexuality began to speak on its own behalf, to demand that its legitimacy of "naturality" be acknowledged, often with the same vocabulary, using the same categories by which it was radically disqualified. (p.101)

The next significant event that put the young men closer to involvement in prostitution was their initial association with other gay people and their subsequent exposure to the "public territories" of male homosexuality (Read, 1980). There are specific factors that determine in which subset of the homosexual subculture adolescent male prostitutes will participate. The adolescents in this study were isolated and did not form private support networks of gay friends. They had to resort to the public territories of homosexuality, the streets in particular, in order to interact with other gay people. They were, in fact, channeled to public arenas. Their age excluded them from other avenues of interaction with gays such as bars and baths. They were neither aware, nor sophisticated enough to join the homophile movement if there had been an access point, which there was not. Thus, as we shall see, their introduction to gay life was through the hustling market found on the street and in youth discos that catered to gay adolescents and resembled adult gay bars.

Case Studies

Mark was introduced to gay life at age 13. He was living in a group home in Seattle and had dropped out of school:

> I had heard all about it. I was doing a little discovery and just came downtown. I saw all those drag clothes there. I didn't understand it then. But I was curious.

One month later Mark prostituted. He said he had thought about doing it and had imagined a prostitution scenario:

> About how much they got paid and stuff and me saying something like 25 or 40 bucks. Cause I didn't know how much to ask before. I was a square.

Another hustler told Mark that $25 was too cheap. Mark started "getting hep." He first prostituted in a motel with a friend who had "caught a trick." After this incident Mark said he prostituted again because of the money; he was tired of being broke. But there were other reasons:

> It was mostly to be around other gays. I mean that's the way gays did.

I asked David if he knew any gay people that were not involved in hustling. His response was:

No, well yes, but I mean yes and no because I think that every gay person that there is, is in some kind of prostitution. You know maybe that's not true, but I think everybody experiences it at least once. Maybe not on the street, it could be in the richest house in Beverly Hills, but I can't get into those fences.

Matthew discovered the corner downtown while on a bus. He saw people on the street and decided "this is what I am."

Matthew's experience is representative of other young men in the study. The only way they knew to meet other gay people was through contact with tricks (customers), other youth who were also prostituting, and in the gay youth discos, which were a shallow cover for prostitution activity. One young man estimated that 75% of the kids that went to one disco were involved in prostitution: "It was like everybody. All the hookers went there. Whenever they get off work or whatever you want to say."

Some young men reported not knowing *any* other gay people except tricks:

How did you meet other gay people?
I don't think that I ever had (known) any.

PROSTITUTION

Prostitution provides an identity and mode of conduct that corresponds with the cultural image of the male homosexual. The image of the homosexual is one of distorted and exaggerated sexuality, of promiscuity, and deviance. This image has unfortunately been reinforced with public discussion of homosexual lifestyles resulting from the AIDS epidemic. Within this image one finds consistency with conventional versions of male sexuality plus a deviant lifestyle to accompany the prescribed status of the vilified homosexual.

The male prostitutes in this study took on the world and identity of prostitution because it provided a coherent context linking objective understanding of homosexuality with subjective experience in the social action of prostitution. Given the constraints of their situation: family rejection, sexual exploitation, and homosexual stigma, prostitution made sense. The elation of self-recognition could be heard in the response of one young man's description of his first exposure to gay hustlers: "Yes, this is what I am." They were no longer outcasts, but stars. Male prostitutes "practiced" being gay. As prostitutes, they enacted the myths and reflected the images of stigma they had learned.

The continuity provided by prostitution bonds male prostitutes to the subculture. It may be equated with Berger and Luckman's (1967) example of revolutionary socialization of an individual to a counter-reality. But, as any revolutionary knows, it is an identity that is difficult to maintain. Enthusiasm wanes, intensity falls, and loneliness sets in as opposition by the dominant culture becomes overwhelming. The cases studied show the initial exhilaration of street life and street companions falling short as a permanent solution for the adolescent gay male. The young men found themselves coping with the added stigma of prostitution.

Case Studies

Matthew prostituted daily for 6 months. Prostitution was his primary means of support. His drug usage increased as he needed to "take his mind off his problems." As time went by, Matthew became more depressed and suicidal. He was hospitalized once after slashing his wrists. Later, he was placed in a youth shelter, but went back to the streets.

Matthew met a man in his late twenties at a gay disco. They had a brief sexual affair that turned into a nonsexual friendship. The man became Matthew's friend and gave him a place to stay and financial support contingent upon Matthew quitting prostitution. The last I heard about Matthew, he had stopped prostituting and his drug use was declining.

> I would only do it now if I was really desperate. It (prostitution) really does something to you.

Mark prostituted daily from 8 pm until 6 am for a year. He said he hoped for companionship. Like many male prostitutes he thought he could find a relationship through prostitution. He would often fall in love with his tricks only to be disappointed:

> In the beginning prostitution was easy. It was sort of romantic, if I was attracted to somebody. [And] prostitution is addicting because you can get the money so fast.

> At times it does get sort of rough. There were pimps, and I would butch it up (act more masculine) to protect myself. So many things happened.

Luke didn't think prostitution would affect his life. At first he prostituted to "be with other gays." Luke said: "I loved the sex," but then his feelings began to change.

> I enjoyed sex (with friends he found on the street), but I never really enjoyed sex with the tricks. I just lay there, whatever they want they get.

Luke has tried to get jobs, but he keeps going back to the street. He's afraid he is trapped:

> I've been through a lot of emotional trauma. I feel like I will have a nervous breakdown one of these days. Like yesterday, I just sat down and thought of prostitution. I thought I am a prostitute. I am doing all those things. I sat there and I just started to shake. Then I got up and started working and I was fine. I am quite capable of turning my feelings off and on, you know.

CONCLUSION

I have not been able to discuss all the varied dimensions of prostitution. I have chosen to focus on male prostitution as a cultural phenomenon that is produced from cultural constructions of sex and gender. I have attempted to make homosexual prostitution intelligible by analyzing it as a product of culture. In so doing, I have tried to show how involvement in prostitution makes sense to a young man who is trying to understand what it means to be a homosexual in American culture. My analysis of the social and cultural interactions of male prostitutes has identified their inner feelings of contradiction and their discovery of differentness. This differentness was translated as a sexual difference that led to this self-understanding: What was being said about homosexuality was being said about them.

Self-recognition as a homosexual was in some respects the male prostitutes' own analysis of the cultural system. They tried to make sense of themselves in the world, to answer questions about who they were and what kind of social life was available to them. Their answers were found in one particular sexual subculture, the public territories of male homosexuality. It was within the subculture that male prostitutes found the potential for "wholeness" (Read, 1980). It was here that hustling and prostitution were grasped as part of their reality. The subculture provided both an identity and social interactions that allowed male prostitutes to organize their lives and to find ways to survive psychologically and materially.

The lives I have described are sad ones, but not hopeless ones. My ongoing research includes an analysis of the exit process from street life and the impact of social services directed toward street youth (Boyer, 1986b). In this study, I recently interviewed a 16-year-old black, gay, male who had prostituted for 2 years. During the interview we discussed the counseling he had received from gay staff and recent changes in his life. I asked him what he had learned about himself. He said: "I learned I was a *nice* gay person."

NOTES

1. Uniform Crime Reports are most useful when used as indicators of trends in illegal behavior and not as actual incidents of those behaviors. The reported number of males under age 18 who were arrested for prostitution increased between 1969 and 1978 from 236 to 981 (315%). Between 1974 and 1983, reported arrests went from 742 to 691 showing a 6.9% decrease. Arrests for 1983 show a rise again with 891 arrests. Since 1978 arrests have remained relatively stable with no increase or decrease comparable to the dramatic rise seen between 1969 and 1978.

2. The homosexual preference of the prostitute sample, in contrast to the dominant heterosexual orientation of the control group, suggested that the latter was in some ways an irrelevant comparison group. I did attempt to identify a subsample of youth who were both gay and delinquent through the juvenile system, the gay community, and street contacts. Delinquent gay youths who were not involved in prostitution were extraordinarily difficult to find. I did succeed in interviewing two such youths. Their delinquent involvement was minimal and their problems had been resolved through familial acceptance of their homosexuality. Although

the control group selection may be criticized, I believe it underscores the importance of a homosexual identity as a constraint upon one's reality and options, and its relationship to prostitution. In addition, the data collected from the group of prostitutes, and the interpretations I made, could very well stand alone without the contrast of a control group.

3. I had been told by Seattle police that there were no Native American males known to be involved in prostitution. Also, between 1970 and 1980 there was a 65.4% increase in the population of Native Americans, Eskimos, and Aleuts in the Seattle area (United States Census, 1970, 1980).

4. Another point needs to be made regarding the use of the categories of sexual orientation. I have collapsed the homosexual and bisexual categories together. This is an approach commonly found in studies of homosexuality. It has also been soundly criticized because it implies that homosexuality is a homogenous category and that sexual orientation is a polarized and immutable state (De Cecco, 1981). I may be "less guilty" in my use of these categories than others, because according to De Cecco, I did use the Kinsey scale to form the categories, which recognizes the interrelated dimensions of both homosexuality and heterosexuality (De Cecco, 1981; Bell & Weinberg, 1978). I may be faulted for apparently ignoring the diversity of sexuality by dichotomizing the sample into groups of homosexuals and heterosexuals, but more so for apparently suggesting that bisexuality is the same as homosexuality. My response to this potential criticism is that this is not a study of natural categories, but of cultural ones. Whether one's self-definition as a homosexual is biological or cultural, any homosexual experience has the potential of influencing how one's identity may be constructed. I concur with De Cecco's criticisms, but I will argue that individuals draw upon the existing cultural categories in their attempts to gain a self-understanding. To be either homosexual, bisexual, or the victim of a homosexual assault in this culture, is to be suspect of an aberration. This is evident in the experiences these groups shared. On the basis of these shared experiences and self-perceptions, the category homosexual includes those young men who perceived themselves to be bisexual or homosexual.

5. Correlations linking abuse with adult homosexuality should not be interpreted as a cause-and-effect relationship that results in adult homosexual preference. Seventy percent (n = 23 of 33) of the homosexual prostitutes had their first sexual experience with a male. It is tempting to suggest that this initial experience, whether forced or not, may be the "cause" of their present homosexual orientation. While many of the young men state that they had strong feelings for males at a very early age, I did not ask specifically if their homoerotic interest had preceded their first sexual experiences. Some other studies shed light on this issue, however. Simari and Baskin's (1982) study of incestuous experience within a male and female homosexual population, indicated that almost all of the male subjects had identified themselves as actively homosexual before their incestuous experience. They conclude that the sexual learning that takes place during a homoerotic experience may only influence one whose orientation is not firmly established, but otherwise may not "cause" homosexuality. Bell and Weinberg's study (1978) of homosexual males indicates that only 5% reported childhood sex-

ual experiences with adults. The issue is not one of early homoerotic victimization causing homosexuality, but of how abused individuals interpret the meaning of that experience. Finkelhor (1984) found that boys victimized by older men were in fact 4 times more likely to engage in homosexual activity as adults than nonvictims. This relationship, however, did not hold for boys who engaged in peer homosexual activity. It was true only when the partner was much older, which increases the likelihood of long-term traumatic effects (Finkelhor, 1984). Bell et al. (1981) also argue that homosexuality is not the result of atypical sexual experience. The feelings of individuals toward homosexual activity was more significant in signaling adult sexual preference than homosexual activity alone (Bell et al., 1981). The heterosexual prostitutes in my study behaved according to the erroneous assumption that they must be homosexuals because of their homoerotic experience.

REFERENCES

Allen, D. (1980). Young male prostitutes: A psychosocial study. *Archives of Sexual Behavior, 9*(5), 399-426.

Bell, A.P., Weinberg, M.S., & Hammersmith, S.K. (1981). *Sexual preference: Its development in men and women.* Bloomington: Indiana University Press.

Berger, P., & Luckman, T. (1967). *The social construction of reality.* Garden City: Doubleday.

Bloch, I. (1909). *The sexual life of our time.* London: William Heineman.

Boyer, D. (1986a). Male prostitution: A cultural expression of male homosexuality Doctoral Dissertation, University of Michigan. (University Microfilms International No. 8613141).

Boyer, D. (1986). *Street exit project.* Final report to Department of Health and Human Services. (Grant No. 90-CY-0360). Washington, DC: Office of Human Development Services.

Boyer, D., & James, J. (1983). Prostitutes as victims: Sex and the social order. In D.E.J. MacNamara & A. Karman (Eds.), *Deviants: Victims or victimizers* (pp. 109-146). Beverly Hills, CA: Sage Publications.

Bullough, V. (1976). *Sexual variance in society and history.* New York: John Wiley & Sons.

Caukins, S.E., & Coombs, N. (1976). The psychodynamics of male prostitution. *American Journal of Psychotherapy, 30,* 441-451.

Coombs, N. (1974). Male prostitution: A psychosocial review of behavior. *American Journal of Orthopsychiatry, 44,* 782-789.

Craft, M. (1966). Boy prostitutes and their fate. *British Journal of Psychiatry, 112,* 1111-1114.

Crompton, L. (1976). Homosexuals and the death penalty in colonial America. *Journal of Homosexuality, 1,* 277-293.

Cory, D. (1951). *The homosexual in America.* New York: Castle Books.

Cory, D., & LeRoy, J.P. (1963). *The homosexual and his society: A view from within*. New York: Citadel Press.

De Cecco, J.P. (1981). Definition and meaning of sexual orientation. *Journal of Homosexuality, 6*(4), 51-67.

Deisher, R., Eisner, V., & Sulzbacker, S. (1969). The young male prostitute. *Pediatrics, 43*, 936-941.

Ellis, H. (1912). *The taste of social hygiene*. London: Constable.

Ellis, H. (1936). *Studies in the psychology of sex: Vol. 2. Sexual inversion*. New York: Random House.

Finkelhor, D. (1984). *New theory and research*. New York: Free Press.

Fisher, B., Weisberg, K., & Marotta, T. (1982). *Report on adolescent male prostitution*. San Francisco, CA: Urban and Rural Systems Associates.

Foucault, M. (1980). *The history of sexuality: Vol. I. An introduction*. New York: Vantage Books.

Freud, S. (1905). Three essays on the theory of sexuality (1st ed.). New York: Basic Books.

Freund, K. (1977). Should homosexuality arouse therapeutic concern? *Journal of Homosexuality, 2*, 235-240.

Gagnon, J., & Simon, W. (1973). *Sexual Conduct*. Chicago: Aldine.

Ginsburg, K. (1967). The meat rack: A study of the male homosexual prostitute. *Journal of Psychotherapy, 21*, 170-185.

Goffman, E. (1963). *Stigma: Notes on the management of a spoiled identity*. Englewood Cliffs, NJ: Prentice-Hall.

Green, R. (1975). *Sexual identity conflict in children and adults*. New York: Basic Books.

Green, R. (1976). One-hundred ten feminine and masculine boys: Behavioral contrasts and demographic similarities. *Archives of Sexual Behavior, 5*, 425-426.

Green, R. (1980). Patterns of sexual identity in childhood: Relationship to subsequent sexual partner preference. In J. Marmor (Ed.), *Homosexual behavior* (pp. 255-266). New York: Basic Books.

Green, R., & Money, J. (1966). Stage-acting, and effeminate impersonation during boyhood. *Archives of General Psychiatry, 15*, 535-538.

Harry, J. (1982). *Gay children grow up: Gender culture and gender deviance*. New York: Praeger.

Hirschfeld, M. (1936). *Sexual anomalies and perversions*. London: F. Aldor.

Hooker, E. (1967). The homosexual community. In J. Gagnon & W. Simon (Eds.), *Sexual deviance* (pp. 167-184). New York: Harper & Row.

Humphreys, L. (1970). Tearoom trade: *Impersonal sex in public places*. Chicago: Aldine Press.

James, J. (1980). *Entrance into juvenile prostitution*. Final report to the National Institutes of Mental Health (Grant No. 29968). Seattle, WA: University of Washington, Department of Psychiatry and Behavioral Sciences.

James, J., & Meyerding, J. (1979). Early sexual experience as a factor in prostitution. *Archives of Sexual Behavior, 7*(1), 31-42.

Katz, J. (1976). *Gay American history: Lesbians and gay men in the USA*. New York: Thomas Y. Crowell.

Kinsey, A.C., Pomeroy, W.B., & Martin, C.E. (1948). *Sexual behavior in the human male*. Philadelphia: W.B. Saunders.

Knutson, D.C. (1980). Homosexuality and the law: Introduction. *Journal of Homosexuality, 5*, 5-23.

Lebowitz, P. (1972). Feminine behavior in boys: Aspects of its outcome. *American Journal of Psychiatry, 128*(10), 103-109.

Leznoff, M., & Westley, W.A. (1956). The homosexual community. *Social Problems, 3*, 256-263.

Litvinoff, S.I., (Producer). (1968). *The Queen*. [documentary film]. New York: Grove Press, Film Division. Cinema.

MacNamara, D.E.J. (1965). Male prostitution in an American city. A pathological or socioeconomic phenomenon. *American Journal of Orthopsychiatry, 35*, 204.

Marmor, J. (1980). Overview: The multiple roots of homosexual behavior. In Marmor, J. (Ed.), *Homosexual behavior: A modern reappraisal* (pp. 3-22). New York: Basic Books.

Marotta, T. (1981). *The politics of homosexuality*. Boston: Houghton Mifflin.

Masters, W.H., & Johnson, V.E. (1979). *Homosexuality in perspective*. Boston: Little Brown.

Millers, A. (1984). *Thou shalt not be aware: Society's betrayal of the child*. New York: Farrar, Straus, Giroux.

Money, J., & Ehrhardt, A.A. (1968). Prenatal hormonal exposure: Possible effects on behavior. In R.P. Michael (Ed.), *Endocrinology and human behavior* (pp. 32-48). Oxford: Oxford Medical Publications.

(1972). *Man and woman, boy and girl: The differentiation and dimorphism of gender identity from conception to maturity*. Baltimore: Johns Hopkins University Press.

Plummer, K. (1975). *Sexual stigma: An interactionist account*. London: Routledge & Kegan Paul.

Read, K. (1980). *Other voices: The style of a male homosexual tavern*. Novato, CA: Chandler & Sharp.

Rechy, J. (1977). *The sexual outlaw: A documentary*. New York: Grove Press.

Reiss, A.J., Jr. (1961). The social integration of queers and peers. *Social problems, 9*(2), 102-120.

Ross, M. (1978). Stigma, sex and society. *Journal of Homosexuality, 3*, 315-330.

Saghir, M.T., & Robins, E. (1973). *Male and female homosexuality: A comprehensive investigation*. Baltimore: Williams & Wilkins.

Silbert, M. (1980). *Sexual assault and prostitution: Phase one*. Washington, DC: National Institutes of Mental Health.

Simari, G.C., & Baskin, D. (1982). Incestuous experience within a homosexual population: A preliminary study. *Archives of Sexual Behavior, 11*(4), 329-344.

Stroller, R.J. (1967). It's only a phase: Femininity in boys. *Journal of the American Medical Association, 201*, 98-99.

Stroller, R.J. (1968). *Sex and Gender: Vol. 1. On the development of masculinity and femininity*. New York: Science.

Tripp, C.A. (1975). *The homosexual matrix*. New York: McGraw-Hill.

Weeks, J. (1977). *Coming out: Homosexual politics in Britain from the nineteenth century to the present*. London: Quartet Books.

Weeks, J. (1979). *Sex, politics, and society: The regulation of sexuality since 1800*. London: Longman.

Weeks, J. (1981). Inverts, perverts, and maryannes: Male prostitution and the regulation of homosexuality in England in the nineteenth and early twentieth centuries. *Journal of Homosexuality, 6*(1/2), 113-133.

Gay Youth and AIDS

Douglas A. Feldman, PhD

Kew Gardens, New York

SUMMARY. Gay male teenagers face considerable adversity during their "coming out" process due to the AIDS epidemic. They must decide whether to be tested for HIV-1 infection, whether to postpone sexual activity, how to select a partner, and which kinds of sexual practices to engage in. Gay youth often make such decisions based upon misinformation and faulty premises. This paper reviews what is known about gay youth and AIDS, and assesses their possible risk for HIV-1 infection. It is recommended that school and community-based health education programs be developed to teach gay and bisexual youth about safe sex. Moreover, research is needed into sociocultural variations among gay youth in order to develop appropriate and effective intervention strategies for AIDS risk reduction in this diverse population.

I can't imagine what it must be like to be a gay teenager today. I had my street culture. Then, it was okay to hang out on the

Dr. Feldman is a medical anthropologist, international health consultant for AIDS programs, and Chairperson of the AIDS and Anthropology Research Group of the American Anthropological Association. He is the founder and former Executive Director of the AIDS Center of Queens County, Inc. He has conducted AIDS research in New York City and in Rwanda, and is the co-editor of *The Social Dimensions of AIDS: Method and Theory*.

The author would like to thank especially Dr. Ralph DiClemente of the Alpha Institute, San Francisco; Dr. Gilbert Herdt of the Committee on Human Development, the University of Chicago, and Mr. Al Jensen of the Howard Brown Memorial Clinic, Chicago, for their assistance in the completion of this paper. He would also like to thank Phyllis Feifer for her secretarial services. This paper was accepted for publication in February 1987.

Correspondence and requests for reprints may be addressed to the author at 84-47 Abingdon Road, Kew Gardens, NY 11415.

street. Sex was social then. Now it's a social disease. . . . when I was young, sex was fun. I'm glad I'm not a kid now.

Harvey Feinstein, quoted in the *New York Native*, January 19, 1987 (Grubb, 1987).

It was the best of times, it was the worst of times,. . . . it was the spring of hope, it was the winter of despair. . . .

Charles Dickens, *A Tale of Two Cities*, 1859 (Dickens, 1927).

In the late 1970s and early 1980s, it appeared that sociocultural change in America had led to a major shift in the relationship between gay men and the dominant heterosexual society. Anita Bryant was increasingly seen as a buffoon in the mass media and public opinion. Homosexuality was no longer seen as pathological by mental health professionals. The rise and proliferation of gay newspapers, directories, political organizations, legal services, bars, hotels, resorts, and other businesses of various kinds led to the emergence of an infrastructure within the gay community seen only among the most well-entrenched American ethnic groups. Gay had become good in the minds of many gay Americans, and an acceptable alternative lifestyle in the minds of millions of heterosexual men and women.

Then came AIDS. It initially appeared that only gay men living in the "fast lane" were susceptible — the gay baths crowd who had many different sexual partners and used nitrite inhalants and other drugs. By 1982, many gay men in New York City began to decrease their use of nitrite inhalants ("poppers"), their number of sexual partners, and their practice of engaging in receptive anal sex (Feldman, 1985, 1986). Other groups (Haitian-Americans, intravenous drug users, hemophiliacs, and recipients of blood transfusions) were found to develop the disease as well. However, except for the gay press, little was reported to the general public about the disease. By May 1983, at a time when the number of AIDS cases was doubling every 6 months in the United States, the mass media broke the story to the public. It remained front-page news for several days in newspapers and magazines and on radio and television.

Relatively little was known about AIDS at the time, and researchers could not entirely rule out the possibility that the disease could be casually transmitted. Some segments of the press, especially the supermarket tabloids, exploited this growing fear, emphasizing the notion of casual transmission of AIDS while labeling it a "gay plague." Physicians and nurses were commonly shown wearing gloves and masks when visiting their hospital AIDS patients. Male homosexuals, who in the past had been seen by the wider society as sinners, criminals, or mentally ill, were now being seen as diseased and dangerously infectious. The homophobia and anti-gay bias which had begun to wane in the United States was re-emerging under the guise of this growing fear of AIDS.

Even now, when researchers know that AIDS is caused by a sexually transmissible virus and cannot be casually transmitted, anti-gay violence (usually by heterosexual teenagers) continues to escalate, and gay men increasingly find some of their heterosexual acquaintances keeping their physical and psychological distance. Federal policies of discrimination against human immunodeficiency virus, type one (HIV-1) infected persons in the military, Department of State, and the Job Corps has encouraged this social climate. Initiatives by fringe political groups bring to the forefront the issue of quarantining millions of HIV-1 infected Americans.

Within this context, male teenagers with homosexual orientations today face considerable adversity during their "coming-out" process. Not since the mid-1960s have so many obstacles been placed in the path of gay youth during the formation of their gay identity and self-esteem. It appears that as result of the AIDS epidemic, many gay male adolescents are delaying the development of their gay identities and postponing homosexual relationships (Herdt, 1986). Denial of same-sex orientation is often easier for gay youth to cope with than the hostility, stigma, and possible terminal illness facing gay men.

Paul A. Paroski, Jr., a pediatrician who has worked with gay and bisexual adolescents in New York City, reported that for those who do "come out" during their teenage years, there is often a different kind of denial: that the AIDS crisis does not apply to them, but only to older gay men (P.A. Paroski, Jr., personal communication, November, 1986). Part of this misinformation derives from a poor understanding of the prolonged latency period of HIV-1. Only 126 out of 28,905 AIDS cases reported to the Centers for Disease Control (CDC) by December 22, 1986 involved people between the ages of 13 to 19, or 0.4% of the total (CDC, 1986). Moreover, only about half (47.9%) of the teenagers with AIDS were gay or bisexual males (Tom Storcher, CDC, AIDS Surveillance, personal communication, December, 1986). While most gay men, especially in the major cities, have undoubtedly been affected by the AIDS-related death or illness of one or more friends or acquaintances, very few gay or bisexual teenagers likely know someone their own age with AIDS or AIDS-related conditions (ARC). To the unwary teenager, it would seem that only older gay men can get AIDS, and that others their own age are perhaps somehow immune to the disease.

Yet HIV-1 is an insidiously slow acting virus with infection to diagnosis now estimated to average nine years. An 18-year old who becomes HIV-1 infected and gets AIDS would not be expected, on the average, to develop symptoms until he is 27. In other words, a better measure of the scope of HIV-1 infection among gay and bisexual teenage males is the AIDS morbidity and mortality rates for gay and bisexual males in their 20s. Here the pattern is entirely different. About one-fifth (6,056 of 28,905, or 21.0%) of all reported persons with AIDS in the United States are in their 20s. This proportion has remained remarkably stable since much earlier in the epidemic (CDC, 1983).

It is not clear how many gay and bisexual male teenagers are HIV-1 seropositive (i.e., carrying the virus and presumably infectious to others). The Hetrick-Martin Institute (formerly the Institute for the Protection of Lesbian and Gay Youth) and Gay and Lesbian Youth of New York, both in New York City, discourage gay youth from taking the serological test for HIV-1 (Joyce Hunter and Damien Martin, personal communication, May, 1986; Stan Isaac, personal communication, October, 1986). Indeed, when it is considered that Gibson (1986) concluded that gay and bisexual youth are three times more likely than heterosexual youth to attempt suicide during their teen years, the ethics of encouraging gay youth to take an anti-HIV-1 test is extraordinarily complicated given that they would have about a one in four chance of developing AIDS in approximately 5 years ("AIDS," 1986).

On the other hand, O'Reilly, Sanders, Ward, Allen, Cates, and Grindon (1986) have shown on data from HIV-1 positive blood donors that positive test results do appear to reduce certain unsafe sexual practices. In gay and bisexual adolescents who do not have a history of attempted suicide or suicidal thoughts, health care professionals should consider the advantages of epidemiologic surveillance, possible reduction of unsafe sexual practices, and health status monitoring of the HIV-1 infected individual. HIV-1 serological testing should then be promoted, provided pretest and posttest counseling is employed and both repeated ELISA and confirmatory Western blot methods are utilized. All tests, of course, must be anonymous or vigilantly confidential.

About half of all gay men in major North American cities with large gay communities are HIV-1 seropositive (34% of a Vancouver sample, 55% of a New York City sample, and 73% of a San Francisco sample) (Jeffries, Willoughby, Boyko et al., 1985; *Morbidity and Mortality Weekly Report* [MMWR], 1985; New York City Department of Health, 1985). A cohort of HIV-1 negative gay and bisexual male teenagers who have unsafe sex only among themselves would remain HIV-1 negative. But even if only one person in the group is HIV-1 positive, the others in the group could become HIV-1 positive very quickly. So the practice by some gay and bisexual teenagers of restricting sexual partners to only those who are about the same age is by no means a guarantee against seroconversion. Furthermore, the common practice by many gay and bisexual teenagers today of restricting sexual partners to only those who look healthy (Mid-Hudson Valley AIDS Task Force, personal communication, October, 1986) is ineffective in screening out HIV-1 positive partners because nearly all HIV-1 infected persons appear to be well. Teenagers tend to be very susceptible to sexually transmissible diseases (Bell and Holmes, 1984). Therefore, it is entirely possible that the sexually active gay and bisexual male teenagers of today have a higher rate of HIV-1 positivity than do gay and bisexual men in their 20s, 30s, and 40s.

Teenagers in general are fairly ill-informed about AIDS and safe-sex practices. Though Price, Desmond, and Kulkulka (1985) report a relationship among high school students between close geographic proximity to cities where AIDS is common and greater knowledge about AIDS, DiClemente, Zorn, and Temoshok (1986) found, in a study of 1,326 high school students in San Francisco, that adolescents have a poor understanding of AIDS and safe-sex practices. Only 60% were aware that using a condom during sex can lower the risk of getting AIDS. Only 66% were aware that it cannot be spread by using someone's personal belongings, and only 68% were aware that you cannot get AIDS by shaking hands. In another study of 58 high school students in the San Francisco area, DiClemente (1986) found that those with the least knowledge of AIDS were, as well as reporting the greatest self-perceived risk of disease, also least likely to seek out AIDS information or discuss AIDS with their family or friends.

Some school districts and municipalities have begun to include AIDS in their high school curricula, but often the material taught is inadequate. In New York City, for example, two 40-minute lessons on AIDS are taught in the 11th grade by specially trained instructors who undergo a 3-hour training program. The lessons are given in the hygiene course and focus on what AIDS is, and on public policy issues relating to AIDS. Clearly, time limitations permit only a superficial discussion of some of the major issues in this multifaceted and highly complex health crisis.

Political considerations also may affect AIDS educational policy. The planned showing in all New York City high schools of a widely acclaimed video by ODN Productions, "Sex, Drugs, and AIDS," was postponed in order to add a statement on the value of virginity (Kornhauser, 1986). The title was also changed to "AIDS: Just Say No." Furthermore, it is unlikely that any school district in the United States is currently prepared to teach junior high and high school students explicitly *how* to have safe sex.

There is no evidence to suggest that gay and bisexual high school students are any less naive about AIDS and safe-sex techniques than are their heterosexual classmates (Stan Isaac, Gay and Lesbian Youth of New York, personal communication, October, 1986). Gay and bisexual adolescents often may not have other gay or bisexual friends, read gay publications, or have access to the same kinds of formal and informal social networks and informational channels that adult gay men usually have (Ralph DiClemente, personal communication, November, 1986). Gay bars and bathhouses, places where gay men can learn about AIDS and safe-sex techniques, are usually closed to gay and bisexual teenagers.

No systematic research ascertaining what gay and bisexual teenagers actually know, or do not know, about AIDS has yet been published (as of January, 1987). Dr. Robert Deisher (personal communication, November, 1986) indicated that some teenage male prostitutes in Seattle told him that they no longer engage in receptive anal sex with their older clients. As mentioned previously, a common myth held by many gay and bisexual teenagers is that if the sex partner is healthy, or appears healthy, then it is all right to have sex with the individual.

Early in the course of the epidemic in New York City, younger gay men (under 30) admitted to being less familiar with the symptoms of AIDS than were older gay men (30 or over) ($p < .05$) (Feldman, 1985). There is no evidence to suggest that this pattern has changed, or that it is not valid for urban areas outside New York City.

It is also likely that this lack of adequate information translates into unsafe sexual practices. While the American gay community has undergone a major social revolution in strongly embracing the condom as a central tool in safer sex encounters (an object of sharp derision only a few years ago), it is not clear if gay and bisexual teenagers are also using condoms in any significant numbers. At the Howard Brown Memorial Clinic in Chicago during the period May-October 1986, 31% of all gay and bisexual men with positive gonorrhea results (rectal and urethral) were under 25 years of age (Al Jensen, personal communication, January, 1987).

The biopsychosocial process of establishing sexual orientation in males takes place well before puberty (Money, 1963). It would certainly be psychologically damaging to the gay individual if his fear of AIDS prevents him from normal homosexual development during his teenage years. On the other hand, the message that sex between males should be practiced safely with condoms and spermicidal lubricants urgently needs to reach all gay and bisexual teenagers.

It has become a matter of wellness or ill-health, of life or death. School- and community-based health education programs directed at gay and bisexual male teenagers need to be developed throughout America to teach them not only *what* is safe sex, but *how* to do it. In a discussion of gay youth, Kogan (1986) adroitly reminded us that "these kids are our [the gay community's] future and we must invest in them."

Research on gay youth and AIDS is needed in order to determine precisely what gay youth do know and do not know about AIDS, and to what extent they are already HIV-1 infected. We need to know more about the sociocultural variation among American gay youth (i.e., ethnicity, socioeconomic status, educational status, residence, and so on) in order to develop socially appropriate and effective intervention strategies for AIDS risk reduction in the various segments of this diverse population.

It is essential that gay-supportive social scientists put aside their laissez-faire attitude toward gay youth, and begin to work with gay youth in carrying out this much-needed research and in formulating AIDS health education and promotion programs. In spite of the inevitable homophobic peer pressure from not so well-meaning colleagues, such work must be done.

REFERENCES

AIDS. (1986, July 5). *Lancet*, p. 51.

Bells, T.A., & Holmes, K.K. (1984). Age-specific risks of syphilis, gonorrhea, and hospitalized pelvic inflammatory disease in sexually experienced U.S. women. *Sexually Transmitted Disease, 11*, 291-295.

Centers for Disease Control. (1983, October 24). *Acquired immunodeficiency syndrome (AIDS): Weekly Surveillance Report*. Atlanta, CDC.

Dickens, C. (1927). *A tale of two cities*. New York: Walter J. Black. (Original work published 1859.)

DiClemente, R. (1986, October). *Adolescents' avoidance of AIDS Information: Counterproductive behavior in the face of a perceived health threat*. Paper presented at the meeting of the American Public Health Association, Las Vegas, NV.

DiClemente, R., Zorn, J., & Temoshok, L. (1986). Adolescents and AIDS: A survey of knowledge, attitudes and beliefs about AIDS in San Francisco. *American Journal of Public Health, 76*, 1443-1445.

Feldman, D.A (1985). AIDS and social change. *Human Organization, 44*, 343-348.

Feldman, D.A. (1986). AIDS health promotion and clinically applied anthropology. In D.A. Feldman & T.M. Johnson (Eds.), *The social dimensions of AIDS: Method and theory* (pp. 145-159). New York: Praeger.

Gibson, P. (1986, June). *Gay male and lesbian youth suicide*. Paper presented at the National Conference on Prevention and Interventions in Youth Suicide, Oakland, CA.

Grubb, K. (1987, January 19). Safe sex with Harvey Fierstein. *New York Native*, pp. 41-44.

Herdt, G. (1986, December). Panel member. Comments at the Symposium on AIDS and Anthropological Research, American Anthropological Association, Philadelphia.

Jeffries, E., Willoughby, B., Boyko, W.J. et al. (1985). The Vancouver lympha-denopathy-AIDS study: Part 2. Seroepidemiology of HTLV-III antibody. *Canadian Medical Association Journal, 132*, 1373-1377.

Kogan, B. (1986, September 15). Investing in our future. *New York Native*.

Kornhauser, A. (1986, December 2). See no evil: The Board of Ed snips gays from an AIDS prevention film. *Village Voice*.

Money, J. (1963). Factors in the genesis of homosexuality. In G. Winokar (Ed.), *Determinants of sexual behavior*. Springfield, IL: Charles C Thomas.

Morbidity and Mortality Weekly Report (MMWR). (1985). Update: Acquired immunodeficiency syndrome in the San Francisco cohort study, 1978-1985. *MMWR, 34*, 573-575.

New York City Department of Health. (1985, April). *The AIDS epidemic in New York City: Surveillance trends. AIDS surveillance team and infection control nurses, physicians, and hospitals of New York City*. Paper presented at the International Conference on AIDS, Atlanta.

O'Reilly, K.R., Sanders, L.L., Ward, J., Allen, J.A., Cates, W., & Grindon, A. (1986, September). *Sexual behavior change after positive HTLV-III antibody tests in blood donors: Report from a longitudinal study*. Paper presented at the meeting of the American Public Health Association, Las Vegas, NV.

Price, J.H., Desmond, S., & Kulkulka, G. (1985). High school students' perceptions and misperceptions of AIDS. *Journal of School Health, 55*, 107-109.

Lesbian and Gay Youth in England

Ken Plummer, PhD

University of Essex

SUMMARY. The experience of being gay and young has been seriously neglected in youth culture research and in youth service provision. This stems in part from the pervasiveness of both the heterosexual assumption and the sexual stigma. Since the advent of the gay movement, however, some modest research into gay youth has been conducted and some has been generated through the activity of gay organizations themselves. This paper reviews the experience and problems of being young and gay in Britain as revealed through three research studies. It outlines some key changes that have occurred during the 1980s, especially the emergence of gay youth organizations. It concludes by suggesting the diversity of the gay youth experience in England.

There is a voluminous literature on youth in England, but an almost total absence of any reference to youthful same-gender desire.[1] Researchers have entered schools, hung around street corners, studied the youth services, and surveyed the workplaces of the young, but amongst their subjects it is hard to find a single lesbian or gay voice. There is a complex documentation of "spectacular"

Dr. Plummer is a lecturer in sociology at the University of Essex.

The author wishes to express his appreciation to Gregg Blachford for his helpful comments on an earlier draft of this article, and his indebtedness to Michael Burbidge, Sharon Bye, Lorraine Trenchard, Jonathan Walters, and Hugh Warren, whose pioneering empirical research on gay and lesbian youth made this paper possible. His greatest debt must be to the young people whose voices are, at last, slowly being heard. A small grant from the Fuller Bequest Fund, University of Essex, assisted in the research for this article.

Correspondence and requests for reprints may be addressed to the author, c/o Sociology Department, University of Essex, Wivenhoe Park, Colchester, Essex, CO4 3SQ, England.

195

youth styles in England since the 1950s: the Teddy Boys, Mods, Rockers, Skinheads, Soccer Hooligans, Hippies, Glamrocks, Punks, New Romantics, Headbangers and Casuals, accompanied by a dense Marxist theorization of these styles, which manages to read them as signs of a working class resistance to the dominant culture.[2] But, again, gay youth are missing. There are even attempts to regain a social history of youth, but it is a history where once more same-gender eroticism continues to be hidden.[3] This absence is all the more serious when it is realized that at least since the 1970s, much of this research purports to be critical and radical. In practice it simply reinforces the centrality of the white, male — and, in this case, working class — world. Only very recently have gender and race been allowed to permeate such research. But still the issue of sexual orientation/identity is missing.[4]

There are a few exceptions. Mike Brake's comprehensive review of youth research does give homosexuality a two-page discussion concluding that "subculture studies of youth never mention homosexuals" (Brake, 1980, p. 152). Likewise a recent overview of youth policy in England does make several passing references to gay youth, only to conclude that they are "simply ignored altogether" (Davies, 1986, p. 111). And some very recent feminist inspired studies of girls have seen lesbianism as an issue and have mentioned it briefly (Griffin, 1985, pp. 58-9; McRobbie & Nava, 1984, p. 86). Otherwise, homosexuality really only appears in two places.

First, most of the literature on youth culture in England is actually about boys and masculinity, not youth at all, and an unarticulated homophobia is a pervasive theme. Youth, indeed, is a masculine construct; "All our images of the adolescent . . . the restless, searching youth, the Hamlet figure, the sower of wild oats, the tester of growing powers — these are *masculine* images . . ." (Hudson, 1984, p. 35). Not only does this lead to the girl largely being defined in the context of the home; it also sets up a standard for boys to achieve. Boys who don't achieve this, and gay boys often don't, become problems (cf. Harry, 1982).[5] Youth culture research documents (and often celebrates) in detail the prowess of being a boy: a toughness, of sport, of sexual bravado, of aggression (Willis, 1976; Wood, 1984); it has also revealed his homophobia. It is probably amongst such boys that "queer bashing" is most likely to emerge (Mungham & Pearson, 1976; Meldrum, 1980). Homosexuality, then, in much research on youth becomes not a topic of legitimate experience in itself, but a pervasive fear that invades the celebration of masculinity.

A second area in which homosexuality appears is a more positive one. For there is one stream of youth style, wavering between the early Mods, the hippies, "glamrock," punk and "gender bending," which has constantly stressed either the weakening of the traditional male role or a sense of androgyny. Since the early days of the Beatles and the Rolling Stones, through David Bowie, and Gary Glitter, and on to Boy George, and Marilyn, the acceptability within one strand of youth culture for boys to be more androgynous and bisexual has become increasingly pronounced.[6] The same has also partially been true of girls. Within this tradition too, some pop stars have been explicitly gay in their act, not just erotically (as many have been), but politically. Most recently, Jimi Sommerville (formerly of Bronski Beat, now of the Communards) has articulated his gayness, both personally and publicly. Earlier, in 1978, Tom Robinson (with his top selling "Glad to be Gay," his explicit talk and his distribution of pamphlets at concerts), served as a very active catalyst for many young people to see gayness. As Stephen, a young gay man in London, said in an interview with Jeffrey Weeks, in the late 1970s:

> I'd just been to a rock concert, 3 or 4 weeks after I started work, by the Tom Robinson Band. I was ever so amazed to read on the front cover of *Sounds*, "GAY POWER," and I thought, that's me. And God, is he really gay . . . and when we went to his concert, he started giving out all these leaflets. I never listened to the songs, I didn't realize what they meant . . . there were all these comments about fascists and anti-Nazi League and all this rubbish again . . . It didn't dawn on me till I got home and read the whole of this thing . . . and right at the top of the leaflet there was Switchboard's number. . . I got so depressed one dinner hour and phoned up. . . [7]

By the mid-1970s, then, gayness was becoming a more conscious presence in the world of youth, even if it hadn't yet entered the minds of social researchers.

Indeed, it is about this time that gay youth in England started to get organized. "Gay Socs" had existed in most polytechnics and universities since the early 1970s, but they only catered to older, and usually, more middle class and *politically correct* youth. In 1975, a youth group within the Campaign for Homosexual Equality (CHE) was formed (publishing for a few years *Youth News*); in February 1976, the London Gay Teenage Group emerged partly as a breakaway group; in 1978, the Joint Council for Gay Teenagers (JCGT) was formed to provide support (mainly from adults) to a range of youth groups that had then come into existence.[8] Such groups not only set up structures to provide support, they also initiated the very first researches into gay young people in England. Both social science and the social services had offered only neglect or prejudice; it was for gay people themselves to initiate the first insights into their own experiences of growing up gay.

GAY YOUTH SPEAKING:
SOME RESEARCH STUDIES

In this article, my prime aim is to consider what it was like to grow up gay in England[9] during the early 1980s. Having previously theorized around this process (Plummer, 1975, 1981a),[10] I plan here to draw upon three exploratory research studies of young lesbians and gay men. All these studies have acknowledged limitations, but they are nevertheless the best information currently available.

In the first study (organized by the Joint Council for Gay Teenagers [JCGT], in 1979), 8 young lesbians and 26 young gay men from throughout England[11] provided unedited accounts of their experience, guided by 19 general questions that ranged from when they first thought they were gay to their experience of antigay abuse. This was the first study of its kind in England and the accounts are both moving, yet curiously predictable. I refer to this as the teenage study (Burbidge & Walters, 1981).

In the second study (funded by the now defunct Greater London Council, organized by Lorraine Trenchard and Hugh Warren, and published by the London Gay Teenage Group), 415 responses (279 male and 136 female) were gathered by a lengthy questionnaire distributed through both the commercial and noncommercial London scene, as well as through friends, during 1983.[12] Most respondents were between 18 and 21 (78%), about one half saw themselves as working class, and about 90% were white (4.5% were Asian, and 5.0% were black). They emerge as a relatively "out" group of young people. I refer to this as the London survey (Trenchard & Warren, 1984).

A final, unpublished undergraduate sociology project by Sharon Bye, solicited 95 life history letters from 55 young gay men and 40 lesbians who lived in isolated areas, all lived at least 15 miles from any gay club or disco, and a little over 25% (27) had no contact with gay people except through letters. The letters were gained from both an informal snowball network linked to a few close friends, and through a magazine for isolated lesbians. Again, about one half of these respondents saw themselves as working class. I refer to this as the Isolates Study (Bye, 1984).

Some Cautionary Caveats

Each of the studies is exploratory, conducted with minimal resources, and very much aware of its limitations. Even the most thorough of them, the London survey, makes it clear that, "We do not imagine that this report constitutes any definitive work on the needs of young lesbians and gay men in London" (Trenchard & Warren, 1984, p. 21). Before considering their limited findings, some general warnings are in order.

First, there are no randomly representative samples in gay research.[13] And what exists in all three of the above studies are samples of youth who are already in some way self-identified as gay and who already belong to some setting (club, friendship network, correspondence magazine) to which researchers have access. Even Bye's "isolates" are not wholly isolated. If they were, then by definition she could not have located them. This means that all the studies only deal, to differing degrees, with the more public, stable and "out" forms of young gay experiences. The more ambiguous, the more isolated, and possibly the more painful experiences, are less likely to enter a researcher's net. There is a whole world of youthful same gender experiences that simply is not discussed by these studies, this article or anybody else, because it remains so deeply hidden. It must be remembered, then, that only *one* pattern of relatively out experience is being discussed.

Secondly, the 1970s and the 1980s have been a period of significant and rapid social change. Not only was the experience of being young and gay completely concealed before the rise of the Gay Movement in the early 1970s, there was also no research to serve as a comparative baseline. Westwood's study (1960) certainly suggests similar phases of coming out as occur today (p. 183), and many of his respondents talk about the homosexual experience at school where 24% of his sample thought it very frequent, and 48% thought it occasional (p. 25). But in general his sample implies that the experience of "becoming gay" was both more secretive and likely to occur later. Generalizations from the early 1980s should neither be used to read back experiences of the past, nor to project the future.

Thirdly, throughout this article I have had a terminological problem. "Gay Youth," "Lesbian Youth," and "Gay Teenagers" will be used as a convenient shorthand, just as they are in the three studies. But I do have serious reservations about the value of such terms. Youth itself is a sociopolitical category of recent invention, and it is known to harbour a plurality of meanings and experiences (Musgrove, 1964; Gillis, 1974). The same is true of "gay" and "lesbian," terms that have useful political functions but analytically hurl together too much diffuse and contrasting experience to be of value (Plummer, 1981). Putting the terms together merely compounds the confusion. Yet they are convenient shorthands, and I will hence be using them.

Finally, there are difficulties in interpreting the comments made by the respondents. It is clear that all their statements were collected through political projects aiming at alleviating the sufferings of young gays and lesbians; they are not neutral, but are necessarily partial and selective. Further, my own selection and rereading of quotations can only render them even more problematic. This issue, the hermeneutics of narratives, is a field of inquiry in its own right, and it cannot be considered here. It means, however, that throughout this article I am engaging in a "naive" reading of those stories.[14]

GROWING UP GAY IN ENGLAND:
THE CONTEXT

The overwhelming feature of growing up gay in English society in the 1980s is still the existence of institutions that are organized around the *heterosexual assumption*: "unless there are very good reasons for thinking otherwise, everybody in our culture will be presumed to be heterosexual," and the *sexual stigma* which, "leads homosexuality to become enmeshed in a network of devaluation, hostility, fear, dread, and even outright loathing."[15]

The iceberg tip of this is legislation: for men, if one of the partners is below 21 then homosexuality is a criminal offence. The law in the U.K. is the most stringent in Europe: in France, for instance, the age of consent is 15, and in Germany, it is 18. Despite the recommendations of a number of prominent organizations[16] that the gay age of consent should be brought into line with either the heterosexual age of consent (16), or the age of majority (18), there are few signs of it being changed. It is true that all prosecutions have to be taken to the Director of Public Prosecutions, and that he can exercise substantial discretionary power, and that in practice many young people are not prosecuted (Crane, 1982).[17] But it nevertheless remains the case that the law hangs ominously and omnipresently over the heads of many gay males. As a Howard League Working Party on Sex Law Reform recently put it:

Because an open admission of sexual activity is effectively an admission of crime, this inhibits youth from confiding in parents, or seeking information or counseling elsewhere, encourages youth organizations to ignore the needs of young homosexuals, or to pretend that they do not exist, and prevent gay bars and clubs from welcoming the young who may be seen as jail bait. The result is that many feel unhappy, socially isolated, guilt ridden, and perhaps tempted to look for sex contacts in lavatories or other unsuitable venues. (Howard League, 1985. p. 37)

The case for changing the law has now been made effectively by several groups (cf. note 16), but the law, is only an iceberg tip. It does not, for instance, officially effect lesbians who by all accounts seem to have at least as hard a time as boys. Much more important because more pervasive are the settings of English society through which youth live their lives: families, education, community, media and workplace. For each of these settings works on the experiences of gay youth to structure out even the possibility of being gay. This is true more so of the past than now, and it is clear that many young people manage to become gay in spite of such settings. But, nevertheless, it is these settings that are the central source of problems for gay youth. I will discuss some of these problems in the next section, but here I would like to focus on four major mechanisms at work that organize youthful lives around the heterosexual assumption. These are:

1. The hidden curriculum, which transmits a message about the centrality of family life, clear gender roles and heterosexuality.
2. The absence of role models who are gay or lesbian.
3. The concrete presence of peer relations organized through heterosexuality.
4. The mechanisms of homophobia that serve, in the last resort, to coerce, control, and ultimately punish those who step over the line.

Any young person's life in England can hence be located in a matrix of settings (family, school, workplace, community, television and other media), each of which gives messages, role models, and concrete experiences that "organize out" the plausibility of gayness, and that present ultimate sanctions, should it appear. There is no space here to develop this fully, but I will give some examples from one setting: the school.[18]

Structuring Out Homosexuality in the School

The "hidden" curriculum has been widely discussed in social science, but primarily as a mechanism for reproducing class relations in schools. The most cursory look, however, at school curricula in England makes it clear that whereas standard gender relations are reproduced (Deem, 1980; Stanworth, 1983), issues around same gender experiences are typically excluded. English studies will ignore the homoerotic influences on Shakespeare, or Wilde, or Woolf, and historical studies will ignore the new "gay history." It is not a total exclusion, but in one London study only 35 respondents (out of a total of 416) found that homosexuality was talked about at schools in ways they found helpful, 60% said it was avoided completely; of the remaining 40%, 80 said they did not find the mention helpful (Trenchard & Warren, 1984, Chap. 4). Nevertheless, more recently in 1986, there have been attempts by more radical local authorities to introduce "gay texts" into the classroom, such as Susanne Bosche's *Jenny Lives with Eric and Martin* a tale of a little girl living with her father and his male lover. Such attempts caused much controversy, even a moral panic, but they do signpost some potential changes.

The second mechanism concerns the absence of gay role models. In the United States this has been one of the most controversial areas in gay politics: both in the Dade County decision and the Briggs initiative, the idea of gays acting as role models for youth, especially by being teachers, and thereby either mentally corrupting or physically seducing them, was of central concern (Shilts, 1982). Although such state-wide voting cannot happen in England, a National Council for Civil Liberties survey conducted in 1975 of local education authorities[19] did conclude that discrimination in employment against homosexuals was probably more evident in teaching than anywhere else (except perhaps the highest grades of the civil service) (Daly, 1983, p. 45). It was not so much that teachers have their jobs terminated for simply being gay; it is rather that authorities objected to teachers being "known about" or openly discussing the issue.[20] Yet it is precisely this quality of "being out" that is required in schools if gay teenagers are to have the heterosexual assumption at least punctured, and, more practically, if they are to have access to adults who may help them discuss their gay feelings and develop. Such role models are also absent in families (hence the debate about fostering), in the youth service (hence the debate about gay youth clubs), and in the media (hence the debate about gay-sponsored television programs and so forth).

A third mechanism to structure out homosexuality is less ideological and more concrete: in every setting, the peer groups of gay adolescents come to practice and embody *how youth behaves*. One of the key messages of this culture by the fourth and fifth years of secondary school is that "one should start to go out with the opposite sex." It is one of the key ways of validating ones normality. Some comments from the teenage study show this clearly: As Julie, 16, from Walthamstow said, "it really is horrible at school because everyone keeps on at you about whether or not you have a boyfriend and if not, why not?" (p. 17). Or as Terry, 17, from Croydon said, "No one knew about me, at first, but I soon got a reputation at school, not because I looked or acted queer, but because I never boasted about this girl or that" (p. 51).

Or Germaine, 19, from Hampshire,

> "When, on the odd occasion, I used to be chatted up by one of the boys, I always felt rather embarrassed . . . One of them, John, I think his name was, asked me to go out with him, I was quite upset, and I told him to stop being silly. He got really narked and told his mates I was 'one of those.'" (p. 54)

Such pressures to conform to the heterosexual assumption, of curriculum, of staff, of peers, lead many English gay youth to feel isolated and withdrawn. In the London survey, 25% of those at school experienced this.

Peter, 19, from Leicester said:

> "Between the ages of 13 and 15 I closed myself off from the outside world. I would rarely go out and would never dare to go places where other people of my own age would be. The only thing I knew was that homosexuality was bad." (Burbidge & Walters, 1981, p. 52)

But there is a fourth and final mechanism that comes into force if all else fails, and this entails a direct homophobic response through the harassment of gay youth by teachers and "friends." In the London survey, for example, about half of the respondents had been either beaten-up, teased, verbally abused, or ostracized at school.

Peter continues:

"The biggest shock came when I went to a comprehensive school and discovered words like 'queer,' 'pouf' etc. etc. and realized that I was one of these 'vile, disgusting perverts' and as far as I knew the only one. I was very often physically and mentally bullied at school and several times narrowly escaped violent attacks by some of the 'tough' boys. Because of the abuse, I shut myself off from the outside, not only at school, but at home as well. I began to question myself and wondered if I was ill or abnormal. The sex education talks at school never mentioned homosexuality and I assumed that it was so uncommon it wasn't worth mentioning." (Burbidge & Walters, 1981, p. 52)

As with each of the other mechanisms for structuring out gayness, direct homophobic response occurs in every setting a young person encounters. From mockery and abuse to physical violence; from being rejected by parents to losing one's job; from psychiatric treatment to imprisonment, all these remain distinct possibilities for those who dare to breach the heterosexual assumption.

GROWING UP GAY IN ENGLAND: THE EXPERIENCE

Given these contexts and mechanisms in which gay youth grow up, it is clear that their experiences, at least initially, are likely to be enmeshed in problems. I will examine next some of these problems as they appear in research accounts.

"I Know That I'm Gay . . ."

At the outset, a key theme to emerge in reading these accounts is the overwhelming sense that many young people know they have a preference for their own sex during their early teenage years or even earlier. And this happens in spite of all the socialization they experience that directs them to heterosexuality. Of the 34 accounts provided in the teenage survey, there are only seven who do not make comments like the following:[21] Alan, "I realized when I was 10 or 11 that I was attracted to men but I couldn't put a label on it that time. I finally put a label on it when I was 12 or 13" (Burbidge &

Walters, 1981. p. 7); Elizabeth, "My first homosexual experience was when I was 13, but I'd realized earlier that there was something different" (p. 10); Dermot, "Well, I think I knew I was gay when I was a little boy, but I really knew when I was about 13" (Dermott, p. 11); Peter, "I can remember my first feelings about another boy when I was six or seven in infant school" (p. 12); Paul, "Since about the first year in school I've had some suspicion that I was gay" (p. 14); Glyn, "Never have I felt any heterosexual feelings towards women . . . my first concrete 'gay' experience was when I was eight or nine" (p. 15).

There are, of course, problems with such observations. They may be retrospective interpretation, a reconstruction of the past to fit the present and the future (Plummer, 1981. pp. 67-72). There may be maturation, by which homosexual interest may be transformed a little later in life. And there may be sampling bias, people who respond to surveys of these kinds may constitute a select experience. But all this notwithstanding, such accounts are presented so frequently that I am sure it is valid for a significant portion of homosexual experience. There are certainly many people who grow up in a heterosexual society feeling that they are "really" gay.[22]

Apart from the more obvious problems of direct harassment that confronts many, there are also many more insidious, indirect problems that may be generated. These include a negative self-image, secrecy and isolation, problems of access to like-minded people, and potential suicide.

The Problem of a Negative Self

Gay youth have to grow up with all the negative imagery that surrounds homosexuality. For some this initially means the stereotype serves as a means of distancing oneself from being gay:

> "I knew what homosexual meant, it was an in-joke with the kids I knew. So and so's bent, queer, a pansy, etc. When you're faced with such negative views of gays, it's not surprising that you are filled with terror at the prospect of acquiring a label . . . how could an ordinary girl like myself possibly be one of a group of sick people?" (Cathy, age 18; Bye, p. 29)

But more commonly perhaps the label does slowly come to be taken on and the full weight of hostile meanings can lead to a major trauma:

> "I went through such hell. I thought I was going to have a breakdown. Gradually you attach the label gay to yourself because if you don't you really crack up. I did it gradually after years of torment, but still hated myself for it. Accepting that it could be real was the hardest part of my life. I felt lonely, couldn't turn to anyone through fear of what would happen to me. I didn't know any gays so how could I know that we are just ordinary people. I felt I could only be alone as I wasn't straight but also I wasn't the kind of gay my mates used to laugh and joke about." (Mike, age 19; Bye, pp. 31-2)

As Bye remarks, "In every life history, I was able to discover references to a shared experience of how the young people had grown up viewing gay people. The commonly held view was that homosexuals were 'perverts' and people suffering from mental illness. Every respondent held a negative picture of homosexuals" (Bye, 1984, p. 30).

Many of the comments in the Teenage Survey reveal the same thing: "I was preconditioned like anyone else by things like misrepresentation on T.V." (Alan, 19; p. 7); "I didn't know about the word 'gay' until I was about 18 when I read something about them 'poor, sick people' so I rang Gay Switchboard feeling suicidal, degraded and disgusted with myself" (Michelle, 20; pp. 31-2).

The Problem of Secrecy and Isolation

A second problem was secrecy: "stigma creates silence, ban breeds solitariness" (Plummer, 1984, p. 236). So central is this idea that two of the three research reports that I am quoting from here actually play with this theme in their titles: they are called *Breaking the Silence* (Burbidge & Walters, 1981) and *Something to Tell You* (Trenchard & Warren, 1984). Although young people have a strong sense of their gayness quite early, they initially feel that nobody must find out. Gideon (19) in Bye's (1984) sample put this clearly:

"Most of all my pals and family mustn't ever find out about it. This means no one else can know for fear that it may get back home. I don't want to be cut off from those I care about." (p. 49)

This leads to what I have previously called the paradox of secrecy (Plummer, 1975, p. 194). For as long as stigma leads the experience of gay youth to be kept as a secret, so gay youth will remain invisible. Only once the secrecy is broken down can gay youth become identifiable and bring about social changes that make homosexuality less stigmatized and more plausible. It is precisely such a process that seems to have been happening since the mid 1970s.

The Problem of Access

A third problem was access and availability. For many young people, schools, youth clubs, and the workplace become key locations for finding boyfriends and girlfriends. In contrast, for gay young people, these places are highly alienating as they constantly reinforce their difference and provide no pathways to partners or relevant experiences. Some of these problems are particularly highlighted in the London studies (1984, Chaps. 4-7; Warren, 1985; Trenchard, 1985), but are clearest with Bye's "isolated" group. Although in cities like London, a significant network of gay institutions does exist awaiting discovery by the exploring youth; in smaller towns and rural areas there is nothing on offer. Working on a gay switchboard which covered a fairly rural area, I would often take calls from young people who lived in villages without any major means of transportation and, of course, without much money. If they had either, they could, practically, get to a gay pub or group in a neighbouring city; but a journey of 20 miles or further is not easy for nonmobile, poor, under drinking-age, rural youth.[23] Bye's isolated group however found further difficulties even when a youth had the means to get to a gay pub. Marcus, a driver and 18, says:

"How could I go to X (a local gay disco)? It takes me 45 minutes to drive there and it goes on to 2:00 in the morning. My mum makes me be in by 1:00 a.m. when I go out, and you bet she's up and waiting for me then. I think she sees me as a kid 'cos [sic] I'm at school still. It just isn't worth it all to go to X as it would mean leaving about 12:00 a.m. just to be on the safe side! The disco is just about hotting up then!'' (Bye, pp. 59-60)

Other Problems

I have only highlighted a few of the most general problems that gay youth face. There are many others. For instance, the negative self-image and worry may be so extreme as to lead to thoughts of attempting suicide. Indeed, in the London survey, nearly 1 in 5 had made a suicide attempt; in the Bye's survey of isolates, it was nearly 2 in 5; and in a survey conducted by Parents Enquiry[24] in 1982, some 55% had made a suicide attempt. These are desperate acts and worrying figures that have been indicated in other research studies too (Rofes, 1983). They highlight very concretely just how painful it can be to come to identify oneself as gay in a society that has structured out the possibility and the plausibility of being so.

SOCIAL CHANGE AND "COMING OUT"

So far I have indicated how the heterosexual assumption is at work, both in research and in the everyday settings of youth, and how this can generate enormous problems for young people who sense that they may be gay from quite early ages. Yet the story in England is not quite as pessimistic as this would make it appear. For throughout all the studies there are clear signs that gay youth do not passively accept this suffering and condemnation, but instead make very active paths to construct a gay identity, to enter a gay world, to work for acceptance, and even challenge the heterosexual assumption.

For example, family life is initially painful. But a lot of young people eventually come to tell somebody in their family that they're gay, 284 or 70% of the London survey (51% were "out" to all their family; 21% were "out" to mother alone; but only 1.4% had come "out" to their father alone). The initial response can be good and reasonable (in some 42% of these stories), but it is often bad. Nevertheless, even in cases of negative response there does appear to be a cycle of acceptance by which after a period of time, parents may gradually come to understand more.[25]

Likewise, in schools it seems to have become increasingly possible for gay youth to let others know about their homosexuality and often to be accepted. In the London survey, for example, the authors comment:

> Despite the lack of support and information in schools, the majority of our sample were confident enough about their sexuality to be open about it with at least some of their peers. Fifty-seven percent[26] said that their school friends knew that they were homosexual and 32% said that their teacher knew. (Trenchard & Warren, 1984, p. 62)

One boy, Chris, 18, in the Teenage Survey, captured this alternative view:

> I'm still at school, doing A levels. I get on well with people and like keeping in touch with people. A lot of people at school know I'm gay and there's general gossip. I've taken boyfriends to straight discos. The school is a grammar, gone comprehensive. I even put a lamda badge and a "Glad to be Gay" badge on my pencil case. There's no hostility at school, (Burbidge & Walters, 1981, p. 33)

In some of these accounts, friends and teachers offer support (Rosemary, p. 42). Indeed, since 1974 there has been an active Gay Teachers Group, which campaigns on behalf of such students and teachers.

There are signs, then, that by the early 1980s many young people were finding it easier to come out, to themselves, to others, and to the organized gay community, than was possible in earlier decades. The growth of Gay Switchboards played a particularly prominent role in this. By February 1979, possibly 1 in every 500 males, aged

14 to 20 was contacting a Switchboard (JCGT, 1980, p. 1). That number has probably continued to grow since then,[27] as Switchboards have become more and more part of the national landscape.[28] (Sixty-three percent of the London Survey had contacted a switchboard or advisory service at some stage [Trenchard & Warren, 1984, p. 114].) Nigel captures the importance of this experience:

> After phoning (Alec) in London, I felt as though a whole weight had been taken from me. There was hope for me, gays are just ordinary people living boring lives in boring places. I began to feel that I wasn't so evil after all. I'm just a kid who wants a man not a woman to share life with. The only way I differ (as I see it now) from straights is by my sexual needs. Too big an issue is made out of sex, any young person knows that, straight or gay. (Bye, 1984, p. 35)

Another significant development has been the emergence of Gay Youth Organizations, youth switchboards, youth clubs, and the Lesbian and Gay Youth Movement. The latter national organization is explicitly political and holds meetings and social events, including an annual conference and summer camp. It publishes a regular magazine. Other groups tend to be more social, providing alternatives to both the commercial gay scene and the heterosexual youth services. In mid-1986, for example, there were 15 social groups for lesbians and young gays in London, and 21 groups outside of it. Many got funding from their local authorities, and there were signs of official support from bodies such as the National Association of Youth Clubs and the National Youth Bureau (London Gay Teenage Group, 1982; Kent-Haguley, 1982, 1984). This is a wholly new development, allowing gay and lesbian youth to "come in from the cold." Trenchard and Warren have documented the positive responses of young people at these clubs:

> I phoned Gay Switchboard and explained how I felt, that I was down in the dumps, and they gave me the number for the Gay Teenage Group. I phoned up and went a week later. I was nervous going, but once I was in I felt entirely at home after 10 minutes. I thought "This is it, I'm not the only gay 17-year-old in the world." There were other people of my own age and

we could talk. I was glad, very glad, that I went because I made friends, really close friends that I'd never had before. (Male, 18)

I go to the Young Lesbian Group sometimes . . . I haven't been very often, but I've made lots of friends there. It's easier to talk to them because they talk about their experiences too, and understand how you feel. It's a good laugh because you don't have to pretend, you can be yourself. At other youth clubs, girls sit around trying to look fashionable and pretty, (I used to), and the boys look bored. (Female, 16)

At the London Gay Teenage Group I met other gay teenagers for the first time, and it was very helpful to know I wasn't the only young gay in the world. They knew what problems you go through as they've been through them themselves. (Male, 17; all cited in Trenchard & Warren, 1985, pp. 21-4)

Over the past decade, then, there have been a number of developments to facilitate the coming out process of gay youth.

Nevertheless, all the pieces of research described above were conducted before the growth of an AIDS consciousness. By the end of 1983, there were only 35 recorded cases in Britain (Daniels, 1985, p. 4) and there is no mention of AIDS at all in any of this research. Certainly, gay switchboards were receiving calls from young people who had conflated AIDS with being gay and for whom the problems of coming out had once again become enormous. It is not unreasonable to suggest that there is now a new cohort of young people, an AIDS cohort, who are experiencing their gayness in ways that are significantly different from the experience described above. For some, the symbolic linking of AIDS to homosexuality may be enough to prevent any coming out at all; for others, the more explicit talk about "safer sex" may mean a more helpful clarification of sexual possibilities than was previously feasible. One London Switchboard worker has told me that when the issue of AIDS and safer sex is raised to some young callers they have responded with "Well, thank God I don't have to have anal intercourse because I was worried it would be too complicated and I'm so inexperienced and frightened of fucking." Safer sex may provide a legitimate means of opting out, while simultaneously permitting talk of other sexual possibilities.

CONCLUSION: VARIETIES OF YOUTHFUL GAY EXPERIENCE

In this article, I have attempted to capture, through several research studies, some common experiences of a group of young people between 14 and 21, who generally seem to know they are gay quite early in life. They go through various pains and problems in their families, schools, and workplaces because of the heterosexual assumption and sexual stigma, but they eventually come to terms with their gay desires. But this broad patterning conceals enormous diversity; only at a very early stage of research inquiry is it valuable to depict such gross processes. Behind the labels "gay and lesbian youth" are complex, heterogeneous realities that have scarcely been considered. Hence, to end this article, I will briefly highlight four dimensions that need much further exploration.

Class Divisions

Most research on gay experience both samples and suggests a middle-class world, where money, education, and employment are not seen as problems. Yet the sociology of modern England has persistently emphasized the deeply stratified nature of society, and gay experience cannot remain untouched by this! Indeed, in the London Survey, about half of the respondents were self-defined as working class; most of the sample had very little income (only 20 men had over £55 per week, and only 1 woman had this much); and many were unemployed, 73 men, 43 women, and 40% of the sample (Trenchard & Warren, 1984, p. 30). To talk of youth in general as an affluent period of life, or to see gay youth in particular as part of a glamorous scene of smart discos, fancy clothes, and high living is a serious misconception. Large sections of gay and lesbian youth are poor and unemployed; hence compounding their problems.

Gender Divisions

The experiences of young lesbians and gay men are very different. In general young women are particularly likely to be "lumped together in a *faceless bunch* of *typical girls*, rendered silent and invisible behind a haze of stereotype and assumption" (Griffin, 1985, p. 6). There are several significant consequences for young lesbians of "girl socialization":

1. Girls are much more likely to have to stay in the home than boys. Housework and childcare play a crucial role in most young girls lives (Nava, 1984, p. 11; Griffin, 1985, Chap. 3). There is, therefore, less opportunity for girls to explore the more public aspects of the gay and lesbian world.
2. Girls appear to be pressurized more than boys to get a partner and ultimately marry (Griffin, 1985, Chap. 4). The heterosexual assumption may ultimately be more pervasive.
3. Girls typically rely on female friendship groups. But once they meet a boy, girls gradually lose touch with their girlfriends ("often at the young mans insistence," Griffin, 1985, pp. 60-1). They become more and more dependent on men, and ultimately, in marriage, become emotionally tied.

All of this suggests that girls may have a much tougher time in confronting their lesbianism and in breaking away from the heterosexual tramline (Lees, 1986).

Race and Ethnic Divisions

In the postwar period, England has become a multiracial, multiethnic society; there are around 2 1/2 million members of ethnic minorities (nearly 5% of the total population). Asians, Afro-Caribbeans, and Cypriots constitute the most popularly identified categories, but each category harbours a diversity of cultural, familial and religious tradition. "A Sikh from Punjab and a Muslim from Bangladesh are likely to have as much and as little in common as a Catholic from Spain and a Protestant from Sweden" (Coombe & Little, 1986, p. 37). Each of these groups has a heavy preponderance of young people, an emphasis on family ties that is very central, and a culture of homophobia. Consequently growing up gay in an ethnic minority in England usually produces additional burdens and problems. Although now there do exist various black gay and lesbian groups,[29] in the main the race/ethnic dimensions have been missing in discussions of homosexuality.

Two problems are particularly prominent and need examining. First has been the relative absence of "black images" of gays and lesbians. With some noticeable exceptions, like the successful film of Asian gay youth, *My Beautiful Launderette*, and the gay youth video, *Framed Youth*, gay images are overwhelmingly white and middle-class; institutionalized racism permeates the gay world in Britain. Second, the centrality of religion and family in many ethnic groups makes problems within the family structure even more probable. Many ethnic youth grow up between *three cultures*: the tradition of their home, the different but heterosexual cultures of school and work, and a sense of also belonging to a third, a gay and lesbian culture. The conflicts generated can be enormous. Thus, in the Asian community, the issue of arranged marriages looms large: two families make a contract over the marriage of their children. This contrasts not only with the heterosexual norm of romantic love, the ideological basis of English marriage, but also with any sense at all of gay issues. Again, problems of gay and lesbian youth are compounded.

Youth Divisions

Finally, most youth culture research suggests an array of youth culture styles, from militant, political youth to delinquent youth, from drop out youth to conventional youth (Brake, 1980). Such diversities are likely to significantly shape the gay experience. Thus, there are gay youth who take a strong political stand, often making alliances with anarchism, Marxism, or feminism. There are gay runaways who may become homeless and who may turn to prostitution (Deakin & Willis, 1976). There are gay youth who become involved in the more organized world of gay youth clubs.[30] There are still others who head straight for the glamour of the disco scene. Some become punks, some become casuals, some become headbangers, some become skinheads. And so on. There is a massive heterogeneity awaiting investigation.

What I have suggested in these final few paragraphs is simply that the study of gay youth in England has only just begun. There is a broad understanding of the common problems and processes involved in coming out in the early 1980s. But I have suggested, firstly, that AIDS may alter all that; and, secondly, that there is a whole matrix of youthful gay experience that is shaped by class, gender, race, and youth culture, which remains unexplored. The understanding of gay youth in England has moved quickly in the past decade; but there is still much further to travel.

AFTERWORD

An important development has occurred in England since this article was completed. In December 1987 a clause was inserted into a Local Government Bill which states that:

1. A local authority shall not —
   (a) intentionally promote homosexuality or publish material for the promotion of homosexuality;
   (b) promote the teaching in any maintained school of the acceptability of homosexuality as a pretended family relationship by the publication of such material or otherwise;
   (c) give financial or other assistance to any person for either of the purposes referred to in paragraphs (a) and (b) above.

Despite strong protests, it seems most likely that the Bill will become law by mid-1988. It is clear that such legislation will strengthen the mechanisms of the heterosexual assumption and the sexual stigma that I describe in the article and hence increase the problems and sufferings of lesbian and gay youth.

NOTES

1. There is, of course, little to be surprised about in this. There is substantial documentation of bias in the social sciences against the homosexual dimension. For instance, for psychological bias see Morin (1977); in "social problems"

texts, see Potter (1985); and in sociology generally, see the *American Sociologist* 1982. These are all U.S. references and I have little doubt, impressionistically, that the bias is much stronger in the U.K. Although there is a superficial tolerance of homosexuality in English academic life, few academics would think of incorporating the issue in their research.

2. It would overload this article with references to cite all the U.K. research on youth culture. Key reviews and examples are Brake (1980), Cohen (1986), Hall, Critcher, Jefferson, Clarke, & Roberts (1976), Hebdige (1979), Roberts (1983), and Willis (1976).

3. See especially Geoffrey Pearson's otherwise very significant study (1983). Also Gillis (1974).

4. Even very recent studies continue to ignore this dimension. For instance the Schwendingers' (1985) massive survey and theoretical analysis fails to mention any possibility of "gay youth" emerging under capitalism (cf. Schwendinger & Schwendinger, 1985). Their analysis links the growth of capitalism to the rise of adolescent subcultures, yet a cursory familiarity with the work of D'Emilio (1983), for instance, would suggest similar processes at work for homosexuality, which may connect to the modern emergence of "gay youth." The point, of course, is that studies are generally blind to homosexuality and only "specialists on" homosexuality work in the area, thereby reinforcing its separateness.

5. Although controversial in many respects, Harry's (1982) study has a great deal to offer in pointing to links between gender culture and growing up gay. Some boys grow up not to learn the characteristics of "male culture" and this may make them outcasts. Unfortunately, Harry dubs these boys as "effeminate" which I think prejudices the issue.

6. There is some discussion of this phenomenon in Brake (1980, p. 80), Mungham and Pearson (1976, Chap. 5), and Frith (1983, Chap. 10).

7. In 1978, the Open University commissioned Jeffrey Weeks and myself to make two television programs, a cassette, and a course booklet on "sexuality and life history" for their *Social Science, a second level course called: Introduction to Sociology*. One program involved an interview with an elderly gay, Trevor; another involved an interview with a young gay, Stephen. The programs have been broadcast annually in the U.K. since 1980. The story of Stephen would appear to be a fairly typical life story of a young gay in England in the late 1970s and early 1980s.

8. JCGT went out of existence in 1985.

9. I refer to England, but the situation is probably similar in Wales, Northern Ireland and Scotland.

10. Briefly, in 1975 I suggested four stages in gay development: sensitization, signification, coming out and stabilization. Despite criticisms, others have commented on parallel stages (e.g., Minton & McDonald, 1984) and made connections to lesbian development (e.g., Darty & Potter, 1984). One of my main concerns in the 1981 article was to stress that this developmental process has to be

historically located. Coming out in the 1980s is *not* the same as coming out in the 1930s. In this article, my prime concern is with England in the early 1980s.

11. Several did come from Scotland and Wales. Much of this analysis does apply to the United Kingdom, but there are differences: for simplicity I am restricting my comments to England.

12. 1,700 questionnaires were distributed.

13. The "Kinsey" studies initiated by Gagnon and Simon and executed by Williams, Weinberg and Bell, did try to adopt a sophisticated sampling frame. But in general all studies suffer from inadequate representativeness, not least because homosexuality is a continuum of complex experiences and not a sample of people. (See Plummer, 1981, p. 214.)

14. For illustrative examples of this problem, see Williams (1984) and Gubrium (1986) as well as Plummer (1983, Chaps, 5-6, pp. 130-2) and Plummer (1987).

15. Plummer (1981a, p. 98) outlines these key distinctions. See also the discussion by Adrienne Rich on compulsory heterosexuality (Rich, 1983).

16. There have been many recommendations to lower the homosexual "age of consent" to either 16 or 18. The Policy Advisory Committee on Sexual Offences (1981) to the Criminal Law Revision Committee (1984) urged 18 (par 6.17); while the European Parliament has urged all members of the E.E.C. to maintain a consistent age of consent for heterosexuals and homosexuals. Less formal bodies such as CHE (the Campaign for Homosexual Equality) and the Howard League for penal reform have also recommended lower ages. Yet a recent governmental white paper still refuses to do this.

17. Paul Crane, in a useful review of the U.K. law, notes the D.P.P. as saying to the Royal Commission on Criminal Procedure in 1978:

> My decisions are often strongly influenced by the relative ages of the offender and the "victim." If there is no element of corruption by the former and the latter was a fully consenting party . . . I do not normally prosecute a man of 22 for a homosexual offence against a man of 19, although if, for instance, the elder went into a public toilet intent on finding a partner and the younger was or might become a male prostitute, I would probably decide to prosecute both. (p. 66)

According to the London based weekly Capital Gay (16th January 1987), there were 37 men sent to prison for consensual homosexual relations with men under 21 and above 16 in 1985.

18. A lengthier analysis would have to analyse each of these "settings" for youth (cf. Dorn & South, 1983). Further, schools in England differ widely, and I am here talking only generally. The public school system appears to possess a strong underbelly of homoeroticism, as depicted in Lindsay Anderson's *If* and Julian Mitchell's *Another Country*, and many autobiographies. But it is an underbelly not to be made public or condoned. In the state education sector (overwhelmingly the majority) some local education authorities, such as London do espouse an anti-sexual orientation discrimination policy (G.L.C. Charter, 1985).

However, nowhere in England has the idea of "gay schools" like that of the Harvey Milk School in Manhattan, ever been mentioned.

19. Forty-seven out of 104 replied.

20. See especially the article by Malcolm Dobson (1983), and the discussion by Mike Day of the case of John Warburton (1983, pp. 44-7).

21. The seven are Julie (p. 17), Paul (p. 22), Carrie (p. 23), Michelle (p. 31), Tony (p. 43), Derek (p. 47) and Germaine (p. 53). Though they all are gay in their earlier years, they do not present comparably blunt quotes. These quotes are simply culled from the first six in the booklet (Burbidge & Walters, 1981).

22. This raises the now much discussed problem of essentialism again. What I say here is largely compatible with Whitams' (1986) view, but it is a view that nevertheless worries me. (See my critique of this book, *British Journal of Criminology*, 1987, forthcoming.)

23. In England, the drinking age is 18. Sixteen-year-olds may enter "pubs" providing they do not consume alcohol.

24. An important group established by Rose Robertson to deal with parents enquiries, but which also receives calls from and counsels many young people.

25. Rose Robertson has drawn a parallel between this coming out to parents and the cycle of bereavement. Parents often feel they have "lost" their child.

26. This is based on only a percentage of those who answered the questionnaire. It is not clear from the study how many this was.

27. See the annual reports of the London Lesbian and Gay Switchboard. Note too that when Dank investigated coming out in the U.S.A. in the late '60s, Switchboards didn't figure at all and gay bars, parties, parks and tearooms, along with love affairs, were the most frequently cited contexts for coming out (Dank, 1971). In the London survey, these remained popular settings for first contact with other homosexuals, but to this was now added Switchboard (5.7%) and gay groups (nearly 20%).

28. The June 1986 *Gay Times* lists some 52 helplines in England, and a number of others in Scotland, Northern Ireland, and Wales.

29. Among the many emerging groups in 1986 were the Black Lesbian and Gay Group, the Long Youth Club, and the Turkish Gay Group. Regular details of these and other organizations are provided in the leading U.K. gay magazine, *Gay Times*, each month.

30. The statutory youth service emerged in England in 1939, and under the orbit of Local Educational Authorities has moved through a number of phases, leading increasingly from clubs to community (see Eggleston, 1975). Nowhere in its history, however, has there been any recognition of gay youth and their needs, although recently it has come under attack for this. In 1982, the review group of the Youth Service argued "The Youth Service has the duty to help all young people who have need of it" (HMSO, 1982, p. 47), while simultaneously ignoring the needs of gay youth. A few local authorities, notably ILEA, have gone against this national trend.

REFERENCES

Report of American Sociological Association's task group on homosexuality, (1982). *American Sociologist, 17*, pp. 164-179.

Brake, M. (1980). *The sociology of youth culture and youth subcultures*, (2nd ed.). London: Routledge.

Burbidge, M., & Walters, J. (Eds.). (1981). *Breaking the silence: Gay teenagers speak for themselves*: Joint Council for Gay Teenagers.

Bye, S.L. (1984). *An investigation into the lives of socially and geographically isolated gay teenagers*, Unpublished B.A. project, Sociology Dept. University of Essex.

Bosche, S. (1985). *Jenny lives with Eric and Martin*. London: GMP.

Coombe, V., & Little, A. (1986). *Race and social work: A guide to training*. London: Tavistock.

Cohen, P. (1986). *Rethinking the youth question*. (Working Paper 3). London University, Institute of Education.

Crane, P. (1982). *Gays and the law*. London: Gay Men's Press.

Daly, M. (1983). At Work. In B. Galloway (Ed.). *Prejudice and pride: Discrimination against gay people in modern Britain*. London: Routledge & Kegan Paul.

Daniels, V.G. (1985). *AIDS: The acquired immune deficiency syndrome*. Lancaster: MTP Press.

Dank, B. (1971). Coming Out in the Gay World. *Psychiatry 34*, pp. 180-97.

Darty, T., & Potter, S. (Eds.). (1984). *Women—Identified women*. Palo Alto: Mayfield.

Davies, B. (1986). *Threatening youth: Towards a national youth policy*. Milton Keynes Open University Press.

Deakin, M., & Willis, J. (1976). *Johnny Go Home*. London: Quartet Books.

Deem, R. (1980). *Schooling for women's work*. London: Routledge & Kegan Paul.

D'Emilio, J. (1983). *Sexual politics, sexual communities: The making of a homosexual minority in the United States, 1940-1970*. London: University of Chicago Press.

Dobson, M. (1983). At School. In B. Galloway (Ed.), *Prejudice and pride: Discrimination against gay people in modern Britain*. London: Routledge & Kegan Paul.

Dorn, N., & South, N. (1983). *Of males and markets. A critical review of youth culture theory*. Enfield, Middlesex Polytechnic, Centre for Occupational and Community Research, Research Papers, No. 1.

Eggleston, J. (1975). *Adolescence and community: The youth service in Britain*. London: Edward Arnold.

Frith, S. (1983). *Sound effects: youth, leisure and the politics of rock 'n' roll*. London: Constable.

Galloway, B. (Ed.). (1983). *Prejudice and pride: discrimination against gay people in modern Britain*. London: Routledge & Kegan Paul.

Gillis, J. (1974). *Youth and history: tradition and changes in European age relations, 1770-Present*. London: Academic Press.

G.L.C. Charter. (1985). *Changing the world: A London charter for gay and lesbian rights*. G.L.C. Public Relations Branch.

Griffin, C. (1985). *Typical girls? Young women from school to the job market*. London: Routledge & Kegan Paul.

Gubrium, J.F. (1986). *Oldtimers and Alzheimers': The descriptive organization of senility*, Greenwich, CT: JAI Press.

Hall, S., Critcher, C., Jefferson, T., Clarke, J., & Roberts, B. (1976). *Resistance through rituals*. London: Hutchinson.

Harry, J. (1982). *Gay children grown up: Gender culture and gender deviance*. New York: Praeger.

Hart, J., & Richardson, D. (Eds.). (1981). *The theory and practice of Homosexuality*. London: Routledge & Kegan Paul.

Hebdige, D. (1979). *Subculture: The meaning of style*. London: Tavistock.

Howard League. (1985). *Unlawful sex: Offences, victims and offenders in the criminal justice system of England and Wales*. London: Waterlaw Publishers.

HMSO (1982). *Experience and participation: A report of the review group on the youth service in England*.

Hudson, B. (1984). Femininity and Adolescence. In McRobbie & Nava (Eds.), *Gender and Generation*. London: Macmillan.

Joint Council for Gay Teenagers. (1980). *I know what I am: Gay teenagers the law*. London: JCGT.

Kent-Baguley, P. (1982). Is being gay okay, *Youth and Policy, 14*, pp. 16-21.

Kent-Baguley, P. (1984). The silence broken. *Youth in Society*, Leicester National Youth Bureau.

Lees, S. (1986). *Losing out: Sexuality and adolescent girls*. London: Hutchinson.

Lloyd, R. (1977). *Playland: A study of boy prostitutes*. London: Blond & Briggs.

London Gay Teenage Group. (1982 December.) *Experience and participation: A response by the London Gay Teenage Group*.

Meldrum, J. (1980). *Attacks on gay people*. London: Campaign for Homosexual Equality.

Minton, H.L., & McDonald, G.J. (1984). Homosexual identity formation as a developmental process. *Journal of Homosexuality, 9*(2/3), p. 91.

Morin, S.F. (1977). Heterosexual bias in psychological research on Lesbianism and male homosexuality. *American Psychologist, 32*, pp. 629-37.

McRobbie, A., & Nava, K. (Eds.). (1984). *Gender and Generation*. London: MacMillan.

Mungham, G., & Pearson, G. (Eds.). (1976). *Working class cultures*. London: Routledge & Kegan Paul.

Musgrove, F. (1964). *Youth and the social order*. London: Routledge & Kegan Paul.

National Council for Voluntary Youth Service. (1976). *Report of the Working Party on Young People and Homosexuality*. London: National Council for Voluntary Youth Service.

Nava, M. (1984). Youth service provision, social order and the question of Girls. In McRobbie & Nava, (Eds.). *Gender and Generation*, (pp. 1-30). London: Macmillan.

Pearson, G. (1983). *Hooligans: A history of respectable fears*. London: MacMillan.

Plummer, K. (1975). *Sexual stigma: An interactionist account*. London: Routledge & Kegan Paul.

Plummer, K. (Ed.). (1981). *The making of the modern homosexual*. London: Hutchinson.

Plummer, K. (1981a). Going gay: Identities, lifecycles and lifestyles in the male gay world. In J. Hart and D. Richardson (Eds.). *The theory and practice of Homosexuality* London: Routledge & Kegan Paul.

Plummer, K. (1983). *Documents of life: An introduction to the problems and literature of a humanistic method*. London: Allen & Unwin.

Plummer, K. (1984). Sexual diversity: A sociological perspective. In K. Howells (Ed.). *The Psychology of Sexual Diversity* (pp. 219-253). Oxford: Blackwell.

Plummer, K. (1987). *Beyond childhood: Organizing gayness in adult life*. Paper presented at Homosexuality Beyond Disease, International Conference, Amsterdam, December 1987.

Potter, S. (1985). Distortions in the looking glass: Gay and lesbian presence in social problems texts, *80th Annual Meeting of the A.S.A. Conference*. Washington, DC.

Rich, A. (1984). Compulsory heterosexuality and lesbian existence. In A. Snitow, C. Stansell, & S. Thompson (Eds.), *Desire: The politics of sexuality* (pp. 212-242). London: Virago Press.

Roberts, K. (1983). *Youth and leisure*. London: George Allen & Unwin.

Robertson, R. (1981). Young Gays. In J. Hart & D. Richardson (Eds.) *The theory and practice of homosexuality*. London: Routledge.

Rofes, E.E. (1983). *I thought people like that killed themselves*. San Francisco: Grey Fox Press.

Schwendinger, H. & Schwendinger, J.R. (1985). *Adolescent subcultures and delinquency*. Eastborne: Praeger.

Shilts, R. (1982). *The life and times of Harvey Milk*. New York: St. Martin's Press.

Stanworth, M. (1983). *Gender and schooling: A study of sexual divisions in the Classroom*. London: Hutchinson.

Trenchard, L., & Warren, H. (1984). *Something to tell you . . . The experiences and needs of young lesbians and gay men in London*. London Gay Teenage Group.

Trenchard, L. (Ed.). (1985). *Talking about young lesbians*. London Gay Teenage Group.

Trenchard, L., & Warren, H. (1985). *Talking about youth work*. London Gay Teenage Group.

Warren, H. (1985). *Talking about school*. London Gay Teenage Group.

Westwood, G. (1960). *A Minority: A report on the life of the male homosexual in Great Britain*. London: Longmans.

Whitam, F.L., & Mathy, R.M. (1986). *Male homosexuality in four societies*. New York: Praeger.

Williams, G. (1984). The genesis of chronic illness: Narrative reconstruction. *Sociology of Health and Illness* 6(2), pp. 175-200.

Willis, P. (1976). *Learning to labour: How working class kids get working class jobs*. London: Saxon House.

Wood, J. (1984). Groping towards sexism: Boys' sex talk. In McRobbie and Nava. (Eds.), *Gender and generation*. London: Macmillan.

Gay Liberation and Coming Out in Mexico

Joseph M. Carrier, PhD

University of Chicago

SUMMARY. This article presents information on three sociocultural variables and relates it to gay liberation and the behavior of gay youth in Guadalajara, Mexico's second largest city. A detailed history of the gay liberation movement in Guadalajara is given because it provides an excellent example of the interaction of sociocultural variables and shows how different the outcome of liberation may be for gay people in Mexico. Brief life histories of the "coming out" of two Guadalajaran gay men further illustrate some of the unique ways in which gay identities change the lives of gay youth in Mexico.

The Mexican homosexual world differs in many significant ways from the neighboring Anglo-American homosexual world. Compared with large cities in the United States, like San Francisco, New York, and Los Angeles, large Mexican cities have relatively small gay scenes. Gay neighborhoods do not exist there, for example, and there are only a few gay bars and discos, and almost no exclusively gay bathhouses. Cultural differences account for most of these dissimilarities. "Homosexual Mexicans often prefer their way of interacting to the U. S. forms because of cherished, cultural values" (Taylor, 1986, p. 117).

Gay life in the United States has affected some aspects of Mexican homosexual social organization over the past two decades, but

Dr. Carrier received his PhD in Social Sciences at the University of California at Irvine. He is deeply indebted to José and Pedro for generously allowing the publication of their life histories.

Correspondence and reprint requests may be addressed to the author at 17447 Castellammare Drive, Pacific Palisades, CA 90272.

225

its impact has generally been superficial. One major exception has been the American gay liberation movement, which has implanted in Mexico the idea of establishing certain rights for homosexual and bisexual people. Even then, gay liberation movements have only slowly gotten started in large urban areas outside of Mexico City, and the results of gay liberation have been uniquely Mexican.

A gay liberation movement did not emerge in Guadalajara, Mexico's second largest city with a population around 4 million, until the spring of 1981. Even now, many homosexually involved people think it remarkable that it could take place at all and still survive in such a traditional, politically conservative city, a city located in the macho state of Jalisco where mariachi music, tequila, and the "charro" (Mexican cowboy) tradition originated, and where men are believed to defend their honor or *machismo* unhesitatingly with a pistol.

Three important sociocultural variables related to the organization of gay social life in Mexico are the society's view of homosexuality and bisexuality, family attitudes and behavior toward homosexuality, and societal beliefs and laws related to public manifestations of homosexual behavior. This article presents some information on these variables and relates it to gay liberation and the behavior of gay youth in Guadalajara at present.[1] A detailed history of the gay liberation movement in Guadalajara is given because it provides an excellent example of the interaction of cultural variables and shows how different the outcome of liberation may be for gay people in Mexico. Case histories of the "coming out" of two Guadalajaran gay males further illustrate some of the unique ways in which gay identities change the lives of gay youth in Mexico.

Only gay male behavior is dealt with here because information available on lesbian behavior is too meager. A study of lesbian behavior by the author is currently underway in Guadalajara.

SOCIETY'S VIEW OF HOMOSEXUALITY AND BISEXUALITY

In Guadalajara all people exhibiting traits of the opposite sex are considered to be homosexual. Feminine males are especially denigrated because it is almost unthinkable that a masculine male could be a "real homosexual." Generally speaking, only male receivers in homosexual intercourse are considered "homosexual." A noted essayist and poet, Octavio Paz (1961), concisely summarized the view held by many Mexicans: "Masculine homosexuality is regarded with a certain indulgence insofar as the active agent is concerned. The passive agent is an abject, degraded being. Masculine homosexuality is tolerated, then, on condition that it consists in violating a passive agent" (pp. 39-40). One consequence of this societal belief appears to be an unspoken widespread acceptance of bisexual behavior.

The anal receptive sexual role in homosexual encounters is by inference, through the cultural equivalence of effeminacy with homosexuality, prescribed for feminine males. The beliefs linking feminine males with homosexuality are culturally transmitted by a vocabulary that provides the appropriate labels, by homosexually oriented jokes and word games, and by the mass media. From early childhood on, Mexican males are made aware of the labels used to denote males homosexual, and the connection is always clearly made that these homosexual males (usually called *putos* or *jotos*) are guilty of unmanly feminine behavior. It thus becomes a self-fulfilling prophecy of the society that feminine males (a majority?) are eventually, if not from the beginning, pushed toward exclusive homosexual behavior.[2] Some do engage in heterosexual intercourse and some marry and set up households, but they probably are a minority of the obviously feminine males in the mestizoized segment of the Mexican population. Feminine males clearly provide easily identifiable sexual targets for interested males in Mexico.

Because of the lack of stigmatization in Mexico of the anal inserter participant in homosexual encounters, most Mexican males are not fearful of bisexuality. They do not believe that "one drop of homosexuality" makes one totally homosexual as long as the appropriate sex role is played; that they must show erotic distaste toward other males as long as they are masculine, and play the inserter role in homosexual encounters. And most are not especially concerned about homosexual reaction eradicating heterosexual responsiveness as long as they do not become too involved in homosexuality. Thus, although heterosexuality is considered superior to homosexuality in Mexico, a Mexican male's gender identity is not necessarily threatened by his homosexual behavior (Carrier, 1985).

Sexual behavior between males is facilitated in Mexico by socialization patterns that tend to be all male in character, both before and after marriage. Peer-group relationships, of particular importance in adolescence, remain essentially unchanged by marriage. "In social life a Mexican man's marital status is of little practical importance, as a man carries on virtually the same sort of social life after marriage as he did before — and one in which the women have little part" (Peñalosa, 1968, p. 83).

Many Mexican males begin an active sex life at an early age. From birth onward they are made aware of different kinds of sexual relationships by way of joking and the public media. And machismo, a culturally defined hypermasculine ideal model of manliness through which a Mexican male may measure himself, his sons, and his male relatives and friends against such attributes as courage, dominance, power, aggressiveness, and invulnerability, is expressed sexually "through an emphasis on multiple, uncommitted sexual contacts which start in adolescence" (Espín, 1984, p. 157). At the first signs of puberty, Mexican adolescent males may be pressured by their brothers, male cousins, friends, or all three, to prove their masculinity by having sexual intercourse with either prostitutes or available neighborhood girls. By this time they are also made aware of the availability and acceptability of feminine males as sexual outlets.

The available data suggest that perhaps a majority of feminine homosexual males start their sexual lives prior to puberty; many between the ages of 6 to 9 (Carrier, 1976a). These early homosexual relationships are often with postpubertal cousins, uncles, or neighbors. And they may be long lived, for several years rather than just one or two sexual encounters.

The sexual partners Mexican males choose at any time depends on such obvious factors as sexual excitement, attractiveness, mutual interest, timing, and cost. Over time, some may choose female partners only, others male partners only, and still others both female and male partners. Since a Kinsey-type survey of male sexual behavior has never been done in Mexico, there are no data from which to estimate for any given age group the percentage of the sexually active male population who at some time have used both female and male sexual outlets. However, judging from the socio-cultural factors described above, it appears that for any given age group, more sexually active single males in Mexico have had sexual intercourse with both genders than have Anglo-American males. The Kinsey et al. (1948, p. 258) "data suggest that about 15% of single sexually active Anglo-American males between 15 and 25 have mixed sexual histories. The percentage of Mexican males with mixed histories may be as high as 30% for the same age group" (Carrier, 1985).

GUADALAJARA'S GAY SCENE

Like other cities in Mexico, Guadalajara has only a few gay establishments—four discos and one bar, which is gay only after dark. Gay neighborhoods do not exist there, and there are no exclusively gay bathhouses.

But in Guadalajara there are, nevertheless, wide-ranging opportunities for gay males seeking sexual partners along the boulevards and streets downtown, in city parks, in movie houses, and in many "straight" restaurants, cantinas, and bars. And many gay youth looking for homosexual encounters turn to their crowded neighborhoods as choice locations for finding sexual partners.

Gay male youth have traditionally met and socialized in several straight downtown restaurants. The most long-standing and popular of these has been an outdoor cafe in the Umbrellas Plaza located in the center of the city. Several other locations exist but change over time because of harassment by owners and police for what is considered to be scandalous behavior by groups of feminine gay males.

As will be seen below, one major result of the gay liberation movement has been the creation and continuation of special meeting places for gay people. This is particularly important in a society where single people continue to live at home with their families on into adulthood, and where, because of space limitations or prejudice, socialization at home for most gay people is difficult.

THE IMPORTANCE OF FAMILY

Most gay people in Guadalajara (and all of Mexico for that matter) live in crowded circumstances with the family of origin until their late 30s or 40s, and some all of their lives.[3] Family attitudes and behavior toward homosexuality thus have an important effect on their sexual and social activities.

Given that homosexuality is generally viewed with shame, most gay youth must cope over time with the dissonance generated by their behavior and their family's treatment of the homosexual as a shameful being. Masculine gay males have a different set of problems dealing with their families than do feminine gay males because they are not as easily identified as "homosexual," and are thus much more concerned about being exposed as a homosexual. They must spend more time worrying about avoiding situations that might "burn" or "scorch" their reputation. The masculine Mexican males who face the greatest amount of dissonance in their lives, however, are those who, in addition to being homosexually involved, also play the anal passive sex role. They must worry about exposure and contend with the role conflict generated by being masculine and playing the female role sexually.

Acceptance of their homosexual behavior by family members — or at least an accommodation with respect to it — is a matter of particular urgency for gay youth. When acceptance or accommodation occurs, which appears to be the case in most families when the youths' homosexual behavior is known, gay youth and their families often cope with the problem by using a conspiracy of silence about homosexuality. In social functions with relatives and neighbors, gay youth are frequently treated by their families as though they were straight. Family tension in these situations is oftentimes relieved by joking relationships between the gay youth and friendly siblings, relatives, or neighbors.

Because most gay youth grow up and continue to live in crowded neighborhoods, over a great part of their lifetimes they must also deal with neighbors who have negative attitudes toward homosexuality. As will be seen in some of the excerpts from the two life histories presented below, however, in spite of generally negative societal attitudes, there is a certain tolerance and acceptance of gay youth on the part of many. This seems to be particularly true for bisexual male neighbors.

GAY BEHAVIORAL PATHWAYS

Two different paths of behavior have been distinguished for Guadalajaran male youth who eventually identify themselves as gay. Although not the only pathways taken by gay youth, they are the most salient ones.

Gay youth following one behavioral pathway start with early feminine mannerisms and homosexual experiences during childhood (some as early as 6 to 9 years old) that are then continued on into adolescence and adulthood. Gay youth following the other pathway start with early masculine mannerisms during childhood that are then continued on into adolescence and adulthood. Most heterosexual or homosexual experiences (or both) occur for this group at the time of puberty.

Gay youth following the first pathway generally develop a strong preference for playing the *pasivo* (anal receptive) sexual role; those following the second a strong preference for playing the *activo* (anal insertive) sexual role. Although oral and anal sexual techniques are used, anal intercourse is the ultimate sexual practice preferred in homosexual encounters by both groups.[4]

Some gay male youth in Guadalajara may follow other pathways prior to their gay identification. Some may also change, or do not develop sex role preferences and are thus both passive and active sexually. Gay people consider their sexual behavior both foreign and unique enough, however, to be commonly called *internacionales* (internationals).

Gay Mexican males who fall into the *internacionales* category are difficult to assess as a group. The author's data suggest that most of them are masculine rather than feminine and during the early years of their sex lives play only the "activo" sexual role — the "pasivo" sexual role being incorporated later as they become more involved in homosexual encounters. Many "internacionales" state that although they may play both sex roles, they nevertheless retain a strong general preference for one over the other.

THE GAY LIBERATION MOVEMENT

The gay liberation movement in Guadalajara began in June of 1981. A national rumbling against political oppression had occurred in October 1968 when an estimated two to three hundred students and workers, some of whom were gay, were killed by police and soldiers while peacefully demonstrating for political rights in Mexico City just prior to the Olympic Games. One result of this massacre was the creation of gay rights groups that later evolved in the middle and late 1970s into the Homosexual Liberation Movement (Movimiento de Liberación Homosexual) in Mexico City and elsewhere. The movement finally took hold in Guadalajara in the early 1980s.

Exceptional police oppression in the spring and early summer of 1981 was the catalyst of the movement in Guadalajara. Large numbers of gay people were being extorted and arrested by police in the largest downtown park, a traditional gay cruising area. Customers in the oldest gay bar in the city were also being increasingly harassed by the police.

A group was finally formed by gay men and women in June and July 1981 to initiate the first public fight in Guadalajara against police repression and in favor of the civil rights of the homosexual community. By the end of 1981, the group numbered about 40. Close to half were "street people" from relatively poor families, but all social classes were represented. Police oppression was a potential problem for all homosexually involved people regardless of age, income, or social class.

The July 1982 national elections were a rallying point for the group, which aligned itself politically with the newly recognized Revolutionary Workers Party (PRT) and named itself the Committee of Lesbians and Homosexuals in Support of Rosario Ibarra (CLHARI). Rosario was the feisty and charismatic female presidential candidate of the PRT. Two local gay candidates for the National Chamber of Deputies were put on the PRT slate in Jalisco.

The arrest of seven flamboyant and feminine gay men in a straight restaurant in early April 1982 brought about the first gay demonstration in Guadalajara. The restaurant had become a popular meeting place and hangout for gay people. For some time the manager had tried to get gay patrons, especially the feminine ones, to stop congregating in and around his open-patio restaurant. Being unsuccessful, he called the police and the seven gay men were arrested. Homosexuality between consenting adults is not illegal anywhere in Mexico, so arrests of gay people by police are usually made for immoral or scandalous behavior, or for disturbing the peace.[5]

In response to the arrests, several militant members of the committee staged a peaceful demonstration in the restaurant on April 24th. On being refused service, they pointed out to the restaurant's manager that it was a violation of the Federal Consumer Protection law to deny them service systematically just on the basis of their sexual orientation. Police were once again called. After being roughly handled and verbally abused, they were arrested and jailed. Because one of them was the PRT candidate for the National Chamber of Deputies, the event was widely reported in the local press.

The committee then called for the first gay protest march ever held in Guadalajara, for 6 p.m., during the rush hour on May 8, 1982. On that day, despite the possible consequences on their personal lives, 120 courageous gay and lesbian demonstrators marched down Avenida Juárez from the Umbrellas Plaza to the site of the arrests. Bold banners announced their cause: STOP POLICE HARASSMENT, LESBIANS AND HOMOSEXUALS ARE NEITHER SICK NOR CRIMINALS, STOP THE REPRESSION AGAINST LESBIANS AND HOMOSEXUALS, LESBIANS AND HOMOSEXUALS ARE EVERYWHERE.

The second gay protest march was held June 4th at the end of a week of campaigning for PRT candidates. Over 150 lesbian and gay demonstrators, some holding the bold banners, walked down Avenida Juárez during the evening rush hour from the Umbrellas Plaza to the Revolution Park. At a meeting in the park, they denounced the maltreatment of the gay community by the police, press, robbers, and extortionists. They specifically accused Guadalajara patrol officers of arresting "homosexuals" and then getting payoffs to let them go free.

Rough times lay ahead for the homosexual community in Guadalajara. A gay leader met with newly installed government officials early in 1983. They were found to be even more homophobic than the previous ones. *All* gay bars were closed by order of the new governor in March 1983 on the grounds that such establishments violated the moral codes of the people. Police repression not only continued but increased. Jalisco's new Penal Code of September 1982, which made the government the proprietor of public morals, facilitated corruption and abuses by authorities.

Some discord occurred within the gay liberation movement at this time. Political alignment with the Revolutionary Workers Party (PRT) disturbed many members. And friction developed between very radical openly gay members, many of whom were very feminine, and those who wanted to be less open and stay in the closet with respect to their families and work. Part of the discord was resolved by renaming the organization "Group Pride for Homosexual Liberation" [Grupo Orgullo Homosexual de Liberación (GOHL)], and by establishing absolute independence between GOHL and PRT.

A police raid of a large upper-class gay party on July 23, 1983 was a turning point for gay liberation in Guadalajara. The police photographed and extorted money from each of the 300 guests, sending some to jail even though they had paid bribes.

GOHL used the police raid to publicize problems existing between law enforcement agencies and the gay community. Guadalajara's most important newspapers published letters by GOHL members outlining the community's major grievances with the police. They also published objective and positive new articles about the gay community by leading journalists.

In early August 1983, at a gay and lesbian demonstration in Guadalajara's Cathedral Plaza, GOHL demanded that police harassment be stopped and gay bars be reopened. In December 1983, the gay bars were reopened and GOHL opened a private disco for its members and friends.

Major changes in the behavior of the police, however, did not occur until the autumn of 1984. GOHL's work, plus outside letters of protest to the governor, caused him to institute major reforms to police activity. The arrest of many of his friends on homosexual charges also helped change his opinion about the evils of police harassment and corruption.

Harassment of the gay community by the police lessened, and direct links established between the gay community and the police benefited many gay people in trouble. The general public at times also openly supported gay activists. For example, angry citizens stopped police from blocking the start of the gay pride parade in January 1985. They prevented a policeman from handcuffing a gay leader who was stopping traffic on a main boulevard to let 200 lesbian and gay marchers start the parade.

The civil authorities tried once again to deny gay people in Guadalajara their civil liberties in February and March, 1986. The offices of gay liberation groups and three gay discos were closed by the police. It was only after another series of demonstrations that city administrators backed down and allowed the offices and gay discos to reopen.

Although there are several gay and lesbian groups in Guadalajara at present, GOHL, under the leadership of Pedro Preciado, has clearly established its primacy in the gay liberation movement. Since the summer of 1986, a direct link between GOHL and the police chief has been maintained. The police chief apprises GOHL's leader weekly about law enforcement problems related to gay people and seeks his advice as to how they might be resolved. And Pedro negotiates directly with the chief for the release of gay people and others when they are illegally arrested by police officers who habitually harass and try to extort money from "homosexuals." In January 1987, for example, he foiled an attempted extortion by police officers by successfully bringing about the release from jail of a large number of wealthy men who had been illegally arrested while attending a gay party.

Another important service provided by GOHL at present is education concerning AIDS (referred to as SIDA), and how homosexually involved males can, through adopting safer-sex practices, reduce the risk of contracting it. Along with other gay groups, they have been participating in a study conducted by the Institute of Infectious Diseases, University of Guadalajara Medical School, to determine what percentage of bisexual and homosexual males have been exposed to the AIDS virus.

GOHL currently rents a large two-story house in the center of Guadalajara in which it operates its adjunct Gay Community Assistance Center (Centro de Apoyo a la Comunidad Gay), an afternoon gay refreshment bar for teenagers during the week, and a disco on weekends (BOOP'S). GOHL's house has become the major center for gay activities in the city, and the location for semiannual gay pride celebrations.

The current major objectives of GOHL are (a) to maintain respect for the civil rights of all gay people (gente gay), (b) to continue to exercise their rights, (c) to try to get more people in the Gay Community (Communidad Gay) to participate in the movement, (d) to furnish a number of useful services to the gay community, and (e) to help build a National Gay Movement (Movimiento Gay Nacional). The next major test of the organization and of gay liberation in Guadalajara will be changes brought about in city administration by the July elections of 1988.

We will now turn to the life histories of two Guadalajaran gay males. Both histories are presented with the permission of the respondents, who read what was written about them and chose not to disguise their names.[6,7]

GAY LEADER'S COMING OUT

Pedro was born in the fall of 1956 to relatively prosperous parents in an upper-middle-class neighborhood of Guadalajara. He has an older brother and sister, and three younger brothers. At the age of 25, he became a leader in the gay rights movement and a candidate for the National Chamber of Deputies. He has a college degree in economics. Until he lost his job as a result of his gay activism, he was a secondary school teacher. His father is a well-known lawyer.

Pedro is a brawny good-looking young man, slightly taller than average (about 5'10"), with long dark black hair and a large moustache. He speaks in a masculine way with a deep resonant voice. Based on his physical appearance, most Mexicans would be surprised to learn that he is gay. As a child, he remembers himself as being like all the other boys his age.

Pedro divides his life into two phases: before and after "coming out of the closet" (salir del closet). In recently reflecting on coming out, he was aware that although it happened several years ago, the pain of it lingers. He remembers the events leading up to it with great clarity. In talking about it, he divides the world into two groups, the straight (buga) and the gay. To him, the "buga" world is heterosexual and macho, and naive about homosexuality. The gay world, on the other hand, is revolutionary and allows him the freedom to follow his true sexual orientation.

Before coming out in his early 20s, Pedro thinks that, like most Mexicans who suppress their homosexual feelings, he was anguished and frustrated:

> I was going through life with a heterosexual mask, knowing that deep down I had incomprehensible desires and emotions that, in some way, should give a man pleasure. This caused me such distress, and was such a threat to my emotional equilibrium, that it repressed me and put me low spiritually. I was living a life like that of any straight person. But, in my case, I was an anguished straight person (buga angustiado) because I did not understand what was going on inside me.

A long time before he came out, Pedro knew he was different from others his age. Since kindergarten he remembers:

> I knew already a profound, profound attraction — I don't think sexual, but yes of pleasure — to be with my little boy companions, with other boys. In my mind, clearly, I didn't yet think myself to be a homosexual but neither did I think myself odd (raro) feeling that. Yet I didn't sufficiently swallow the heterosexist education that was subsequently given me, and that made me feel different and like something apart.

As time passed, gradually, from 17 to 23, Pedro began to learn about the homosexual world and how he might be related to it; much of what he learned made him feel bad about himself. Referring to what he had read about homosexuality, he reports:

> That was my first contact, I identified myself with what was being said in books — even though many things I read were venomous. For example, they say in encyclopedias that the homosexual is sick, dirty (lugarcete comun), you understand, and specifically that homosexuality is a perversion. And in medical books they give all kinds of explanations that make you feel bad.

During his 23rd year, Pedro went through a homosexual panic. He describes it as follows:

> I thought myself very bad, and many times I was at the point of suicide. I don't know if I really might have killed myself, but many times I thought about it and believed it was the only alternative. This caused me problems with many friends. I felt they thought me to be different, homosexual, and really sick. It made me separate from them. I felt myself inferior and thought I was the only one these things happened to.
>
> Some weeks before I left the closet, I went into a terrible panic. A panic that overwhelmed me above all, I was hysterical, psychotic. One morning I woke up yelling . . . in a cold sweat, stiff, eyes rolling. My family came into my room and asked me: What happened? What's going on? There were no medical explanations. And no other kind of explanation other than the strong anguish I felt over being what, at that moment, I did not want to be; and that I was rejecting . . . a product of the education I had received.
>
> I had an enormous fear that they might discover me . . . that my family or a friend might *know* something about me. Many times in the few family reunions I used to go to, talk would always turn to the subject of the "joto," the homosexual, or something related and I was forced to conceal myself. Everyone was saying bad things about homosexuals. I used to stay quiet then, distressed.

Pedro overcame his bad feelings about being homosexual, just as he had overcome his feelings of being "an anguished straight person, a heterosexual who did not know what was going on inside." It came about in part as a result of telling a heterosexual childhood friend of his dilemma of being a homosexual. His friend gave him some positive articles to read about gay people. Referring to them, Pedro recalls:

> I remember reading in *El Viejo Topo* some articles by Carlo Forti, and others in *Sábado de Uno Más Uno*, that were truly revelatory. I was able to identify myself and know more of myself. They were excellent, and permitted me to know my

homosexuality from a political point of view. I knew I didn't have to reject myself just for being gay.

Pedro still had another problem to surmount: coming out sexually. Although at some level he could accept being gay, as an ordinary masculine person he had not been able to face the trauma of physically acting out his inner sexual longings with other males. He had masturbated since puberty and once told a priest in the confessional about it. But,

> clearly I never told him that the fantasies which stimulated my masturbation were homosexual. I simply told him I masturbated, and he almost laughed. So I then told him my masturbation was obsessive. But I thought to myself what really was obsessive was my inability to touch and explore another masculine body.

In finally coming out to himself, Pedro started looking for homosexual encounters in the street (el ligue en la calle). He remembers his first attempts to find sexual partners as excruciating experiences. He knew the special signals, "intense looks, lustful ones that say something." And he knew where to go to find them. "I knew that things happened in the center of Guadalajara . . . that here in this city the zone most open for an encounter is the street; there are very few places for gay people here."

He describes the very first time he set out to look for a sexual companion:

> The first time I tried to make it with someone was horrible. I crossed Avenida Juárez and in a dark side street found a "chavo," very feminine for sure. I saw him and said to myself: fuck my prejudices, fuck my education, fuck everything. I want to go to bed with a man now, and I'm going to do it.
>
> He, she, was a "loquita"; and I was standing close to her. But it was difficult for me to approach. With every step I took, I was feeling more flushed in my head and felt it growing. I was very nervous because I didn't know what to say to the "chavo," I didn't know how to begin the conversation. The only thing I could think to say was hey, "carnal." I thought

the word *carnal* was also used between homosexuals. He turned around. I looked at him, but couldn't say another word. My jawbone was paralyzed. I wanted to say something strong, to express how I felt, but I couldn't. My brain thought I was saying things; but I couldn't hear anything. No sound left my mouth. A horrible sensation. For fractions of seconds of course, but they seemed like long ones. I felt bad, my head was going around. And then what I did was to go running. I was running desperately, like a "loca"!

Pedro's first homosexual affair was with an older American professor who worked in Guadalajara in the summertime. It lasted for several years, and he felt very comfortable with the sexual part of it because it involved only fellatio. Although he has tried receptive anal intercourse a few times since becoming sexually active, Pedro generally prefers fellatio or playing only the "activo" sex role. Even now he is unable to deal with the psychological dissonance that results from his playing the "pasivo" role.

Pedro's final coming out was to his family, who he believed were not aware of his homosexuality, or at least who knew or were suspicious but never mentioned it. This changed dramatically during the latter part of his 23rd year when one of his younger brothers came home unexpectedly and found him having sex with a boyfriend. Both his father and eldest brother were told about the incident. A family crisis ensued, with lots of bitter remarks, tears, and rejection. But because by then Pedro had completely accepted himself as gay, he felt ready to confront his family. He first explained the situation to his father, then later to his brothers and sister as a group. Pedro, his father, and his brothers and sister, however, decided to keep his homosexuality a secret from his mother who was in Mexico City at the time. She did not learn of Pedro's homosexuality until 2 years later.

Pedro had decided not to tell his mother because she and his father were estranged and he did not want to burden her further. He felt very protective toward his mother then because his father treated her in such a chauvinistic way. Pedro deeply resented the way his father treated his mother, and he often upbraided him about it. In the fall of 1981, just one month prior to his 25th birthday, Pedro's father asked him to leave. Pedro claims, ironically, it had nothing to do with his homosexuality.

One of Pedro's younger brothers, who had gotten into some legal difficulties and become estranged from his father, joined him and they rented an apartment together. A short time later, their mother moved in with them on a temporary basis.

It was at this time that Pedro's mother discovered his homosexuality. In an interview several years later (Mother, 1984), she recalled to Pedro how she had had "small indications" that left her wondering and uneasy:

> some telephone calls, some friends of yours who came to the house, who I saw [as like] homosexual. Then I thought to myself . . . why do they visit my son? . . . Why do they call by telephone? why? I wanted to cloud it over, it was not like you . . . not you. And I was rebeling and saying to myself, no! I looked for explanations . . . you were very sociable, you had all kinds of friends. When I finally realized, it was a tremendous shock for me.

Later in the interview, Pedro asked his mother, "What feelings or emotions did you experience when you discovered that a very beloved son of yours was a homosexual? Do you remember that day? Can you describe it?" She replied:

> Yes, son . . . I am never going to forget that day. Can you imagine . . . among my family I had discovered a homosexual . . . a son of mine . . . very dear, very special as you are . . . was homosexual. Given what I thought about homosexuality all of my life, you must know how it shocked me and took me a long time to get over . . . a shock that included much rejection of you, very nearly . . . like . . . blaming you insofar as you might hurt me personally with this. And later I thought of you even as a cynic in the way you treated me. I don't know son . . . I wished . . . maybe to attack you, beat you. How was it possible that you could be so bad, I thought to myself . . . because for me this was homosexuality. I was going through a terrible personal crisis when I discovered it. Then, this came to give me yet more pain.

Pedro's mother then noted her eventual acceptance of her son's homosexuality: "At first I was very hard with you . . . severe. Later, little by little I began to understand you, I was . . . grasping it . . . I was understanding all that you had also suffered before . . ."

Pedro overcame the final barrier to acceptance by his family in the spring of 1982 when he became a leader of the gay liberation movement and a candidate for the National Chamber of Deputies. The notoriety associated with these positions disarmed his family for awhile. But believing in the cause he pursued, they set aside their fears and prejudices about homosexuality and accepted and supported him in his role as a leader of the movement. Pedro states that now, "They do not just tolerate me . . . they admire me."

Since that time, Pedro has maintained a close relationship with his family, visiting them weekly. His mother and several of his brothers in turn visit him regularly at the Group Pride for Homosexual Liberation Movement's (GOHL) headquarters, a two-story rented house in the center of Guadalajara, where he lives, and they occasionally participate in some of the group's activities. They also know his current male lover. Antagonisms between Pedro and his father continue, but they relate mostly to the father's treatment of the mother.

Although disappointed that he lost his teaching position, Pedro has found that running a gay liberation organization is a full-time job. Maintaining an accommodation with the police in Guadalajara requires a continuing weekly dialogue with the relevant civil authorities and the chief of police. And on a daily basis, he must also oversee GOHL's gay support services and refreshment bar, and on weekends the operation of its disco, a major source of income for the organization.

Pedro feels strongly about the importance of the educational objectives of the gay liberation movement, and so maintains a telephone hot line to counsel youth having problems related to their homosexuality and coming out, and to provide information about AIDS. He also organizes semiannually gay pride week lectures and exhibits. He feels strongly about providing a place in Guadalajara for gay youth to congregate. Both the refreshment bar during the week and the disco on weekends fill this need.

Pedro's leadership role and living arrangement do not allow him a great deal of privacy. The inconvenience, however, is far out-weighed, he feels, by GOHL's success.

JOSÉ'S COMING OUT

José was born in the fall of 1954 to relatively poor parents in an old lower-middle class neighborhood of Guadalajara that has been continuously occupied since the city was founded by Spaniards in the 16th century. Located a short distance from the center of the city, the neighborhood is mainly made up of four- to five-room single story Spanish style adobe brick houses that adjoin sidewalks and have interior courtyards. Neighborhood youth socialize on the sidewalks in front of houses each evening while buses, trucks, and cars rumble through the narrow streets. Many old customs are still followed. For instance, families give "sweet 15 parties" for their daughters, and boys serenade their girlfriends. Families also still worry about the virginity of their daughters and supervise as much of their behavior as possible given the times.

Along with his mother, father, and 10 brothers and sisters, José has lived most of his life in the house where he was born. During his late teens and early 20s he lived on and off in the United States for 5 years, but moved back to live with his family in Guadalajara in 1978, where he has lived since then. Since he returned to Mexico he has held a number of different jobs. He worked several years in a well known restaurant as a waiter and singer. He currently works as a tailor at his house and is employed part time with an "estudian-tina" sponsored by the city.

At present José is a slim, nice looking young man, about average in size (about 5'6" tall). He has maintained a trim physique all his life. Most people judge him to be much younger than he is. He dresses in a very flashy, sometimes feminine way with skin-tight pants and blousy shirts. He believes his only obviously feminine trait, however, to be his manner of walking. Like Pedro, he speaks in a masculine way with a deep resonant voice.

José established a gay identity in his late teens. Part of his moti-vation for going to the United States after "coming out" to himself, family, and friends at the age of 17 was to experience the freedom of living completely as a "gay" person in New York with a European male lover he had previously met in Guadalajara. After 5 years, however, his longing to be back with his family in his old neighborhood was so intense that, after breaking up with his lover, he returned home.

José explains his return:

> Even though I had a lot of gay and straight friends, a nice apartment, car . . . I was lonely. I'm sure it sounds crazy . . . to give all that up to come back to a poor family and share a small bedroom with two younger brothers. But my lover and I had broken up . . . and I really missed being with my family. Also, a neighborhood of straight young guys were back here waiting for me . . . available . . . most know I'm gay.

José's earliest homosexual experiences occurred prior to puberty, between 4 and 13 years of age, with neighborhood youths who were between 14 and 18. He remembers "sucking off" three teenage neighborhood brothers when he was 4 and being anally penetrated by a 16-year-old neighbor when he was 6. He further remembers his initial anal experiences as being frightening and painful, and feeling disgusted with himself afterwards for having allowed the older boy to do it to him.

Before reaching puberty at the age of 13, he also remembers being penetrated anally by several other neighborhood youth, but only a few times. He gradually became comfortable with the anal passive role and no longer felt repulsed by it. But he does not remember having a strong sexual role preference. He believes he ended up playing the passive role because he was sexually excited by the older neighborhood youth who would only play the active role.

Reflecting on his masculinity, José reports that he has "always been in the middle, neither macho nor feminine." As a boy, he liked playing with both girls' and boys' toys, but when a teenager he mostly liked playing male sports. He acknowledges, however, that in his neighborhood he was probably viewed by many of his friends as being "slightly feminine." And when he was 16, his cousin of the same age told him that he "acted like a homosexual," which meant, José said, that he "was acting feminine."

José's first ejaculation occurred when he masturbated with some older neighborhood boys at the age of 13. He remembers his early mutual masturbatory experiences with considerable pleasure and little guilt.

During the first 2 years following the onset of puberty, José became actively involved in homosexual behavior. He established a pattern of weekly sexual encounters, generally with very masculine neighborhood youths whose ages ranged from 14 to 19. When first interviewed by the author at age 15, he remembered having homosexual encounters with 14 different youths the first year; 10 different ones the second year. Although on occasion he performed fellatio on some, it was only preliminary to the anal intercourse that he and his sex partners enjoyed most. He continued to play only the anal receptive role. During those two years, casual social contacts with neighborhood youths led to most of José's homosexual encounters. He almost never went out deliberately looking for sexual partners in his neighborhood, but rather had sexual encounters with the same youth three or four times.

When he was 15 years old, José told the author that only a first cousin knew about his homosexual behavior, and that the rest of his family neither knew nor suspected anything. He worried a lot about their finding out. To cover himself, he had girlfriends in the neighborhood and made a point of introducing them to his family and friends. If his parents found out about his homosexuality, he said, "I would leave home at once and never return because I wouldn't be able to face the shame."

Two years later, when he was 17, José's family found out about his homosexual behavior. News about his homosexual contacts with neighborhood youths had finally reached his older brothers, and one of them told his parents. José's father was very angry with him, so he decided to leave forever. Although distraught about his homosexuality, his mother was not angry with him and did not want him to leave. He left believing he would never return. Not long after leaving, however, he learned through relatives that the family's furor over his homosexuality had subsided. He therefore decided to return home, hoping somehow he would be accepted by his family.

After being back home a while, his relationship with his mother, older sister, and six younger siblings returned to normal. He remained estranged from his three older brothers, however, and for several years his father and second oldest brother almost never spoke to him. His homosexuality was not mentioned by anyone. José started seeking sexual contacts with males living outside his neighborhood during this time.

A few months later, accepting that he had never had any real sexual interest in women and had no intention of getting married and having children, José decided that he was what he had known himself to be for a long time, a homosexual, and so should learn more about the "gay world." He envisioned the gay world as a place where he could be as feminine or as masculine as he wanted, where he could be around people like himself and thus not have to put up a false front. José refers to the events of the following month as his "coming out of the closet" and establishing a "gay identity" (los de Ambiente).

After coming out, José spent the next few months socializing with several young "queens" he had met in Guadalajara's only gay bar and adopted a feminine nickname "la chepa." He recalls his behavior during this time as being "muy loca" (extremely effeminate). He then met and started a sexual relationship with an older European man, became his lover, and decided to live with him in New York. José felt he could live there freely as a gay person. With his lover's help, he was able to enter the United States legally and get a job.

Although he enjoyed many aspects of his new life in the United States, José missed his family and neighbors. During his 5 years residence in New York, he returned to Guadalajara every Christmas and on other occasions when possible to assuage his homesickness. His lover often traveled with him and became acquainted with his family. They knew the foreigner was José's lover, but nevertheless were hospitable, and no one confronted José about his homosexual relationship.

As time passed, José had a falling out with his lover. Though sexually compatible, he found his older lover to be possessive and jealous of his younger friends. Differences in social backgrounds and interests also contributed to the breakup. José's homesickness increased.

Shortly after breaking up with his lover, José decided to return home. On returning, except for his father and second oldest brother, he found his family delighted to have him home for good. He easily reintegrated himself back into family life, establishing a close bond with his mother and very warm relationships with his sisters and their husbands. Whenever he and one of his brothers-in-law got together, they often joked about his sexual availability.

After returning home, José's presentation of self to family and neighbors differed from before. He was still not blatantly homosexual, but he never denied being gay and was no longer ashamed of being gay.

He found few changes in his neighborhood, and resumed his old pattern of spending most of his free time socializing with neighborhood friends and having homosexual encounters with some of them. Shortly after his return, he started what turned out to be a long-term affair with a local youth who at the same time carried on active courtships with girlfriends. Both he and the youth were teased by neighborhood friends about their affair but no one tried to break it up. The affair continued for many years, but tapered off when the youth became engaged and then married.

José was aware of the gay liberation movement from the time it started in 1981, but has never been an active participant. Some neighborhood youths had seen the first gay demonstration in the Umbrellas Plaza. They were curious and astonished, but not hostile. They questioned José as to what brought it on and wanted to know what he thought about it and why he had not participated. He said he told them, "I'm in favor of gay rights . . . gay people only have a few places they can go and be together, like Pancho's place where I've taken some of you. But the police close down gay bars and extort and arrest lots of gay people for nothing."

José made no reply to them about not actively participating in the gay liberation movement. He prefers to spend most of his time socializing with neighborhood straight friends rather than with gay friends. He only occasionally goes to gay bars, and he finds all the sexual partners he wants among youths in his own neighborhood. Thus, although he supports gay rights, he has never felt involved enough in the struggle to become an active participant.

At present, José is having an affair with an 18-year-old bisexual youth in the neighborhood. He maintains a close relationship with the youth and the youth's girlfriend, who lives next door. The girlfriend knows that José is gay and spends a lot of time with her boyfriend. She apparently does not mind sharing him with José. When she and her boyfriend are in the midst of a quarrel, she often approaches José as an intermediary.

José's boyfriend and some of his male cousins occasionally go to the gay disco run by GOHL, and have been seen in the neighborhood in the company of "queens." José is not at all pleased by this. One of the major reasons José is attracted to his boyfriend is that he is, by José's standards, heterosexual. If the young man turns out to be gay, José is not at all sure he will continue to be interested in him sexually.

DISCUSSION

An uneasy accommodation now exists between gay people and civil authorities over gay rights in Guadalajara. Only after the election and change in city administrations in 1988 could it be known how long the accommodation would last. Gay leaders know they must continue to maintain vigilance over potential abuses by homophobic elements in their society. They are also aware of the continuing need to educate homosexual people and the general public about the positive aspects of being gay.

An ongoing problem *within* the gay liberation movement reflects differences between those homosexual males who are open and feminine and those who are not. Public demonstrations of feminine behavior by young gay males who consider it a basic part of their makeup is disturbing to those gay males who prefer to comport themselves in more masculine ways and thus be less obvious in straight settings.

Leaders of gay liberation must therefore deal with the need to accept the rights of young feminine gay males, who have provided major support for the gay rights movement, to behave in public as they want, as well as the right of other gay males to behave in public in more conservative ways, even stay in the closet if they choose to. Although attempts have been made in the gay liberation movement to get its more masculine members to view feminine male behavior in a more positive way, they have had little success.

The predicament has its roots in a rather pervasive cultural belief system. Although Mexicans are traditionally quite permissive about sexual behavior in private or in regulated urban zones (zonas rojas), as previously noted they have strong feelings against public displays of behavior which are considered immoral, scandalous, or publicly disturbing. Masculine gay males who are not out of the closet to family members, neighbors, or friends may thus be concerned about having their reputations burned by the "scandalous behavior" of young feminine gay males in public. They may participate in "campy" feminine behavior among themselves in private, but would only do so in public with great care.

Although differing considerably in the paths followed, Pedro's and José's biographies reveal that prior to coming out both were generally concerned about their families, neighbors, and friends finding out about their homosexual behavior. And even after coming out of the closet, they still carefully control their gay behavior at home and in public so as not to offend the sensibilities of others. For example, even though José is openly gay in his neighborhood, he still conducts himself "seriously" (meaning not in a campy gay manner) in the presence of his family, with whom he still lives, and in most social settings involving straight neighbors. Pedro also continues to conduct himself in a masculine way with his family and, as a leader of the gay liberation movement, with public officials and the general public.

A comparison of Pedro's and José's biographies further points out an important behavioral difference between young gay Mexican males: The amount of cognitive dissonance generated by being homosexual appears to differ considerably between them. Although some go through the kind of homosexual panic experienced by Pedro before coming out, many do not. José, for example, never really thought of himself as heterosexual prior to coming out, and so did not go through the kind of identity crisis that Pedro experienced.

Some critical variables related to cognitive dissonance generated when gay youth are contemplating homosexual or gay identities prior to coming out include (a) degree of masculinity, (b) heterosexual identity, (c) number of homosexual experiences, (d) age when first meaningful homosexual experiences occurred, and (e) sex role played.

Feminine male youth, who only play the "pasivo" sexual role

(i.e., receptive anal intercourse in Mexico) and begin meaningful homosexual relations prior to puberty, appear never to think of themselves as being heterosexual, accepting homosexual identities in their early teens and thereby experiencing less cognitive dissonance. They appear to have fewer concerns with establishing gay identities and coming out.

Masculine male youth, on the other hand, who start out playing only the "activo" sexual role (i.e., insertive anal intercourse) and begin (or contemplate having) meaningful homosexual relations while adolescents, appear to think of themselves as being heterosexual and thus are more likely to experience considerable cognitive dissonance over their homosexual thoughts or behavior. They may reduce dissonance by having successful heterosexual intercourse or by limiting their homosexual contacts and by playing only the insertive sexual role. However, as Pedro's biography illustrates, sufficient dissonance may occur and homosexual panic generated when a youth with no sexual experiences just contemplates acting out homosexual desires and thus fears not being heterosexual. Another pathway involving panic occurs when a bisexual youth becomes increasingly involved homosexually and incorporates the receptive anal role into his sexual repertoire; that is, becomes an "internacional."

Finally, the two biographies illustrate differences of opinion about gay liberation. Although José recognizes the need for a liberation movement for many gay people, he has not been an active participant and feels that, given *his* gay life-style, its outcome has no particular relevance to him. Pedro, on the other hand, as a gay activist believes the outcome is not only important to him, but to all homosexually involved people in Guadalajara.

NOTES

1. Information presented on sociocultural variables and gay behavioral pathways is based mainly on participant-observation and interview data gathered by the author on middle- and lower-class mestizo Guadalajaran male respondents and their families over a period of 17 years. See Carrier (1985, 1976a, and 1976b) for additional information on Mexican male bisexual and homosexual behavior.

The behavior of several respondents has been observed from age 15. They were 32 years old at the time of this writing, and all have gay identities. The history of the gay liberation movement is based on interviews with one of its leaders, Pedro Preciado, and on newspaper reports.

2. One cannot assume that all exclusively homosexual males in Mexico are the result of this self-fulfilling prophecy. Exclusively homosexual males exist who remember themselves masculine as children and who would be judged masculine with any set of criteria as adults. Some of those who are feminine believe their sexual orientation is innate and thus would have been the same with or without the society's association between effeminate behavior and homosexuality. Whatever the causation of feminine behavior, however, be it innate or learned or both, the fact is that heterosexual feminine males in Mexico generally have to prove their sexual orientation.

3. At the time of the 1980 census in Guadalajara, family size averaged seven members — the large majority of whom lived in small two- to four-room houses. Single people choosing to live away from their family of origin generally move to another city or to the United States.

4. In Mexico the use of the words "activo" and "pasivo" by males involved in homosexual behavior is never qualified by the type of sex practiced, the assumption being that the labels refer only to insertive and receptive anal intercourse.

5. On the question of Mexican legal attitudes toward sex, Taylor (1986) asked, "Considering how liberal the Mexican legal attitude toward sex is, how can we account for the constant repression of overt homosexual expression?" The answer lies, he noted,

> In the nature of "the minimum ethics indispensable to maintaining society." For the laws state that overt behavior must conform to the prevailing norms, values, folkways, and mores. Whether homosexual, bisexual or heterosexual, people must not engage in behavior which disturbs the peace, scandalizes others, or is generally considered immoral conduct (falta de moral). Thus, sex in private is inviolate, but public manifestations of sexual interests are subject to prevailing customs and values. (p. 133)

6. Based on interviews of Pedro conducted by the author and by Gonzalo Valdés (1984). It is remarkable that a leading newspaper in Mexico would publish Valdés' candid interview of Pedro.

7. The author has followed José as a research subject since 1970, when he was 15 years old. His neighborhood has been studied by the author since the spring of 1982.

REFERENCES

Carrier, J. M. (1985). Mexican male bisexuality. In F. Klein & T. Wolf (Eds.), *Bisexualities: Theory and research* (pp. 75-85). New York: The Haworth Press.

Carrier, J. M. (1976a). Family attitudes and Mexican male homosexuality. *Urban Life, 5,* 359-375.

Carrier, J. M. (1976b). Cultural factors affecting urban Mexican male homosexual behavior. *Archives of Sexual Behavior, 5,* 103-124.

Espín, O. M. (1984). Cultural and historical influences on sexuality in Hispanic/Latin women: Implications for psychotherapy. In C. Vance (Ed.), *Pleasure and danger: Exploring female sexuality* (pp. 149-164). Boston: Routledge & Kegan Paul.

Kinsey, A. C., Pomeroy, W. B., & Martin, C. E. (1948). *Sexual behavior in the human male.* Philadelphia: W. B. Saunders.

Mother (1984, February). Confesiones de mi madre acerca de mi homosexualidad. *Crisálida: De y para la comunidad gay,* pp. A-D. (GOHL, Guadalajara, Jalisco, Mexico).

Paz, O. (1961). *The labyrinth of solitude: Life and thought in Mexico.* New York: Grove Press.

Peñalosa, F. (1968). Mexican family roles. *Journal of Marriage and Family, 30,* 680-689.

Taylor, C. L. (1986). Mexican male homosexual interaction in public contexts. In E. Blackwood (Ed.), The many faces of homosexuality (pp. 117-136). New York: Harrington Park Press.

Valdés, G. (1984, July 7). El movimiento gay en Guadalajara. Sábado de Uno Más Uno (Guadalajara, Jalisco, Mexico).

Growing Up Gay or Lesbian
in a Multicultural Context

Bob Tremble, CCW

Sexual Orientation and Youth Program, Toronto, Ontario

Margaret Schneider, PhD, C Psych

Ontario Institute for Studies in Education, Toronto, Ontario

Carol Appathurai, MS

Central Toronto Youth Services

SUMMARY. This study is an investigation of the influence of ethnicity on the relationships of gay and lesbian young people and their families. A framework for conceptualizing the influence of culture is presented. Modes of family responses are described and the conflicts involved in maintaining an ethnic identity, and a gay or lesbian identity, are discussed. Implications for researchers and practitioners are identified.

The study of the gay and lesbian experience in North America has been most often the study of the white, middle-class experience. Until recently, the impact of ethnic and racial differences among gay males and lesbians has remained largely unexamined.

Bob Tremble is Training and Development Coordinator of the Sexual Orientation and Youth Program. Margaret Schneider is Assistant Professor in Applied Psychology at the Ontario Institute for Studies in Education. Carol Appathurai is Research and Policy Analyst at Central Toronto Youth Services.

The authors would like to thank Joyce Hunter, Director of Social Services at the Hetrick-Martin Institute for her comments and suggestions.

Correspondence and reprint requests may be addressed to Dr. Schneider, c/o Ontario Institute for Studies in Education, 252 Bloor Street W., Toronto, Ontario Canada M5S 1V6.

However, as anecdotal evidence has emerged among social service providers and in the gay and lesbian communities, occasional articles have begun to appear in the gay press and in professional journals. Some thorny issues for racial and ethnic minorities have been identified. These include: (a) particular difficulties in coming out to the family; (b) finding a niche in the gay and lesbian community in the face of discrimination; (c) difficulties in reconciling sexual orientation and ethnic or racial identity.

The impact of ethnic and racial differences on the coming-out process is particularly relevant in a country such as Canada which is characterized by much racial and ethnic diversity and where government policy actively encourages and supports the retention of discrete ethnic groupings. In Canada, the concept of the melting pot has been eschewed in favor of a cultural mosaic. Since the 1970s when a Ministry of State for Multiculturalism was created, there has been a strong and distinct recognition in government policies that the nation should be held together by recognizing, emphasizing, and glorifying ethnic identity (Smith, 1981).

For the vast majority of immigrants to Canada, the transition from one country to another involves coming face-to-face with a new language, new culture, a new value system, and the realities of an urban setting. Very few first generation immigrants complete that transition. In the context of the government's policy on multiculturalism, each immigrant group can remain ethnically, residentially, occupationally, and socially segregated.

The ethnic mosaic is obvious in Toronto, a city of over 2,000,000, where this research was conducted. Many parts of the city are ethnic enclaves. To the east are the Greek, Indo-Pakistani, and Chinese communities. To the west are the Italian, Portuguese, Polish and Caribbean neighborhoods. The Eastern European, Korean, and Vietnamese communities are notably present as well. Each geographical area is characterized by ethnic restaurants, grocery stores, theatres, and businesses carried out in the language of origin. Even the street signs are bilingual in some districts. Radio and television provide multicultural programming and a variety of ethnic festivals are celebrated throughout the year. Public schools offer heritage language programs for children. Many new Canadians can and do function without ever learning English.

These new Canadians, often from rural backgrounds, with little formal education, bring with them Old World values and traditions. Within each group, traditional life-styles, values, and customs remain strong. The emphasis on strong kinship ties, conformity to traditional gender roles, and the personal duty to continue the ancestral line through marriage and procreation are cornerstones of social and family life within these groups (Fong, 1973: Skeoch & Smith, 1983). Religious faith and practice is an important element of family and community life. None of these values per se are inconsistent with prevailing North American values. The difference lies in the strength of adherence to these values and the insular lifestyle that protects the values from external influences. These values also fend off the threat of cultural assimilation at the same time. After all, one can abandon traditional values in Portugal and still be Portuguese. If they are abandoned in the New World, the result is assimilation.

What are the consequences for the gay or lesbian ethnic[1] youngster? Every adolescent, regardless of ethnic affiliation, must resolve a number of issues as part of the coming-out process. These include: (a) deciding whether or not to disclose to the family, (b) finding a niche among gay and lesbian peers, and (c) reconciling sexual orientation with other aspects of identity. For the child of immigrant parents, the coming-out process takes place against the backdrop of ethnic traditions, values, and social networks. For some, this adds a dimension of complexity to the issues. Homosexuality, often in conflict with North American religious and cultural mores, seems even more incongruous and unacceptable in the context of conservative, Old World values. Furthermore, the rift that occurs between parent and child over sexual orientation is set in the context of an existing conflict as the child pulls away from the Old World culture to espouse the North American way of life.

The purpose of this paper is to examine the complexities of coming out in a multicultural context, to explore some ways in which ethnic parents and their homosexual youngsters can come to terms

with each other, and to formulate some hypotheses regarding ethnicity and the coming-out process.

THEORETICAL FRAMEWORK

"Do you know what my father would do to me if he found out I
was gay?" These are the words of a Portuguese-Canadian boy, age
16, echoed by many young people with immigrant parents from
Greece, Italy, Hong Kong, and so on. We believed that these parents would never be able to accept their gay or lesbian child. In the
course of our project's outreach to the gay and lesbian community,
we had met youngsters who had encountered resistance and hostility from their parents, and many more who would never dare broach
the subject in family circles. Yet, after lengthy interviews with
youngsters of various ethnic backgrounds who had come out to their
parents, the picture became more optimistic. In many instances,
when apparently intractable cultural strictures collided with the
facts of life, the parents' response was more flexible, complex, and
subtle than we had expected. We could account for hostility. How
could we account for the acceptance?

From the interview material emerged a framework for conceptualizing the influence of cultural milieu on the coming-out process.
Levels of conflict form the basis of the framework. All youngsters
experience conflict during the coming-out process. They are in conflict with: (a) themselves, (b) their family, and, (c) their culture, or,
in the case of ethnic youngsters, tied to the New World by such
things as the school system, two cultures. None of these levels of
conflict are independent of each other. To their intrapsychic struggle, youngsters bring their interpretation and internalization of society's dictums regarding homosexuality as well as their personal experiences, strengths and weaknesses. For the parents, perceptions
of cultural dictates will interact with their experience of their
youngster, mediated by family dynamics that were established long
ago. Reactions of the community will depend on community standards as well as the community's knowledge and perception of the
youngster. For example, we have known popular, active youngsters
who have come out in their high schools with relatively little hostil-

ity or censure. We have also known of socially marginal youngsters who were ostracized and harassed for being gay or lesbian. Cultural sanctions are not fixed values. They are perceived and interpreted by individuals, families, communities, and are modified in application by the perceived characteristics of the individuals involved.

The cultural milieu is one of many factors that determines the youngster's ultimate acceptance as a homosexual within the family and the community. However, the cultural milieu is mediated by those immersed in it. For ethnic youngsters, the family represents the Old World culture. It perceives, filters, and interprets that culture for the child. Youngsters themselves internalize and modify cultural mores. Thus, the influence of culture is also the influence of perceptions and interpretation of culture. Herein lies the flexibility to come to terms with homosexuality.

A number of variables may be predictors of culturally-based attitudes toward homosexuality. These include demographics such as: rural versus urban experiences, the number of generations in North America, education, and degree of assimilation. Joyce Hunter, Director of Social Services at the Hetrick-Martin Institute suggests that socioeconomic status is a very important variable. For example, she notes that the young gay males who cross-dress are most often from the lower end of the scale. This likely reflects the greater polarity of gender roles within this subgroup in many cultures. However, we hypothesize that expectations regarding gender role, religious values, and social expectation regarding marriage and family are the pivotal predictors of attitudes toward homosexuality. Specifically, homosexual youngsters will be most in conflict with their cultures when religious beliefs are orthodox, when there exists a strong expectation to reside with the family until marriage, and to get married and have children, and when gender role expectations are polarized and stereotypical.

Paradoxically, these values also provide the pathway to reconciliation between homosexual children and parents. When the love of children and the value of family ties are strong, nothing, including homosexuality, will permanently split the family. Ultimately, when the family system is bound by love and respect, a way is found to embrace the homosexual member.

METHOD AND PARTICIPANTS

Ten young people between the ages of 16 and 21 were interviewed for this research. Their cultural backgrounds were Asian, Portuguese, Greek, Italian, and Indo-Pakistani. Although we attempted to contact equal numbers of males and females, seven of the participants were male. This imbalance reflects the membership of Lesbian and Gay Youth Toronto, the youth group through which we made most of our contacts. Some of our observations are also based on many informal contacts with young people in the gay and lesbian community.

The sample of 10 is neither random nor representative. These youngsters are a minority among their ethnic peers in that they are out to their parents and all but one has maintained a relatively amicable relationship. We focused on the success stories in order to investigate the ways that ethnic youngsters and their parents can coexist openly and harmoniously.

Relatively unstructured interviews were used because of the exploratory nature of the study. During the course of the interview, which lasted from 1 to 2 hours, participants were asked to describe their families, their relationships with their parents, their parents' perceptions of homosexuality, the importance of their ethnic heritage, the importance of religion, perceptions of gender roles, and how their families reacted to the youngsters' sexual orientation. The focus was on the parents' reactions, with less attention paid to the responses of siblings or other significant family members.

THE PARENTS' RESPONSE

In the course of our work with young people we have encountered ethnic youngsters with a variety of experiences with their parents. Many are afraid to disclose and may never do so. Some, who have come out, are met with hostility and rejection. However, this discussion will focus on the success stories.

Success means that the parents have not rejected the youngster and that the parent-child relationship has remained intact. At the very least, the parents have reached a personal understanding of their child's sexual orientation that, distorted or not, enables them to come to terms with it. Although a complete understanding and a positive feeling may not exist, sexual orientation is no longer a constant focus of attention and conflict. What are the factors that influence the process?

The way in which parents prioritize their values seems to be a strong predictor of acceptance. In the determination to find a way to keep "the black sheep within the fold" the recurring theme was, "You are my child and I love you no matter what." Love for the child was given priority over all other values and expectations. Conflicting feelings are resolved through the transformation and re-interpretation of values. A 17-year-old Portuguese-Canadian male describes his mother's reaction:

> I thought she would be disgusted and spit in my face or something. But she said that she was afraid that my life would be very hard, and that I would be hurt. She was concerned about *me*, that I would be lonely without a family of my own. If anything she felt she loved me more because of all the hurdles and everything I would have to face.

For this mother, the importance of the family was articulated as companionship and safekeeping rather than carrying on a name and tradition for its own sake. With this interpretation of family values, some of her concerns could be allayed as she became aware that the traditional nuclear model is not the only type of family. Being able to understand the function of values gives them flexibility.

In some instances parents have precedents and experiences to draw upon. The next two quotations demonstrate how diverse precedents can be relevant:

> Both my parents knew gay people from their culture. My dad had a good friend who finally told him he was gay. My dad said that they were very close and that the guy had always been a good friend and had never come on to him. The guy is my godfather. In fact, he stood up for me at my confirmation. My dad knew he was gay at the time. My mother had a good friend from their village who turned out to be bisexual and my mother has always known. (Portuguese-Canadian male, age 18)

I would like to move out and live closer to downtown next year, but I'm afraid of hurting my parents. They won't understand why I'm moving out and they'll be worried about what the neighbors will say. . . . The neighbors will think we had a fight or something. But I do have two older cousins who aren't married and they don't live at home, and my parents have gotten used to that. So I'm hoping that maybe that will help make things OK. (Italian-Canadian female, age 18)

Members of some ethnic groups find it inconceivable that any of them could be homosexual. Being black, Muslim, Greek, and so forth, and being homosexual, are perceived to be mutually exclusive. The myth remains unchallenged as long as homosexuals remain closeted. To resolve the dissonance created by a gay or lesbian child, ethnic parents may blame the dominant culture. A 20-year-old Pakistani-Canadian male explains, "My parents are hurt. They see homosexuality as being against the Muslim faith. They think of it as a white people's thing. Being gay is something I picked up from my white friends." Homosexuality is perceived as the result of a decadent, Western urban society. It is one of the penalties exacted for seeking a better life in North America. Rather than being an integral part of identity, it may be seen as a form of rebellion, as in this case:

My family holds Western culture somehow responsible for off-beat youth. They think my being lesbian is my being young, and confused, and rebellious. They feel it has something to do with trying to fit into white culture. It's one aspect among many that they don't like about me: I'm left-wing, radical, politically active. And they're waiting for me to stop rebelling and to be heterosexual, go out on dates, and come home early. (East Indian-Canadian female, age 16)

It may also be seen as akin to a bad habit, "My sister saw my sexuality as an addiction. She felt I had an uncontrollable urge of some kind" (Pakistani-Canadian male, age 20).

The myth of sexual seduction is another way of disowning homosexuality: "My parents thought I had probably been seduced or molested. They didn't think it was something you were born with.

It was more like drug abuse or drinking too much'' (Greek-Canadian male, age 17).

Attributing homosexuality to an external source does not make parents any happier, nor could these rationales be called a real understanding, but they do seem to remove responsibility from themselves and their child. The child can be accepted as part of the family, albeit uneasily at times.

Although these youngsters maintained a place in the family, their relationship with their ethnic community and culture was often a different story. In spite of the cultural pride which several expressed, they felt removed from their culture. They usually excluded themselves from cultural activities in order to avoid shaming the family in front of friends. The consequences of this alienation will be discussed later.

Often parents do not understand what it means to be gay or lesbian. Homosexual behavior per se, is not infrequent among adolescent males in some cultures because of the premium placed on female virginity. But to prefer homosexuality as a sexual and affectional orientation is difficult to comprehend. Many people expect gay males to be effeminate, and parents often believe that their gay son wants to be a woman. The idea of lesbianism is even more difficult to grasp. Some people are unaware that lesbians even exist, and parents may believe that their lesbian daughter wants to be a man. In cultures where men are supposed to be macho and women are supposed to be passive and submissive, deviance from gender role is particularly alarming. Parents are somewhat reassured if their child does not behave in the sterotypical gay or lesbian image. Ironically, however, when gender roles are polarized, gay or lesbian youngsters are more likely, themselves, to believe in and act out the homosexual stereotypes.

Perhaps the most elusive aspect of homosexuality is to understand it as a pattern of relationships. An Italian-Canadian male commented:

> The big contradiction is not getting married and having kids. I think they would find it easier to accept a married bisexual guy, who fooled around but had a family, than they would a 50-year-old straight guy, who never married.

In summary, parents have several mechanisms for ameliorating the conflict between homosexuality and cultural values. These include (a) prioritizing and reinterpreting values, (b) finding precedents, and (c) externalizing the blame. Youngsters can (a) withdraw from cultural activities and (b) promote a better understanding of homosexuality, particularly by separating the issue of gender role from sexual orientation. Likely, further investigation would reveal more strategies. However, in the final analysis, the success of the process is reduced to the qualities of the family and the individuals involved. Are they flexible, open-minded, willing to communicate?

> My dad seemed more embarrassed but he was able to say that he didn't understand me. Then he thought about it and said that he didn't know why *he* liked women or why he liked some women and not others. So he said maybe he didn't have to understand why I liked men. He said maybe he could have been gay just as easily as straight, that it's not something of choice. (Portuguese-Canadian male, age 17)

Ultimately, if given the chance, time will demonstrate that gay and lesbian youngsters are still the same people that they always were:

> Everybody in my family knows. I appeared in a TV interview. At first it was really uncomfortable. After a long time and the fact that nothing ever happened to shock them, they all resumed their old ways with me. (Italian-Canadian male, age 19)

CULTURAL IDENTITY

These youngsters have been accepted within their families, but are distanced from their culture to some extent. They stay away because they want to protect their families and because some find little in common with peers who socialize in traditional patterns. They separate from their culture in search of gay and lesbian peers, a process that takes place in the general context of cultural assimilation:

> I'm glad everyone knows. All that is out of the way now. I am
> more separated from them because I'm gay, but part of that is
> because I looked for new, gay friends, and I was breaking
> away from the old traditions anyway. (Greek-Canadian male
> age 19)

The ethnic communities are not large enough to sustain gay or lesbian subcultures of their own. Although there are support groups in Toronto for gay Asians and gay Blacks, ethnic youngsters find themselves in a largely white, middle-class, Protestant milieu. They find few opportunities to meet gay or lesbian role models from their own culture. Thus, in their efforts to integrate their sexual orientation into the rest of their identity, they are often on their own to answer the question, "What does it mean to be gay and Greek, or lesbian and Italian?" Often these youngsters are victimized by the stereotypes within their own culture. They believe that being gay or lesbian means being gender role reversal. They go through a phase of extreme cross-gender behavior, which distresses or alienates their parents, or may leave them open to harassment or victimization.

An unspoken myth exists that the homosexual community, as a culture of people who know oppression, is tolerant and accepting of differences. To a large extent this is actualized in the lesbian community, where ethnic and racial heritage is celebrated in the visual and performing arts. Yet even the lesbian community has its intolerances (Beck, 1982). The reality is that visible minorities in particular, blacks, Asians, and Indo-Pakistanis, have experienced discrimination in the gay community. In 1986 alone, *The Body Politic*, a Toronto-based magazine serving the gay and lesbian community, ran two separate articles on racism against Blacks and Asians within the gay community. A gay Chinese adolescent from Hong Kong states, "I am a double minority. Caucasian gays don't like gay Chinese, and the Chinese don't like the gays. It would be easier to be white. It would be easier to be straight. It's hard to be both." A recent article on gay black men suggests that this double discrimination may result in inadequate coping techniques, poor self-concept, and stereotyped behavior (Icard, 1986).

Where does the ethnic youngster find a sense of belonging? Some look to their countries of origin, "My culture? My culture is over there in Portugal. I would really like to be a lesbian in Portugal. I hear that it's really easy over there" (Portuguese-Canadian female, age 19). In fact, being gay and Portuguese in Portugal or gay and Italian in Italy would be easier because the gay community would consist of Portuguese or Italians. To the Portuguese-Canadian youngster who knows no other gay people from his or her own culture, a homosexual identity and a cultural identity seem mutually exclusive.

The ethnic youngster, particularly from a visible minority, has a foot in each culture without feeling a complete sense of belonging in either. The effect on sense of identity, self-esteem, and sense of well-being, needs further study.

DISCUSSION:
IMPLICATIONS FOR RESEARCH AND PRACTICE

Self-disclosure to the family almost always poses difficult and complex issues for everyone. The results ultimately depend upon the qualities of the family, and the unique characteristics of each individual. Ethnic youngsters are not the only ones for whom the process is conflict-ridden. However, we do contend that the values inherent in many ethnic cultures in North America are a backdrop that can make a difficult situation even more so, and will certainly make the situation appear to be almost insurmountable. All things being equal, youngsters from the Greek-, Portuguese-, Italian-, and Indo-Pakistani-Canadian cultures will face a greater challenge than their counterparts in mainstream North America. We know less about the various Asian and black cultures, although we do know that gays and lesbians from visible minorities are subject to unique stresses.

Mention of religious values has been conspicuously absent from this discussion. Religious practice was an important part of family life in all instances, and most parents expressed some sense that homosexuality was morally wrong. Yet religious values, per se, were rarely invoked as a focus of conflict between parent and child. An Italian-Canadian youth offered this explanation:

> My mother goes to church all the time. Religion is very impor-
> tant to her. We have a Bible in the house. But Italians are
> religious without knowing anything about religion. They never
> open a Bible let alone read one. They couldn't tell you where
> the Bible says homosexuality is a sin.

Although this may explain the absence of religious references in
this small sample, the importance of religious orthodoxy and ways
of addressing it require further investigation.

Young ethnic lesbians have been underrepresented in this research. To some extent this reflects the proportion of lesbians in the
youth group from which the sample was recruited. Generally, girls
have less freedom than boys to come and go as they please, especially at night. In cultures where women's freedom is even more
attenuated, young lesbians would have even more difficulty contacting a youth group. Perceptions of women's sexuality in some
cultures may make it more difficult for females to recognize same-
sex sexual preferences. Many of our respondents stated that their
parents were unaware that lesbians existed, even though they knew
about male homosexuality. A cross-cultural study of lesbians within
the context of women's sexuality in general is suggested by the
relative invisibility of ethnic lesbians.

This exploratory research has some implications for the service
provider who is counseling an ethnic gay or lesbian youngster.

1. Ethnic background is not necessarily a barrier between the gay
or lesbian youngster and the parents, even when values, beliefs, and
traditions mitigate against the acceptance of homosexuality. Consider the family as a unique, individual unit. Assess the strengths
and weaknesses and ask a number of questions. What is the quality
of the family dynamics? Does this family function well when there
is a crisis or conflict? Do the members communicate effectively? A
foundation of healthy family dynamics is necessary if the outcome
of disclosure is to be successful. How does the family prioritize its
values? Is there flexibility in the use and understanding of these
values? What do the family members understand about homosexuality?

2. What are the criteria for a successful outcome with this family? The parents may never approve of the youngster's sexual orien-

tation. They may only achieve tolerance, not acceptance, and may demand that the youngster keep his or her gay life-style separate from family life. Is the youngster prepared to compromise? Are you and the youngster prepared to be flexible with regard to outcome?

3. Has the youngster lost an important connection with his or her culture? What are the present and future psychological and practical consequences of this loss? Does the youngster have a place among gay or lesbian peers in which to feel at home?

4. In this present attempt to broach the topic of homosexuality and multiculturalism, we have made sweeping generalizations about a variety of cultures in order to generate some broadly applicable counseling and research strategies. Nonetheless, we recognize that each ethnic group and the subgroups within each must be treated as unique entities, with obvious as well as subtle differences and similarities. We must become conversant with the cultural perspective of each client in order to do effective work.

Demographic studies have demonstrated that the composition of the gay and lesbian population in North America is very much like the entire population (Bell & Weinberg, 1978). Ethnic gays and lesbians may be less visible, but they do exist. By recognizing and researching this portion of the population, we will become better service providers, helping parents of all cultures to be better able to respond to the gay and lesbian youth who were always there. In the words of a Pakistani-Canadian youngster, "The important thing is that my parents think that being gay is a white man's thing. My culture has to be shown that it's not . . . that it's a *human* thing."

NOTE

1. Although all people have an ethnicity, the term is used here to denote people who have immigrated to Canada in the last few generations and still retain many of the customs and traditions of their country of origin.

REFERENCES

Beck, E. T. (1982). *Nice Jewish girls, A lesbian anthology*. Trumansburg, NY: The Crossing Press Feminist Series.
Bell, A. P., & Weinberg, M. S. (1978). *Homosexualities*. New York: Simon & Schuster.

Fong, S. L. M. (1973). Assimilation and changing social roles in Chinese Americans. *Journal of Social Issues*, *29*, 115-127.

Icard, L. (1986). Black gay men and conflicting social identities: Sexual orientation versus racial identity. *Journal of Social Work & Human Sexuality*, *4*, 83-93.

Skeoch, A., & Smith, T. (1983). *Canadians and their society*. Toronto: McClelland & Stewart.

Smith, A. (1981). National images and national maintenance: The ascendancy of the ethnic idea in North America. *Journal of Political Science*, *14*, 227-258.

Youth, Identity, and Homosexuality: The Changing Shape of Sexual Life in Contemporary Brazil

Richard Parker, PhD

University of California, Berkeley

SUMMARY. This essay examines the relationship between homosexuality and adolescence in contemporary Brazil, focusing on a distinction between two rather different systems of sexual meanings that have structured the experience of same-sex relations: a traditional model of the sexual universe that continues to dominate sexual life in rural areas, and a more modern set of notions that has become increasingly important in the cities. It examines the ways in which these rather different systems have affected the experience of same-sex desires and practices during youth or adolescence, and suggests some of the ways in which the emergence of a gay subculture in

Dr. Parker is affiliated with the Department of Anthropology, University of California, Berkeley.

Field research in Brazil was conducted from July 1982 to August 1982, August 1983 to July 1984, and July 1986 to August 1986. It was made possible by grants from the Tinker Foundation and the Center for Latin American Studies, a Robert H. Lowie Scholarship from the Department of Anthropology, a Traveling Fellowship in International Relations, and a Graduate Humanities Research Grant from the Graduate Division, all at the University of California, Berkeley, as well as a Fulbright Full Grant and a Grant-in-Aid from the Wenner-Gren Foundation for Anthropological Research. The author would like to thank Vagner João Benício de Almeida, Robert N. Bellah, Stanley Brandes, Roberto Da Matta, Alan Dundes, Peter Fry, Paul Kutsche, Ondina Fachel Leal, Rosemary G. Messick, and Nancy Scheper-Hughes for their helpful discussions of many of the issues examined in this essay. Responsibility for the specific interpretations developed here is, of course, entirely the author's.

Correspondence and reprint requests may be addressed to the author c/o the Department of Anthropology, 232 Kroeber Hall, University of California, Berkeley, CA 94720.

urban Brazil has transformed the range of sexual possibilities and choices currently available to young men and women.

I

While the relationship between youth or adolescence and sexuality has been a focus of cross-cultural research for some time, the more specific question of homosexuality among young people has received less cross-cultural attention. Such inattention is hardly surprising given the nature of the popular prejudices concerning homosexuality that continue to play themselves out in our own society. But it is nonetheless unfortunate, particularly in light of the significant insights that have emerged over the course of recent years from historical and anthropological research on homosexuality more generally (see, e.g., Blackwood, 1986; Herdt, 1981, 1984; Plummer, 1981; Weeks, 1977, 1981).

Central to such research has been the growing conviction that the experience of homosexuality, like the experience of sexual life more generally, must be understood less as a natural given than as a highly variable social and cultural construct (see Hansen, 1979; Plummer, 1981; Weeks, 1977, 1981). Precisely because this is the case, the experience of homosexuality among young people must clearly vary as well, and some understanding of such variations could potentially offer important insights — not only about homosexuality, but about the very dynamics of sexual life — that we have thus far largely failed to take into account.

A number of these issues have emerged with particular clarity in my own ethnographic research on the social and cultural construction of sexual life in contemporary Brazil (see Parker, 1984, 1985, 1987). As my research developed and I began to make my way within the system of symbols and meanings that maps out the sexual field in Brazilian life, I became increasingly convinced that it must be understood as comprised of multiple subsystems, multiple discourses, or cultural frames of reference that exhibited rather specific social and historical relationships and that exerted a central influence in shaping the sexual experiences and understandings of different individuals (see, in particular, Parker, 1984). Responding, perhaps above all else, to the complex interplay between tradition and modernity in a rapidly changing society, these multiple frames of reference seem often to both contradict and yet at the same time intersect one another, opening up not a single, unique sexual reality, but a set of multiple realities. Nowhere can this multiplicity be seen more clearly than in the case of homosexuality, which, in Brazil at least, must be characterized less as a unitary phenomenon than as a fundamentally diverse one — a case, at the very least, of a variety of somewhat different homosexualities rather than of a single, unified homosexuality (Parker, 1985, 1987).

In the pages that follow, I will try to explicate these rather abstract assertions a bit more fully while paying special attention to the ways in which the particular construction of sexual meanings in Brazil influences the shape of homosexual experience among young people. I will argue, in particular, that at least two quite distinct systems of sexual meaning currently shape the experience of same-sex sexual interactions in Brazil, and will examine some of the (quite different) ways in which both of these systems, at least when compared with our own traditions in the industrialized West, seem to allow perhaps an unusual degree of fluidity or flexibility in the constitution of sexual realities among adolescents. Ultimately, however, I will suggest that the impact of this fluidity or flexibility in opening up the potential for shaping one's own sexual identity is quite clearly strongest for young people in Brazil's larger, more highly modernized and industrialized cities, where, thanks to the contingencies of the current historical moment, a rather unusual wealth of choices seems to characterize the contemporary experience of sexual life.[1]

II

In seeking some understanding of the experience of homosexuality among young people in Brazil, it is absolutely essential to realize that the very notion of homosexuality itself is, in fact, but a rather recent development. In Brazil, as in the nations of the industrialized West, homosexuality has a history. While a whole set of ideas related to homosexuality (and, by extension, to heterosexuality as well) have recently taken root in Brazilian culture, these ideas have in fact been imported from the industrialized West — modeled, as we shall see, on patterns that had already emerged in Europe and the United States. As relatively recent imports, such notions are far from the only, or even the dominant, way of conceiving the sexual universe in Brazilian culture.

On the contrary, this more modern, more highly rationalized way of thinking about sexual life that was originally developed in the West and only later imported to Brazil coexists there with what is perhaps a far more deeply rooted set of traditional ideas about the nature of things sexual. Such traditional notions can perhaps best be described as a kind of folk model of the sexual universe, and clearly contrast in a number of important ways with more modern notions. This folk model has, until quite recently, served as the central frame of reference that Brazilians have used in articulating and interpreting the significance of their sexual experience (see Fry, 1982, 1985; Parker, 1984, 1985, 1987).

Within the folk model of sexual life in Brazil, cultural emphasis seems to have been focused not merely on sexual practices in and of themselves, but on the relationship between sexual practices and gender roles—in particular, on a distinction between masculine *atividade* (activity) and feminine *passividade* (passivity) as central to the organization of sexual reality. It is in terms of this distinction between atividade and passividade that notions of *macho* (male) and *fêmea* (female), of *masculinidade* (masculinity) and *feminilidade* (femininity), and the like, have typically been organized in Brazil. In daily life, however, these notions have been constructed rather less formally in the discourse of popular culture. They have been less a product of self-conscious reflection than of the implicit values encoded in the language that Brazilians commonly use to speak about the body and its practices, about the combination of bodies, and about the classificatory categories that flow from such combinations (see Parker, 1984, 1985, 1987).

Perhaps nowhere is this distinction between atividade and passividade more evident than in the popular language that Brazilians use in describing sexual relations, in verbs such as *comer* (literally, to eat) and *dar* (literally, to give). Comer, for example, is used to describe the male's active penetration of the female during sexual intercourse. It implies a kind of symbolic domination that is typical of Brazil's traditional culture of gender, and can be used as a synonym, in a number of different contexts, for verbs such as *possuir* (to possess) or *vencer* (to vanquish, conquer). Dar, on the other hand, is used to describe the female's passive submission to her male partner, her role of being penetrated during intercourse. Just as comer is used to describe various forms of domination through reference to the relations of gender, dar can be used to imply submission, subjugation, and passivity in any number of settings. Drawing on these categories (and any number of others that function in precisely the same way), then, the sexual universe is continually structured and restructured, in even the simplest and most common verbal exchanges, along the lines of a rigid hierarchy: a distinction between sexual atividade and passividade that is translated into relations of power and domination between machos and fêmeas, between *homens* (men) and *mulheres* (women) (see Fry, 1985; Fry & MacRae, 1983; Parker, 1984, 1985).

What is particularly important to understand in the present context, however, is not simply the structure of this hierarchy, but the fact that, within the traditional context of Brazilian popular culture, it has been used to organize and conceptualize sexual relations both between members of the opposite sex, *and* between members of the same sex. The symbolic structure of male/female interactions seems to function in many ways as a kind of model for the organization of same-sex interactions in Brazilian culture. Within the terms of this model, what is centrally important is perhaps less the shared biological gender of the participants than the social roles that they play out — their atividade or passividade as sexual partners and social persons. A homem who enters into a sexual relationship with another male does not necessarily sacrifice his masculinidade — so long as he performs the culturally perceived active, masculine role during sexual intercourse and conducts himself as a male within society. And a mulher who conforms to her properly passive, feminine sexual and social role will not jeopardize her essential feminilidade simply by virtue of occasional (or even ongoing) sexual interactions with other biological females (see Fry, 1982, 1985; Fry & MacRae, 1983; Parker, 1984, 1985, 1987).

The same cannot be said, however, of the errant partners in such sexual exchanges. On the contrary, the male who adopts a passive, female posture, whether in sexual intercourse or social interaction, almost inevitably undercuts his own masculinidade, just as a female, in adopting an active, dominating, masculine posture undercuts her feminilidade. By upsetting the culturally prescribed fit between biological gender and social gender, both must sacrifice their appropriate categorization as homem and mulher. The failed homem comes to be known as a *viado* (from *veado*, or, literally, deer) or a *bicha* (literally, worm or intestinal parasite, but also, instructively, the feminine form of *bicho* or animal, and thus a female animal) thanks to his inappropriate femininity, while the inadequate mulher is known as a *sapatão* (literally, big shoe) or even a *coturno* (army boot), due to her unacceptable masculinity. Both figures are seen, in a very strong sense, as failures on both social and biological counts — as unable to realize their biological potential because of inappropriate social behavior, yet equally unable to cross the boundaries of social gender due to inadequate anatomy. Not surprisingly, both are thus subject to among the most severe stigmatization to be found anywhere in Brazilian society (see Fry, 1982, 1985; Fry & MacRae, 1983; Parker, 1984, 1985, 1987).

Within the framework of this relatively traditional model, then, there exists a fairly explicit cultural construction of same-sex desires and practices. What is perhaps most striking, at least from our own vantage point, is that an individual's same-sex object choice seems to be, in some ways, rather less significant than his or her sexual role; less significant, in other words, than the connection between anatomical and social gender as played out in terms of atividade and passividade. In light of these facts, it is hardly surprising that central cultural emphasis should traditionally have been given in Brazil to the problem of assuring the atividade of *meninos* (little boys) and the passividade of *meninas* (little girls). While average Brazilians are of course unlikely to reflect upon the psychodynamic processes involved in the formation of gender identities, they tend to view the masculinidade of the menino as almost constantly threatened by too close contact with female relatives such as his mothers and sisters, and Brazilian men, in particular, make a rather conscious effort to encourage active, aggressive, masculine behaviors on the part of their young male relatives. Feminilidade, on the other hand, seems to be seen less as threatened than as threatening — a rather perplexing force, tied to natural rhythms and female reproductivity, and in need of almost constant repression. If masculinidade must be built, feminilidade must be controlled. The passividade of the menina, no less than the atividade of the menino, must be encouraged, shaped, and molded in society.

The consequences of the social shaping of active and passive stances among boys and girls become fully evident only as children begin to take part in sexual activities. Upon entering adolescence, *rapazes* (boys or young men) who have successfully built up (or in whom society has successfully built up) an "active" stance in relation to their gender identity are clearly expected to demonstrate and even follow through on their desire for the opposite sex, as are *moças* (girls or young women) who have succeeded in adopting a properly "passive" stance, though the actual activities of adolescent girls continue to be closely guarded and controlled by their male relatives, who are thought to exercise rightfully absolute authority over the sexual powers of their female relatives. As they progress through adolescence and on into full adulthood (most commonly marked in Brazil by marriage), however, these same individuals will not uncommonly *also* take an interest in sexual play with members of the same sex. Indeed, such play is frequently reported by informants as at least one important part of their early sexual educations.

Among rapazes, same-sex play and exploration is almost institutionalized through games such as *troca-troca* (literally, exchange-exchange), in which two (or more) boys take turns, each inserting the penis in their partner's anus. It is perhaps even more obvious in the expression, *Homem, para ser homem, tem que dar primeiro* (A man, to be a man, has to give [in passive anal intercourse] first), which is often used by older boys seeking to comer their slightly younger playmates. And while such practices are perhaps less explicit among groups of moças, early sexual play with same-sex partners is cited nearly as frequently by female informants as by males. Such experiences seem relatively widespread and, as a game such as troca-troca would indicate, offer participants with at least some room to explore both active and passive roles. Assuming that the cultural system has, in fact, successfully carried out its mandate, however, such early adolescent play is quite explicitly *not* expected to disrupt fundamentally the process of development that will ultimately transform the rapaz into an active homem and the moça into a passive mulher.

If, however, we have learned anything at all from psychoanalytic theory, it is precisely that cultural systems often *fail* to carry out their mandate (see, in particular, Weeks, 1985). For the rapaz who, for whatever reasons, has failed to acquire a properly active stance, or a moça who has been unable to adopt a passive stance, it is in such adolescent sexual play, as well, that psychological disposition begins to be transformed into a distinct social role. For these individuals, however, the available roles are not the positively sanctioned categories of homem and mulher, but the negatively stigmatized categories of bicha and sapatão. Failure to perform properly (i.e., in active/passive terms) in early sexual interactions seems to translate rather rapidly, on the part of these individuals, into an emphasis, during all social performances, on the social style of the opposite sex. Viados or bichas, defined initially in terms of their passive performances during sexual intercourse, rather quickly begin to adopt an exaggerated effeminate style in their more public social interactions as well, just as sapatões, defined by their activity, take on many of the most explicit symbols and characteristics of an exaggerated masculinity. They set out upon a life course that is culturally recognized and institutionalized, yet at the same time stigmatized and often even openly oppressed (see Fry & MacRae, 1983; Parker, 1987).

Within the context of this traditional, folk model of the sexual universe in Brazil, then, same-sex desires and practices clearly have an important place in the sexual experience of many, if not most, young men and women. The specific cultural configuration of such desires and practices is quite different, though, from our own modern conception of homosexuality, with its focus on sexual object choice as definitive of sexual identity. On the contrary, within this traditional system, sexual object choice seems unusually fluid or variable, especially during adolescence. One's object choice is clearly less important than what might be described as one's gender role, atividade or passividade, in organizing or structuring same-sex interactions. The categorical distinctions that shape the experience of *both* young and old within this system are not those between heterosexuals and homosexuals, but between homens, mulheres, viados, and sapatões. It is perhaps above all else during the sexual experimentation of youth or adolescence that individuals begin to sort themselves out (not so much psychologically, of course, as socially) within the framework of these categories, transforming private desires into public identities, and develop an understanding of their place within what will rather quickly become a fairly rigid hierarchy of gender that will continue to exert profound influence on them throughout the course of their lives.

III

While certainly subject to at least some regional variation in terminology and usage, the basic form or structure of the folk model of sexual reality that we have described has clearly been central throughout Brazilian history. As a number of writers have suggested, this model seems to have dominated the sexual landscape in Brazil throughout the 19th and early 20th centuries, and continues to function, even today, both in rural areas as well as among the lower classes (many of whom are themselves migrants from the countryside) in Brazil's larger, more modernized and industrialized cities (see, in particular, Fry, 1982; Parker, 1985). Since at least the first decades of the 20th century, however, and increasingly during the course of the past 10 to 15 years, this traditional system has gradually begun to give way to—or, perhaps more accurately, to coexist with—a far more rationalized manner of thinking about the nature of things sexual: a model rooted, perhaps above all else, in the conceptions of modern medical science, and imported to Brazil from Western Europe and the United States (see Fry, 1982; Fry & MacRae, 1983; Parker, 1984, 1985, 1987; Trevisan, 1986.)

Introduced in Brazilian culture, at least initially, through the writings of medical doctors, therapists, and psychoanalysts (see, e.g., Pires de Almeida, 1906; Doyle, 1956; Ribeiro, 1938), and translated only gradually into the wider discourse of popular culture, this new medical/scientific model seems to have marked a fundamental shift in cultural attention or emphasis away from a distinction between active and passive roles as the building blocks of gender hierarchy, and toward the importance, along European and North American lines, of sexual object choice as central to the definition of the sexual subject (on Europe and the United States, see, of course, Foucault, 1979; Weeks, 1977, 1981; on Brazil, see Fry, 1982; Parker, 1985, 1987; Trevisan, 1986). In practical terms, perhaps its greatest impact has been the creation of a new set of classificatory categories—notions such as *homossexualidade* (homosexuality), *heterossexualidade* (heterosexuality), and *bissexualidade* (bisexuality)—for mapping out and interpreting the sexual landscape.

By the mid-20th century, these new categories had become central to the medical and scientific discussion of sexual life throughout Brazil, and had been fully incorporated into the language of law and government as well. But, until perhaps the late 1960s or the early 1970s, their influence seems to have been limited almost entirely to a small, highly educated elite—the same segment of the Brazilian population that has traditionally maintained contact with and been most influenced by European and North American culture. Restricted to this elite, notions such as homossexualidade (understood not merely as a sexual behavior, but as a class of people, or even a distinct way of being in the world) had largely failed to penetrate the language of daily life in Brazil. Up until perhaps the 1970s, the system of sexual classifications that is so familiar to us in Europe and the United States simply failed to play a significant role in Brazilian popular culture or to influence the lives and experiences of the vast majority of Brazilians (see Fry, 1982; Fry & MacRae, 1983; Parker, 1985, 1987; Trevisan, 1986).

Even while this is the case, however, precisely at the same time that this new conception of same-sex relations was first making itself felt among the elite, an almost secretive (or semisecretive) sexual subculture organized around same-sex preferences and practices was itself beginning to take shape, principally among the popular classes in such large, rapidly industrializing and modernizing cities as Rio de Janeiro and São Paulo (see Trevisan, 1986; for glimpses of this subculture, see also, Freyre, 1981; Manta, 1928). Reproducing the distinctions between atividade and passividade as central to the organization of sexual relations between members of the same sex, and, indeed, exaggerating the importance of such distinctions almost to the point of caricature, this subculture seems to have placed less emphasis on a shared identity common to all its participants than on the simple fact of same-sex sexual contacts. It was shared sexual behavior within its protective spaces that seemed to tie the members of this subculture together, rather than some sense of themselves as somehow members of the same sexual species because of this behavior, and the symbolic center of this urban underworld was thus less psychological than spatial: the cafés or bars, the plazas and streets where individuals seeking such sexual contacts were known to meet. Protected, at least up to a point, by the increased anonymity of urban life, a loosely organized, flexible, and constantly shifting sexual community began to take shape in the streets of Brazil's larger cities at the same time that a notion of homossexualidade as a distinct mode of sexual being was beginning to form in the saloons and studies of the well-to-do and well-educated. (For the fullest discussion of these developments that is yet available, see Trevisan, 1986.)

Thus, throughout the early and mid-20th century, two new models for the conceptualization and organization of same-sex desires and practices had begun to emerge in Brazil. These two models seem to have contrasted rather sharply both with one another as well as with the traditional model of same-sex interactions available in popular culture. By the late 1960s or early 1970s, however, as a result of developments both within Brazil itself as well as in the outside world, the histories of these new models began to merge. On the one hand, it was at this point that the Brazilian middle class, which had been developing gradually since the end of the 19th century, really began to exercise dominant influence in Brazilian society as a whole. Always concerned with and sensitive to the latest styles and developments in the so-called developed world, the members of this newly dominant class did not fail to take note of a series of significant changes that had begun to take place in Western Europe and the United States: the emergence of urban gay culture and the gay liberation movement as significant forces in contemporary Western society.

For more conservative Brazilians, as for conservative Americans or Europeans, such developments were a sign of decadence and decay. For individuals drawn to same-sex relations, however, and oppressed or stigmatized by the restrictions of Brazil's traditional sexual universe, the model offered by gay life in Paris, New York,

San Francisco, or what have you, was in fact profoundly powerful. The notion of a *communidade gay* (gay community) organized around an *identidade homossexual* (homosexual identity) or an *identidade gay* (gay identity) rather quickly became, for members of the middle class, a point of convergence where the elite appropriation of modern medical/scientific classifications and the popular reality of a sexual subculture organized around same-sex practices could be brought together and, at least up to a certain point, merged. Throughout the 1970s and on into the 1980s, these various currents would continue to flow together and mix, making possible the progressive formation of what is now probably the largest and most visible gay subculture anywhere outside of the industrialized West (see, e.g., Altman, 1980; Fry, 1982; Fry & MacRae, 1983; Lacey, 1979; MacRae, 1982, 1983; Parker, 1985, 1987; Trevisan, 1986; Whitam, 1979; Young, 1973).

It would be a mistake, however, to view this Brazilian subculture as nothing more than an importation from abroad, a tropical version of the gay community as it exists in Europe or the States. On the contrary, it has continued to respond in a variety of ways to the particularities of Brazil's own social and cultural context. Perhaps nowhere is this more evident than in its reproduction of such traditional distinctions as atividade and passividade in a profusion of sexual categories or types. Terms such as viado, bicha, and sapatão are reproduced, and other, even finer distinctions are added. Effeminate bichas, for instance, are contrasted with *bofes* (perhaps best translated as studs or hunks), who are characterized in terms of their aggressive masculinity and their active sexual role. The man-like sapatão is contrasted to the more feminine *sapatilha* (literally, slipper) roughly like a butch dyke is contrasted to a fem. And in the increasingly prominent world of male prostitution (which is, of course, a function not merely of desire, but also of poverty, at least in the underdeveloped world), a sharp distinction is drawn between the *travesti* (transvestite) and the *michê* (in this context, hustler) — between an exaggerated, feminine figure who clearly prefers a passive sexual role and an almost equally exaggerated masculine figure thought to be generally available for the active role but unwilling to perform the passive role (see Parker, 1987).

A set of active/passive distinctions that is unusually elaborate thus typifies this subculture and clearly emphasizes its specifically Brazilian character. Yet even here, it is important to emphasize just how different this is from the traditional model of the sexual universe that continues to dominate life in rural Brazil. The distinctions that characterize this urban subculture are never seen as absolute. It is part and parcel of the ideology that structures this world that such active/passive oppositions can always be inverted, that bofes or michês can be convinced to dar while travestis and bichas comem, and so on. The overturning of such categorical distinctions is possible because, unlike the distinctions of traditional culture, these categories are determined and defined from *within* the subculture itself. While the viado or the sapatão in traditional culture are defined from without, stigmatized and labeled by the other members of the wider society, and ultimately excluded from the world of proper homens and mulheres, here, within this more modern subculture, *one essentially defines oneself*, on the basis of one's sexual and erotic preferences and within the community of one's fellows. And the company of one's fellows, in turn, provides at least some form of protection from the kinds of hostility and oppression that one might still have to face when confronting the wider social world.

This sense of community comes through perhaps most clearly in the fact that all such elaborate categories can be subsumed under the more general heading of *entendido* or, in the case of women, *entendida* (literally, one who knows or one who understands). This more general category had apparently been present for some time within the relatively secretive, almost underground subculture that began to take shape in the early-20th century. It began to be used much more frequently, however, with the great expansion and the increasing visibility of this subculture in the 1970s. At least since that time, it has been used by the members of this subculture themselves as an all-encompassing term referring to anyone who, to whatever extent, participates in — and thus, by extension, knows or understands the nature of — this specific community.

Significantly, then, the term entendido applies both to those individuals (again, mostly middle class) who have adopted a strictly homosexual or gay identity based on the model provided by the industrialized West, as well as to anyone else who has come to take part in this particular subculture even sporadically, without necessarily limiting themselves to it or defining themselves solely through their relationship to it. In short, it is a category that can apply to individuals who engage exclusively in same-sex interactions, as well as to individuals who engage in sexual relationships with both sexes. Indeed, the entendido and the entendida are thus almost mirror images of the traditional homem and mulher (who inevitably engage in relationships with the opposite sex, but who enjoy a certain freedom to interact with members of their own biological sex as well).

Ultimately, then, what seems to have emerged over the course of the past decade in large urban centers such as Rio or São Paulo — and only to a slightly lesser extent in smaller cities such as Porto Alegre, Recife, or Salvador — is a relatively complex sexual subculture that, while surely woven from Brazilian cloth, nonetheless provides a model for the organization of sexual reality that is clearly very different from the more traditional patterns of Brazilian culture. While this new subculture tends to retain much of the fluidity or flexibility of sexual desire that seemed so typical in traditional culture, it organizes it and links it to the formation of identities in rather different ways. And it clearly offers those individuals whose lives it touches a radically different set of possibilities and choices in the constitution of their own sexual and social lives.

The effect of these changes has surely been felt by Brazilians of all ages, though middle aged and older individuals, who also experienced the patterns of traditional life more deeply, are perhaps more consciously aware of the *mudanças* (shifts or changes) that have taken place around (and often within) them. While they may well be less cognizant of such historical dimensions, however, it is a younger generation that has felt the impact of these developments most forcefully, as perhaps nowhere have the rules of the game changed quite so profoundly as for adolescents seeking to shape their own understandings of themselves and of their place within the wider social world.

The experiences of adolescents within this more modern, urban setting are surely not entirely divorced from those of young Brazilians growing up in more traditional settings. On the contrary, even in the most modernized sectors of Brazilian society, the sexual classifications and values of traditional culture are well known and implicitly understood by all Brazilians. And the sexual play of children and young adolescents that seemed so central to the shaping of public identities based on sexual preferences in traditional Brazil continues to be an important part of one's sexual education and maturation in urban settings. In the more modern context of the cities, however, the significance of such interactions seems rather reduced because of the vastly expanded opportunities for the exploration of one's sexual desires. The existence of a relatively complex and varied sexual subculture where young men and women can begin to explore their own sexuality not only through specific sexual practices, but as part of a much more all inclusive social experience, has radically transformed the process through which adolescents both shape as well as understand their own sexual realities.

Almost invariably, it is during adolescence (especially for boys, though perhaps somewhat less frequently for girls, whose sexuality continues to be more guarded and repressed even in the cities) that individuals first come into contact with the entendido subculture. One's point of entry into this subculture varies greatly, both from individual to individual, as well as from one social class to another. For boys who come from the urban poor or who have migrated to the cities from the countryside, for instance, some form of prostitution is a typical rite of passage serving both erotic and financial ends, and the specific streets, plazas, and bars that serve as a focus for male prostitution in any given city provide many lower-class males with their earliest exposure to this new world. For both boys and girls from the middle or upper classes, more expensive clubs or discos and, at least in coastal cities, the gay sections of the beaches, are perhaps more likely settings. Within such more or less protected or protective spaces, same-sex sexual contacts can be initiated and carried out in relative safety, and without much fear of negative social sanction or stigmatization because one's activities are obscured from the view of the wider society. For anyone who experiences same-sex desires, then, the appeal of this subculture can hardly be underestimated.

The presence of same-sex desires, then, linked, of course, to economic need in the case of male prostitution, first draws young women and men to this urban subculture, and same-sex sexual transactions provide the focus for any individual's continued participation within it. Yet even though this must thus be described as a sexual subculture, a subculture organized first and foremost around a specific set of sexual preferences and practices, there is an ironic sense in which the importance of sex itself is in some ways less absolute here within this subculture than was the case in more traditional settings where no such subculture existed. This is because here, in this urban subculture, sexual conduct becomes linked to an entire social milieu, a community, if you will, though certainly not quite as bounded or well defined a community as those of the industrialized West.

Within this community, a sense of self is built up not only through the meanings attached to one's sexual role (though, as we have seen, such meanings do not cease to exist), but through the nature of one's relationships. Perhaps nothing quite so profoundly differentiates the experience of adolescents in contemporary urban Brazil from those in more traditional areas as this shift of emphasis from acts to relations. Within this more modern sexual subculture, ongoing relationships are constructed that may or may not be sexual in nature, but which play a central role in the shaping of social identities.[2]

While these relationships are no doubt as varied as the individuals who form them, for adolescents they nonetheless seem to take shape in at least two significant directions: horizontally and vertically. On the one hand, as young men and women enter the gay subculture, they quickly form friendships with groups of peers roughly their own age, more often than not from the same class background, and almost invariably their same sex, who also consider themselves entendidos or entendidas. Sexual interactions may take place from time to time between such peer group members, but are generally less significant to the nature of such relationships than is a shared sense of comradeship, a shared sense of understanding and friendship.

At the same time as they are forming these horizontal relationships with their peers, young entendidas and entendidos also tend to form vertical relationships based on age and class differences, relationships with individuals who are either older, more well-to-do, or, typically, both. Perhaps even more frequently than in the case of horizontal relationships among peers, these vertical relationships often begin as sexual relationships, then gradually transform themselves into ongoing and often extremely deep friendships. Such vertical relations tend to be extremely important in initiating younger men and women into the wider world of this subculture, and older individuals are sometimes willing to take on and teach their younger partners almost as is if they were apprentices. And as is perhaps to be expected in an extremely hierarchical society such as Brazil, there is often a certain patron/client quality to such relationships as well, with more well-to-do individuals sometimes going out of their way to provide financial support, educational and vocational opportunities, as well as love and friendship, to their younger partners.

The construction of such profound, ongoing relationships within the urban gay subculture distinguishes the experience of young entendidos and entendidas from that of viados and sapatões in traditional Brazil perhaps more sharply than any other single factor. Thanks to such relationships, and to the sexual subculture, the protected social space that makes them possible, adolescents drawn to same-sex sexual practices in contemporary Brazil inhabit a world that is radically different from that inhabited by their counterparts in more traditional settings, a world in which it is far more possible to shape and reshape one's own identity through both sexual and social interactions with one's fellows. It would be completely incorrect to suggest that this new world is a world without prejudice or social stigma. On the contrary, like the traditional system of sexual meanings itself, traditional prejudices continue to exist, and new ones have certainly evolved as well (see Parker, 1985, 1987). But the ability that young women and men now have actively to shape their own sexual realities, as well as the social world within which these realities will be lived out, surely contrasts quite sharply with that more traditional system of meanings in which the possibilities open to one were largely predetermined and often absolute.

IV

Ultimately, the major point that I want to emphasize is the fact that the relationship between homosexuality and adolescence in contemporary Brazil, as anywhere else in the contemporary world, is hardly a simple one. On the contrary, to even begin to approach this relationship, it is necessary to situate it within a much broader context, and to examine it in terms of the profoundly complex meanings and symbolic transformations that it inevitably entails. This task is all the more necessary in a setting such as Brazil precisely because of the complex interplay between tradition and modernity that characterizes so much of the industrializing world. In such contexts, systems of sexual meaning are often less unified than multiple, values are less fixed than constantly changing. This is certainly the case in Brazil, and perhaps nowhere is it more evident than in relation to homosexuality and the sexuality of the young more generally.

What one finds in Brazil, then, is not only one, but at least two, relatively distinct, though not entirely unrelated, systems or models for the organization of sexual life: a traditional model that continues to dominate in rural areas and perhaps in very small cities, and a more modern model heavily influenced by the patterns of the industrial West but already deeply rooted in Brazil's larger, more industrialized cities. In the first of these two models or systems, emphasis is placed, perhaps above all else, on the sexual act itself, and on the culturally conceived roles of the participants in this act. On the basis of such considerations, social identities are built up, principally during youth or adolescence, that codify sexual reality in a number of rather specific ways, offering relative sexual freedom to those males and females whose behavior is seen to be properly tied to their biological gender, but seriously stigmatizing those who have failed to live up to such social expectations.

This situation has been changing radically for some time in urban Brazil, however, where the sexual classifications of modern medical science and the patterns of social relations characteristic of the gay communities of the industrialized West have exerted increasing influence and have been adapted to the specific circumstances of contemporary Brazilian life. Here, in the sexual subculture that has emerged in larger cities such as Rio and São Paulo, a new social space seems to be emerging in which a vastly expanded set of choices and possibilities are available to adolescents seeking to pursue sexual contacts with members of their own sex. Within this subculture, the importance of sexual acts has perhaps given way, at least up to a certain extent, to a new emphasis on social relationships as centrally important in shaping the experiences of young men and women. One's sexual role has been treated, not unlike desire itself, as far less fixed than fluid or variable, and social identities tied to one's erotic preferences have perhaps become less a matter of external imposition on the part of a wider, and often hostile, society, than a matter of negotiation and construction within a far more supportive social setting.

One can only speculate, of course, about the ways in which the various developments we have examined will continue to play themselves out in the future. For the moment, however, suffice it to say that while the modernization of sexual life in Brazil has brought with it its own unique dilemmas, it has nonetheless helped to open up for many Brazilians, and especially for the young, a whole range of new opportunities and choices. Whether from our own perspective as outside observers, or from the perspective of Brazilians themselves, it is impossible to ignore the significance of these changes.

NOTES

1. My concern in this essay will *not* be the question of how homosexual desire initially takes shape, though the question is obviously a crucial one. For a helpful discussion which has shaped my own understanding of this issue, see Herdt and Stoller (1985). My central concern here is not the origin of homosexual desires, but the ways in which such (preexisting) desires manifest themselves and play themselves out in specific social settings. I am interested in the various channels that Brazilian society has opened up for such desires, the ways in which it has sought to organize them culturally, particularly during the crucially important period of adolescence.

2. While the context is, of course, quite different, my understanding of this distinction between acts, relations, and, ultimately, choices has been heightened by the discussions of both Foucault (1982/1983) and Weeks (1985). Clearly, neither writer intended to typify distinct cultural configurations as I have here, but such a characterization can nonetheless be useful if it helps us to understand the different emphases of these rather distinct ways of conceptualizing the sexual universe in Brazil.

REFERENCES

Altman, D. (1980). Down Rio way. *Christopher Street, 4*(8), 22-27.

Blackwood, E. (Ed.). (1986). *Anthropology and homosexual behavior*. New York: The Haworth Press.

Doyle, I. (1956). *Contribuição ao estudo da homossexualidade feminina* (Contribution to the study of female homosexuality). Rio de Janeiro: Compositora Gráfica LUX Ltda.

Foucault, M. (1979). *The history of sexuality, Volume 1: An introduction*. New York: Random House.

Foucault, M. (1982/1983). Sexual choice, sexual act: An interview with Michel Foucault. *Salmagundi, 58/59*, 10-24.

Freyre, G. (1981). *Sobrados e mucambos*, sexta edição (The mansions and the shanties). Rio de Janeiro: Livraria José Olympio Editora.

Fry, P. (1982). Da hierarquia à igualdade: A construção histórica da homossexualidade no Brasil (From hierarchy to equality: The historical construction of homosexuality in Brazil). In P. Fry (Ed.), *Para Inglês ver: Identidade e política na cultura Brasileira* (pp. 87-115). Rio de Janeiro: Zahar Editores.

Fry, P. (1985). Male homosexuality and spirit possession in Brazil. *Journal of Homosexuality, 11*(3/4), 137-153.

Fry, P. & MacRae, E. (1983). *O que é homossexualidade* (What homosexuality is). São Paulo: Editora Brasiliense S.A.

Hansen, B. (1979). The historical construction of homosexuality. *Radical History Review, 20*, 66-73.

Herdt, G. H. (1981). *Guardians of the flutes: Idioms of masculinity*. New York: McGraw-Hill.

Herdt, G. H. (Ed.). (1984). *Ritualized homosexuality in Melanesia*. Berkeley and Los Angeles: University of California Press.

Herdt, G. H. & Stoller, R. J. (1985). Theories of origins of male homosexuality: A cross-cultural look. In R. J. Stoller (Ed.), *Observing the erotic imagination* (pp. 104-134). New Haven: Yale University Press.

Lacey, E. A. (1979). Latin America: Myths and realities. *Gay Sunshine, 40/41*, 22-31.

MacRae, E. (1982). Os respeitáveis militantes e as bichas loucas (Respectable militants and crazy queens). In A. Eulalio et al. (Eds.), *Caminhos Cruzados: Linguagem, Antropologia e Ciências Naturais* (pp. 99-111). São Paulo: Editora Brasiliense S.A.

MacRae, E. (1983). Em defesa do gueto (In defense of the ghetto). *Novos Estudos CEBRAP, 2*(1), 53-60.

Manta, I. (1928). *A arte e a neurose de João do Rio* (The art and the neurosis of João do Rio). Rio de Janeiro: Livraria Francisco Alves.

Parker, R. (1984, November). The body and the self: Aspects of male sexual ideology in Brazil. Paper presented at the annual meeting of the American Anthropological Association, Denver.

Parker, R. (1985). Masculinity, femininity, and homosexuality: On the anthropological interpretation of sexual meanings in Brazil. *Journal of Homosexuality, 11*(3/4), 155-163.

Parker, R. (1987). Acquired Immunodeficiency Syndrome in Urban Brazil. *Medical Anthropology Quarterly*, new series, *1*(2), 155-175.

Pires de Almeida, J. R. (1906). *Homossexualismo: A libertinagem no rio de Janeiro* (Homosexualism: Libertinism in Rio de Janeiro). Rio de Janeiro: Leammert & C.

Plummer, K. (Ed.). (1981). *The making of the modern homosexual*. Totawa, NJ: Barnes & Noble.

Ribeiro, L. (1938). *Homossexualismo e endocronologia* (Homosexualism and endocrinology). Rio de Janeiro: Francisco Alves.

Trevisan, J. S. (1986). *Devassos no paraíso: A homossexualidade no Brasil, da colônia à atualidade* (Perverts in paradise: Homosexuality in Brazil, from the colonial period to the present). São Paulo: Editora Max Limonad Ltda.

Weeks, J. (1977). *Coming out: Homosexual politics in Britain from the nineteenth century to the present*. London: Quartet.

Weeks, J. (1981). *Sex, politics and society: The regulation of sexuality since 1900*. London: Longman.

Weeks, J. (1985). *Sexuality and its discontents: Meanings, myths, and modern sexualities*. London: Routledge & Kegan Paul.

Whitam, F. L. (1979). The entendidos: Middle class gay life in São Paulo. *Gay Sunshine, 38/39*, 16-17.

Young, A. (1973). Gay gringo in Brazil. In L. Richmond & G. Noguera (Eds.), *The gay liberation book* (pp. 60-67). San Francisco: Ramparts Press.

To Be 20 and Homosexual in France Today

Jean Le Bitoux

Paris, France

Terrance Brown, MD (translator)

SUMMARY. Being young and gay in Paris today poses a duality: The new generation of gay men and women have forgotten the historical consciousness of the gay liberation movement, yet their cultural identity and new way of life in a more modern France is a positive point. Thus, a new generation of gay young people growing up in a new cultural landscape and progressive attitudes of heterosexuals permit being optimistic.

> I was twenty, and I forbid
> anyone to say that it is the
> most beautiful time of life.
>
> *Paul Nizan*

Trying to study today's young gays in France requires inquiry that is not only sociologically oriented but compassionate. The evolution of homosexuality in this country during the last ten years, and specifically, the young gays, necessitates a modernization of the ways we think. It is my hope that this study has taken into full account the more fluid and complex reality that exists for today's young gays.

Jean Le Bitoux is a gay activist living in Paris.

Correspondence and requests for reprints may be addressed to the author at 45 Rue Benard, 75014 Paris, France.

291

THE RETURN OF PRIVACY

Christophe is 17. He lives with his parents, who are lower-middle-class people, in the northern suburbs of Paris. Christophe's first attraction to a male was at a very young age when he became fascinated by a youth leader on his block. In addition to this first sexual attraction, Christophe had good memories of other sexual encounters in Paris. About a year ago, he decided to accept his homosexuality. He made this decision because he wanted to be clear about who he was and what his desires were. This decision was also influenced by the desire to escape the "sad fate" of living a double life, like some of the older homosexuals in his neighborhood. The latter had made furtive advances that he refused. When Christophe spoke about his life, he spoke with clarity and authenticity, although the social aspects of his homosexuality were strangely absent. When I pursued the conversation further, I found that Christophe's interests were not intertwined with his love life. He wanted a career in advertising when he finished his baccalaureate, which he hoped would be this year. He also wanted to travel and get to know other cultures. He was particularly attracted to the Middle Eastern cultures and had listened at length to the young Arabs on his block describe their customs and ways. For Christophe, homosexuality was not a problem; it was a concrete way to fulfill his manly passions of "rock" and swimming. And he hoped to one day build a life with another young man. Christophe preferred to seduce the young men in his neighborhood to spending frustrating and dissatisfied nights in Parisian gay spots. When we discussed gay issues, such as the history of homosexual liberation or the existence of a gay culture, Christophe was indifferent. For Christophe, homosexuality remains a private matter of deepest subjective choice. There was no question of announcing his sexual tastes to his family or his friends. To do so would risk creating breaks with his environment, his roots, and his friendships. He is not convinced that he has to make himself understood and accepted by others on an issue that is perceived as exhibitionist and risky, and which remains stigamatized. Christophe believes he would have the courage to be more open when he moved to Paris for his studies, but never wants to risk complete rupture or to have to justify certain homosexual images that repulse him (i.e., leather queens and militant discussions with tricks). He is confident of his future love life and counts on social integration and current tolerance to enable him to build a happy life. Christophe is a modern young man.

Nadine is a 16-year-old who declares herself lesbian. Two years ago she had her first sexual encounter with one of her mother's female friends. This awakened in her a passion for women. She is now involved with a high school friend. Her Parisian bourgeois upbringing is not really a problem and no one brings up the question of her sexual identity, which suits her perfectly. Moreover, her lesbianism in no way commits her to any sort of feminism. She admits loving women and finds no major fault with the patriarchal society in which she lives. She dreams of being an engineer and of continuing her relationship with her high school friend. In her free time she rides horses and does photography. Although she is aware of the existence of lesbian bars and of a monthly magazine on lesbianism, she expressed no interest in them. She lives out her lesbianism in ways that do not seem to her to break with the bourgeois values with which she grew up. Nadine looks serenely forward to her future.

THE NEW CONFORMISTS

Philippe is 20 years old. Five years ago he organized a group of gay minors. The homosexual press spread the news and the group quickly became a great success. The group was watched by the police for a long time. They wanted to see if any adults attended the group so that a scandal would be created and the group dissolved. But Philippe protected the autonomy of the group with fervor and a strong communicative atmosphere developed. The group's discussions reflected the problems encountered by young gays: family surveillance, lack of places to meet one another, and the difficulties of spending the night away from home without the risk of arrest for their adult companions. At the same time, Philippe found that gay young people of his generation were in no way out of step culturally with their heterosexual counterparts: that is in their choice of pastimes and ways in which they led their love lives. Nothing hindered their return to respecting their parents or holding conformist values. The youths' demands arose from specific circumstances and did not reflect the desire to lead lives bolder than those of older gays.

In personal terms, Philippe began his own sexual life when he was very young. From the age of 12, Philippe's tendencies were toward men whom the law calls pedophiles and whom the courts persecute savagely. His mother was understanding and didn't attempt to discourage him. Philippe is one of those rare young men I have met who openly regrets his generation's lack of social consciousness. Philippe, however, is concerned about the hostility, more discrete today but still present, of a society that continues to hold family and heterosexuality as the two quasi-obligatory passports to social acceptance. Although this situation could be mitigated somewhat by the evolution within the homosexual community, Philippe was not optimistic. Throughout our long conversation, Philippe developed a number of grievances that explain the disengagement and disenchantment of gays of his generation. He also talked about current dangers of loss of a collective gay consciousness. These dangers include: corrosion of the gay movement's political discourse, outrageous commercialization of gays' need to meet, monotonous prattle about the merits of "gay culture," lack of solidarity with the younger and the older gays, and absence of true safe-sex campaigns to stop the spread of AIDS (there were 1,000 "official" cases of AIDS reported in 1986, and 3,000 "unofficial" cases: the highest in Europe). According to Philippe, the homosexual vigilance of several years ago had evaporated and in its place was a cozy dream of utopian integration. He believes that the gay movement's "tactics without strategy" became obsolete with the French socialists' rise to power in 1981. Since the political Right came to power in March 1986, there is more caution and fear: gays avoid social provocation, dangerous sexual encounters, and huddle up with domestic routines and careers that are uncomplicated by social issues. Thus, today's 20-year-olds find themselves holding conformist ideals that are strangely convergent with the ideals of the preceding generation: They aim at social integration in the "supposedly" tolerant environment that has permeated the current social and political culture in France.

DIFFERENCE AND INDIFFERENCE

This study would be completely partial as well as pessimistic if we did not carefully examine the concepts on which we have based our reflections. Let's begin with the concepts of "young" and "homosexual," both of which were invented more than a century ago, at a time when bourgeois humanism was formulating ideas of social protection. The idea was to protect children legally from sexual exploitation by adults and from exploitation and degradation in the work place. This resulted in the socially decontextualized concepts of "youth" and "homosexual" on which two extreme attitudes regarding homosexual youth have hinged: the need to revolt and the dream of integration.

At the beginning of this century, European homosexual movements were engaged in political and cultural agitation. This resulted in counteroffensives launched by the German and French governments as well as the medical profession. Even the movement of May 1968, which was a political and cultural revolt, was carried out by young people, and a new wave of homosexual territorial claims were rapidly staked out. The recent student rebellion in December 1986 witnessed the emergence of a new consciousness, perhaps together with a radical new movement of young gays. But only time will tell.

However, because of the constraints imposed by such labels, today's adolescent, who discovers himself to be homosexual, is in an extremely delicate situation. To begin with, becoming aware of a desire for men may produce fear or internal panic that is dissipated by rituals of conformity and "being normal." It is generally among such troubled individuals that one finds lifelong hostility or reactionary attitudes to any liberalization of mores. Happily, in France, there is no link between these isolated attitudes and any social movement.

In France today there exists a fringe of gay youth situated between the "new conformists" and the "eternally repressed." These young people are able to react by constructing a consciousness from a homosexual point of view. The adolescent who feels neither fear of himself nor of the eruption of his impulses will frequently be inclined to rejoin a culture that recognizes, integrates, and validates his desires. Others, who are more courageous and lucid, are aware that this lifestyle, this choice of erotic polarity, is at odds with a hostile society. They choose to organize themselves against movements that oppose all alternatives to heterosexual destiny.

THE NEW MASCULINE CULTURE

Finally, it is necessary to place this diversity of young gay people's lives within the context of an aging French society and a worldwide depoliticization of society. Should we become discouraged because the achievements of homosexual activism no longer create great interest on the part of young gays? Today, more than ever, there are other serious problems that need resolution: unemployment, what to study in school, pocket money. Such considerations explain the strategic retreat of today's young people into the traditionalism of family values and social respectability. We might also ask whether a specific culture, a gay press, or a nocturnal urban life such as exists in the major French cities, are truly adapted to today's problems. The evidence suggests that they are not. Today's young gays reject the homosexual society of plenty: the exciting, yet antiquated, civilization of pleasure has been derailed by cultural progress and evolving lifestyles.

If the questions of this generation are directly opposite our own, it is because the environment has become less oppressive about sexuality and homosexuality. In the absence of a truly organized moral movement, such as the Moral Majority in the United States, homosexuality is marginally accepted as debauchery. It is more through a cultural and media evolution than through a political strategy that living openly as a homosexual has become a real, though still fragile, possibility. Consider the spectacular image of today's man. The marketing message that now penetrates almost every aspect of a man's life (his clothing, perfume, hairstyles, sports, dance, music, photography, and so forth).

Nor have young heterosexuals escaped unscathed. At last they can now acknowledge their feelings and tenderness for other men without being stamped with the label of homosexual; something that would have occurred not too long ago. More and more, males have the opportunity to construct loving friendships with one another, the ambiguity of which they willingly admit. It is a positive sign of the times that homosexuality ceases to be the property of homosexuals, that it ceases to be captive to their discourse only. Before that happened, the question was privatized to the detriment of the whole society. The evolution of masculine culture, the visible signs of a new masculine narcissism, allows elaboration of a new behavioral mold and a bachelor lifestyle wherein all the signs of gay culture can now exist without contradiction. This new configuration of man, whereby he consents to become an object after having worn himself out claiming to be a subject, proposes a masculine erotism whose cultural audience goes beyond the worn-out stereotypes of aesthete dandy or classic macho. It is as if men had rediscovered one another on the same road traveling the same seductive path after a worrisome separation.

Young gays, the people who fashioned this reconciliation, this conceptual transcendence of sexual and gender identities, position themselves squarely at the crossroads of this happy modernization.

Gay Youth in Four Cultures:
A Comparative Study

Michael W. Ross, PhD

South Australian Health Commission

SUMMARY. Young and older homosexual men in four countries (Sweden, Finland, Ireland, and Australia) were compared on a number of psychological, social, and psychometric indices to determine what differences existed between them, and the effect of culture on any such differences. Data show that there are greater differences between younger and older homosexual men as the culture appears more antihomosexual, and that younger homosexual men are less likely to accept their sexual orientation and more likely to accept myths surrounding homosexuality. Younger homosexual men were also more likely to have had gonorrhea (regardless of their number of sexual partners), to prefer receptive anal intercourse, and to have contacted partners by cruising. These data confirm that mental health consequences of antihomosexual environments are most negative where homosexuality is most severely stigmatized.

Martin and Hetrick (1988), in reviewing the psychological and social concomitants of being young and homosexual in the United States, noted the major difficulties such individuals face. In a society that is homophobic and in which there are few if any role models for the homosexual adolescent to follow, the process of identifying oneself as a homosexual person may be both difficult and painful. The cognitive task of developing a positive self-image

Dr. Ross is Director of Research and Evaluation, STD Services, South Australian Health Commission, and Clinical Senior Lecturer in Psychiatry and Primary Health Care, Flinders University Medical School, Adelaide, South Australia.

Correspondence and reprint requests may be addressed to the author c/o STD Services, South Australian Health Commission, P.O. Box 65, Rundle Mall, Adelaide 5000, Australia.

in an atmosphere of prejudice will almost certainly produce cognitive dissonance and ego-dystonic reactions in those individuals who are homosexual: in some 20%, internalized self-hatred will lead to attempts at suicide, and it is impossible to estimate how many successful suicides are related to sexual orientation. The difficulties related to becoming homosexual, Martin and Hetrick noted, include the fact that there are no role models as in the case of other minority groups — where at least parents are able to provide a basis for group membership and for a "we" versus "them" support system — and the subsequent cognitive isolation. Those individuals who do recognize that they are homosexual are prey to inaccurate and damaging myths about what homosexuals are and may expect from life, including, Martin and Hetrick commented, the pervasive belief that "if a male is attracted to a male, then he must be feminine." Other myths regarding what homosexual men are and what they do, including the myths of an unhappy and lonely lifestyle, that homosexual men are child molesters, and that they are social outcasts, not only produce dysphoria, but may also lead to violence against the homosexual adolescent by parents, siblings, and peers.

Martin (1982) noted that the socialization of the gay person occurs during adolescence, rather than at birth as for most other groups, and that society's traditional view of homosexuality as a stigma, along with the absence or denial of role models prevents the easy attainment of such identity. Other problems which Martin identified for the gay adolescent include the fact that gay male adolescents are unable to develop social networks of sympathetic others until old enough to attend gay bars, and that unlike heterosexual adolescents, who learn to date with sexual contact as the end point, the homosexual adolescent starts with the end result and then attempts to develop the relationship. At a medical level, most concern for the gay adolescent has concentrated on sexually transmissible diseases (STDs) (Owen, 1985) and on the limited ability of gay adolescents to recognize STD symptoms, as well as denial of risk (O'Reilly & Aral, 1985).

The difficulties in socialization and adjustment of the gay adolescent would thus appear to be directly related to the degree of societal stigmatization of homosexuality and to the degree of openness of a society to information on homosexuality. Do homosexual adolescents face greater psychological difficulties, internalize myths more often, and have more STD problems in less accepting societies? Male homosexual adolescents in four western societies (Sweden, Finland, Australia, and Ireland) were compared with older gay men in an attempt to answer these questions.

STUDY POPULATION

The study population consisted of 176 Swedish, 158 Australian, 149 Finnish, and 121 Irish homosexual men (604 respondents in total), whose personal characteristics are detailed in Table 1.

Questionnaires with stamped addressed envelopes for return were given to homosexual rights and social clubs in Stockholm, Melbourne and Brisbane, Helsinki, and Dublin. In each case the club was the main homosexual rights or social organization in that city, and the aims and functions of the five clubs selected appeared to be almost identical. The response rate was 46.6% for Stockholm, 44% for Melbourne and Brisbane, 54% for Helsinki, and 48.6% for Dublin. This response rate was based on the number of questionnaires given to each club, one for each member on its mailing list.

QUESTIONNAIRE

The questions asked were part of an anonymous wider questionnaire comparing homosexual men in Sweden, Australia, Finland, and Ireland. The full questionnaire form is reproduced in Ross (1986). Questions included a range of demographic, psychological, and social variables, along with the Bem Sex Role Inventory (Bem, 1974) and the Sex Role Survey (McDonald, 1974). Ten questionnaires from each sample in which respondents identified themselves were subsequently compared with interviews with the men as a check on accuracy; no discrepancies were found. Swedish questionnaires were translated into Swedish by two people and checked for accuracy by a third. Translation of the Finnish questionnaire followed a similar procedure. Questionnaires in Australia and Ireland were in English.

DATA ANALYSIS

Analysis was by the X^2 test for the categorical data and by Student's *t* test for the data that had interval or ratio scales. Young homosexual men were defined as being age 22 or younger, older men as being age 23 or over, and all analyses involved comparisons between these two groups.

RESULTS

The results are presented in Tables 1 to 5. Some differences were apparent between the study populations (see Table 1). One way analysis of variance showed that there were significant differences between Australia and Finland in ages of the respondents (3 to 6 years on average), in years of education between Sweden and Ire-

Table 1

Sample Characteristics (Mean ±SD)

Variable	Sweden	Australia	Finland	Ireland	Differences
Age	30.9±7.4	32.0±11.2	28.4±7.8	29.1±9.7	Aus-Fin*
Years Education	12.7±5.3	13.3±3.6	13.2±4.4	13.5±5.9	Ire-Swe*
Age Became Sexually Active	20.8±7.4	19.3±12.1	20.4±7.2	20.9±6.8	
Age realized was homosexual	14.1±5.7	12.5±7.0	13.9±5.4	15.6±6.0	
Kinsey Scale Level	6.6±0.8	6.7±1.0	6.5±0.9	6.2±1.0	
Sexual partners/ month, past year	3.3±6.2	2.7±3.5	1.7±2.6	2.0±3.6	Swe-Fin*
Religion: Practising	11(6.7)	52(32.4)	10(7.1)	37(31.4)	
(%) Nominal	91(55.5)	51(33.6)	66(47.1)	48(40.7)	
None	62(37.8)	49(32.2)	64(45.7)	33(28.0)	
		X^2=66.6, df=6**			
Social class: Upper	32(18.9)	8(5.2)	4(2.8)	15(12.4)	
(%) Middle	80(47.3)	89(58.2)	66(45.8)	72(59.5)	
Working	57(33.7)	56(36.6)	74(51.4)	34(28.1)	
		X^2=40.1, df=6**			

*p<.05   **p<.01

Table 2

Differences between Young and Older Swedish Homosexual Men

	Young	Older
I have a harder time than other people in gaining friends	2.9±0.5	2.6±0.8
How much do you think homosexuality violates conformity in general?	4.1±1.8	4.9±2.4
Age realised some people think homosexuality is wrong, deviant or different	11.5±1.9	13.3±3.2
Thinks of self now as feminine	4.1±1.4	3.5±1.5
Ever cross-dressed - as a child	2.8±0.9	2.2±1.1
- since adolescence	3.6±0.7	3.1±0.9
Conservatism	9.9±4.3	8.1±4.2

land (0.8 years on average), and in number of sexual partners per month over the past year between Sweden and Finland (1.6 per month on average). There were also significant differences between the four countries in terms of the social class of respondents, with more Swedes and Irishmen reporting that their parents were upper class, and in terms of religious involvement, with more Australians and Irishmen reporting that they were practicing members of religions. The proportion of young homosexual men in each sample was Sweden, 12.5%; Australia, 27.2%; Finland, 24.4%; and Ireland 32% (X^2 = 18.1, p < .05).

DISCUSSION

Of particular interest is the pattern of significant differences between the four societies, with Sweden (the most liberal with regard to attitudes toward homosexuality and information on homosexuality) having the fewest differences between homosexual adolescents and older homosexual men, and Ireland and Australia (the least

Table 3

Differences between Young and Older Australian Homosexual Men

	Young	Older
From how many heterosexuals do you try to conceal your homosexuality?	3.3±1.1	2.7±1.1
Would there be problems at work if people found out?	2.7±1.0	2.2±1.1
Do you think people are likely to break off a social relationship with someone they consider homosexual?	3.8±0.6	3.6±0.8
A person is born homosexual or heterosexual	1.8±0.8	2.2±0.9
I have a harder time than other people in gaining friends	2.6±0.8	2.3±0.9
Influence of female friends own age on behavior	6.4±2.2	5.7±1.9
How much do you think homosexuality violates conventional morality?	5.8±2.5	5.0±2.7
Age realized some people think homosexuality is wrong, deviant or different	12.5±2.9	14.4±4.9
Most homosexuals tend to imitate the heterosexual world and its values too much	3.9±2.3	4.8±2.1
When publicly became homosexual, level of fear it would make you feel small and lower your prestige	6.1±2.3	6.9±1.6
Mean rank, meeting other homosexuals		
- bars and clubs	1.6±0.7	2.0±1.0
- beats or conveniences	4.2±1.2	3.4±1.4
- bathhouses	2.4±1.8	4.2±1.7
Proportion of leisure time spent in homosexual subculture	59.6±19.1	67.3±20.6
Partners per month	3.6±4.3	2.4±3.1
Conservatism	35.0±12.5	41.7±13.1
Sex-Role Conservatism: Social and Domestic	6.8±4.4	8.1±4.1

TABLE 3 (continued)

	Young	Older
Sex-Role Conservatism: Sex Appropriate Behavior	10.3±5.5	15.1±5.9
Depressed maladjustment[a]	4.7±1.2	3.9±1.3
Episodes of gonorrhea	1.8±0.4	1.6±0.5

[a]See Ross (1985)

liberal) each having three times as many significant differences. Finland, midway between the two in liberalism at the time these data were collected, is midway between Sweden on the one hand, and Australia and Ireland on the other, in terms of number of significant differences between gay adolescents and older gay men. Those broad differences between cultures do suggest that in the more homonegative societies, there will be greater differences between young and older homosexual men, almost certainly as a function of the difference between pre- and post-gay socialization. For homosexual youth in the most homonegative societies, these differences reflect the gap between the level of functioning of the adult homosexual man in a social support network and the functioning of the gay adolescent developing his identity. The greater the gap, the more stigmatized is the adolescent first identifying as homosexual.

There are, however, interesting patterns that emerge within each culture that are useful in describing the position of gay youth in the four societies studied.

Sweden

There are minimal differences between gay adolescents and their older peers in Sweden, which is almost certainly a consequence of that society's more positive attitude toward homosexuality both in law and in beliefs. Homosexual youth tended to feel they had a harder time in gaining friends, still thought their homosexuality violated conformity in general more, and realized that homosexuality was stigmatized earlier in their lives than for older men. This, how-

Table 4

Differences between Young and Older Finnish Homosexual Men

	Young	Older
Kinsey scale	5.1±1.0	5.5±0.8
Has (or would) being labeled homosexual bother you?	1.4±0.5	1.6±0.5
How much do you think homosexuality violates conventional morality?	4.7±2.3	3.8±2.0
How much influence did male friends your own age have on your behavior?	4.8±1.9	5.5±1.9
How much influence did female friends your own age have on your behavior?	6.0±1.9	5.1±1.8
How old were you when you realized some people think homosexuality is wrong, deviant, or different?	12.7±2.3	14.3±3.5
Male homosexuals often act as if they are more feminine than male heterosexuals	4.5±2.0	3.4±1.6
Most people think that male homosexuals are feminine to some extent	3.2±1.3	2.3±0.8
Because individuals may think male homosexuals are more feminine than heterosexual males, the homosexual ones tend to act that way	5.0±2.1	4.1±2.0
Have you ever cross-dressed? - as a child?	3.2±1.1	2.8±1.0
Extent Finns are antihomosexual	4.0±1.5	3.4±1.4
When publicly became homosexual, level of fear about losing friends	5.4±2.2	3.9±1.6
Partners per month	1.1±0.7	2.1±3.2
Depressed inadequacy[a]	3.3±1.3	3.9±1.3

[a]See Ross (1985)

Table 5

Differences between Young and Older Irish Homosexual Men

	Young	Older
Has (or would) being labeled homosexual bother you?	1.8±0.4	1.6±0.5
How much do you think homosexuality violates conventional morality?	5.5±2.5	4.4±2.5
How much influence did male friends your own age have on your behavior?	3.9±2.2	5.0±2.4
How much influence did female friends your own age have on your behavior?	6.4±2.0	5.6±2.4
How much influence did teachers or school have on your behavior?	5.7±2.3	4.8±2.3
At what age did you realize that some people think homosexuality is wrong, deviant, or different?	12.7±2.5	14.7±2.9
When you first became active homosexually, did you think of yourself as passive?	5.6±2.5	4.4±2.1
Most people think that male homosexuals are feminine to some extent	2.7±1.5	2.2±0.8
Because individuals think male homosexuals are more feminine than heterosexual males, the homosexual ones tend to act that way	4.3±2.2	5.1±2.3
Most homosexuals tend to imitate the heterosexual world and its values too much	3.9±1.9	4.8±2.5
Extent Irish laws are antihomosexual	3.6±1.5	3.0±1.2
Extent Irish people are antihomosexual	2.4±1.1	2.1±0.6
When publicly became homosexual, level of fear it would make you feel small and lower your prestige	5.6±2.4	6.8±2.1
Mean rank, meeting other homosexuals		
- beats or conveniences	4.1±1.1	3.2±1.1
- gay activist meetings	2.5±1.0	3.3±1.2
Partners per month	1.0±1.1	2.5±4.2

TABLE 5 (continued)

	Young	Older
Family acceptance of homosexuality[a]	4.5±6.5	4.8±4.8
Acceptance of own homosexuality	6.5±8.6	6.8±7.5
Episodes of gonorrhea	1.9±0.3	1.7±0.5

[a]See Ross (1985)

ever, was probably an artifact of sampling, because those who realized homosexuality was stigmatized earlier tended to identify as homosexual earlier and to come out into the gay subculture earlier.

As predicted by Martin (1982), younger gay men thought of themselves as more feminine than older gay men, and tended to have cross-dressed more. This, however, may also have been a function of those individuals who, being more feminine, were identified, or identified themselves, as homosexual earlier. There is some evidence to suggest that being more effeminate may lead to internal or external labeling at an earlier stage, although cause and effect cannot be disentangled in these data. Gay adolescents were also more conservative than their older peers. These data show few significant differences between Swedish gay adolescents and older homosexual men.

Finland

Finnish homosexual adolescents have much in common with Swedish homosexual adolescents in that, probably for the same reasons, they became aware that homosexuality was stigmatized at an earlier age than their older peers (although later than Swedes). In addition, however, they were more concerned at being labeled homosexual and considered themselves more bisexual than older homosexual men. The evidence suggests that there is less reliance on male peers and more reliance on female peers, probably because of less rejection or more identification as feminine. In line with this, the younger group responded to three questions that confirmed that they see a number of social pressures operating that put young homosexual men under greater pressure to act in a feminine way. For example, cross-dressing as a child was, as in the Swedish sample, more common in the younger group, suggesting that, as Martin (1982) has noted, the more effeminate youth tend to come out (or be labeled) as homosexual earlier.

Awareness that Finns tend to be antihomosexual was expressed more strongly by the younger group, and such individuals were also concerned about losing their friends when they became publicly homosexual. Lower partner numbers (perhaps reflecting lack of opportunity) and a stronger belief that homosexuality violates conventional morality also characterized the younger group. Thus, in the Finnish sample, the effects of societal pressure against a homosexual orientation became apparent in comparison with the Swedish sample.

Australia

In the Australian sample, the effects of a more homonegative society were clearly seen in comparison with the Swedish and Finnish samples. Younger gay men attempted to conceal their homosexuality more, believed there would be more problems at work if people found out, and expected more social repercussions if their sexuality were known. They also believed more often than older gay men that a person is born homosexual or heterosexual, and felt that they have a harder time than the older group in gaining friends. Like the Finnish sample, they also reported more influence of female peers on their behavior and a stronger belief that homosexuality violates conventional morality. These findings also indicate that young gay men in Australia became aware of the stigmatized nature of homosexuality at an earlier age than did their older peers. Unlike the two Scandinavian samples, though, there was no evidence of increased femininity or beliefs that homosexuals are more feminine.

One possible explanation for this may be the more dominant idiom of masculinity in Australian culture; however, the more probable explanation is the different sexual pattern that the Australian sample displays. Homosexual adolescents spend less time than older homosexual men in the gay subculture, but have significantly

more partners per month (and significantly more episodes of gonorrhea), tend to meet partners more often on "beats" (cruising) or in
conveniences, and less often in bath houses, bars, and clubs. Similarly, in contrast to previous data, the young Australian sample was
less conservative and less concerned with being exposed as gay and
losing their friends.

These data suggest that a different group of young people have
been sampled in Australia, and that those who come onto the "gay
scene" there are tougher, more sexually active and more accultured
into cruising. This may be a function of sample bias, but it does
identify the fact that there are probably two subgroups of young gay
men, those who are labeled by their femininity or adopt a feminine
role in response to societal myths, and those who become sexually
active and are not as conservative or concerned about their sexual
proclivities. It is unclear, however, whether this is a function of
societal differences or of sampling differences.

Ireland

The Irish sample of young gay men illustrated the extreme of the
European trend toward the members of the most homonegative societies having the greatest concern about being exposed as homosexual and accepting the feminine myth to the greatest extent.
Young Irish homosexual men believed, as did the younger homosexual men in Australia and Finland, that homosexuality violates
conventional morality. Young Irish gay men reproduced the pattern
of having been more influenced by female peers and less by male
peers, suggesting that a consistent pattern of feminine identification
or greater acceptance may occur, or that the more feminine tend to
identify as homosexual earlier. Again, they also identified earlier
their society's stigmatization against homosexuality, and a large
number of their responses to our survey questions confirmed that
they see themselves as more passive and feminine, and as following
a heterosexual model to a greater extent. As would be expected in
Ireland given its status as one of the most homonegative societies in
this study, younger gay men there recognized, to a greater extent
than their older peers, that Irish laws and the Irish population are
antihomosexual and show greater concern over exposure. Interest-

ingly, the younger gay men expressed less embarrassment over people seeing them as homosexual than did the older men.

Frequency of sexual behavior in Ireland was, in contrast to Australia, lower in terms of partner numbers in the adolescent homosexual men, although, as in Australia, contact was less commonly made at "beats" and conveniences and more at gay activist meetings. As would be anticipated, the younger men accepted their homosexuality less than the older men and, despite having fewer partners, also reported more cases of gonorrhea. This latter finding tends to confirm the suggestion of O'Reilly and Aral (1985) that younger people are less aware of the risks associated with STDs. In general, the Irish homosexual adolescents appeared to display more signs of the effects of societal stigma than their colleagues in the two other Scandinavian societies with which they can be most closely compared.

Interpretation of these data must be approached with some caution. First, there may be a cohort effect operating, although with the progressive temporal liberalization of attitudes toward homosexuality the data trend would be in the opposite direction of that shown. This may account for the lesser concern or fear about coming out in some samples, notably the Australian one. Second, these comparisons are specific to each country, and while each country is its own control, the degree of stigmatization for the adults may not be that much lower than for the adolescents, making it difficult to achieve statistical significance. Third, by the sampling procedure used, the sample is biased toward those who are "out" and thus have social support within a gay community.

Notwithstanding these qualifications, the data from each country do confirm that a "stigmatization gap" exists between gay adolescents and adults that increases with the level of homonegativity of the society. This stigmatization gap manifests particularly in the degree to which individuals are concerned about exposure, and in the degree to which myths such as the effeminate nature of homosexuals are accepted. In this context, it is particularly important to note that Ross (1983) found that homosexual men were more feminine in sex role rigid and antihomosexual societies as compared to sex role liberal and less antihomosexual societies, where they did not differ in this regard from heterosexual controls. These data suggest that stigmatization may magnify this effect in younger homosexual men even when using a within-country analysis.

The STD data also suggest that in the two more homonegative societies, denial of risk, which may be associated with a degree of denial of a stigmatized status such as homosexuality, is associated with a higher gonorrhea infection rate—regardless of whether or not there are significant differences in partner numbers.

Combined Samples

Analysis using the four country samples, collapsed into a total young versus old sample, was utilized to look at general trends across cultures. Such an analysis summarizes the major differences between the younger and older homosexual men. It is apparent that, apart from demographic variables that might be expected to be different (e.g., younger men being less likely to be in a relationship for more than two years and having less education), younger men had a significantly more negative attitude toward their homosexuality and were less accepting of their sexual orientation, although they were less conservative than the older men. They also realized they were homosexual at a younger age and became actively homosexual earlier than the older group. This clearly suggests that the younger group sampled here was atypical and did not include those who "came out" later.

In general, the younger homosexual men also thought homosexuality violated conventional morality, religious morality, and general conformity less than did the older group, although this may be a function of a cohort effect, less conservatism, or the previously noted bias toward those who came out younger. As found in the individual country analyses, the younger group also indicated that they thought homosexual men often acted as if they were more effeminate, and that they believed that people thought male homosexuals were effeminate to some extent, confirming the suggestion of Martin (1982) that younger homosexual men internalize societal myths to a greater extent.

Sexually, a number of differences were reported between the groups. The younger group was less likely to cruise public conveniences for partners and more likely to frequent bars and clubs in order to make contact. Sexual behaviors for younger individuals included a significantly greater preference for receptive anal sex and full body contact, and a significantly lower preference for inserter anal sex. Gonorrhea was more common among the younger group despite there being no difference in partner numbers between the two groups. These data suggest that, as previously implied, STDs are likely to constitute a greater problem in younger gay people. As a matter of conjecture, this may be due to less discriminating partner choice, or less awareness of STDs and their symptoms in partners, or related to a preference for receptive anal intercourse.

CONCLUSIONS

In summary, these data suggest that homosexual adolescents are likely to have more problems in the more antihomosexual countries, and that they are also likely to be less accepting of their sexual orientation and less positive about homosexuality than older homosexual men. Similarly, adolescents are more likely to accept the popular myths about homosexuality, although they are less likely to believe that homosexuality violates conventional morality or conformity. Sexually, they are less likely to contact partners by cruising, and more likely to prefer receptive anal intercourse and to have contracted gonorrhea.

The suggestions of Martin (1982) and Martin and Hetrick (1988) that homosexual adolescents are at greater risk of internalizing antihomosexual stereotypes and of decreased acceptance of their sexual orientation appear to be correct. The findings in this sample, biased toward those who already have access to (and were recruited from) gay subcultures, strongly suggest that those homosexual adolescents who do not have access to such social support and demythologizing networks will have even greater difficulties. Indirect evidence supporting this conjecture is the finding that young homosexual men have greater and more numerous difficulties in societies that are more antihomosexual. Unfortunately, the difficulty of obtaining respondents who are not part of a homosexual community or who have not become actively homosexual precludes more direct confirmation. However, the evidence from this study consistently suggests that the psychological disadvantages the homosexual adolescent faces is cross-culturally consistent in western societies, and appear to be a direct function of the degree of stigmatization of a homosexual orientation through both the internalisation of societal stigma and acceptance of popular myths through lack of appropriate models.

REFERENCES

Bem, S. L. (1974). The measurement of psychological androgyny. *Journal of Consulting and Clinical Psychology, 42,* 155-162.

McDonald, A. P. (1974). Identification and measurement of multidimensional attitudes toward equality of the sexes. *Journal of Homosexuality, 1,* 165-182.

Martin, A. D. (1982). Learning to hide: The socialization of the gay adolescent. In S. C. Feinstein, J. G. Looney, A. Z. Schwartzberg, & A. D. Sorosky (Eds.), *Adolescent Psychiatry* (Vol. 10, pp. 52-65). Chicago: University of Chicago Press.

Martin, A. D., & Hetrick, E. (1987). The stigmatization of the gay and lesbian adolescent. In M. W. Ross (Ed.), *Homosexuality and Psychopathology in Homosexuality* (pp. 163-183). New York: The Haworth Press, Inc.

O'Reilly, K. R., & Aral, S. (1985). Adolescence and sexual behavior: Trends and implications for STD. *Journal of Adolescent Health Care, 6,* 262-270.

Owen, W. F. (1985). Medical problems of the homosexual adolescent. *Journal of Adolescent Health Care, 6,* 278-285.

Ross, M. W. (1983). Societal relationships and gender role in homosexuals: A cross-cultural comparison. *Journal of Sex Research, 19,* 273-288.

Ross, M. W. (1986). *Psychovenereology: Personality and lifestyle factors in sexually transmitted diseases in homosexual men.* New York: Praeger.

The Life Course
of Gay and Lesbian Youth:
An Immodest Proposal
for the Study of Lives

Andrew M. Boxer, PhD (cand.)
Bertram J. Cohler, PhD

The University of Chicago

SUMMARY. The authors raise questions about several fundamental assumptions and methods regarding study of the development of gay and lesbian youth. Primary among these are the validity of reliance on respondents' recollections regarding their childhood and ad-

Andrew M. Boxer is Program Coordinator of the Clinical Research Training Program in Adolescence at Michael Reese Hospital and The University of Chicago; Associate Director of the Center for the Study of Adolescence at Michael Reese Hospital and Medical Center; and doctoral candidate in the Committee on Human Development at The University of Chicago. He is Project Director of the ongoing investigation, "Sexual Orientation and Cultural Competence in Chicago." Bertram J. Cohler is the William Rainey Harper Professor of Social Sciences in the College, and Professor in the Departments of Behavioral Sciences (Committee on Human Development), Education, Psychiatry, and Divinity, at The University of Chicago.

Preparation of this manuscript was facilitated by an Institutional Training Grant from the National Institute of Mental Health (5T32 MH14668-12) entitled, Clinical Research Training Program in Adolescence, awarded to the Department of Psychiatry at Michael Reese Hospital and Medical Center, and the Committee on Human Development (Department of Behavioral Sciences) at The University of Chicago. Illustrative data presented in this article are drawn from the ongoing investigation, "Sexual Orientation and Cultural Competence in Chicago" (conducted by Gilbert Herdt, Andrew M. Boxer, and Floyd S. Irvin), funded by a grant from the Spencer Foundation. The authors are grateful to Judith A. Cook,

315

olescent experiences; inferences about developmental processes and outcomes made on the basis of cross-sectional samples; the time-specific, cohort-bound nature of many previous constructs and findings; and the persistent search for continuities between childhood gender behavior and adult sexual orientation. In consequence, the emerging body of theory is largely a developmental psychology of the remembered past. Strategies are suggested for longitudinal, prospective research on homosexual adolescents, shifting attention from child-based, "causal" models to those of adolescent and adult-centered perspectives. Aimed at understanding life changes and the developmental processes and course of negotiating them, longitudinal methods will more accurately reflect current experiences of gay and lesbian youth coming of age in a unique historical context. Findings from studies of the life course have direct implications for modification of current developmental theories, particularly those that can inform gay and lesbian-sensitive clinical services for all age groups.

We have come to a time when the basic processes of human learning have been used to develop science and technology far beyond the dreams of our ancestors. This has made possible the emergence of modern societies very different from the societies of our past. As a byproduct of these developments — an authentic paradox of success — we have inadvertently made the process of growing up in some ways more complicated than ever before — there are now so many changes within a lifetime, so many requirements for learning and relearning, so many moving targets to hit . . . Thus, adolescence, as the critical passage from childhood to adulthood, more than ever deserves careful, patient attention and responsible innovation. (Hamburg, 1986, p. 13)

Gilbert Herdt, Joanne Marengo, and Judith LeFevre, for their critical comments on earlier versions of this manuscript. Special thanks also go to Gilbert Herdt and Monte Hetland for their editorial assistance. Some of the ideas in this manuscript have evolved from initial discussions with the staff of the Chicago Youth Project. Thanks go to them for their dedicated commitment.

Correspondence and reprint requests may be addressed to Andrew M. Boxer, Center for the Study of Adolescence (PPI), Michael Reese Hospital and Medical Center, Lake Shore Drive at 31st Street, Chicago, IL 60616.

INTRODUCTION:
GAY AND LESBIAN YOUTH
AND ADOLESCENT RESEARCH

Several national publications, particularly those serving gay and lesbian communities across the United States, have recently focused attention on the emergence, problems, and prospects of gay and lesbian youth (see Hippler, 1986; Kogan, 1986; Olson, 1986; Sadownick, 1986; Suggs, 1987). From a life span perspective, these youth are a group of pioneers negotiating uncharted territory that, indeed, requires new and complex learning and creative innovation. The new groups of self-identified gay and lesbian youth underscore that previous researchers of adolescence have, perhaps unwittingly, made *heterosexual assumptions* with regard to their samples and research questions. At the same time, various social changes are occurring which differentially affect the development of all adolescents in our society (Boxer, Gershenson, & Offer, 1984). The label "gay" or "lesbian" *adolescent* appears to represent a unique cultural category in history. It seems unlikely that past groups of "pre-Stonewall" youth would have labeled themselves gay or lesbian, let alone had the same opportunities for organized, collective socializing or socialization that some do today. Thus, this aspect of the life course, self-identification as gay or lesbian during adolescence, may be a unique developmental process found only in current cohorts of some homosexual youth (see Herdt, 1988, herein) and carry different consequences for later life course development. For that reason alone, studies of gay and lesbian youth are a timely occurrence.

The developmental study of adolescence, in general, is currently burgeoning.[1] Research on this phase of the life course has come of age. In partial consequence of the increasing attention directed to its study by interdisciplinary researchers, adolescence is now the focus of varying kinds of new public attention, from the drama of the humanities and popular journalism (Spacks, 1981; Coons, 1987), to the sway of blue ribbon presidential commissions (see Coleman et al., 1974). A recent example of this concern is represented by an issue of the *Journal of the American Medical Association* (1987) devoted to research on adolescent health concerns. Most obviously, little of this work has directly addressed the concerns of gay and lesbian youth.

However, the accumulating body of research findings on adolescence has been particularly useful in joining public health and education interventions in beginning to address national concerns regarding youth, such as teen pregnancy and parenting, substance abuse, school failure, and most recently, it is hoped, with regard to education about AIDS. But without a "remapping" of adolescent development, sustaining the efforts such as those represented in this present volume (Herdt, 1988), the experience and needs of a significant group of youth cannot be understood and addressed.

Recently there has been increased interest in the study of lives from the perspective of the life span as a whole, rather than as based on cross-sectional studies of human development. This new focus may be traced in large part to the failure of much previous research to account for significant changes in personality and adjustment from childhood to adulthood (see Cohler, 1982, 1983). Studies of both cognitive and affective development (Lennenberg, 1967; Kagan & Klein, 1973; Clarke & Clarke, 1976) and of early childhood deprivation (Rutter, 1987; Dennis, 1973) all show that there may be remarkably little consistency between early childhood development and later adult outcomes. Longitudinal research all too often has been concerned with the demonstration of stability of lives over time and, perhaps for this reason, has failed to address the most interesting question, that of conditions accounting for change in lives. As Baltes (1979) has suggested, on the basis of a thorough review of developmental research, there is no single point in the life cycle that can claim such primacy for developmental change (see also Kohlberg, Ricks, & Snarey, 1984).

The search for developmental continuities[2] has implicitly characterized many investigations of adult homosexual men and women, which focus on delineating childhood correlates of adult sexual orientation (see section 3 below for a brief review of this work). This is in striking contrast to the discontinuities and changes that characterize the lives of many gay and lesbian adults, particularly when internalized societal expectations and early socialization experiences require strategies for dealing with the many cultural discontinuities experienced throughout the adult life course (Bell & Weinberg, 1978; Bell, Weinberg, & Hammersmith, 1981; Cass, 1979, 1984; Humphreys & Miller, 1980; Martin, 1982; Minton & Mc-Donald, 1983/1984; Troiden, 1979; Weinberg & Williams, 1974).

Contemporary studies of lives have recognized the importance of providing a more complete ecology of the life course, including study of individuals' wishes and intents as shaped by development and maturation, aspects of social context, and, in particular, those historical circumstances which so dramatically affect the lives of persons within a specific generation or age-linked cohort (Cohler & Boxer, 1984). There is, consequently, increased interest in the study of those factors that might be associated with individual differences in stability and change over time.

The determinants of continuity and discontinuity are also related to factors of vulnerability and resilience (Cohler, 1987). Of particular interest for the study of gay and lesbian youth are those qualities and features associated with the capacity to remain resilient when confronted by adverse life circumstances. Such resilience has been identified as a characteristic of many older gay and lesbian adults, developed as a result of their dealing with the adversity of various types of discrimination, homophobia, and other social stigmata throughout a significant portion of their lives (see e.g., Berger, 1982; Kelly, 1977; Kimmel, 1978, 1980; Lee, 1987; Robinson, 1979; Weinberg & Williams, 1974). The study of resilience and coping requires consideration of the characteristics associated with particular life changes, as well as their timing and synchronization. These characteristics of events must be considered together with attributes of persons at particular points in the life course. This predictive approach, based on information regarding the type of life change, the social context in which particular changes take place, and the developmental attributes of persons, must be complemented by a narrative or interpretive approach, that is concerned with the manner in which persons experience and interpret or "make sense" of these life changes.

Little is known of the manner in which persons create a narrative that renders adversity coherent in terms of experienced life history, or the manner in which presently constructed meanings of life changes may be altered in order to maintain a sense of personal integration (Cohler, 1981, 1982, 1987). For some persons, the experience of adverse life events may be used as an explanation for the failure to realize personal goals. For others, this misfortune becomes the impetus for increased effort in order to attain these goals. The value of an interpretive approach as a complement to the predictive one becomes even greater as a result of findings emerging from longitudinal studies (Emde, 1981; Jones, Bayley, MacFarlane, & Honzik, 1971; Kagan & Moss, 1962; Livson & Peskin, 1980; Moss & Sussman, 1980; Rutter, 1987), showing that lives are not as ordered and predictable over time as had previously been assumed. To the extent that lives show predictability, this order may be more a function of shared understanding regarding the linear organization of the expectable course of life in this culture, than of continuity reflected by data collected at multiple observation points. (For a more comprehensive review, see Cohler, 1987; Anthony & Cohler, 1987.)

The concept of life course, which is socially structured, must be differentiated from such terms as life cycle or life span, which refer only to change over time, without consideration of the normative cultural element implicit in making sense of such change. It is clear that age as a chronological marker is of little significance for the study of the life course, except as represented by the socially shared meanings attached to particular ages across the life cycle. Without such cultural and historical knowledge, age itself becomes an "empty" variable in the study of lives. It is precisely this social definition of the course of life which transforms the study of the life span or life cycle into the study of the *life course.*

In this paper our focus is on the study of gay and lesbian youth from the perspective of life course social science. We argue for the necessity of prospective, longitudinal, life span investigations (employing both predictive and interpretive methodologies), which will have an impact not only on our understanding of vulnerability, resilience, and well-being for gay and lesbian youth as well as for adults, but will also carry important implications for models, methods, and theories within the social sciences for the study of lives (see for example, Lee, 1987). First, from the vantage point of the life course, we delineate some critical developmental questions emerging from our current knowledge of gay and lesbian youth. We briefly examine applications of the developmental paradigm to homosexuality, which have been primarily focused on causal inferences based on adult retrospections. To illustrate the potential benefits from employment of longitudinal methods, we review longitudinal perspectives as applied to adolescence. Finally, the significance of developmental research to the provision of adequate gay and lesbian-sensitive clinical services is highlighted.

GAY AND LESBIAN YOUTH:
SOME QUESTIONS ON THE COURSE OF DEVELOPMENT

The papers collected here (Herdt, 1988) constitute some of the first major advances in our understanding of a heretofore neglected group of youth coming of age. They leave us, however, wanting to know more. For example, what happens to adolescents after they have traversed the coming out phases as outlined by Troiden (1988)? How do gay and lesbian youth further negotiate their relationships with mothers and fathers during young adulthood and well after, having come out to family members (Savin-Williams, 1988)? How will the differing life biographies and self-representations of "José" and "Pedro" in Mexico, elaborated by Carrier (1988), evolve as adults? How and in what form will the young lesbian, discussed by Schneider (1988), create the life she desires as "normal and gay"? More generally, what we do not yet know is how the experiences of gay and lesbian youth are evolving through the course of adolescence, how continuity and change are prefiguring their lives, how resilience and vulnerability are at work. In short, little is yet known about how they experience their lives as they are living them, rather than as they are *remembered*? Nor do we know how the experience of these youth will be different from or similar to other gay and lesbian individuals who have grown up in different settings and historical periods.

In addition, a frequently asked and still unanswered question is: How do gay and lesbian adolescents differ from their heterosexual peers? Is the normative adolescent "storm and stress" exacerbated among these youth?[3] The studies represented in this issue clearly describe groups of gay and lesbian youth in various contexts and ecologies, from diverse ethnic and social groups. They sensitize us to important variations in development as a function of cultural and ecological factors (Barker, 1968; Bronfenbrenner, 1977; LeVine, 1973) or what used to be called the individual's "total life space" (Lewin, 1946).

We are left, though, with the question of what happens to these youth over time, and especially after initial "coming out" experiences. How will the individual's adulthood be affected by his or her adolescent experiences, and more specifically, how will coming out in the current sociocultural and historical context shape expectations and hopes for the future? How will intimacy, sexual expression, and friendships develop for a cohort of youth coming of age during the AIDS crisis and knowing no other historical context of life experience? More specifically, how does a teenager's initial life adjustment to coming out relate to later outcomes, to patterns of achievement and cultural competence, to resilience and vulnerability, in young adulthood? How do those who fall victim to physical or emotional abuse because of their sexual orientation, negotiate relationships later in adult life? Does the specific context of individual socialization into gay and lesbian communities relate to patterns of successful aging and life satisfaction during middle and later life? What kinds of effects do gay- and lesbian-sensitive service providers have on the youth who make use of these, albeit limited, services?

The rise of AIDS both as an illness and as an historical context makes coming out in the 1980s unlike any other time in recent history. While we tend to associate the current cultural ethos of AIDS only with individual life event illness outcomes, it is also part of a general cultural and historical context for both male and female adolescents who are currently coming out. In an ongoing study of 200 gay and lesbian youth in Chicago (Herdt, Boxer, & Irvin, 1986), one gay male adolescent, Marc, stated it this way in response to the question of how AIDS had affected his coming out:

> It has politicized me. It forced me or sobered me. I came out at a critical time. Six months earlier if I had come out, I might have gone through a slutty period. In my case it wasn't an option. People I met were into getting serious, not just dating. The tone of the community was alerted and cautious. My sexual behavior didn't change. It's been consistent.

This young man's experience, inevitably, is both similar to and different from that of a gay man who grew up 20 years or even 10 years earlier. In response to a question about his feelings regarding coming out he said:

> There was an awareness that things aren't always the way you are told they are. It's like being an expatriate in another country and you can view your own country from that distance. The isolation I experienced in being gay and feeling there was no one to go to, resulted in my mustering up my own resources. Mustering up that fiber once was important.

His perceptions on his own development highlight the importance of examining the impact of historical and cultural changes on the course of lives. This man discussed his relative ease in being open to others about being gay, after his initial reticence, while at the same time drawing on social support from certain "role colleagues" who he met at a gay and lesbian youth group, a circumstance quite different than what he would have encountered 10 years earlier. He is also aware of the danger and constraints which AIDS has created. So while there is a component of "danger to life" associated with the expression of sexuality, there is also the opportunity for the expression and consolidation of his gay identity. This cultural context of AIDS, obviously, has differential effects on women as well, and may hold different meanings for them than for males. One lesbian youth, Jana, in the Chicago project put it this way:

> I'm concerned about it not only because males are getting it, but also because lesbians are getting it . . . But a friend of mine died of AIDS. We were really close. He was like 17. When he died I didn't know much about it. It really did scare me. Friends would say he was a fag that's why he died of AIDS. It still scares me but not as much as it did before. I'm more educated so I feel a lot better about it. It's hard with lesbians, how do you have safe sex? I'm not sure what lesbians can do. I'm about as safe as I can get.

Additionally, this cultural context becomes not only a fear of death and "plague," but also an adverse life event for those peers, like Jana, who may experience various aspects of loss, grief, and bereavement.

All existing studies of gay and lesbian youth (and of gay and lesbian adults as well), however, portray slices of experience at one point *in time*, rather than their construction or development *across time*. The questions we have delineated regarding the gay and lesbian life course have either been neglected, or have been investigated through the use of retrospective methods, a highly questionable procedure for the type of knowledge that is needed, and a method that has been severely criticized for the distortions and biases that may result (see, e.g., Yarrow, Campbell, & Burton, 1970; Ross, 1980; Spanier, 1976).[4] It is no surprise, then, that up to the present time our understanding of the development of gay and lesbian individuals across the entire life course has been constructed using cross-sectional and retrospective findings, through which processes are inferred across stages or age groups. For example, in the development of gay or lesbian identity, current coming out schemes and ideal types are typically based on data gathered from respondents at one point in time, who are at varying phases of this process.

It is worth digressing here momentarily to comment on a lesson that developmentalists of adulthood have learned with regard to inferences of development from cross-sectional findings. Studies of intellectual development in adulthood were initially based on data collected at one point in time from cross-sectional samples. These findings were viewed as developmental sequences across different age groups, suggesting a general decrement in intellectual functioning across the latter half of life. However, longitudinal and cross-sequential analyses (Baltes, 1968; Schiae, 1965) of the same group of individuals across time demonstrated that such initial inferences, across age groups, regarding the decline in intelligence were erroneous. Cohort effects, such as that of educational level, were strongly associated with different groups (see Botwinick, 1977; Schaie, 1965; Horn & Donaldson, 1980) which resulted in the misinterpretation of cross-sectional data. Our understanding of intellectual development across the adult years is now quite different as a result of longitudinal studies.

The developmental psychology of the gay and lesbian life course is, in consequence, largely a psychology of the *remembered past*. It now seems necessary to link studies of adulthood with those of adolescence, through prospective research rather than inference. Therefore, the study of contemporary cohorts of gay and lesbian youth provide the opportunity to begin systematic investigation of individuals at a critical transition phase of the life cycle and to trace their development into adulthood, and beyond to old age. This mapping of gay and lesbian life span trajectories will no longer necessitate reliance on the *reconstructed past*. The resulting picture may be quite different from our current body of retrospective knowledge. For example, previous gender differences in age at first homosexual experience (see Troiden's review, 1988) may be a result of different cultural ideologies of men and women (in addition to historical changes). Relationship and connection have been identified as more salient cultural categories for many women, whereas autonomy and differentiation have been more important for men (Chodorow, 1978; Gilligan, 1982); this may affect the ways in which adult men and women reconstruct the memories of their adolescent sexual experiences. Longitudinal study of gay and lesbian youth may yield a different picture, with a narrower range of gender differences (see for example, Pratch, 1987).

From a life course point of view, the newly expanding visibility of gay and lesbian youth strongly suggests that the time has come to reassess certain key developmental concepts, including the "coming out" process itself, as well as the generalized concepts of "gay" and "lesbian" identity. Perhaps because they have been the first of more recent, developmentally informed investigations of homosexuality, these concepts now appear, ironically, to have a static and ahistorical timelessness that will ultimately render them meaningless unless such factors as historical time, social structure, and the individual's position in the life course are taken into account (Elder, 1975, 1980).

In a recent historical overview of adolescent studies, Glenn Elder (1980) has commented:

> Adolescence is intimately linked to matters historical: the evolution of social age categories, the emergence of youth related institutions, the impact of social change on lives . . . In what sense can we presume to understand the psycho-social development of youth without systematic knowledge of their life course and collective experience in specific historical times? (pp. 3, 4)

Regarding the historical changes in gay and lesbian life course trajectories we may ask, for example: Is coming out in 1987 as a 16-year-old adolescent in Chicago the same process as that for someone who came out in 1970 in San Francisco as a 40-year-old? Some researchers (e.g., Dank, 1971; Kimmel, 1978) have suggested that Stonewall is a critical historical marker distinguishing the manner of coming out for different "cohorts" of individuals. To a large extent, these processes have been studied independently of other life span developmental issues. There is no doubt that, depending upon the individual's life cycle position, the psychological issues are different. A middle-aged man must reconcile the time that has passed and is behind him with the limited future time left to live (Neugarten, 1967). An adolescent, on the other hand, is reckoning with the future in a new way (Greene, 1985, 1986) and must deal with the personal and social meanings of time and time mastery, looking toward the life that is yet to be lived. Too often we have presumed that creating a positive self-representation is the same for a middle-aged man or woman as that of an adolescent or young adult (see also, Cass, 1979, 1983/1984, 1984; Plummer, 1981; Herek, 1985; Weinberg, 1984).[5] Other research suggests significant differences in the coming out experiences between urban, suburban, and rural groups within the same historical period (reviewed in Herdt, 1988; see also Lynch, 1987; Murray, 1984; Troiden, 1988). More frequently overlooked is the question of how the individual's identity has evolved years subsequent to the initial coming out process.

HOMOSEXUALITY
AND THE DEVELOPMENTAL PERSPECTIVE

Homosexuality has been the subject of much developmental analysis but little prospective longitudinal research, particularly across age groups or life stages (Morin, 1977; Watters, 1986). Such lacunae have also been noted in the study of sexuality in general. To the extent that the findings of developmental research have had an impact on either social theory or clinical practice, they have served primarily to provide what is believed to be scientific verification of particular assumptions regarding the origins of homosexual behavior in early childhood. Thus far, this use of a developmental perspective is a result of combining both longitudinal and retrospective findings, rendering the developmental perspective as a problematic "history of confusion" and a confusion of "histories." Investigators employing a developmental paradigm have been principally focused on linking various derivatives of early experience (e.g., maternal and paternal identification) including aspects of infancy and early childhood, to adult homosexual behavior. This line of inquiry, then, represents concern with causality, and delineation of continuities through functions and mechanisms presumed to give rise to emergent adult forms of homosexuality.

Indeed, one of the only longitudinal studies (and of lengthiest duration) explicitly aimed at developmental understanding of homosexuality is that conducted by Green (1987). This work implicitly follows an earlier line of developmental research that attempted to link aspects of childhood sex-role interests and identifications, to adult gender roles and sexual orientation (Bieber et al., 1962; Chang & Block, 1960; Gebhard, Gagnon, Pomeroy, & Christenson, 1965; Holeman & Winokur, 1965). Developmental hypotheses elaborated in Green's (1987) study are concerned with whether and how gender identity precedes the emergence and development of sexual orientation, albeit in a clinically constituted sample. The predominant paradigm of this study is child-centered, with major emphasis on longitudinal changes in gender role atypical "sissy males" (a term employed by Green to describe a constellation of atypical behaviors, i.e., a syndrome), examining parent and child variables that predict to adult homosexuality.

A major problem of method apparent in the Green (1987) study is the quite different sources of data employed for childhood and adult measurements. While there are statistically significant correlations between some child and adult variables, overall they account for little explained variance. The sample selection procedures themselves precluded examination of homosexual individuals who did not manifest effeminate behavior in early childhood.[6] (For a critical review of these issues, see De Cecco, 1987.) Because of the selection criteria, this study of males represents one subtype of homosexuality and likely excludes many others. In contrast to the focus of our discussion, Green's work is not primarily concerned with gay or lesbian identity development and the life course of youth subsequent to adolescence. The focus on origins and causes in this line of research meant that Green was unable to provide more detailed description and understanding of the life course subsequent to childhood.

Kagan and Moss's (1962) analysis of 25 years of longitudinal data from the Fels Research Institute in Ohio was actually one of the first contemporary reports on personality and gender role development from childhood to adulthood, employing both longitudinal design and complex methods of data analysis. This study employed ratings of home visits and laboratory observations across several points in early and middle childhood, together with detailed assessment of personality in adulthood. High correlations were reported, in particular, between boys' childhood and adult gender role behaviors and interests. The Fels report, with its numerous variables, has been criticized as maximizing chance relationships and, similar to the Green (1987) study, as reflecting largely cultural definitions of gender roles and personality traits, rather than genuine aspects of continuity or change in such attributes over time.

Aside from these studies, the bulk of the developmental research on homosexuality is retrospective and based on adults' reconstructions of their childhoods. Causal inferences made from retrospective data are highly problematic, because adults' self-representations and understandings are infused with current cultural constructs and ideologies.[7] Additionally, recent findings in family research suggest that influences within families are bidirectional (Bell & Harper, 1977; Boxer, Cook, & Cohler, 1986; Cohler & Geyer, 1982; Cook, 1988; Cook & Cohler, 1986; Hagestad, 1981). Causal inferences typically only consider the *forward direction of effects* in socialization, from parent to child. The concept of *reciprocal socialization* (Cook & Cohler, 1986) specifies that children influence parents in as many but different ways as parents influence children. A growing corpus of research provides evidence that across the family life cycle, parents are actively socialized by their children from infancy throughout adulthood in diverse ways, from behavioral discipline strategies to political values (see, e.g., Bugental & Shennum, 1984; Cook & Cohler, 1986; Dawson & Prewitt, 1969; Troll & Bengtson, 1982).

Because of this disproportionate focus on development in childhood, the early development of gay men is still the focus of much attention. There is little comparable research on lesbians, and existing studies raise questions as to whether there are parallel factors operating for women (see, e.g., Ponse, 1978; Sophie, 1985/1986).[8] Based on newer and more refined studies of adults, gay men's early development is now being reinterpreted employing an *implicit* concept of reciprocal socialization. Isay (1985, 1986, 1987), for example, on the basis of detailed clinical case studies, suggests that adult gay men report the lack of close bonds with their fathers in childhood, due to defensive distortions of their early erotic attachments to their fathers. A normal developmental issue of these men's childhood, Isay posits, is cross-gender behavioral characteristics such boys manifest in order to acquire and maintain the attraction and attention of their fathers. The primary supposition is that the father or father surrogate, not the mother, becomes the main object of the child's sexual attention.

Thus, while supporting Green's findings regarding cross-gender childhood behavior, Isay (1987) posits that sexual orientation precedes the development of gender identity. Silverstein (1981), based on interviews with a nonclinical sample of adult gay men, has also maintained that the absent/distant father relationship, reported by the majority of his sample of 190 males, was a result, not a cause, of the adult men's homosexuality. Similarly, Bell, Weinberg, and Hammersmith (1981) have, on the basis of retrospective reports, called attention to the strong manifestations of early childhood cross-gendered behavior as reported by adult male homosexuals. Harry's (1982) recent study of "gay children grown up" makes similar conclusions about childhood effeminacy. All four authors, then, suggest that sexual orientation is a biological, or at least very early, emergent phenomenon, that sets the course of many different aspects of later development, at least in the samples studied.

These more recent studies discussing the early development of gay men, with the exception of Green's (1987), were focused upon adults who were asked to retrospect backward in time. We therefore may know more about remembered childhoods than the experienced adult present. Because of this, we must be very wary of the influence of cultural conceptions of homosexuality/"inversion" upon the reconstructed life history (Herdt, 1988). The developmental models emphasizing causal linkages in adult homosexuality are employing a system of explanation and generalization based on descriptive, narrative modes of understanding, ordering the material of life histories into a coherent account.

We caution that retrospective and prospective data may render quite different life histories. The origin of this confusion is commonly attributed to Freud (1955), although he himself pointed out:

> So long as we trace the development from its final outcome backwards, the chain of events appears continuous, and we feel we have gained an insight which is completely satisfactory or even exhaustive. But if we proceed the reverse way, if we start from the premises inferred from the analysis and try to follow these up to the final result, then we no longer get the impression of an inevitable sequence of events which could not have been otherwise determined. We notice at once that there might have been another result, and that we might have been just as well able to understand and explain the latter. (p. 167)

It is particularly interesting to note that despite recent conclusions of a number of developmental and personality researchers (Brim & Kagan, 1980; Cohler, 1981; Gergen 1982; Neugarten, 1977, 1979) on the lack of continuity across the life cycle, most developmental research on homosexuality has focused on examining continuities related to sexual orientation between childhood and adulthood. In contrast, there is a paucity of accumulated data regarding the experience of individual change and the impact of life events through the life course. Thus, with concern fixed on childhood, little attention has been devoted to studying either adolescence or adulthood as other than an *outcome* of childhood, nor with experiences across the life course. It appears we would do well now to apply to adolescence what Neugarten (1969) said nearly 20 years ago about the study of adulthood:

> We shall not understand the psychological realities of adulthood by projecting forward issues that are salient in childhood neither those issues that concern children themselves, nor those that concern child psychologists as they study cognitive development and language development and the resolution of the Oedipal. (p. 121)

Livson and Peskin (1980), in their comprehensive review of adolescent longitudinal research, commented: "In both the theoretical and empirical underpinnings of birth-to-maturity longitudinal study, the adolescent years may have been unduly hidden or homogenized in the grist of consistencies over time, weakening their psychosocial and psychobiological claim to status as a separate phase" (p. 64). While the value of longitudinal research in understanding the influences of childhood on the subsequent life course has been recognized, the emphasis on childhood causation has focused research on the demonstration of continuity. This presumes that development proceeds in a linear manner, with future attainments or changes directly associated with those of past years. Several investigators have recently called this assumption into question (Gergen, 1982; Kagan, 1980; Cohler, 1981, 1982; see also Weinberg, 1984), noting the limitations associated with linear assumptions regarding development. Gergen (1982) has suggested that the course of development is largely unpredictable and subject to chance. A major task across the course of life is to make "sense" of such chance events, weaving these events into a narrative that provides meaning and coherence.

From this perspective, the most interesting question in longitudinal research is that of factors influencing the maintenance of an internally consistent account of the course of life at different life cycle positions (Cohler, 1982). Understanding the manner in which persons maintain a sense of self-cohesiveness and identity remains a key problem in the study of lives. Together with the experience of particular normative and eruptive life events, these developmental factors contribute to successive *revisions* of the person's own narrative of the life course, resulting in significant alterations over time in the subjective account of a life history. Such revisions include alterations in the remembered past and the anticipated future, so as to provide a continuing sense of continuity of the life as a whole.

For example, it is important to keep in mind that every adult retrospectively develops a picture of what his or her parents were like (Cohler, 1980). This picture of one's parents fluctuates across the life cycle: adolescents expectedly view their parents in terms of distantiation, autonomy, and dependency (Greene & Boxer, 1986; Montemayer, 1986; Steinberg & Silverberg, 1986), whereas many older persons view their parents in highly idealized terms (Lieberman & Falk, 1971; Prosen, Martin, & Prosen, 1972). Throughout the passage of time across the life course, persons' self-representations are redefined in relation to dimensions of the past, present, and future in differing ways, depending upon their position in the life course (Back & Gergen, 1963; Boxer & Cohler, 1980; Butler, 1963; Cohler, & Boxer, 1984; Lens & Gailly, 1980; Revere & Tobin, 1980/1981). The relativity of time itself colors differential perceptions of experience, as a function of the individual's life cycle position. For an adolescent 1 year out of 16 will seem longer than 1 year out of 80 for an octogenarian (Janet, 1877).

The process by which the personal narrative is successively reconstructed, from childhood to old age, is similar in some respects to the writing of history, for discrete events are significant only as they become part of a narrative that is understood as coherent and makes sense to the readers of a particular time (Ricoeur, 1977). Just as there is a shift over time in the interpretation of historical events, similar shifts can be observed across the life course, both in the narration of personal events, and also in the interpretation provided for the relationship among these events (Cohler, 1982).

Therefore, because of these complexities of reminiscence, the study of individuals' remembered past is likely to result in "developmental histories" different from those constructed from the *prospective*, longitudinal study of lives through time. Predictive and interpretive approaches may each make an important contribution to the developmental study of lives (Cohler, 1987). However, it is necessary to differentiate these two perspectives in order to understand fully the transformations and changes that constitute human development. Predictive studies have the virtue, at least in theory, of being verifiable in terms of external criteria beyond the coherence of a narrative itself. In an effort to provide verifiable findings, predictive studies, concerned with "a laws and instances ideal of explanation" (Geertz, 1983), are unable to account for many aspects of the life history that may be most important in understanding such characteristics as resilience, vulnerability, personal success, and achievement. They fail to include shifting meanings attributed to past experiences across the course of life as determinants of present adjustment. Interpretive studies are critical, as Geertz (1983) has stated, "for connecting action to its sense rather than behavior to its determinants" (p. 34).

ADOLESCENCE
AND THE LONGITUDINAL PERSPECTIVE

Longitudinal research on youth, both short-term prospective studies within the adolescent age period, as well as longer-term studies following groups of youth into maturity, have examined various domains of adolescent experience. Despite their intensive focus, investigators conducting longitudinal research on adolescent development typically have not examined the sexual development of the respondents under investigation.[9] Livson and Peskin (1980) have catalogued this work by major foci that include: (a) pubertal-induced behavior; (b) consistency and change over time; (c) prediction of adaptation, psychopathology, and social deviance; (d) youth and school culture; (e) identity formation, sex-role identification, and vocational planning; (f) later separation and autonomy; (g) environmental and family stress; and (h) retrospection. In spite of this neglect of sexuality, a number of important findings have emerged as a result of longitudinal research.

Through examining the *course* of adolescence itself, more refined understanding is possible (Greene & Boxer, in press). For example, evidence suggests that multiple, simultaneous transitions can be particularly stressful for young adolescents (Simmons, Blyth, Van Cleave, & Bush, 1979; see also Coleman, 1980). One large study found that the convergence of school transitions, pubertal development, and new social relationships resulted in difficulties, particularly for young adolescent girls. Longitudinal studies also suggest that while puberty may be an important "developmental organizer" for youth, the experience of puberty and its psychological outcomes are strongly influenced/mediated by the social and cultural contexts in which adolescents live (Clausen, 1975; Petersen & Crockett, 1985). The longitudinal perspective has modified earlier views of parent-youth conflict; although only a small percentage of adolescents experience severe turmoil and conflict with their families, many adolescents may experience time-limited perturbations in relations with their fathers and mothers (Steinberg, 1981; Steinberg & Hill, 1978). Short-term longitudinal studies of adolescents' daily lives reveal that they may experience emotional highs and lows in different and perhaps more intense ways than adults (Csikszentmihalyi & Larson, 1984; Larson, Csikszentmihalyi, & Graef, 1980).

Through the longitudinal method, it has been demonstrated that developmental trajectories through adolescence are quite variable. In one study of adolescent males (Offer, 1969; Offer & Offer, 1975), it was found that there were three developmental routes through the course of adolescence: continuous, surgent, and tumultuous growth patterns. The presumption of "raging hormones" resulting in a stormy and stressful adolescent phase appears to be a reality for only a small group of youth. This body of research also questions the direct effects model of adolescent development (Petersen & Taylor, 1980), which assumes that biological changes act directly upon behavior, without consideration of the psychosocial and cultural processes that mediate these changes, nor with bidirectional or transactional effects.

Questions regarding the relations between pubertal change and psychosocial outcome[10] predominated some of the earliest concerns on adolescence in G. Stanley Hall's (1904) early work. These are still the subject of much research (see, e.g., Brooks-Gunn, Petersen, & Eichorn, 1985a, 1985b), particularly regarding the effects of pubertal timing on adolescent psychosocial development. It is interesting to note that similar questions were echoed as an early concern of Alfred Kinsey and his associates (Kinsey, Pomeroy, & Martin, 1948).

Kinsey viewed the onset of puberty and early adolescence as important turning points, at least for male homosexuality. In his cross-sectional sample, Kinsey found a high positive correlation between the earlier onset of puberty and the frequency of homosexuality during adolescence and later life. This high correlation was not found among the female respondents. Kinsey also linked this correlation into the fact that the occurrence of peak sexual activity for males was between the ages of 16 and 20. Sexual behavior was thus viewed as reinforced by high sexual drives. Correlational data in the male sample (Kinsey et al., 1948, p. 317) demonstrated that the earlier the onset of puberty, the greater was the accumulated incidence of homosexual behavior.

Other associates of Kinsey have attempted to account for this relationship by positing a kind of environmental conditioning hypothesis (Gebhard, 1965; Tripp, 1975). This quasi theory states that boys who begin masturbating early build a "crucial" associative connection between maleness and male genitalia, and these in turn are linked to a set of associations that are sexually arousing and exciting. Tripp (1975) has hypothesized that these associations build into an eroticism that is "ready" to extend itself to other male attributions and later to a same-sex partner. Thus, heterosexual interests are preempted. The retrospective, correlational data of Kinsey may have been demonstrating a spurious correlation or, though less likely, a result rather than a cause of sexual orientation. It should be noted that there is no longitudinal evidence that indicates pubertal timing is associated with a higher incidence of homosexuality among youth.

More importantly, the awareness of one's homosexual desires may initiate a crisis of feeling different, i.e., being "off-course," rather than "off-time." Most gays and lesbians have experienced this discontinuity in some form. What is different today is that adolescents coming out now have the opportunity to integrate aspects of their sexuality with other components of their developing identities *during* the adolescent phase of the life course.

A Sample Case

One of the earliest developmental investigations of adolescence was pioneered at the Institute of Human Development (then the Institute of Child Welfare) at the University of California at Berkeley. This longitudinal project is one of the longest-running and most comprehensive developmental study of lives ever conducted on a nonclinical sample in this country. As an illustrative example, it demonstrates the inherent potential of such research efforts.

The Adolescent Growth Study (later renamed the Oakland Growth Study) was begun in 1931 by Harold E. and Mary C. Jones and Herbert Stolz on a sample of 212 fifth and sixth graders attending schools in Oakland, California. The initial questions of the investigators were directed to the experience of youth growing up,[11] and specifically focused upon physical growth and personality development, as well as social relationships (see, e.g., Jones, 1940; Stolz & Stolz, 1951), examining the influences of biological, pubertal-induced changes on psychological development (see, e.g., Mussen & Jones, 1957; Jones & Mussen, 1958). Subsequent follow-ups of the sample have been conducted when the study subjects were approximately 33 and 38 years old. This study has recently been merged with other long-term longitudinal samples, now combined into one intergenerational panel of (who are now) middle-aged and older adults, and includes some of the study subjects' parents as well as their children. It is a unique data set in both the range of data collected as well as the period of time covered across the life course.

Some analyses conducted on the Berkeley data have attempted to relate specific aspects of adolescence to adult outcomes and adjustment (Peskin & Livson, 1981; see other recent analyses of the adult data in Eichorn, Clausen, Haan, Honzik, & Mussen, 1981). For example, Peskin and Livson (1981) examined both adolescent and adult data from this study, and found that particular personal resources and modes of coping used during adolescence became salient once again and were further drawn upon in midlife. It would not have been possible to examine these so-called "sleeper" effects without longitudinal observation.

The impact of sociocultural and historical events has also been investigated with various subsamples of these respondents. Glen Elder's (1974) classic volume, *Children of the Great Depression*, and subsequent analyses building upon this (see for example, Elder, 1979, 1980; Elder, Downey, & Cross, 1986; Elder & Rockwell, 1979), examined the impact of the Depression on the lives of children and adolescents. Economic privation among members of the sample had differential effects on males and females, depending upon whether the respondents were adolescents or children at the time of the economic loss. Erik Erikson and his colleagues (Erikson, Erikson, & Kivnick, 1986) recently tested the revised Eriksonian life cycle model against the experiences of the oldest generation of parents (of the original study subjects), employing 50 years of archival data for the analyses.

Problems of Method in Longitudinal Research

The neglect and omission of sexuality in longitudinal research is likely due to several reasons in addition to the guiding assumptions of heterosexuality. The study of sexuality or any related phenomena in a group of legal minors presents numerous obstacles. Typically, adolescent researchers draw their samples through school systems or other social institutions (e.g., summer camps, church groups, and so on). Many of these groups manifest strong resistance to investigation of a topic they perceive their constituency of parents will find unacceptable (Petersen, Tobin-Richards, & Boxer, 1983). In addition, ethical considerations and federal guidelines requiring informed consent by parents of study subjects makes many investigators reticent even to enter into such research, and many parents may be suspicious of researchers' studying their children's sexuality. As Deisher (1988) has indicated, the problems are compounded in the case of gay and lesbian youth. For example, many of them have not come out to their parents and are therefore unwilling to have a parent sign a consent form.

We are aware that longitudinal research is no panacea; it can be a complex, time-consuming and costly endeavor. The many complexities and methodological problems inherent in the use of longitudinal methods are probably further responsible for the paucity of such work to date. A primary consideration is the tracking and monitoring of respondents' whereabouts, and sample attrition. There may also be many self-selection processes operating among respondents, in that longitudinal studies require continued cooperation for participation in a number of examinations, interviews, tests, and so on. Maintaining a research alliance (Offer & Sabshin, 1967) with respondents is always important, however with gay and lesbian youth, who may not have come out to many others, sensitivity and understanding are critical.

Developmentalists who study the life span have increasingly focused their attention on differentiating those behaviors that are age related (and in this sense developmental) and those that may result from the impact of sociohistorical and cultural events (Baltes, 1968; Schaie, 1965; Schaie & Hertzog, 1982). Many studies are unable to differentiate cultural-environmental and maturational influences upon developmental change. In other words, the components of age change, cohort differences, and environmental influences are typically confounded. Attempts to differentiate these effects are often lacking in current longitudinal work.

One remarkable exception, disaggregating maturational and contextual effects, is the study of adolescent personality development conducted by Nesselroade and Baltes (1974). Their study examined 1,800 children born between 1954 and 1957. Respondents in this study were tested 3 times during a 2-year period. Developmental changes in personality were found to be more influenced by historical effects than by ontogenetic, age-related changes. However, the implications of this study have been directed largely to issues of method, rather than to substantive issues of defining particular sociohistorical forces that have an influence on the life course of youth (see Boxer, Gershenson, & Offer, 1984; Cohler & Boxer, 1983).

A major problem to date has been the definition of the cohort to be studied (Kertzer, 1983; Nydegger, 1977; Rosow, 1978; Ryder, 1965). While two groups of persons born as little as one year apart may suffice as separate cohorts according to critics of longitudinal research, the definition of cohort to be used in a particular study depends, in large part, on the questions addressed by the research (Cohler & Boxer, 1984). The personal significance of particular historical circumstances is likely of greater critical importance in the very definitions that persons have of their own lives (Elder, 1974, 1975, 1980). However, it is an open question as to exactly how the concept of cohort functions among communities of gay and lesbian individuals over the life course. While some researchers have identified "pre" and "post" Stonewall groups as different cohorts, other events or historical markers, including "pre" and "post" AIDS crisis are also likely to be salient in distinguishing the experience of different cohorts (see Murray, 1984, for a discussion of historical markers).

From its very point of initiation, a longitudinal design guides a group of researchers on a given course, and while it should be flexible enough to be subject to modifications, the consequences of any given research strategy may be felt 30 to 50 years later. As new measures come into existence, researchers question the use of old ones. In many longitudinal studies, continuity of data was favored, even when an instrument was found to be faulty or inaccurate. In addition, using one instrument to measure an attribute at several ages does not guarantee that the same process will be measured at each age level. Nor do many investigators control for the practice effects of repeated measures. Longitudinal studies, with their accumulating data banks, do offer possibilities of reanalysis and reinterpretation of data within the limited perspectives available. In a 1971 analysis of the Berkeley longitudinal studies (Block with Haan, 1971), it was noted that not even one-half of the data available had been subject to complete analysis. In an article written 30 years ago (Jones, 1958), Harold Jones, co-founder and long-time director of the Adolescent Growth Study, cited many pertinent issues that plagued his longitudinal research design, but concluded that: "If we wish, as we should, to achieve a body of developmental theory, we cannot eliminate developmental observation" (p. 98). While the longitudinal method presents itself with a multitude of problems for the study of development, the costs incurred appear to be worth every effort. Our current knowledge of development will only be advanced through the longitudinal study of change as it is occurring throughout people's lives.

Clinical Services and the Development
of Gay and Lesbian Youth

Developmental research has generally had a profound impact on the delivery of services to adolescents. Since Anna Freud's (1958) comment that adolescence was the "stepchild of developmental theory," more sophisticated and comprehensive understandings of adolescence have emerged in research, theory, and clinical services. Accompanying the recognition of adolescence as being distinctly different from both childhood and adulthood is the emerging idea that what is "normal" or expectable for an adolescent is different from what is normal or expectable for an adult (Offer & Sabshin, 1984; Offer, 1987). The longitudinal perspective on adolescence has had particularly important implications for mental health practitioners and service providers in providing a baseline in terms of which the origin, course, and treatment of psychological distress and disturbances may be evaluated. This perspective has been particularly useful in informing diagnosis and assessment of psychopathology during the adolescent years. The tendency among clinicians has been to base their understanding of problems characteristic of this decade upon generalizations derived from small psychopathological samples (Offer, Ostrov, & Howard, 1981).

The use of findings from developmental research has led to the realization that not all adolescents must necessarily experience severe identity crises and the accompanying turmoil. This view of inevitable turmoil during adolescence, held by many mental health professionals, has been questioned on the basis of several developmental studies (Csikszentmihalyi & Larson, 1984; Douvan & Adelson, 1966; Kandel & Lesser, 1972; Offer & Offer, 1975). Continued endorsement of this view by those working with adolescents sometimes makes it difficult for troubled teenagers to obtain care addressed to their particular concerns. Thus, major psychopathology may not always be differentiated by clinicians from concerns characteristic of the adolescent epoch. The needs of adolescents can only be addressed when service providers are informed by a broad understanding of development across the adolescent decade, including the complex interplay between maturational and personality processes, and the reciprocal impact of increasingly complex, socially defined expectations regarding major roles upon self-conceptions and individual well-being.

However, conspicuously missing is a developmental understanding of what is "normative" and expectable for gay and lesbian youth growing up in our society today. In understanding the problems of this group, we should consider both the nature of life changes, as well as the means by which adolescents cope more or less effectively with such changes.

Some evidence suggests that gay and lesbian teenagers are "at risk" for adjustment problems such as drug abuse, sexually transmitted diseases, physical abuse, prostitution, and psychiatric disorders (see Kourany, 1987; Martin & Hetrick, 1987; Roesler & Deisher, 1972). For example, one recent, developmentally informed, series of studies of self-identified gay male adolescents (Remafedi, 1987a, 1987b) indicates that they are at high risk for physical and psychosocial dysfunction as a result of experiencing strong negative attitudes (e.g., homophobia) from parents and peers. In addition, some of these youth reported verbal abuse, physical assaults, and discrimination. While this work raises important questions, it is based primarily on a small, cross-sectional sample of males. Existing studies (including those based on retrospective methods or on clinically constituted samples) do support this hypothesis of higher risk, and yet no longitudinal, naturalistic investigations have been conducted to determine the validity of this point of view over time. Research is needed, in other words, to determine how gay and lesbian adolescents negotiate their life course around school, family, and peer relations. It remains an open question as to what subsequently happens to those who are physically or emotionally abused by friends, family, or society at large. How does the teenager's initial resilience and vulnerability relate to subsequent coping processes and life experiences in young adulthood? This and other related questions, such as the impact of service providers on the adjustment of gay youth, can only be answered by following a group of youth across time, through repeated interviews and observations.

As we have emphasized, there is little existing research on the development of gay and lesbian individuals over time.[12] Such an effort would help answer questions regarding the outcomes of youth who may be at risk for various biological, social, and psychological stressors. The relationship between positive life satisfactions and successful aging can also be examined by repeated study of cohorts of youth moving into adulthood. AIDS is now an especially critical factor to be considered. The use of longitudinal methods would provide an ideal way of delineating the psychosocial impact of AIDS on youth coming of age during the current AIDS epidemic (see Feldman, 1988; Millan & Ross, 1987). The needs of groups of lesbians and gay males can only be determined through assessment that examines changes in life-style, behavior, and development over time.[13]

CONCLUSION:
TIME, AGE, AND LIFE COURSE

In summary, we suggest that longitudinal, life span investigations are necessary for a revision of our current developmental understanding of gay and lesbian youth. These studies will also assist in remapping gay and lesbian adult life course trajectories. The developmental perspective can be a useful framework from which to examine the effects and interrelations of historical time and sociocultural contexts on individual development. This requires both quantitative and qualitative research strategies to understand better a previously hidden and neglected group of youth. Many past research findings, based on cross-sectional samples, retrospective methods, or both, may be radically altered by studying lives through time.

Young adults today must negotiate a complicated series of decisions concerning the sequencing of events in the transition to adulthood (Greene & Boxer, 1986). During late adolescence, school, career, and family-related decisions appear to be interwoven, and thereby make late adolescence and young adulthood a time of multiple and simultaneous role changes. Gay and lesbian adolescents are therefore faced with negotiating these decisions, as well as those involving the meaning, management, and expression of their sexuality. The restructuring of personal expectations and anticipations for the future life course may be a unique developmental task for these youth. The first generation of gay and lesbian youth currently coming of age during the AIDS crisis are likely to become some of those with the longest life time histories of a gay or lesbian identity. It is now time to embark with them as consociates in developmental studies as they grow up, enter adulthood, and grow old.

NOTES

1. The proliferation of adolescent research is evidenced by the recent formation of a new, interdisciplinary adolescent research society (The Society for Research on Adolescence), new journal publications (e.g., *The Journal of Early Adolescence, The Journal of Adolescent Research*), the formation of policy promoting bodies (The Carnegie Council on Adolescent Development, The Youth Policy Institute), and more thorough and specialized texts and handbooks for students and scholars (see, e.g., Adelson, 1980; Conger & Petersen, 1984; Kimmel & Weiner, 1985; Leigh & Petersen, 1986; Steinberg, 1985) as well as for parents (Lerner & Galambos, 1984).

2. There are many different ways to examine continuity. Kagan (1980, 1981) has discussed three ways to infer continuity. The first regards hypothesizing the persistence of changeless elements beneath surface phenomena; a second is to uncover changing mechanisms which operate in different contexts across time. The third strategy rests on assuming that two or more events are related because some structural properties in an earlier event are found also in a later one. Alternatively, earlier events may lay the foundation for establishing conditions that result in a later event (Kagan, 1981).

3. It should be noted that several decades of research on nonclinical samples of adolescents demonstrate that not all adolescents experience high levels of stress and turmoil and that there are multiple developmental pathways through adolescence (see, e.g., Douvan & Adelson, 1966; Kandel & Lesser, 1972; Offer & Offer, 1975).

4. From the perspective of life course social science, these so-called biases or distortions become the subject of study; we are interested in those factors determining particular accounts of persons' presently understood course of development. From the perspective of predictive developmental inquiry, focused on the forward course of life, the use of retrospective approaches poses serious constraints on the conclusions which may be drawn. Interpretive and predictive modes of inquiry are both important and add to understanding of lives over time. However, it is important to distinguish between the methods and goals of each approach to the study of lives. This endorsement of a pluralistic mode of social science inquiry, recognizing the contributions of each approach, must be differentiated from positions such as that adopted by Spence (1982), who argues that narrative perspectives should be employed only because human science study will not permit realization of controlled experimental, natural science modes of study, rather than because such inquiry provides findings of intrinsic significance.

5. There are exceptions to this, such as Kimmel's (1978, 1980) studies of middle-aged and aging homosexual men, which examined certain developmental issues related to coming out, as well as the individual's position in the life cycle, in the context of cultural and historical influences (see also Berger, 1982; Kehoe, 1986; Robinson, 1979).

6. Green's (1987) study illustrates our earlier point regarding the difficulties with changing theoretical perspectives within the history of a longitudinal study. The original purpose for initiating this work, as he indicated, was to understand the development of transsexualism.

7. It is not surprising to learn that culturally defined attributes of behaviors such as sex-role definitions are so important in organizing adult personality, in that internalization of the situation is a major determinant of personal expression, as recognized by symbolic interactionist perspectives in social science (Cooley, 1902; Janowitz, 1966; Strauss, 1964).

8. It is unfortunate to note that this new line of research has primarily been directed to the study of males, a circumstance that follows the earlier historical masculine bias of developmental research (see, e.g., Gilligan, 1982; Chodorow, 1987).

9. Conversely, specialized investigations of adolescent sexuality ethnocentrically presume the heterosexuality of respondents, and usually do not situate the subject matter of sexuality in the context of other aspects of the respondents' lives (see Herdt, 1988). These investigations have been problem-focused with the bulk of this work directed to teen pregnancy and parenthood (Coates, Petersen, & Perry, 1982; Dreyer, 1982). In addition, general surveys of adolescent sexual behavior (for a comprehensive review, see Dreyer, 1982) are typically only quantitative in approach and neglect the meaning of sexuality to adolescents, or the ways in which sexuality is related to other aspects of the adolescents' lives, such as their identity development. (For an unusual exception to this, see D'Augelli & D'Augelli, 1979.)

10. For a comprehensive review of this literature, see Petersen & Taylor, 1980; Boxer & Petersen, 1986; Petersen, 1987.

11. This study also pioneered participant observational field methods applied to youth in intensive longitudinal efforts to document and understand growth and change over time. In the Adolescent Growth Study, a Club House was maintained by Institute study staff near the study sample's school (Jones, 1940; Newman, 1946).

12. One exception to this is a recent study by Lee (1987), who has followed a group of middle-aged homosexual men for 4 years, examining aspects of adult development and aging.

13. Some investigators have discussed the potential follow-up of adult respondents from their previous studies (e.g., Silverstein, 1981; McWhirter & Mattison, 1984).

REFERENCES

Adelson, J. (Eds.). (1980). *Handbook of adolescent psychology*. New York: John C. Wiley & Sons.

Anthony, E. J., & Cohler, B. J. (Eds.). (1987). *The invulnerable child*. New York: Guilford Press.

Baltes, P. H. (1968). Longitudinal and cross-sequential sequences in the study of age and generation effects. *Human Development, 11*, 145-171.

Baltes, P. H. (1979). Life-span developmental psychology: Some converging observations on history and theory. In P. Baltes, & O. G. Brim, Jr. (Eds.), *Life-span development and behavior* (Vol. 2, pp. 256-281). New York: Academic Press.

Back, K., & Gergen, K. (1963). Apocalyptic and serial time orientations and the structure of opinions. *Public Opinion Quarterly, 27*, 427-442.

Barker, R. G. (1968). *Ecological psychology: Concepts and methods for studying the environment of human behavior*. Stanford, CA: Stanford University Press.

Bell, R. Q., & Harper, L. (1977). *Child effects on adults*. Hillsdale, NJ: L. Erlbaum.

Bell, A. P., & Weinberg, M. S. (1978). *Homosexualities: A study of diversity among men and women*. New York: Simon & Schuster.

Bell, A. P., Weinberg, M. S., & Hammersmith, S. K. (1981). *Sexual preference: Its development in men and women*. Bloomington, IN: University Press.

Berger, R. M. (1982). *Gay and gray: The older homosexual man*. Urbana, IL: University of Illinois Press.

Bieber, I., Dain, H., Dince, P. R., Drellich, M. G., Grand, H. B., Gundlach, R. H., Kremer, M. W., Rifkin, A. H., Wilbur, C. B., & Bieber, T. B. (1962). *Homosexuality: A psychoanalytic study*. New York: Basic Books.

Block, J., with Haan, N. (1971). *Lives through time*. Berkeley, CA: Bancroft Books.

Botwinick, J. (1977). Intellectual abilities. In J. E. Birren & K. W. Schaie (Eds.), *Handbook of the psychology of aging* (pp. 580-605). New York: Van Nostrand Reinhold.

Boxer, A. M., Cook, J. A., & Cohler, B. J. (1986). Grandfathers, fathers, and sons: Intergenerational relations among men. In K. Pillemer & R. Wolf (Eds.), *Elder abuse: Conflict in the family* (pp. 93-121). Dover, MA: Auburn House.

Boxer, A. M., & Cohler, B. J. (1980, November). Personal time orientations and intergenerational conflicts in three-generation families. Paper presented at the Annual Meetings of The Gerontological Society of America, San Diego, CA.

Boxer, A. M., Gershenson, H. P., & Offer, D. P. (1984). Historical time and social change in adolescent experience. In D. Offer, E. Ostrov, & K. Howard (Eds.), *Patterns of adolescent self-image. New directions for mental health services* (Series No. 22, pp. 83-95). San Francisco, CA: Jossey-Bass.

Boxer, A. M., & Petersen, A. C. (1986). Pubertal change in a family context. In

G. K. Leigh, & G. W. Petersen (Eds.), *Adolescence in families* (pp. 73-103). Cincinnati, OH: South-Western.

Brim, O. H., Jr., & Kagan, J. (1980). Constancy and change: A view of the issues. In O. G. Brim, Jr., & J. Kagan (Eds.), *Constancy and change in human development* (pp. 1-25). Cambridge, MA: Harvard University Press.

Bronfenbrenner, U. (1977). Toward an experimental ecology of human development. *American Psychologist, 32,* 513-531.

Brooks-Gunn, J., Petersen, A. C., & Eichorn, D. (Eds.). (1985a). Timing of maturation and psychosocial functioning in adolescence, Part I. *Journal of Youth and Adolescence, 14*(3), 149-264.

Brooks-Gunn, J., Petersen, A. C., & Eichorn, D. (Eds.). (1985b). Timing of maturation and psychosocial functioning in adolescence, Part II. *Journal of Youth and Adolescence, 14*(4), 267-371.

Bugental, D. P., & Shennum, W. A. (1984). "Difficult" children as elicitors and targets of adult communication patterns: An attributional-behavioral transactional analysis. *Monographs of the Society for Research in Child Development, 49* (Serial No. 205).

Butler, R. (1963). The life review: An interpretation of reminiscence in the aged. *Psychiatry, 26,* 65-76.

Carrier, J. (1988). Gay liberation and coming out in Guadalajara, Mexico. *Journal of Homosexuality, 17*(1/2), 225-252.

Cass, V. C. (1979). Homosexual identity formation: A theoretical model. *Journal of Homosexuality, 4,* 219-235.

Cass, V. C. (1983/1984). Homosexual identity: A concept in need of definition. *Journal of Homosexuality, 9*(2/3), 105-126.

Cass, V. C. (1984). Homosexual identity formation: Testing a theoretical model. *Journal of Sex Research, 20,* 143-167.

Chang, J., & Block, J. (1960). A study of identification in male homosexuals. *Journal of Consulting and Clinical Psychology, 24,* 307-310.

Chodorow, N. (1978). *The reproduction of mothering: Psychoanalysis and the sociology of gender.* Berkeley, CA: University of California Press.

Clarke, A., & Clarke, A. D. B. (Eds.). (1976). *Early experience: Myth and evidence.* New York: Free Press.

Clausen, J. A. (1975). The social meaning of differential physical and sexual maturation. In S. Dragastin & G. H. Elder, Jr. (Eds.), *Adolescence in the life cycle* (pp. 25-47). Washington, DC.: Hemisphere.

Coates, T. J., Petersen, A. C., & Perry, C. (1982). *Promoting adolescent health: A dialog on research and practice.* New York: Academic Press.

Cohler, B. J. (1980). Developmental perspectives on the psychology of the self in early childhood. In A. Goldberg (Ed.), *Advances in self psychology* (pp. 69-115). New York: International Universities Press.

Cohler, B. J. (1981). Adult developmental psychology and reconstruction in psychoanalysis. In S. I. Greenspan, & G. H. Pollock (Eds.), *The course of life: Psychoanalytic contributions towards understanding personality development,*

Vol. 3. Adulthood and aging (pp. 149-201). Washington, DC: Department of Health and Human Services, U.S. Government Printing Office.

Cohler, B. J. (1982). Personal narrative and life course. In P. Baltes & O. G. Brim, Jr. (Eds.), *Life-span development and behavior* (Vol. 4., pp. 205-241). New York: Academic Press.

Cohler, B. J. (1983). Autonomy and interdependence in the family of adulthood: A psychological perspective. *The Gerontologist, 23,* 33-39.

Cohler, B. J. (1987). Vulnerability, resilience, and the study of lives. In E. J. Anthony & B. J. Cohler (Eds.), *The invulnerable child* (pp. 363-424). New York: Guilford Press.

Cohler, B. J., & Boxer, A. M. (1984). Middle adulthood: Settling into the world—Person, time and context. In D. Offer & M. Sabshin (Eds.), *Normality and the life cycle* (pp. 145-203). New York: Basic Books.

Cohler, B. J., & Geyer, E. S. (1982). Psychological autonomy and interdependence within the family. In F. Walsh (Ed.), *Normal family process* (pp. 196-288). New York: Guilford Press.

Coleman, J. C. (1980). *The nature of adolescence.* New York and London: Methuen.

Coleman, J. S., Bremner, R. H., Clark, B. R., Davis, J. B., Eichorn, D. H., Griliches, Z., Kett, J. F., Ryder, N. B., Doering, Z. B., & Mays, J. M. (1974). *Youth: Transition to adulthood. Report of the panel on youth of the President's Science Advisory Committee.* Chicago: The University of Chicago Press.

Conger, J. J., & Petersen, A. C. (1984). *Adolescence and youth: Psychological development in a changing world.* New York: Harper and Row.

Cook, J. A. (1988). Who mothers the chronically mentally ill. *Family Relations, 37,* 42-49.

Cook, J. A., & Cohler, B. J. (1986). Reciprocal socialization and the care of offspring with cancer and with schizophrenia. In N. Datan, A. L. Greene, & H. W. Reese (Eds.), *Life-span developmental psychology: Intergenerational relations* (pp. 223-243). Hillsdale, NJ: L. Erlbaum.

Cooley, C. H. (1902). *Human nature and the social order.* New York: Scribner.

Coons, N. (1987, June). Modern Prom: A night to forget. *Chicago,* 162-173.

Csikszentmihalyi, M., & Larson, R. (1984). *Being adolescent: Conflict and growth in the teenage years.* New York: Basic Books.

Dank, B. (1971). Coming out in the gay world. *Psychiatry, 34,* 180-197.

Dawson, R. E., & Prewitt, K. (1969). *Political socialization.* Boston: Little, Brown.

De Cecco, J. P. (1987). Homosexuality's brief recovery: From sickness to health and back again. *The Journal of Sex Research, 23,* 106-129.

Deisher, R. (1988). Adolescent Homosexuality: Preface. *Journal of Homosexuality, 17*(1/2), xv-xvii.

Dennis, W. (1973). *Children of the Creche.* New York: Appleton-Century Crofts.

Douvan, E., & Adelson, J. (1966). *The adolescent experience.* New York: John C. Wiley.

Dreyer, P. (1982). Sexuality during adolescence. In B. B. Wolman (Ed.), *Handbook of developmental psychology* (pp. 559-601). Englewood Cliffs, NJ: Prentice-Hall.

D'Augelli, J., & D'Augelli, A. (1979). Sexual development and relationship involvement: A cognitive developmental view. In R. Burgess, & T. Huston (Eds.), *Social exchange in developing relationships* (pp. 307-349). New York: Academic Press.

Eichorn, D., Clausen, J., Haan, N., Honzik, M. P., & Mussen, P. H. (1981). *Present and past in middle life*. New York: Academic Press.

Elder, G. H., Jr. (1974). *Children of the Great Depression*. Chicago: University of Chicago Press.

Elder, G. H., Jr. (1975). Age differentiation and the life course. *Annual Review of Sociology* (pp. 165-190). Palo Alto, CA: Annual Reviews Inc.

Elder, G. H., Jr. (1979). Historical change in life patterns and personality. In P. Baltes & O. G. Brim, Jr. (Eds.), *Life-span development and behavior* (Vol. 2, pp. 117-159). New York: Academic Press.

Elder, G. H., Jr. (1980). Adolescence in historical perspective. In J. Adelson (Ed.), *Handbook of adolescent psychology* (pp. 3-46). New York: John C. Wiley & Sons.

Elder, G. H., Jr., Downey, G., & Cross, C. E. (1986). Family ties and life chances: Hard times and hard choices in women's lives since the 1930s. In N. Datan, A. L. Greene, & H. W. Reese (Eds.), *Life-span developmental psychology: Intergenerational relations* (pp. 151-183). Hillsdale, NJ: L. Erlbaum.

Elder, G. H., Jr., & Rockwell, R. W. (1979). Economic depression and postwar opportunities in men's lives: A study of life patterns and health. In R. G. Simmons (Ed.), *Research in community and mental health* (pp. 249-304). Greenwich, CT: JAI Press.

Emde, R. (1981). Changing models of infancy and the nature of early development: Remodeling the foundation. *Journal of the American Psychoanalytic Association, 29*, 179-219.

Erikson, E., Erikson, J., & Kivnick, H. (1987). *Vital involvement in old age*. New York: W. W. Norton.

Feldman, D. A. (1988). Gay youth and AIDS. *Journal of Homosexuality, 17* (1/2), 185-193.

Freud, A. (1958). Adolescence. *Psychoanalytic Study of the Child, 16*, 225-278.

Freud, S. (1955). The psychogenesis of a case of homosexuality in a woman. In J. Strachey (Ed. and Trans.), *The standard edition of the complete psychological works of Sigmund Freud* (Vol. 18, pp. 145-172). London: Hogarth Press. (Original work published 1920.)

Geertz, C. (1983). Blurred genres: The refiguration of social thought. In C. Geertz (Ed.), *Local knowledge* (pp. 19-35). New York: Basic Books.

Gebhard, P. H. (1965). Situational factors affecting human sexual behavior. In F. A. Beach (Ed.), *Sex and behavior* (pp. 65-78). New York: John Wiley and Sons.

Gebhard, P. H., Gagnon, J. H., Pomeroy, W. B., & Christenson, C. V. (1965). *Sex offenders: An analysis of types*. New York: Harper & Row.

Gergen, K. (1982). *Toward transformation in social knowledge*. New York: Springer-Verlag.

Gilligan, C. (1982). *In a different voice: Psychological theory and women's development*. Cambridge, MA: Harvard University Press.

Green, R. (1987). *The "sissy boy" syndrome*. New Haven, CT: Yale University Press.

Greene, A. L. (1985, March). *Great expectations: Age norms in expected future life events in mid and late adolescence*. Paper presented at the 56th Annual Meeting of the Eastern Psychological Association, Boston, MA.

Greene, A. L. (1986). Future time perspective in adolescence: The present of things future revisited. *Journal of Youth and Adolescence, 15*, 99-113.

Greene, A. L., & Boxer, A. M. (1986). Daughters and sons as young adults: Restructuring the ties that bind. In N. Datan, A. L. Greene, & H., W. Reese (Eds.), *Life-span developmental psychology: Intergenerational relations* (pp. 125-149). Hillsdale, NJ: L. Erlbaum.

Greene, A. L., & Boxer, A. M. (Eds.). (in press). *Transitions through adolescence: Research and theory in life-span perspective*. Hillsdale, NJ: L. Erlbaum.

Hagestad, G. O. (1981). Problems and promises in the social psychology of intergenerational relations. In R. W. Fogel, E. Hatfield, S. B. Kiesler, & E. Shanas (Eds.), *Stability and change in the family* (pp. 11-46). New York: Academic Press.

Hall, G. S. (1904). *Adolescence: Its psychology and its relation to physiology, anthropology, sociology, sex, crime, religion and education*. New York: Appleton.

Hamburg, D. A. (1986). Preparing for life: The critical transition of adolescence. *1986 Annual Report of the Carnegie Corporation of New York*. New York: Carnegie Corporation.

Harry, J. (1982). *Gay children grown up*. New York: Praeger.

Herek, G. M. (1985). On doing, being, and not being: Prejudice and the social construction of sexuality. *Journal of Homosexuality, 12*(1), 135-151.

Herdt, G. (1988). Introduction: Gay and lesbian youth, emergent identities, and cultural scenes at home and abroad. *Journal of Homosexuality, 17*(1/2), 1-42.

Herdt, G., Boxer, A. M., & Irvin, F. S. (1986). *Sexual orientation and cultural competence in Chicago*. Proposal for funding submitted to the Spencer Foundation, Chicago.

Hetrick, E. S., & Martin, A. D. (1987). Developmental issues and their resolution for gay and lesbian adolescents. *Journal of Homosexuality, 14*(1/2), 25-43.

Hippler, M. (1986, September 16). The problems and promises of gay youth. *The Advocate*, 42-57.

Holeman, R. E., & Winokur, G. (1965). Effeminate homosexuality: A disease of childhood. *American Journal of Orthopsychiatry, 35*, 48-56.

Horn, J. L., & Donaldson, G. (1980). Cognitive development in adulthood. In O.

G. Brim, Jr. & J. Kagan (Eds.), *Constancy and change in human development* (pp. 445-529). Cambridge, MA: Harvard University Press.

Humphreys, L., & Miller, B. (1980). Identities in the emerging gay culture. In J. Marmor (Ed.), *Homosexual behavior: A modern reappraisal* (pp. 142-156). New York: Basic Books.

Isay, R. A. (1985). On the analytic therapy of homosexual men. *Psychoanalytic study of the child, 40,* 235-254.

Isay, R. A. (1986). The development of sexual identity in homosexual men. *Psychoanalytic study of the child, 41,* 467-489.

Isay, R. A. (1987). Fathers and their homosexually inclined sons in childhood. *Psychoanalytic study of the child, 42,* 275-294.

Janet, P. (1877). Une illusion d'optique interne (The illusion of the inner image). *Revue Philosophie, 1,* 497-502.

Janowitz, M. (Ed.). (1966). *W. I. Thomas on social organization and social personality.* Chicago: University of Chicago Press.

Jones, H. E. (1939). The adolescent growth study: I. Principles and methods, II. Procedures. *Journal of Consulting Psychology, 3,* 157-159, 177-180.

Jones, H. E. (1940). Educational research at the Institute of Child Welfare. *Journal of Educational Research, 34,* 158-159.

Jones, H. E. (1958). Problems of method in longitudinal research. *Vita Humana, 1,* 93-99.

Jones, M. C., Bayley, N., MacFarlane, J. W., & Honzik, M. (Eds.). (1971). *The course of human development: Selected papers from the longitudinal studies, Institute of Human Development, University of California, Berkeley.* Waltham, MA: Xerox College Publishing.

Jones, M. C., & Mussen, P. H. (1958). Self-conceptions, motivations, and interpersonal attitudes of early- and late-maturing girls. *Child Development, 29,* 491-501.

Journal of the American Medical Association. (1987). *257*(24).

Kagan, J. (1980). Perspectives on continuity. In O. G. Brim, Jr., & J. Kagan (Eds.), *Constancy and change in human development* (pp. 26-74). Cambridge, MA: Harvard University Press.

Kagan, J. (1981). Issues in psychological development. In F. Schulsinger, S. A. Mednick, & J. Knop (Eds.), *Longitudinal research: Methods and uses in behavioral science* (pp. 66-92). Boston: Martinus Nijhoff.

Kagan, J., & Klein, M. (1973). Cross-cultural perspectives on early development. *American Psychologist, 28,* 947-961.

Kagan, J., & Moss, H. A. (1962). *Birth to maturity.* New York: John C. Wiley.

Kandel, D., & Lesser, G. S. (1972). *Youth in two worlds.* San Francisco: Jossey Bass.

Kehoe, M. (1986). Lesbians over 65: A triply invisible minority. *Journal of Homosexuality, 12*(3/4), 139-152.

Kelly, J. (1977). The aging male homosexual: Myth and reality. *The Gerontologist, 17,* 328-332.

Kertzer, D. I. (1983). Generation as a sociological problem. *Annual Review of Sociology, 9*, 125-149.

Kimmel, D. C. (1978). Adult development and aging: A gay perspective. *Journal of Social Issues, 34*, 113-130.

Kimmel, D. C. (1980). Life history interviews of aging gay men. *International Journal of Aging and Human Development, 10*, 239-248.

Kimmel, D. C., & Weiner, I. B. (1985). *Adolescence: A developmental transition*. Hillsdale, NJ: L. Erlbaum.

Kinsey, A. C., Pomeroy, W. B., & Martin, C. E. (1948). *Sexual behavior in the human male*. Philadelphia: W. B. Saunders.

Kohlberg, L., Ricks, D., & Snarey, J. (1984). Child development as a predictor of adaptation in adulthood. *Genetic Psychology Monographs, 110*, 91-173.

Kogan, B. (1986, September 15). Investing in our future. *The New York Native*, p. 23.

Kourany, R. F. C. (1987). Suicide among homosexual adolescents. *Journal of Homosexuality, 13*(4), 111-117.

Larson, R., Csikszentmihalyi, M., & Graef, R. (1980). Mood variability and the psychosocial adjustment of adolescents. *Journal of Youth and Adolescence, 9*, 469-490.

Lee, J. A. (1987). What can homosexual aging studies contribute to theories of aging? *Journal of Homosexuality, 13*(4), 43-71.

Leigh, G. K., & Petersen, G. W. (Eds.). (1986). *Adolescence in families*. Cincinnati, OH: South-Western.

Lennenberg, E. (1967). *Biological foundations of language*. New York: John C. Wiley & Sons.

Lens, W., & Gailly, A. (1980). Extention of future time perspective in motivational goals of different age groups. *International Journal of Behavioral Development, 3*, 1-17.

Lerner, R. M., & Galambos, N. L. (Eds.). (1984). *Experiencing adolescents: A sourcebook for parents, teachers, and teens*. New York: Garland Press.

LeVine, R. A. (1973). *Culture, behavior, and personality*. Chicago: Aldine.

Lewin, K. (1964). Behavior and development as a function of the total situation. In K. Lewin (Ed.), *Field theory in social science* (pp. 238-304). New York: Harper Torchbooks. (Original work published 1946.)

Liberman, M., & Falk, J. (1971). The remembered past as a source of data for research on the life-cycle. *Human Development, 14*, 132-141.

Livson, H., & Peskin, H. (1980). Perspectives on adolescence from longitudinal research. In J. Adelson (Ed.), *Handbook of adolescent psychology*. (pp. 47-98). New York: John C. Wiley & Sons.

Lynch, F. R. (1987). Non-ghetto gays: A sociological study of suburban homosexuals. *Journal of Homosexuality, 13*(4), 13-42.

Martin, A. D. (1982). Learning to hide: The socialization of the gay adolescent. *Adolescent Psychiatry, 10*, 52-65.

McWhirter, D. P., & Mattison, A. M. (1984). *The male couple: How relationships develop*. Englewood Cliffs, NJ: Prentice-Hall.

Millan, G., & Ross, M. W. (1987). AIDS and gay youth: Attitudes and lifestyle modifications in young male homosexuals. *Community Health Studies, 11,* 50-53.

Minton, H. L., & McDonald, G. J. (1983/1984). Homosexual identity formation as a developmental process. *Journal of Homosexuality, 9*(2/3), 91-104.

Montemayor, R. (1986). Family variation in parent-adolescent storm and stress. *Journal of Adolescent Research, 1,* 15-31.

Morin, S. F. (1977). Heterosexual bias in psychological research on lesbianism and male homosexuality. *American Psychologist, 32,* 629-637.

Moss, H., & Sussman, E. (1980). Longitudinal study of personality development. In O. G. Brim, Jr., & J. Kagan (Eds.), *Constancy and change in human development* (pp. 530-595). Cambridge, MA: Harvard University Press.

Murray, S. O. (1984). *Social theory, homosexual realities.* New York: Gay Academic Union.

Mussen, P. H., & Jones, M. C. (1957). Self-conceptions, motivations and interpersonal attitudes of late- and early-maturing boys. *Child Development, 28,* 243-256.

Nesselroade, J., & Baltes, P. (1974). Adolescent personality development and historical change: 1970-1972. *Monographs of the Society for Research in Child Development, 39* (Serial No. 154).

Neugarten, B. L. (1967). The awareness of middle age. In R. Owen, (Ed.), *Middle age.* London: British Broadcasting Co (pp. 23-28). (Reprinted in B. Neugarten [Ed.]. [1968]. *Middle age and aging: A reader in social psychology* [pp. 93-98].)

Neugarten, B. L. (1969). Continuities and discontinuities of psychological issues into adult life. *Human Development, 12,* 121-130.

Neugarten, B. L. (1977). Personality and aging. In J. E. Birren & K. W. Schaie (Eds.), *Handbook of the psychology of aging* (pp. 626-649). New York: Van Nostrand-Reinhold.

Neugarten, B. L. (1979). Time, age, and the life cycle. *American Journal of Psychiatry, 136,* 887-894.

Newman, F. B. (1946). The adolescent in social groups: Studies in the observation of personality. *Applied Psychology Monographs, 9,* 1-94.

Nydegger, C. (1977, November). *Multiple cohort membership.* Paper presented at the Annual Meetings of the Gerontological Society, San Francisco.

Offer, D. (1969). *The psychological world of the teenager: A study of normal adolescent boys.* New York: Basic Books.

Offer, D. (1987). In defense of adolescents. *JAMA, 257*(24), 3407-3408.

Offer, D., & Offer, J. (1975). *From teenage to young manhood: A psychological study.* New York: Basic Books.

Offer, D., Ostrov, E., & Howard, K. (1981). The mental health professional's concept of the normal adolescent. *Archives of General Psychiatry, 38,* 149-152.

Offer, D., & Sabshin, M. (1967). Research alliance versus therapeutic alliance: A comparison. *American Journal of Psychiatry, 12,* 1519-1526.

Offer, D., & Sabshin, M. (Eds.). (1984). *Normality and the life cycle*. New York: Basic Books.

Olson, W. C. (1986, September 15). The turning point. *The New York Native*, p. 21.

Peskin, H., & Livson, N. (1981). Uses of the past in adult psychological health. In D. Eichorn, J. Clausen, N. Haan, M. P. Honzik, & P. H. Mussen (Eds.), *Present and past in middle life* (pp. 153-181). New York: Academic Press.

Petersen, A. C. (1988). Adolescent development. *Annual Review of Psychology, 39*, 583-607.

Petersen, A. C., & Boxer, A. M. (1982). Adolescent sexuality. In T. J. Coates, A. C. Petersen, & C. Perry (Eds.), *Promoting adolescent health: A dialog on research and practice* (pp. 237-253). New York: Academic Press.

Petersen, A. C., & Crockett, L. (1985). Pubertal timing and grade effects. *Journal of Youth and Adolescence, 14*, 191-206.

Petersen, A. C., & Taylor, B. (1980). The biological approach to adolescence: Biological change and psychological adaptation. In J. Adelson (Ed.), *Handbook of adolescent psychology* (pp. 117-155). New York: John C. Wiley & Sons.

Petersen, A. C., Tobin-Richards, M., & Boxer, A. M. (1983). Puberty: Its measurement and its meaning. *Journal of Early Adolescence, 3*, 47-62.

Plummer, K. (1981). Going gay: Identities, life cycles, and lifestyles in the male gay world. In J. Hart & D. Richardson (Eds.), *The theory and practice of homosexuality* (pp. 93-110). Boston: Routledge & Kegan Paul.

Ponse, B. (1978). *Identities in the lesbian world: The social construction of self*. Westport, CT: Greenwood.

Pratch, L. (1987). *Gender differences in the coming-out relationships of 12 homosexual youth*. Unpublished master's thesis. Committee on Human Development, The University of Chicago, Chicago.

Prosen, H., Martin, R., & Prosen, M. (1972). The remembered mother and the fantasized mother: A crisis of middle age. *Archives of General Psychiatry, 27*, 791-794.

Remafedi, G. (1987a). Male homosexuality: The adolescent's perspective. *Pediatrics, 79*, 326-330.

Remafedi, G. (1987b). Adolescent homosexuality: Psychosocial and medical implications. *Pediatrics, 79*, 331-337.

Revere, V., & Tobin, S. (1980/1981). Myth and reality: The older person's relationship to his past. *International Journal of Aging and Human Development, 12*, 15-26.

Ricoeur, P. (1977). The question of proof in Freud's psychoanalytic writings. *Journal of the American Psychoanalytic Association, 25*, 835-872.

Robinson, M. K. (1979). *The older lesbian*. Unpublished Master's thesis. California State University, Dominguez Hills, CA.

Roesler, T., & Deisher, R. W. (1972). Youthful male homosexuality. *JAMA, 219*(8), 1018-1023.

Rosow, I. (1978). What is a cohort and why? *Human Development, 21*, 65-75.

Ross, M. W. (1980). Retrospective distortion in homosexual research. *Archives of Sexual Behavior, 9*, 523-531.

Rutter, M. (1987). Continuities and discontinuities in socioemotional development from infancy to adulthood. In J. Osofsky (Ed.), *Handbook of infant development* (pp. 1256-1296). New York: John C. Wiley & Sons.

Ryder, N. B. (1965). The cohort as a concept in the study of social change. *American Sociological Review, 30*, 843-861.

Sadownick, D. (1986, September 15). Gay generation gap? *The New York Native*, p. 19.

Savin-Williams, R. C. (1988). Parental influences on the self-esteem of gay and lesbian youths: A reflected appraisals model. *Journal of Homosexuality, 17* (1/2), 93-109.

Schaie, K. W. (1965). A general model for the study of developmental problems. *Psychological Bulletin, 64*, 92-107.

Schaie, K. W., & Hertzog, C. (1982). Longitudinal methods. In B. B. Wolman (Ed.), *Handbook of developmental psychology* (pp. 91-115). Englewood Cliffs, NJ: Prentice-Hall.

Schneider, M. (1988). Sappho was a right-on adolescent: Growing up lesbian. *Journal of Homosexuality, 17*(1/2), 111-130.

Silverstein, C. (1981). *Man to man: Gay couples in America*. New York: William Morrow.

Simmons, R. G., Blyth, D. A., Van Cleave, E. F., & Bush, D. M. (1979). Entry into early adolescence: The impact of school structure, puberty, and early dating on self-esteem. *American Sociological Review, 44*, 948-967.

Sophie, J. (1985/1986). A critical examination of stage theories of lesbian identity development. *Journal of Homosexuality, 12*(3/4), 39-51.

Spacks, P. M. (1981). *The adolescent idea: Myths of youth and the adult imagination*. New York: Basic Books.

Spanier, G. B. (1976). Use of recall data in survey research on human sexual behavior. *Social Biology, 23*, 244-253.

Spence, D. T. (1982). *Narrative truth and historical truth: Meaning and interpretation in psychoanalysis*. New York: W. W. Norton.

Steinberg, L. (1981). Transformations in family relations at puberty. *Developmental Psychology, 17*, 833-840.

Steinberg, L. (1985). *Adolescence*. New York: Alfred A. Knopf.

Steinberg, L., & Hill, J. (1978). Patterns of family interaction as a function of age, the onset of puberty, and formal thinking. *Developmental Psychology, 14*, 683-684.

Steinberg, L., & Silverberg, S. B. (1986). The vicissitudes of autonomy in early adolescence. *Child Development, 57*, 841-851.

Stolz, H. R., & Stolz, L. M. (1951). *Somatic development of adolescent boys*. New York: Macmillan.

Strauss, A. (Ed.). (1964). *George Herbert Mead: On social psychology*. Chicago: University of Chicago Press.

Suggs, D. (1987, March 24). More than friends: Conversations with lesbian and gay youth. *Village Voice,* p. 18.

Tripp, C. A. (1975). *The homosexual matrix.* New York: McGraw-Hill.

Troiden, R. R. (1979). Becoming homosexual: A model of gay identity acquisition. *Psychiatry, 42,* 362-373.

Troiden, R. R. (1988). The formation of homosexual identities. *Journal of Homosexuality, 17*(1/2), 43-74.

Troll, L., & Bengtson, V. L. (1982). Intergenerational relations throughout the life span. In B. Wolman (Ed.), *Handbook of developmental psychology* (pp. 890-911). Englewood Cliffs, NJ: Prentice-Hall.

Weinberg, M. S., & Williams, C. J. (1974). *Male homosexuals: Their problems and adaptations.* New York: Oxford University Press.

Weinberg, T. S. (1984). Biology, ideology, and the reification of developmental stages in the study of homosexual identities. *Journal of Homosexuality, 10*(3/4), 77-84.

Watters, A. T. (1986). Heterosexual bias in psychological research on lesbianism and male homosexuality (1979-1983), utilizing the bibliographic and taxonomic system of Morin. *Journal of Homosexuality, 13*(1), 35-58.

Yarrow, M. R., Campbell, J. D., & Burton, R. V. (1970). Recollections of childhood: A study of the retrospective method. *Monographs of the Society for Research in Child Development, 35* (Serial No. 138).